Innovations in Financial and Economic Networks

NEW DIMENSIONS IN NETWORKS

Series Editor: Anna Nagurney, *John F. Smith Memorial Professor, Isenberg School of Management, University of Massachusetts at Amherst, USA*

Networks provide a unifying framework for conceptualizing and studying problems and applications. They range from transportation and telecommunication networks and logistic networks to economic, social and financial networks. This series is designed to publish original manuscripts and edited volumes that push the development of theory and applications of networks to new dimensions. It is interdisciplinary and international in its coverage, and aims to connect existing areas, unveil new applications and extend existing conceptual frameworks as well as methodologies. An outstanding editorial advisory board made up of scholars from many fields and many countries assures the high quality and originality of all of the volumes in the series.

Titles in the series include:

Supernetworks
Decision-Making for the Information Age
Anna Nagurney and June Dong

Innovations in Financial and Economic Networks
Edited by Anna Nagurney

Innovations in Financial and Economic Networks

Edited by

Anna Nagurney

University of Massachusetts at Amherst, USA

NEW DIMENSIONS IN NETWORKS

Edward Elgar
Cheltenham, UK • Northampton, MA, USA

Published by
Edward Elgar Publishing Limited
Glensanda House
Montpellier Parade
Cheltenham
Glos GL50 1UA
UK

Edward Elgar Publishing, Inc.
136 West Street
Suite 202
Northampton
Massachusetts 01060
USA

A catalogue record for this book
is available from the British Library

Library of Congress Cataloguing in Publication Data
Innovations in financial and economic networks / edited by Anna Nagurney.
        p. cm. — (New dimensions in networks)
    Includes bibliographical references.
    1. Finance—Mathematical models. 2. Economics, Mathematical. 3. Equilibrium (Economics) I. Nagurney, Anna. II. Series.

    HG106.I56 2003
    330'.01'5195—dc22   2003061220

ISBN 1 84376 415 6
Printed and bound in Great Britain by MPG Books Ltd, Bodmin, Cornwall

Editorial Board

Janny Leung, Associate Professor, Department of Systems Engineering and Engineering Management, The Chinese University of Hong Kong, Hong Kong

Lars-Goran Mattsson, Professor and Chair, Division of Systems Analysis and Economics, Royal Institute of Technology (KTH), Stockholm, Sweden

Patricia L. Mokhtarian, Professor, Department of Civil and Environmental Engineering, University of California, Davis, USA

Panos Pardalos, University Professor, Department of Systems and Industrial Engineering, University of Florida, Gainesville, USA

Padma Ramanujam, Product Manager, i2 Technologies, Inc, Dallas, Texas, USA

Mauricio G. C. Resende, Technology Consultant, Algorithms and Optimization Research Department, AT&T Labs Research, Florham Park, New Jersey, USA

Berc Rustem, Professor, Department of Computing, Imperial College of Science, Technology & Medicine London, UK

Les Servi, Member of the Technical Staff, MIT Lincoln Laboratory, Lexington, Massachusetts, USA

Stavros Siokos, Managing Director and Head of Global Portfolio Trading Strategies, Citigroup, London, UK

Katia Sycara, Principal Research Scientist and Professor, School of Computer Science and Director, Advanced Agent Technology Laboratory, Carnegie Mellon University, Pittsburgh, Pennsylvania, USA

Leigh Tesfatsion, Professor of Economics and Mathematics, Department of Economics, Iowa State University, Ames, USA

Andrew B. Whinston, Hugh Cullen Chaired Professor of Information Systems, Economics and Computer Science, Graduate School of Business, University of Texas, Austin, USA

Ding Zhang, Associate Professor, Department of Management and Marketing, School of Business, State University of New York at Oswego, USA

Contents

7   International Financial Networks with Electronic Transactions   136

Anna Nagurney and Jose Cruz

8   Using Financial Options to Hedge Transportation Capacity in a Deregulated Rail Industry   169

Stephen M. Law, Alexandra E. MacKay, and James F. Nolan

Part II   Economic Networks   195

9   A Supply Chain Network Economy: Modeling and Qualitative Analysis   197

Ding Zhang, June Dong, and Anna Nagurney

13 Capacity Provision Networks: A Technology Framework and Economic Analysis of Web Cache Trading Hubs   **286**

Xianjun Geng, Ram Gopal, R. Ramesh, and Andrew B. Whinston

List of Figures

List of Tables

Preface

The study of networks and their applications has had a long tradition in engineering, operations research/management science, and in computer science. More recently, the fields of finance and economics have come to be rich and fascinating sources of network-based problems and applications. Interest from such disciplines has been supported, in part, by the greater availability of powerful network-based methodologies and tools that allow for enhanced modeling as well as computation of their solutions.

The role of networks in finance and economics has gained new prominence for a variety of reasons, including: the emergence of network industries from transportation and logistics to telecommunications; the recognition of the interdependence among many network systems, such as telecommunications with finance and telecommunications with transportation in the form of electronic commerce; new relationships between economic decision-makers in terms of cooperation and competition which are yielding new supply chains as well as financial networks; the realization of the importance of networks and the pricing of their usage, and interest surrounding networks and their evolution over space and time.

The growing attention to financial and economic networks is happening at a time when few volumes exist on such a topic. This book seeks to remedy this situation and brings together leading edge researchers. The idea for this book originated at the Eighth International Conference for Computational Economics (Computing in Economics and Finance) held in Aix-en-Provence, France, June 27-29, 2002. The editor of this volume organized two sessions on Network Economics for that venue and several of the papers presented there (but now in refereed and revised format) appear here as chapters.

This book is organized into two parts, with the first focusing on financial networks and the second on economic networks. The book contains a variety of innovations in terms of theory and applications. It should be a valuable resource to researchers and students, as well as to practitioners and to those who would like to know more about financial and economic networks.

Acknowledgments

The editing of this volume was supported by a National Science Foundation Grant No. IIS-0002647 and a 2002 AT&T Foundation Industrial Ecology Fellowship. This support is gratefully acknowledged.
The editor is indebted to the referees of the papers submitted for consideration as chapters in this volume for their hard work, timeliness, and diligence, without which this volume would not have been possible. As a token of appreciation and acknowledgments, the referees and their affiliations are listed below. The editor is also grateful to the authors of the contributions to this volume, which vividly demonstrate both the breadth and the depth of research on financial and economic network topics. The contributors, their affiliations, and addresses are given below.

Referees

Martin Arlitt, Hewlett-Packard Laboratories, Palo Alto, California

Ben Branch, Department of Finance and Operations Management, Isenberg School of Management, University of Massachusetts, Amherst, Massachusetts

Jose Cruz, Department of Finance and Operations Management, Isenberg School of Management, University of Massachusetts, Amherst, Massachusetts

June Dong, Department of Management and Marketing, School of Business, State University of New York at Oswego, Oswego, New York

Emmanuel Fragniere, School of Management, The University of Bath, Bath, United Kingdom

Richard B. Freeman, National Bureau of Economic Research, Cambridge, Massachusetts

Ladimer S. Nagurney, Department of Electrical and Computer Engineering, University of Hartford, West Hartford, Connecticut

Padma Ramanujam, i2 Technologies, Inc., Dallas, Texas

Mauricio G. C. Resende, Algorithms and Optimization Research Department, AT&T Labs Research, Shannon Laboratory, Florham Park, New Jersey

Andrzej Ruszczynski, Department of Management Science, Rutgers University, New Brunswick, New Jersey

Leigh Tesfatsion, Department of Economics, Iowa State University, Ames, Iowa

W. David Walls, Department of Economics, University of Calgary, Calgary, Alberta, Canada

Bill Yurcik, National Center for Supercomputer Applications (NCSA), University of Illinois at Urbana-Champaign, Illinois

Ding Zhang, Department of Management and Marketing, School of Business, State University of New York at Oswego, Oswego, New York

List of Contributors

Floortje Alkemade   The Netherlands National Research Center for Mathematics and Computing Science (CWI), PO Box 94079, 1090 GB, Amsterdam, The Netherlands

Hans M. Amman   School of Technology Management, Technical University Eindhoven, PO Box 513, 5600 MB Eindhoven, The Netherlands

Vladimir Boginski   Industrial and Systems Engineering Department, University of Florida, 303 Weil Hall, Gainesville, Florida 32611

Sergiy Butenko   Industrial and Systems Engineering Department, University Of Florida, 303 Weil Hall, Gainesville, Florida 32611

Stijn Claessens   The Finance Group, University of Amsterdam, Roetersstraat 11, 1018 WB Amsterdam, The Netherlands

Jose Cruz   Department of Finance and Operations Management, Isenberg School of Management, University of Massachusetts, Amherst, Massachusetts

Patrizia Daniele   Department of Mathematics and Computer Sciences, University of Catania, Viale A. Doria, 6-95125, Catania, Sicily

Gergely Dobos   Groupe de Recherche en Economie Mathématique et Quantitative, Universite de Toulouse 1 – Sciences Sociales, Bureau MF 007, Manufacture des Tabacs, 31042 Toulouse Cedex, France

June Dong   Department of Management and Marketing, School of Business, State University of New York at Oswego, Oswego, New York, 13126

Xianjun Geng   Center for Research in Electronic Commerce, Department of Management Science & Information Systems, University of Texas at Austin, Austin, Texas 789712

Ram Gopal   Department of Operations and Information Management, Room 376, School of Business, University of Connecticut, 2100 Hillside Road, U-1041 IM, Storrs, Connecticut 06269-2041

Nalan Gülpinar   Department of Computing, Imperial College of Science, Technology and Medicine, 180 Queen's Gate, London SW7 2RH, United Kingdom

Soulaymane Kachani   Department of Industrial Engineering and Operations Research, Columbia University, New York 10027

Daniela Klingebiel   The World Bank, 1818 H Street NW, Washington, DC 20433

J. (Han) A. La Poutré   The Netherlands National Research Center for Mathematics and Computing Science (CWI), PO Box 94079, 1090 GB Amsterdam, The Netherlands

Luc Laeven   The World Bank, 1818 H Street NW, Washington, DC 20433

Stephen M. Law   Department of Economics, Mount Allison University, Sackville, New Brunswick, E4L 1A7 Canada

Alexandra E. MacKay   Rotman School of Management, University of Toronto, 105 St George Street, Toronto, Ontario, M5S 3E6 Canada

John M. Mulvey   Department of Operations Research and Financial Engineering, Bendheim Center for Finance, Princeton University, Princeton, New Jersey, 08544

Anna Nagurney   Department of Finance and Operations Management, Isenberg School of Management, University of Massachusetts, Amherst, Massachusetts 01003

James F. Nolan   Department of Agricultural Economics, University of Saskatchewan, 51 Campus Drive, Saskatoon, Saskatchewan, S7N 5A8 Canada

Panos M. Pardalos — Industrial and Systems Engineering Department, University of Florida, 303 Weil Hall, Gainesville, Florida, 32611

Bill Pauling — Towers Perrin, Centre Square, 1500 Market Street, Philadelphia, Pennsylvania 19102

Georgia Perakis — Sloan School of Management, MIT, Room E53-359, Cambridge, Massachusetts 02139

Mark Pingle — Department of Economics, University of Nevada, Reno, Nevada 89557-0016

R. Ramesh — Department of Management Science & Systems, School of Management, State University of New York at Buffalo, Buffalo, New York 14260

Berç Rustem — Department of Computing, Imperial College of Science, Technology and Medicine, 180 Queen's Gate, London SW7 2RH, United Kingdom

Reuben Settergren — Department of Computing, Imperial College of Science, Technology and Medicine, 180 Queen's Gate, London SW7 2RH, United Kingdom

Koray D. Simsek — Department of Operations Research and Financial Engineering, Princeton University, Princeton, New Jersey 08544

Leigh Tesfatsion — Department of Economics, Iowa State University, Ames, Iowa 50011-1070

Andrew B. Whinston — Center for Research in Electronic Commerce, Department of Management Science & Information Systems, University of Texas at Austin, Austin, Texas 78712

Ding Zhang — Department of Management and Marketing, School of Business, State University of New York at Oswego, Oswego, New York, 13126.

1 Financial and Economic Networks: An Overview

Anna Nagurney

1.1 Background

Networks throughout history have provided the physical means by which humans conduct their economic activities. Transportation and logistical networks have allowed for the movement of individuals, goods, and services, whereas communication networks have enabled the exchange of messages and information. Energy networks have provided the fuel for the transactions to take place.

The emergence and evolution of myriad physical networks over space and time and the effects of human decision-making on such networks through their utilization and management thereof has given rise, in turn, to the development of rich theories and scientific methodologies that are network-based. Networks, as a science, have impacted disciplines ranging from engineering, computer science, applied mathematics, and even biology to finance and economics. The novelty of networks is that they are pervasive, providing the fabric of connectivity for our societies and economies, while, methodologically, network theory has developed into a powerful and dynamic medium for abstracting complex problems, which, at first glance, may not even appear to be networks, with associated nodes, links, and flows.

The topic of networks as a subject of scientific inquiry originates in the paper by Euler (1736), which is credited with being the earliest paper on *graph* theory. By a graph in this context is meant, mathematically, a means of abstractly representing a system by its depiction in terms of vertices (or nodes) and edges (or arcs, equivalently, links) connecting various pairs of vertices. Euler was interested in determining whether it was possible to stroll around Königsberg (later called Kaliningrad) by crossing the seven bridges over the River Pregel exactly once. The problem was represented as a graph (cf. Figure 1.1) in which the vertices corresponded to land masses and the edges to bridges.

Interestingly, not long thereafter, Quesnay (1758), in his *Tableau Economique*, conceptualized the circular flow of financial funds in an economy as a network and this work can be identified as the first paper on the topic of

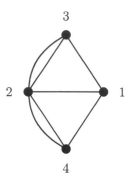

Fig. 1.1. The Euler graph representation of the seven bridge Königsberg problem

financial networks. Quesnay's basic idea has been utilized in the construction of financial flow of funds accounts, which are a statistical description of the flows of money and credit in an economy (see Cohen (1987)).

The concept of a network in economics was implicit as early as the classical work of Cournot (1838), who not only seems to have first explicitly stated that a competitive price is determined by the intersection of supply and demand curves, but had done so in the context of two spatially separated markets in which the cost associated with transporting the goods was also included. Pigou, subsequently, in 1920 studied a network system in the form of a transportation network consisting of two routes and noted that the decision-making behavior of the the users of such a system would lead to different flow patterns. Hence, the network of concern therein consists of the graph, which is now directed, with the edges or links represented by arrows, as well as the resulting flows on the links.

Monge, who had worked under Napoleon Bonaparte in providing infrastructure support for his army, published in 1781 what is probably the first paper on the transportation model (see, e.g., Buckard, Klinz, and Rudolf (1996)). In particular, he was interested in minimizing the cost associated with backfilling n places from m other places with surplus brash with cost c_{ij} being proportional to the distance between origin i and destination j. Much later, and following the first book on graph theory by König in 1936, the economists Kantorovich (1939), Hitchcock (1941), and Koopmans (1947) considered the network flow problem associated with this classical minimum cost transportation problem, provided insights into the special network structure of such problems, and yielded network-based algorithmic approaches. Hence, the study of network flows precedes that of optimization techniques, in general, with seminal work done by Dantzig in 1948 in linear programming with the simplex method and, subsequently, adapted for the classical transportation problem in 1951.

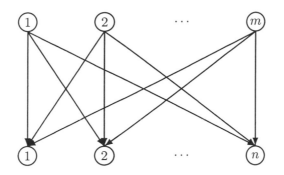

Fig. 1.2. A bipartite network with directed links

In 1952, Copeland in his book recognized the conceptualization of the interrelationships among financial funds as a network and raised the question, "Does money flow like water or electricity?" Moreover, he provided a "wiring diagram for the main money circuit." Note that Kirchhoff is credited with pioneering the field of electrical engineering by being the first to have systematically analyzed electrical circuits and with providing the foundations for the principal ideas of network flow theory. Interestingly, Enke in 1951 had proposed electronic circuits as a means of solving spatial price equilibrium problems, in which goods are produced, consumed, and traded, in the presence of transportation costs. Such analog computational devices, were soon to be superseded by digital computers along with advances in computational methodologies, notably, algorithms, based on mathematical programming, and including not only the aforementioned linear programming techniques but other optimization techniques, as well.

Samuelson (1952) provided a rigorous mathematical formulation of the spatial price equilibrium problem and explicitly recognized and utilized the network structure, which was bipartite (the same structure as in the classical transportation problems), that is, consisting of two sets of nodes (cf. Figure 1.2). Interestingly, he depicted the changing network of trade as the excess demand for the commodity at a particular market increased. In spatial price equilibrium problems, unlike classical transportation problems, the supplies and the demands are variables, rather than fixed quantities. The work was subsequently extended by Takayama and Judge (1964, 1971) and others (cf. Asmuth, Eaves, and Peterson (1979), Florian and Los (1982), Nagurney (1999), and the references therein) to include, respectively, multiple commodities, and asymmetric supply price and demand functions, as well as other extensions, made possible by such advances as quadratic programming techniques, complementarity theory, as well as variational inequality theory (which allowed for the formulation and solution of equilibrium problems for which no optimization reformulation of the governing equilibrium conditions was available).

Beckmann, McGuire, and Winsten (1956), in turn, in their book, provided a rigorous treatment of congested transportation networks, and formulated their solution as mathematical programming problems. Their contributions added significantly to the topic of network equilibrium problems, which was later advanced by the contributions of Dafermos and Sparrow (1969), who coined the terms *user-optimization* versus *system-optimization* and provided computational methods for the determination of the resulting flows on such networks. Subsequent notable contributions were made by Smith (1979) and Dafermos (1980) who allowed for asymmetric interactions associated with the link travel costs (resulting in no equivalent optimization reformulation of the equilibrium conditions) and established the methodology of variational inequalities as a primary tool for both the qualitative analysis and the solution of such and other related problems. For additional background, see the book by Nagurney (1999).

1.2   Financial Networks

We now further elaborate upon historical breakthroughs in the use of networks for the formulation, analysis, and solution of financial problems. Such a perspective allows one to trace the methodological developments as well as the applications of financial networks and provides a platform upon which further innovations can be constructed and evaluated. We begin with a discussion of financial optimization problems within a network context and then turn to financial network equilibrium problems.

1.2.1   Optimization Problems

Network models have been proposed for a spectrum of financial problems characterized by a single objective function to be optimized such as in portfolio optimization and asset allocation problems, currency translation, and risk management problems, among others. We now briefly highlight this literature recognizing that it was, of course, the innovative work of Markowitz (1952, 1959) that started a new era in financial economics and became the basis for many financial optimization models that exist today.

Interestingly, although many financial optimization problems (including the work by Markowitz) had an underlying network structure, and the advantages of network programming were becoming increasingly evident (cf. Charnes and Cooper (1958)), not many financial network optimization models were developed until some time later, with the exception of several early models due to Charnes and Miller (1957) and Charnes and Cooper (1961). Indeed, it was not until the last years of the 1960s and the first years of the 1970s that the network setting started to be extensively used for financial applications.

Among the first financial network optimization models that appear in the literature were a series of currency translating models. Rutenberg (1970) suggested that the translation among different currencies could be performed through the use of arc multipliers. The network model developed by Rutenberg was a multiperiod one with linear costs on the arcs (a characteristic common to the earlier financial networks models). The nodes of such generalized networks represented a particular currency in a specific period and the flow on the arcs the amount of cash moving from one period and/or currency to another. Related financial network models were subsequently introduced by Christofides, Hewins, and Salkin (1979) and Shapiro and Rutenberg (1976), among others. In most of these models, the currency prices were determined according to the amount of capital (network flow) that was moving from one currency (node) to the other.

Networks were also used to formulate a series of cash management problems (cf. Barr (1972) and Srinivasan (1974)), with a major contribution being the introduction (cf. Crum (1976)) of a generalized linear network model for the cash management of a multinational firm. The links in the network represented possible cash flow patterns and the multipliers incorporated costs, fees, liquidity changes, and exchange rates. A series of related cash management problems were modeled as network problems in subsequent years (see, e.g., Crum and Nye (1981), Crum, Klingman, and Tavis (1983)), thereby, further extending the applicability of network programming in financial applications. The focus therein was on linear network flow problems in which the cost on an arc was a linear function of the flow. Crum, Klingman, and Tavis (1979), in turn, showed how contemporary financial capital allocation problems could be modeled as an integer generalized network problem, in which the flows on particular arcs were forced to be integers.

We emphasize that in many financial network optimization problems the objective function must be nonlinear due to the modeling of the risk function and, hence, typically, such financial problems lie in the domain of nonlinear, rather than linear, network flow problems. Mulvey (1987) presented a collection of nonlinear financial network models that were based on previous cash flow and portfolio models in which the original authors (e.g., Rudd and Rosenberg (1979) and Soenen (1979)) did not realize (nor exploit) the underlying network structure. He also emphasized that the Markowitz (1952, 1959) mean-variance minimization problem was, in fact, a network optimization problem with a nonlinear objective function. Here, for completeness, we recall the classical Markowitz models and cast them into the framework of network optimization problems. See Figure 1.3 for the network structure of such problems.

Markowitz's model was based on mean-variance portfolio selection, where the average and the variability of portfolio returns were determined in terms of the mean and covariance of the corresponding investments. The mean is a measure of an average return and the variance is a measure of the distribution

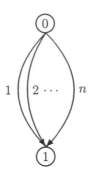

Fig. 1.3. Network structure of classical portfolio optimization

of the returns around the mean return. Markowitz formulated the portfolio optimization problem as associated with risk minimization with the objective function given by:

$$\text{Minimize} \quad V = X^T Q X$$

subject to constraints, representing, respectively, the attainment of a specific return, a budget constraint, and that no short sales were allowed, and, mathematically, given by:

$$R = \sum_{i=1}^{n} X_i r_i$$

$$\sum_{i=1}^{n} X_i = 1$$

$$X_i \geq 0, \quad i = 1, \ldots, n.$$

Here n denotes the total number of securities available in the economy, X_i represents the relative amount of capital invested in security i, with the securities being grouped into the column vector X, Q denotes the $n \times n$ variance-covariance matrix on the return of the portfolio, r_i denotes the expected value of the return of security i, and R denotes the expected rate of return on the portfolio. Within a network context (cf. Figure 1.3), the links correspond to the securities, with their relative amounts $X_1, \ldots, X_n$ corresponding to the flows on the respective links: $1, \ldots, n$. The budget constraint and the nonnegativity assumption on the flows are network conservation equations. Since the objective function here is risk minimization, it can be interpreted as the sum of the costs on the n links in the network. Obsrve that the network representation is abstract and does not correspond (as in the case of transportation) to physical locations and links.

In his work, Markowitz suggested that, for a fixed set of expected values r_i and covariances of the returns of all assets i and j, every investor can find an (R, V) combination that better fits his taste, solely limited by the constraints of the specific problem. Hence, according to the original work of Markowitz (1952), the efficient frontier had to be identified and then every investor had to select a portfolio through a mean-variance analysis that fitted his preferences.

A related mathematical optimization model (Markowitz (1959)) to the one above, which can be interpreted as the investor seeking to maximize his returns while minimizing his risk can be expressed by the quadratic programming problem:

$$\text{Maximize} \quad \alpha R - (1 - \alpha) V$$

subject to:

$$\sum_{i=1}^{n} X_i = 1$$

$$X_i \geq 0, \quad i = 1, \ldots, n,$$

where α denotes an indicator of how risk-averse a specific investor is. Of course, this model is also a network optimization problem with the network as depicted in Figure 1.3.

Many versions and extensions of Markowitz's model have appeared in the literature, a collection of which can be found in Francis and Archer (1979), with $\alpha = 1/2$ being a frequently accepted value. A recent interpretation of the model as a multicriteria decision-making model along with theoretical extensions to multiple sectors can be found in Dong and Nagurney (2001).

Lastly, a part of the optimization literature on financial networks focused on variables that were stochastic and had to be treated as random variables in the optimization procedure. Clearly, since most financial optimization problems are of large size, the incorporation of stochastic variables made the problems more complicated and difficult to model and compute. Mulvey (1987) and Mulvey and Vladimirou (1989, 1991), among others, studied stochastic financial networks, utilizing a series of different theories and techniques (e.g., purchase power priority, arbitrage theory, scenario aggregation) that were then utilized for the estimation of the stochastic elements in the network in order to be able to represent them as a series of deterministic equivalents. The large size and the computational complexity of stochastic networks, at times, limited their usage to specially structured problems where general computational techniques and algorithms could be applied. See Rudd and Rosenberg (1979), Wallace (1986), and Rockafellar and Wets (1991) for a more detailed discussion on aspects of realistic portfolio optimization and implementation issues related to stochastic financial networks.

1.2.2 Equilibrium Problems

In 1969, Thore introduced networks, along with the mathematics, for the study of systems of linked portfolios. His work benefited from that of Charnes and Cooper (1967) which showed that systems of linked accounts could be represented as a network, where the nodes depict the balance sheets and the links depict the credit and debit entries. Thore considered credit networks, with the explicit goal of providing a tool for use in the study of the propagation of money and credit streams in an economy, based on a theory of the behavior of banks and other financial institutions. The credit network recognized that these sectors interact and its solution made use of linear programming. Thore (1970)) then extended the basic network model to handle holdings of financial reserves in the case of uncertainty. The approach utilized two-stage linear programs under uncertainty introduced by Ferguson and Dantzig (1956) and Dantzig and Madansky (1961). See Fei (1960) for a graph theoretic approach to the credit system.

Storoy, Thore, and Boyer (1975), in turn, developed a network representation of the interconnection of capital markets and demonstrated how decomposition theory of mathematical programming could be exploited for the computation of equilibrium. The utility functions facing a sector were no longer restricted to being linear functions. Thore (1980) further investigated network models of linked portfolios, financial intermediation, and decentralization/decomposition theory. However, the computational techniques at that time were not sufficiently well-developed to handle such problems in practice.

Thore (1984) proposed an international financial network for the Euro dollar market and viewed it as a logistical system, exploiting the above-mentioned ideas of Samuelson (1952) and Takayama and Judge (1971) for spatial price equilibrium problems. In this paper, as in Thore's preceding papers on financial networks, the micro-behavioral unit consisted of the individual bank, savings and loan, or other financial intermediary and the portfolio choices were described in some optimizing framework, with the portfolios being linked together into a network with a separate portfolio visualized as a node and assets and liabilities as directed links.

Notably, the above-mentioned contributions focused on the use and application of networks for the study of financial systems consisting of multiple economic decision-makers. In such systems, equilibrium was a central concept, along with the role of prices in the equilibrating mechanism. Rigorous approaches that characterized the formulation of equilibrium and the corresponding price determination were greatly influenced by the Arrow-Debreu economic model (cf. Arrow (1951), Debreu (1951)). In addition, the importance of the inclusion of dynamics in the study of such systems was explicitly emphasized (see, also, Thore and Kydland (1972)).

The first use of finite-dimensional variational inequality theory for the computation of multi-sector, multi-instrument financial equilibria is due to Nagurney, Dong, and Hughes (1992), who recognized the network structure underlying the subproblems encountered in their proposed decomposition scheme. Hughes and Nagurney (1992) and Nagurney and Hughes (1992) had, in turn, proposed the formulation and solution of estimation of financial flow of funds accounts as network optimization problems. Their proposed optimization scheme fully exploited the special network structure of these problems. Nagurney and Siokos (1997) then developed an international financial equilibrium model utilizing finite-dimensional variational inequality theory for the first time in that framework.

Finite-dimensional variational inequality theory is a powerful unifying methodology in that it contains, as special cases, such mathematical programming problems as: nonlinear equations, optimization problems, and complementarity problems. Moreover, with projected dynamical systems theory (see the book by Nagurney and Zhang (1996)) one can then also trace the dynamic behavior prior to an equilibrium state (formulated as a variational inequality). In contrast to classical dynamical systems, projected dynamical systems are characterized by a discontinuous right-hand side, with the discontinuity arising due to the constraint set underlying the application in question. Hence, this methodology allows one to model systems dynamically which are subject to limited resources, with a principal constraint in finance being budgetary restrictions.

Dong, Zhang, and Nagurney (1996) were the first to apply the methodology of projected dynamical systems to develop a dynamic multi-sector, multi-instrument financial model, whose set of stationary points coincided with the set of solutions to the variational inequality model developed in Nagurney (1994); and then to study it qualitatively, providing stability analysis results.

The book by Nagurney and Siokos (1997) presents the foundations of financial networks to that date as well as an overview of the basic methodologies for the formulation, analysis, and solution of such problems with a particular focus on equilibrium problems. Additional background can be found in Nagurney (2001). Finally, Nagurney and Ke (2001, 2003) focus on financial networks with intermediation and utilize variational inequalities in that problem domain.

1.3 Economic Networks

As the preceding discussion has noted, the development of the study of economic networks has been based heavily on transportation networks as well as on spatial price equilibrium networks in the form of interregional commodity trade. Extensive references on the subject as well as a variety of models and applications can be found in Nagurney (1999). Here, we recall two economic equilibrium problems and provide their network equilibrium formulations. The first is a Walrasian price equilibrium problem, which is an example of general equilibrium, whereas, the second is a spatial price equilibrium problem, which is a partial equilibrium problem.

1.3.1   Equilibrium Problems

Zhao and Nagurney (1993) (see also Zhao and Dafermos (1991)) considered the general economic equilibrium problem known as the Walrasian price equilibrium problem as a network equilibrium problem with precisely the network structure given in Figure 1.3. However, the flows on the network representing this problem correspond to prices of different commodities. For completeness and easy reference we briefly review the pure exchange economic equilibrium model and also give its variational inequality formulation. We consider a pure exchange economy with n commodities, price vector $p = (p_1, p_2, \ldots, p_n)^T$ taking values in the positive orthant R_+^n, and the induced aggregate excess demand function $z(p)$, with components $z_1(p), \ldots, z_n(p)$. Under certain technical assumptions (such as requiring that $z(p)$ be homogeneous of degree zero in p), we may normalize the prices so that they take values in the unit simplex, that is,

$$S^n = p : p \in R_+^n, \sum_{i=1}^{n} p_i = 1.$$

As is standard in general economic equilibrium theory, the aggregate excess demand function must satisfy Walras's law:

$$\langle p^T, z(p) \rangle = 0, \quad \forall p \in S^n,$$

with $\langle \, , \, \rangle$ denoting the inner product with the aformentioned equation being equivalent to: $\sum_{i=1}^{n} p_i z_i(p) = 0$.

We now recall the definition of a Walrasian equilibrium.

Definition 1.1: Walrasian Price Equilibrium
A price vector $p^* \in S^n$ is a Walrasian equilibrium if the market is cleared for valuable commodities and is in excess supply for free commodities, that is,

$$z_i(p^*) = 0, \quad if \quad p_i^* > 0$$

$$z_i(p^*) \leq 0, \quad if \quad p_i^* = 0.$$

The following theorem, due to Dafermos (1990), shows the equivalence between Walrasian price equilibria and solutions of a variational inequality problem.

Theorem 1.1: Variational Inequality Formulation of Walrasian Price Equilibrium
A price vector $p^* \in S^n$ is a Walrasian price equilibrium if and only if it satisfies the variational inequality: determine $p \in S^n$ such that

$$\langle -z(p^*), p - p^* \rangle \geq 0, \quad \forall p \in S^n.$$

This example vividly illustrates that fundamental economic equilibrium problems can be cast into a network equilibrium framework. We now (due to its importance in the development of economic network models) recall the spatial price equilibrium problem and provide its variational inequality formulation (for further details, see Florian and Los (1982), Dafermos and Nagurney (1987), and Nagurney (1999)).

Consider the spatial price equilibrium problem in quantity variables with m supply markets and m demand markets involved in the production and consumption of a homogeneous commodity under perfect competition. Denote a typical supply market by i and a typical demand market by j. Let s_i denote the supply and π_i the supply price of the commodity at supply market i. Let d_j denote the demand and ρ_j the demand price at demand market j. Group the supplies and supply prices, respectively, into a column vector $s \in R^m$ and a row vector $\pi \in R^m$. Similarly, group the demands and demand prices, respectively, into a column vector $d \in R^n$ and a row vector $\rho \in R^n$. Let Q_{ij} denote the nonnegative commodity shipment between the supply and demand market pair (i, j), and let c_{ij} denote the unit transaction cost associated with trading the commodity between (i, j). The unit transaction costs are assumed to include the unit costs of transportation from supply markets to demand markets, and, depending upon the application, may also include a tax/tariff, duty, or subsidy incorporated into these costs. Group the commodity shipments into a column vector $Q \in R^{mn}$ and the transaction costs into a row vector $c \in R^{mn}$. The network structure of the problem is depicted in Figure 1.2.

Assume that the supply price at any supply market may, in general, depend upon the supply of the commodity at every supply market, that is, $\pi = \pi(s)$, where π is a known smooth function. Similarly, the demand price at any demand market may depend upon, in general, the demand of the commodity at every demand market, that is, $\rho = \rho(d)$, where ρ is a known smooth function. The unit transaction cost between a pair of supply and demand markets may depend upon the shipments of the commodity between every pair of markets, that is, $c = c(Q)$, where c is a known smooth function.

The supplies, demands, and shipments of the commodity, in turn, must satisfy the following feasibility conditions, which are also referred to as the *conservation of flow equations*:

$$s_i = \sum_{j=1}^{n} Q_{ij}, \quad i = 1, ..., m$$

$$d_j = \sum_{i=1}^{m} Q_{ij}, \quad j = 1, ..., n$$

$$Q_{ij} \geq 0, \quad i = 1, ..., m; j = 1, ..., n.$$

In other words, the supply at each supply market is equal to the commodity shipments out of that supply market to all the demand markets.

Similarly, the demand at each demand market is equal to the commodity shipments from all the supply markets into that demand market.

Definition 1.2: Spatial Price Equilibrium
Following Samuelson (1952) and Takayama and Judge (1971), the supply, demand, and commodity shipment pattern (s^*, Q^*, d^*) constitutes a spatial price equilibrium, if it is feasible, and for all pairs of supply and demand markets (i, j), it satisfies the conditions:

$$\pi_i(s^*) + c_{ij}(Q^*) \begin{cases} = \rho_j(d^*), & if \quad Q_{ij}^* > 0 \\ \geq \rho_j(d^*), & if \quad Q_{ij}^* = 0. \end{cases}$$

Hence, if the commodity shipment between a pair of supply and demand markets is positive at equilibrium, then the demand price at the demand market must be equal to the supply price at the originating supply market plus the unit transaction cost. If the commodity shipment is zero in equilibrium, then the supply price plus the unit transaction cost can exceed the demand price.

The spatial price equilibrium can be formulated as a variational inequality problem. Precisely, we have following Florian and Los (1982), Dafermos and Nagurney (1987):

Theorem 1.2: Variational Inequality Formulation of Spatial Price Equilibrium
A commodity supply, shipment, and demand pattern $(s^*, Q^*, d^*) \in K$ is a spatial price equilibrium if and only if it satisfies the following variational inequality problem:

$$\langle \pi(s^*), s - s^* \rangle + \langle c(Q^*), Q - Q^* \rangle + \langle -\rho(d^*), d - d^* \rangle \geq 0, \quad \forall (s, Q, d) \in K,$$

where $K \equiv \{(s, Q, d) : feasibility\ conditions\ hold\}$.

An Example

For illustrative purposes, we now present a small example. Consider the spatial price equilibrium problem consisting of two supply markets and two demand markets. Assume that the functions are as follows:

$$\pi_1(s) = 5s_1 + s_2 + 1, \quad \pi_2(s) = 4s_2 + s_1 + 2$$

$$c_{11}(Q) = 2Q_{11} + Q_{12} + 3, \ c_{12}(Q) = Q_{12} + 5,$$

$$c_{21}(Q) = 3Q_{21} + Q_{22} + 7, \ c_{22}(Q) = 3Q_{22} + 2Q_{21} + 9$$

$$\rho_1(d) = -d_1 - d_2 + 21, \quad \rho_2(d) = -5d_2 - 3d_1 + 29.$$

It is easy to verify that the spatial price equilibrium pattern is given by:

$$s_1^* = 2,\ s_2^* = 1,\ Q_{11}^* = 1,\ Q_{12}^* = 1,\ Q_{21}^* = 1,\ Q_{22}^* = 0,\ d_1^* = 2,\ d_2^* = 1.$$

In one of the simplest models, in which the Jacobians of the supply price functions, $\left[\frac{\partial \pi}{\partial s}\right]$, the transportation (or transaction) cost functions, $\left[\frac{\partial c}{\partial Q}\right]$, and minus the demand price functions, $-\left[\frac{\partial \rho}{\partial d}\right]$ are diagonal and positive definite, then the spatial price equilibrium pattern coincides with the Kuhn-Tucker conditions of the strictly convex optimization problem:

$$\text{Minimize}_{Q \in R_+^{MN}} \quad \sum_{i=1}^{M} \int_0^{\sum_{j=1}^{N} Q_{ij}} \pi_i(x)dx + \sum_{i=1}^{M} \sum_{j=1}^{N} \int_0^{Q_{ij}} c_{ij}(y)dy$$

$$\sum_{j=1}^{N} \int_0^{\sum_{i=1}^{M} Q_{ij}} \rho_j(z)dz.$$

We note also that the classical Cournot (1838) (see also Nash (1950, 1951)) oligopoly problem which possesses a variational inequality formulation (cf. Gabay and Moulin (1980)) can also be cast into a network framework (cf. Nagurney (1999)) with the structure as given in Figure 1.3. Numerous spatial oligopoly problems including those having the network structure given in Figure 1.2) have also been developed and algorithms that exploit the network structure proposed (see Dafermos and Nagurney (1987) and Nagurney, Dupuis, and Zhang (1994), and the references therein).

Finally, it is worth mentioning that a variety of migration problems in economics have a network structure as do knowledge network problems (cf. Nagurney (1999)).

1.4 The Internet and New Directions

The advent of the Internet, along with associated communication methodologies, has further elevated the interest in networks and the importance thereof. It has brought greater focus to the study of financial and economic networks, the interaction among networks (as in the case of supernetworks (cf. Nagurney and Dong (2002)), and to the entire field of network economics, including network industries (cf. Shapiro and Varian (1999)). Entirely new subject areas such as electronic commerce (cf. Whinston, Stahl, and Choi (1997)) and electronic finance (cf. Claessens and Jansen (2000)) have been born whereas others such as supply chain networks (cf. Nagurney et al. (2002)) have evolved both in dimension and complexity. In such contexts the role of intermediaries becomes increasingly important as well as the dynamics and network structures.

Coupled with the growth of the Internet have come new and more powerful tools for the modeling, analysis, and solution of financial and economic network problems. Such tools, some of which are revealed in this volume, provide new methodologies, both analytical and conceptual, from which further advances can be expected. Above we have provided an overview of financial and

Table 1.1. Methodologies utilized in this volume

Methodology	Chapter
Agent-based simulation	11, 12
Fluid dynamics	10
Game theory	5, 7, 9, 11 – 13
Graph theory	2, 9
Network theory	4, 7, 9 – 12
Optimization	2 – 5, 7 – 11, 13
Stochastic programming	3, 4
Variational inequalities	5, 7, 9

economic networks from both optimization and equilibrium perspectives with a view towards historical developments. It is worth noting also the growth of simulation approaches, notably, those based on agent-based computational economics (ACE), which provide computational studies of economies modeled as evolving systems of autonomous interacting agents (cf. Tesfatsion (2002)) for the study of economic network phenomena.

1.5   Outline of the Volume

This volume presents a broad collection of recent innovations in the study of financial and economic networks by leading scholars in different parts of the world.

Part I of this book focuses on financial networks, ranging from the use of graph theory to provide a new perspective on the stock market, to the conceptualization, modeling, and solution of international financial networks with electronic transactions, and, finally, to the use of financial options to hedge transportation capacity in the rail industry. Part II of this book turns to economic networks, beginning with new frameworks for supply chain and distribution problems, to the use of agent-based computational economics for the study of trade with intermediaries (and varying amounts of information) and for the evolution of worker-employer networks. This part as well as the volume concludes with a market framework for trade in demand-side Web caching.

The innovations in this volume are broad, original, and timely and include conceptual, theoretical, methodological, empirical, as well as application-based contributions. Table 1.1 lists the principal methodologies utilized and in what chapters they may be found. Table 1.2, in turn, highlights some of the applications in this volume.

In addition, for the convenience of the reader, we provide a snapshot of

Table 1.2. Applications in this volume

Application	Chapter
Capacity provision networks	13
Competition	5, 6, 7, 9, 11, 13
Corporate planning	4
Distribution systems	9, 10
Electronic transactions	6, 7, 11, 13
Equilibrium analysis	5, 7, 9
Financial planning	3, 4, 6, 7, 8
Financial services	6, 7
Hedging instruments	8
Intermediation	6, 7, 9, 10, 11, 13
International finance	6, 7
Internet effects	6, 7, 11, 13
Labor markets	12
Network industries	6, 8
Pension planning	4
Policy analysis	6, 12
Portfolio optimization	3, 4, 5, 7
Pricing	7 – 11
Risk management	3, 4, 5, 7, 8
Stock market	2
Supply chains and logistics	9, 10
Trade networks	11, 13
Transportation networks	8, 10
Worker-employer networks	12

the contents of the volume in Table 1.3 in terms of the type of innovations (conceptual, theoretical, methodological, etc.).

Chapter 2 by Boginski, Butenko, and Pardalos presents a detailed study of the stock market graph, which yields a new tool for the analysis of the market structure through the classification of stocks into different groups. The authors first demonstrate how information generated by the stock market can be used to construct a market graph, consisting of vertices and edges, and based on the cross-correlations of price fluctuations. This graph, which may be massive in size, is then analyzed from the perspective of finding cliques and independent sets. Boginski, Butenko, and Pardalos then make evident, through experiments, that the distribution of the correlation coefficients between the stocks in the US stock market remains very stable over time. The authors also establish, for the first time in the field of finance, the

Table 1.3. Snapshot of innovations in this volume

Chapter	Conceptual	Theoretical	Methodological	Empirical	Applications
2	X	X	X	X	X
3	X		X	X	X
4	X		X	X	X
5	X	X	X		X
6	X				X
7	X	X	X		X
8	X			X	X
9	X	X	X		X
10	X	X	X		X
11	X		X	X	X
12	X		X	X	X
13	X	X			X

applicability of the power-law model, which describes massive graphs arising in telecommunications and the Internet.

Chapter 3 by Gülpinar, Rustem, and Settergren uses multistage stochastic programming in order to model the problem of financial portfolio management with transaction costs, given stochastic data provided in the form of a scenario tree. The mean or variance of the total wealth at the end of the planning horizon can be optimized in view of the transaction costs by solving either a linear or a quadratic stochastic program. Moreover, the incorporation of proportional transaction costs yields a model that reflects the effect of these costs on portfolio performance. Numerical experiments backtesting the optimization strategies at different levels of risk and transaction cost are reported, as well as tests that do not optimize over the affected transaction costs. The results show that the incorporation of transaction costs improves investment performance.

The fourth chapter, by Mulvey, Simsek, and Pauling, also utilizes stochastic programming for financial decision-making, and presents a multi-period stochastic network model for integrating corporate financial and pension planning. The model maximizes the combined company's value over a finite planning time horizon and has certain advantages over general nonlinear programs, especially in regards to the model's understandability. The empirical results demonstrate that the integration of pension planning is feasible and that it can improve a company's performance. Moreover, the authors, by analyzing historical data for some typical pension plans, demonstrate that the recent loss of surplus by many large US companies was largely preventable. The methodology proposed requires three elements: a stochastic scenario generator, a pension/corporate simulator, and a stochastic network optimizer. Solving such stochastic programming problems has become practical due to the large improvements in computer hardware and software.

Chapter 5 shifts from stochastic optimization to the investigation of financial equilibria in the case of multiple sectors and multiple financial instruments. Daniele in this chapter proposes a new framework for the modeling, analysis, and computation of financial equilibria through a novel evolutionary model. In contrast to earlier multi-sector, multi-instrument financial equilibrium models, the new model allows for variance-covariance matrices associated with risk perception to be time-dependent as well as the sector financial volumes. Daniele identifies the network structure of the sectors' optimization problems out of equilibrium and provides the network structure of the financial economy in equilibrium. The methodology utilized for the formulation, qualitative analysis, and solution of such problems is that of infinite-dimensional variational inequalities

Chapter 6 focuses on financial services industries, which have been undergoing rapid change due to globalization and technological advances, including electronic finance, and examines the importance of networks in finance and its effects on competition. Claessens, Dobos, Klingebiel, and Laeven, in this chapter, argue that, as part of the changes, financial services are becoming less special, making policies to preserve the franchise value of financial institutions less necessary while competition policy becomes more feasible. They identify the main characteristics of networks, from an economic perspective, along with related public policy issues. They conclude that as financial services heavily and increasingly depend on networks for their production and distribution, that competition policy for financial services becomes more necessary and will need to resemble that used in other network industries, such as telecommunications. Hence, the institutional and functional approaches to competition in the financial sector need to be complemented with more production-based approaches to competition.

The seventh chapter, by Nagurney and Cruz, is complementary to Chapter 6 in that international finance with intermediaries and electronic transactions is of primary concern. However, rather than a focus on competition and appropriate policies with a view of the financial sector as a network industry, it considers the modeling, analysis, and computation of such international financial network problems when the optimizing behavior of those with sources of funds, that of the intermediaries, as well as the consumers is assumed known and given. The authors identify the international financial network with intermediaries in which transactions can take place either physically or electronically, model the behavior of the various decision-makers (which includes net revenue maximization as well as risk minimization), derive the equilibrium conditions, and establish the governing finite-dimensional variational inequality formulation. This formulation is then utilized to obtain both qualitative properties of the equilibrium price and financial flow pattern, as well as a computational procedure. Numerical examples are provided to illustrate both the model and the algorithm. The model is sufficiently general to include as many countries, financial sectors in each country, currencies, and intermediaries, as well as financial products, as needed.

In Chapter 8, Law, MacKay, and Nolan describe a potential derivatives, in particular, financial options, market for rail car capacity pricing in the case of a deregulated rail industry. The authors discuss the rail industry in the United States and Canada, identifying the similarities and differences. They delineate the features of the rail car capacity market that they expect to evolve if there is entry deregulation in this industry, noting the existing capacity allocation mechanisms that will be kept and discussing those that will be entirely new. They draw links between the possible future for the rail industry and the path that has been followed by other network industries, such as natural gas and electricity, that have deregulated in recent years. An empirical example is constructed to show how such a market might actually function, using coal as the commodity to be transported by rail.

Part II of this book, which focuses on economic networks, starts out with Chapter 9.

Chapter 9 develops a new framework for supply chain networks, using concepts from graph theory, optimization theory, and variational inequality theory. Co-authored by Zhang, Dong, and Nagurney, it develops a general network model of a supply chain economy to study supply chain competition. The proposed network framework considers the transformation and pricing of the material flows as they propagate through the network from origins, associated, for example, with raw material suppliers, to destinations – the consumer markets. The network includes both operation links and interface links, with an operation link representing a business operation such as manufacturing, storage, and/or transportation, while an interface link represents a business to business bridge. The model allows for the formulation and analysis of both intra-chain cooperation and inter-chain competition, and predicts the *winning* supply chains, which are those that carry positive chain flows. The model has the notable feature that as many links (and any topology as needed) can be utilized to describe the supply chain structures to capture both cooperation as well as competition. The network model is also analyzed qualitatively in terms of existence and uniqueness of solutions.

Chapter 10, in turn, by Kachani and Perakis, proposes a fluid model of dynamic pricing and inventory control in the context of supply chain management under make-to-stock regime. In particular, the supply chain system that the authors consider is a distribution system that consists of several wholesalers, intermediate distributors, and retailers. All entities are subsidiaries of the same company that is producing and selling multiple products. The model does not require the determination of how prices at each wholesaler, distributor, and retailer affect the corresponding demands. Instead, the model accounts for how price and level of inventory affect the sojourn time of the products at each wholesaler, distributor, and retailer in the distribution system. The model, hence, allows for joint pricing, production, and inventory decisions in a capacitated, multi-product, and dynamically evolving distribution system. Kachani and Perakis also analyze the properties of the model and establish conditions under which the model gives rise to reasonable policies. Finally, the authors discuss how this delay approach connects with more traditional demand models.

The following two chapters utilize agent-based computational modeling within a trade network game simulation framework to investigate economic questions in electronic commerce and in labor institutions, respectively. Chapter 11, by Alkemade, Poutré, and Amman, investigates whether intermediaries can still make a profit in an information economy. In particular, the authors study the influence of the network structure and the information level of the agents, in the form of producers, consumers, and intermediaries, on the level of intermediated trade. The main conclusion of the simulations is that intermediaries that have better knowledge of the market than the average consumer will continue to exist and make a profit if the market dynamics are sufficiently complex. For example, intermediaries that are experts at finding the best price quotes can survive in an electronic trade network where consumers can also form direct links to producers. However, ultimately, most consumers bypass the intermediary if direct trade is more profitable. Interestingly, the authors find that in the case of higher purchase prices, consumers compensate for the higher purchase price by maintaining fewer links, and this has a stabilizing effect on the architecture of the electronic trade network.

Chapter 12, by Pingle and Tesfatsion, applies agent-based computational modeling to analyze the impact of labor institutions. Determining the effects of labor institutions on macroeconomic performance is a central concern of economic policymakers. Specifically, the authors utilize an agent-based computational labor market model to conduct systematic experiments testing the sensitivity of macroeconomic performance to changes in the level of a non-employment payment. The computational experiments are implemented by means of the *Trade Network Game Laboratory*, which is an agent-based computational laboratory for studying the evolution of trade networks via real-time simulations, tables, and graphical displays. The experiments allow the authors to examine the effects of a non-employment payoff on network formation and work-site behaviors among workers and employers participating in a sequential employment game with incomplete contracts.

The final chapter in this volume, authored by Geng, Gopal, Ramesh, and Whinston, introduces Capacity Provision Networks (CPN) as a market framework for demand-side Web cache trading. According to the authors, the need for demand-side cache trading is supported by the fact that there exist positive network externalities across individual Internet Service Providers who provide caching services to their respective users. The need for a CPN market is further supported by the existence of convexity in capacity discounting and the consequential potential for intermediation in cache trading. This chapter develops three critical components in an implementation of Capacity Provision Networks: a technical framework, the economic foundations of such networks, and tactical models of real-time trading, and demonstrates the technical and economic viability of a CPN to effectively support demand-side distributed caching systems through the mechanisms of cache trading and deployment. Possible future research will include futures contract, options, and the development of indices as instruments for Internet Service Providers to coordinate capacity decisions through trading mechanisms.

1.6   Notes

In this chapter we have attempted to provide a preface to the subject matter at hand so that the innovations in this volume can be appreciated. The chapters in this volume contain additional source and background material as well as appropriate references.

In addition to the above-mentioned references and the other citations following each chapter in this book, we also mention several books that provide further interesting material and background on networks. For a history of graph theory and contributions over two centuries, see Biggs, Lloyd, and Wilson (1976). For numerous models, algorithms, and applications of network flows, see the book by Ahuja, Magnanti, and Orlin (1993). For a classical book on network flows, see Ford and Fulkerson (1962).

References

Ahuja, R. K., Magnanti, T. L., and Orlin, J. B. (1993), *Network Flows*, Prentice Hall, Upper Saddle River, New Jersey.

Arrow, K. J. (1951), "An Extension of the Basic Theorems of Classical Welfare Economics," *Econometrica* **51**, 1305-1323.

Asmuth, R., Eaves, B. C., and Peterson, E. L. (1979), "Computing Economic Equilibria on Affine Networks," *Mathematics of Operations Research* **4**, 209-214.

Barr, R. S. (1972), "The Multinational Cash Management Problem: A Generalized Network Approach," Working Paper, University of Texas, Austin, Texas.

Beckmann, M. J., McGuire, C. B., and Winsten, C. B. (1956), *Studies in the Economics of Transportation*, Yale University Press, New Haven, Connecticut.

Biggs, N. L., Lloyd, E. K., and Wilson, R. J. (1976), *Graph Theory 1736-1936*, Clarendon Press, Oxford, England.

Burkard, R., Klinz, B., and Rudolf, R. (1996), "Perspectives of Monge Properties in Optimization," *Discrete Applied Mathematics* **70**, 95-161.

Charnes, A., and Cooper, W. W. (1958), "Nonlinear Network Flows and Convex Programming over Incidence Matrices," *Naval Research Logistics Quarterly* **5**, 231-240.

Charnes, A., and Cooper, W. W. (1961), *Management Models and Industrial Applications of Linear Programming*, John Wiley & Sons, New York.

Charnes, A., and Cooper, W. W. (1967), "Some Network Characterizations for Mathematical Programming and Accounting Approaches to Planning and Control," *The Accounting Review* **42**, 24-52.

Charnes, A., and Miller, M. (1957), "Programming and Financial Budgeting," Symposium on Techniques of Industrial Operations Research, Chicago, Illinois, June.

Christofides, N., Hewins, R. D., and, Salkin, G. R. (1979), "Graph Theoretic Approaches to Foreign Exchange Operations," *Journal of Financial and Quantitative Analysis* **14**, 481-500.

Claessens, S. and Jansen, M., editors (2000), *Internationalization of Financial Services*, Kluwer Academic Publishers, Boston, Massachusetts.

Cohen, J. (1987), *The Flow of Funds in Theory and Practice*, *Financial and Monetary Studies* **15**, Kluwer Academic Publishers, Dordrecht, The Netherlands.

Copeland, M. A. (1952), *A Study of Moneyflows in the United States*, National Bureau of Economic Research, New York.

Cournot, A. A. (1838), *Researches into the Mathematical Principles of the Theory of Wealth*, English Translation, Macmillan, London, England, 1897.

Crum, R. L. (1976), "Cash Management in the Multinational Firm: A Constrained Generalized Network Approach," Working Paper, University of Florida, Gainesville, Florida.

Crum, R. L., Klingman, D. D., and Tavis, L. A. (1979), "Implementation of Large-Scale Financial Planning Models: Solution Efficient Transformations," *Journal of Financial and Quantitative Analysis* **14**, 137-152.

Crum, R. L., Klingman, D. D., and Tavis, L. A. (1983), "An Operational Approach to Integrated Working Capital Planning," *Journal of Economics and Business* **35**, 343-378.

Crum, R. L., and Nye, D. J. (1981), "A Network Model of Insurance Company Cash Flow Management," *Mathematical Programming Study* **15**, 86-101.

Dafermos, S. (1980), "Traffic Equilibrium and Variational Inequalities," *Transportation Science* **14**, 42-54.

Dafermos, S. (1990), "Exchange Price Equilibria and Variational Inequalities," *Mathematical Programming* **46**, 391-402.

Dafermos, S., and Nagurney, A. (1987), "Oligopolistic and Competitive Behavior of Spatially Separated Markets," *Regional Science and Urban Economics* **17**, 245-254.

Dafermos, S. C., and Sparrow, F. T. (1969), "The Traffic Assignment Problem for a General Network," *Journal of Research of the National Bureau of Standards* **73B**, 91-118.

Dantzig, G. B. (1948), "Programming in a Linear Structure," Comptroller, United States Air Force, Washington DC, February.

Dantzig, G. B. (1951), "Application of the Simplex Method to the Transportation Problem," in *Activity Analysis of Production and Allocation*, pp. 359-373, T. C. Koopmans, editor, John Wiley & Sons, New York.

Dantzig, G. B., and Madansky, A. (1961), "On the Solution of Two-Stage Linear Programs under Uncertainty," in *Proceedings of the Fourth Berkeley Symposium on Mathematical Statistics and Probability* **1**, pp. 165-176, University of California Press, Berkeley, California.

Debreu G. (1951), "The Coefficient of Resource Utilization," *Econometrica* **19**, 273-292.

Dong, J., and Nagurney, A. (2001), "Bicriteria Decision-Making and Financial Equilibrium: A Variational Inequality Perspective," *Computational Economics* **17**, 29-42.

Dong, J., Zhang, D., and Nagurney, A. (1996), "A Projected Dynamical Systems Model of General Financial Equilibrium with Stability Analysis," *Mathematical and Computer Modelling* **24**, 35-44.

Enke, S. (1951) "Equilibrium among Spatially Separated Markets," *Econometrica* **10**, 40-47.

Euler, L. (1736), "Solutio Problematis ad Geometriam Situs Pertinentis," *Commetarii Academiae Scientiarum Imperialis Petropolitanae* **8**, 128-140.

Fei, J. C. H. (1960), "The Study of the Credit System by the Method of Linear Graph," *The Review of Economics and Statistics* **42**, 417-428.

Ferguson, A. R., and Dantzig, G. B. (1956), "The Allocation of Aircraft to Routes," *Management Science* **2**, 45-73.

Florian, M., and Los, M. (1982), "A New Look at Static Spatial Price Equilibrium Models," *Regional Science and Urban Economics* **12**, 579-597.

Ford, L. R., and Fulkerson, D. R. (1962), *Flows in Networks*, Princeton University Press, Princeton, New Jersey.

Francis, J. C., and Archer, S. H. (1979), *Portfolio Analysis*, Prentice Hall, Englewood Cliffs, New Jersey.

Gabay, D., and Moulin, H. (1980), "On the Uniqueness and Stability of Nash Equilibria in Noncooperative Games," in *Applied Stochastic Control in Econometrics and Management Science*, pp. 271-294, A. Bensoussan, F.

Kleindorfer, and C. S. Tapiero, editors, North-Holland, Amsterdam, The Netherlands.

Hitchcock, F. L. (1941), "The Distribution of a Product from Several Sources to Numerous Facilities," *Journal of Mathematical Physics* **20**, 224-230.

Hughes, M., and Nagurney, A. (1992), "A Network Model and Algorithm for the Estimation and Analysis of Financial Flow of Funds," *Computer Science in Economics and Management* **5**, 23-39.

Kantorovich, L. V. (1939), "Mathematical Methods in the Organization and Planning of Production," Publication House of the Leningrad University; Translated in *Management Science* **6** (1960), 366-422.

König, D. (1936), *Theorie der Endlichen und Unendlichen Graphen*, Teubner, Leipzig, Germany.

Koopmans, T. C. (1947), "Optimum Utilization of the Transportation System," *Proceedings of the International Statistical Conference*, Washington DC, Also in *Econometrica* 17 (1949), 136-146.

Markowitz, H. M. (1952), "Portfolio Selection," *The Journal of Finance* **7**, 77-91.

Markowitz, H. M. (1959), *Portfolio Selection: Efficient Diversification of Investments*, John Wiley & Sons, Inc., New York.

Monge, G. (1781), "Mémoire sur la Théorie des Déblais et des Remblais," in *Histoire de l'Acadèmie Royale des Sciences, Année M. DCCLXXX1, avec les Mémoires de Mathématique et de Physique, pour la Méme Année, Tirés des Registres de cette Académie*, pp. 666-704, Paris, France.

Mulvey, J. M. (1987), "Nonlinear Networks in Finance," *Advances in Mathematical Programming and Financial Planning* **1**, 253-271.

Mulvey, J. M., and Vladimirou, H. (1989), "Stochastic Network Optimization Models for Investment Planning," *Annals of Operations Research* **20**, 187-217.

Mulvey, J. M., and Vladimirou, H. (1991), "Solving Multistage Stochastic Networks: An Application of Scenario Aggregation," *Networks* **21**, 619-643.

Nagurney, A. (1994), "Variational Inequalities in the Analysis and Computation of Multi-Sector, Multi-Instrument Financial Equilibria," *Journal of Economic Dynamics and Control* **18**, 161-184.

Nagurney, A. (1999), *Network Economics: A Variational Inequality Approach*, Second and Revised Edition, Kluwer Academic Publishers, Dordrecht, The Netherlands.

Nagurney, A. (2001), "Finance and Variational Inequalities," *Quantitative Finance* **1**, 309-317.

Nagurney, A., and Dong, J. (2002), *Supernetworks: Decision-Making for the Information Age*, Edward Elgar Publishers, Cheltenham, England.

Nagurney, A., Dong, J., and Hughes, M. (1992), "Formulation and Computation of General Financial Equilibrium," *Optimization* **26**, 339-354.

Nagurney, A., Dupuis, P., and Zhang, D. (1994), "A Dynamical Systems Approach for Network Oligopolies and Variational Inequalities," *Regional Science and Urban Economics* **28**, 263-283.

Nagurney, A., and Hughes, M. (1992), "Financial Flow of Funds Networks," *Networks* **22**, 145-161.

Nagurney, A., and Ke, K. (2001), "Financial Networks with Intermediation," *Quantitative Finance* **1**, 441-451.

Nagurney, A., and Ke, K. (2003), "Financial Networks with Electronic Transactions: Modeling, Analysis, and Computations," *Quantitative Finance* **3**, 71-87.

Nagurney, A., Loo, J., Dong, J., and Zhang, D. (2002), "Supply Chain Networks and Electronic Commerce: A Theoretical Perspective," *Netnomics* **4**, 187-220.

Nagurney, A., and Siokos, S. (1997), "Variational Inequalities for International General Financial Equilibrium Modeling and Computation," *Mathematical and Computer Modelling* **25**, 31-49.

Nagurney, A., and Zhang, D. (1996), *Projected Dynamical Systems and Variational Inequalities with Applications*, Kluwer Academic Publishers, Boston, Massachusetts.

Nash, J. F. (1950), "Equilibrium Points in N-Person Games," *Proceedings of the National Academy of Sciences* **36**, 48-49.

Nash, J. F. (1951), "Noncooperative Games," *Annals of Mathematics* **54**, 286-298.

Pigou, A. C. (1920), *The Economics of Welfare*, Macmillan, London, England.

Quesnay, F. (1758), *Tableau Economique*, 1758, reproduced in facsimile with an introduction by H. Higgs by the British Economic Society, 1895.

Rockafellar, R. T., and Wets, R. J.-B. (1991), "Scenarios and Policy in Optimization under Uncertainty," *Mathematics of Operations Research* **16**, 1-29.

Rudd, A., and Rosenberg, B. (1979), "Realistic Portfolio Optimization," *TIMS Studies in the Management Sciences* **11**, 21-46.

Rutenberg, D. P. (1970), "Maneuvering Liquid Assets in a Multi-National Company: Formulation and Deterministic Solution Procedures," *Management Science* **16**, 671-684.

Samuelson, P. A. (1952), "Spatial Price Equilibrium and Linear Programming," *American Economic Review* **42**, 283-303.

Shapiro, A. C., and Rutenberg, D. P. (1976), "Managing Exchange Risks in a Floating World," *Financial Management* **16**, 48-58.

Shapiro, C., and Varian, H. R. (1999), *Information Rules: A Strategic Guide to the Network Economy*, Harvard Business School Press, Boston, Massachusetts.

Smith, M. J. (1979), "Existence, Uniqueness, and Stability of Traffic Equilibria," *Transportation Research* **13B**, 259-304.

Soenen, L. A. (1979), *Foreign Exchange Exposure Management: A Portfolio Approach*, Sijthoff and Noordhoff, Germantown, Maryland.

Srinivasan, V. (1974), "A Transshipment Model for Cash Management Decisions," *Management Science* **20**, 1350-1363.

Storoy, S., Thore, S., and Boyer, M. (1975), "Equilibrium in Linear Capital Market Networks," *The Journal of Finance* **30**, 1197-1211.

Takayama, T., and Judge, G. G. (1964), "An Intertemporal Price Equilibrium Model," *Journal of Farm Economics* **46**, 477-484.

Takayama, T., and Judge, G. G. (1971), *Spatial and Temporal Price and Allocation Models*, North Holland, Inc, Amsterdam, The Netherlands.

Tesfatsion, L. (2002), "Economic Agents and Markets as Emergent Phenomena," *Proceedings of the National Academy of Sciences U.S.A.* **99**, Supplement 3, 7191-7192.

Thore, S. (1969), "Credit Networks," *Economica* **36**, 42-57.

Thore, S. (1970), "Programming a Credit Network under Uncertainty," *Journal of Money, Banking, and Finance* **2**, 219-246.

Thore, S. (1980), *Programming the Network of Financial Intermediation*, Universitetsforlaget, Oslo, Norway.

Thore, S. (1984), "Spatial Models of the Eurodollar Market," *Journal of Banking and Finance* **8**, 51-65.

Thore, S., and Kydland, F. (1972), "Dynamic for Flow-of-Funds Networks," in *Applications of Management Science in Banking and Finance*, pp. 259-276, S. Eilon and T. R. Fowkes, editors, Gower Press, England.

Wallace, S. (1986), "Solving Stochastic Programs with Network Recourse," *Networks* **16**, 295-317.

Whinston, A. B., Stahl, D. O., and Choi, S.-Y. (1997), *The Economics of Electronic Commerce*, Macmillan Technical Publications, Indianapolis, Indiana.

Zhao, L., and Dafermos, S. (1991), "General Economic Equilibrium and Variational Inequalities," *Operations Reesarch Letters* **10**, 369-376.

Zhao, L., and Nagurney, A. (1993), "A Network Formalism for Pure Exchange Economic Equilibria," in *Network Optimization Problems: Algorithms, Applications, and Complexity*, pp. 363-386, D.-Z. Du and P. M. Pardalos, editors, World Scientific Publishing Company, Singapore.

Part I Financial Networks

2 On Structural Properties of the Market Graph

Vladimir Boginski, Sergiy Butenko, and Panos M. Pardalos

2.1 Introduction

In the modern world of information, one often encounters serious computational challenges of dealing with massive data sets that arise in a great variety of scientific, engineering, and commercial applications, such as government and military systems, telecommunications, medicine and biotechnology, astrophysics, ecology, geographical information systems, and finance (cf. Boginski, Butenko, and Pardalos (2003), Abello, Pardalos, and Resende (2002)). The pervasiveness and complexity of the problems brought by massive data sets make the topic one of the most challenging and exciting areas of research for years to come.

In many practically important cases, a massive data set can be represented as a very large graph with certain attributes associated with its vertices and edges. These attributes may contain specific information characterizing the given application. Studying the structure of this graph is essential for understanding the structural properties of the application it represents, as well as for improving storage organization and information retrieval.

One of the examples of representing a massive data set as a graph is the *Call graph* arising in the telecommunications traffic data. In this graph, the vertices are telephone numbers, and two vertices are connected by an edge if a call was made from one number to another within a certain period of time. This graph was studied in detail by Abello, Pardalos, and Resende (1999) and by Aiello, Chung, and Lu (2001). Interestingly enough, this graph demonstrated the properties that are described by the *power-law model* (Boginski, Butenko, and Pardalos (2003)).

Moreover, it turns out that the Web graph (where the vertices are websites, and the arcs are links between them) and the Internet graph (where the vertices are routers and the edges are cables in the physical network) also obey the power-law model (Broder et al. (2000), Faloutsos, Faloutsos, and Faloutsos (1999)).

In this chapter, we will concentrate on another important real-life application – the graph representation of the stock market. Every year stock markets generate a huge amount of data, and this information can be used for constructing a graph that will reflect the market behavior.

Although not as obviously as in the examples of the Call graph and the Web graph, the stock market can be represented as a graph. A natural graph representation of the stock market is based on the cross correlations of price fluctuations. A *market graph* can be constructed as follows: each financial instrument is represented by a vertex, and two vertices are connected by an edge if the correlation coefficient of the corresponding pair of instruments (calculated for a certain period of time) exceeds a specified threshold θ, $-1 \leq \theta \leq 1$.

Nowadays, a great number of different instruments are traded in the US stock market, so the market graph representing them is very large. The market graph that we construct has 6546 vertices and several million edges.

In this chapter, we present a detailed study of the properties of this graph. It turns out that the market graph can be rather accurately described by the power-law model. We analyze the distribution of the degrees of the vertices in this graph, the edge density of this graph with respect to the correlation threshold, as well as its connectivity and the size of its connected components.

Furthermore, we look for *maximum cliques* and *maximum independent sets* in this graph for different values of the correlation threshold. Analyzing cliques and independent sets in the market graph gives us very valuable knowledge about the internal structure of the stock market. For instance, a clique in this graph will represent a set of instruments whose prices change similarly over time (a change of the price of any instrument in a clique is likely to affect all other instruments in this clique), and an independent set will consist of instruments that have negative correlations with respect to each other; therefore, they can be treated as a so-called diversified portfolio. Based on the information obtained from this analysis, we will be able to classify financial instruments into different groups, which will give us deeper insight into the stock market structure.

2.2   Notations and Definitions

To facilitate the further discussion, let us introduce some formal definitions and notations. We will denote by $G = (V, E)$ a simple undirected graph with the set of n vertices V and the set of edges E.

The graph $G = (V, E)$ is *connected* if there is a path from any vertex to any vertex in the set V. If the graph is disconnected, it can be decomposed into several connected subgraphs, which are referred to as the *connected components* of G.

Given a subset $S \subseteq V$, by $G(S)$ we denote the subgraph induced by S. A subset $C \subseteq V$ is a *clique* if $G(C)$ is a complete graph, i.e. it has all possible edges. The maximum clique problem is to find the largest clique in a graph. The following definitions generalize the concept of a clique. Namely, instead of cliques one can consider dense subgraphs, or *quasi-cliques*. A γ-*clique* C_γ, also called a *quasi-clique*, is a subset of V such that $G(C_\gamma)$ has at least $\lfloor \gamma q(q - 1)/2 \rfloor$ edges, where q is the cardinality of C_γ.

The maximum clique problem is known to be NP-hard (see Garey and Johnson (1979)). Moreover, it turns out that even the approximation of the maximum clique is NP-hard. For instance, Arora and Safra (1992) proved that for some positive ϵ the approximation of the maximum clique within a factor of n^ϵ is NP-hard. Recently, Håstad (1999) has shown that, in fact, for any $\delta > 0$ the maximum clique is hard to approximate in polynomial time within a factor $n^{1-\delta}$.

These facts, together with practical evidence (see Johnson and Trick (1996)), demonstrate that the maximum clique problem is hard to solve even in graphs of moderate size. The theoretical complexity and the huge sizes of data make this problem especially difficult in large graphs.

Another concept closely related to a clique is an *independent set* which is a subset $I \subseteq V$ such that the subgraph $G(I)$ has no edges. The maximum independent set problem can be easily reformulated as the maximum clique problem in the *complementary* graph $\bar{G}(V, \bar{E})$, which is defined as follows. If an edge $(i, j) \in E$, then $(i, j) \notin \bar{E}$, and if $(i, j) \notin E$, then $(i, j) \in \bar{E}$. Clearly, a maximum clique in $\bar{G}$ is a maximum independent set in G, so in this sense these problems are equivalent, and the complexity results obtained for the maximum clique problem are also valid for the maximum independent set problem.

2.3 Theoretical Models of Real-Life Graphs

In many cases, especially if the size of real-life graphs is large enough, it is useful to construct a proper theoretical model of these graphs. This may help to avoid computational difficulties and to better understand the structure of a real-life graph.

The first attempt to build such a model was based on the concept of so-called *uniform random graphs*. The classical theory of uniform random graphs founded by Erdös and Rényi (1959, 1960, 1961) deals with several standard models. Two such models are $G(n, m)$ and $\mathcal{G}(n, p)$ (Bollobás (1978, 1985)). The first model assigns the same probability to all graphs with n vertices and m edges, while in the second model each pair of vertices is chosen to be linked by an edge randomly and independently with probability p.

In most cases for each natural n a probability space consisting of graphs with exactly n vertices is considered, and the properties of this space as $n \to \infty$ are studied. It is said that a typical element of the space or *almost every* (*a.e.*) graph has property Q when the probability that a random graph on n vertices has this property tends to 1 as $n \to \infty$. It is also said that the property Q holds *asymptotically almost surely (a.a.s.)*.

The asymptotical properties of uniform random graphs have been well studied. Among the results obtained in this field we should mention the connectivity threshold and the emergence of a giant connected component. More specifically, a uniform random graph $\mathcal{G}(n,p)$ is *a.a.s.* connected if $p > \frac{\log n}{n}$ and it is *a.a.s.* disconnected otherwise. Also, if p is in the range $\frac{1}{n} < p < \frac{\log n}{n}$, the graph $\mathcal{G}(n,p)$ *a.a.s.* has a unique *giant connected component*.

Although the uniform random graph model captured some properties of the massive graphs arising in practical applications (such as the emergence of a giant connected component), empirical measurements showed a significant difference in the structures of a real graph and a corresponding uniform random graph with the same number of vertices and edges. For instance, this model cannot handle the property of *clustering* that often takes place in the real graphs (Watts and Strogatz (1998), Watts (1999)). This property means that the probability of the event that two given vertices are connected by an edge is higher if these vertices have a common neighbor (i.e. a vertex which is connected by an edge with both of these vertices). The probability that for a given vertex its two neighbors are connected by an edge is called the *clustering coefficient*. It can be easily seen that in the case of the model $\mathcal{G}(n,p)$ the clustering coefficient is equal to the parameter p, since the probability that each pair of vertices is connected by an edge is independent of all other vertices. In real-life graphs, the value of the clustering coefficient turns out to be much higher than the value of the parameter p of the uniform random graphs with the same number of vertices and edges.

However, the most important drawback of the uniform random graph model is the difference in the vertices degree distribution, as compared to the real massive graphs. It can be easily shown that as the number of vertices in a uniform random graph increases, the distribution of the degrees of the vertices tends to the well-known *Poisson distribution* with the parameter np which represents the average degree of a vertex. But the empirical experiments show that in many real-life graphs the degree distribution obeys a *power law*. That is why another theoretical model was developed for describing real-life graphs – the *power-law random graph model*.

The basic idea of the power-law random graph model $P(\alpha, \beta)$ is as follows. If y is the number of nodes with degree x, then according to this model

$$y = e^{\alpha}/x^{\beta}. \qquad (2.1)$$

Equivalently, we can write

$$\log y = \alpha - \beta \log x. \qquad (2.2)$$

This representation is more convenient in the sense that the relationship between y and x can be plotted as a straight line on a log-log scale, so that $(-\beta)$ is the slope, and α is the intercept.

An important aspect related to the power-law model is the relationship between the parameter β and the size of the largest connected component. It has been theoretically shown that in a power-law graph a giant connected component *a.a.s.* emerges at $\beta \simeq 3.47875$, and a graph *a.a.s.* becomes connected when $\beta < 1$. More specifically, the following results are valid (Aiello, Chung, and Lu (2001)):

- If $0 < \beta < 1$, then a power-law graph is *a.a.s.* connected (i.e. there is only one connected component of size n).

- If $1 \le \beta < 2$, then a power-law graph *a.a.s.* has a giant connected component (the component size is $\Theta(n)$), and the second largest connected component *a.a.s.* has a size $\Theta(1)$.

- If $2 < \beta < \beta_0 = 3.47875$, then a giant connected component *a.a.s.* exists, and the size of the second largest component *a.a.s.* is $\Theta(\log n)$.

- $\beta = 2$ is a special case when there is *a.a.s.* a giant connected component, and the size of the second largest connected component is $\Theta(\log n / \log \log n)$.

- If $\beta > \beta_0 = 3.47875$, then there is *a.a.s.* no giant connected component.

As was pointed out above, the power-law model has proved to be suitable for the Call graph and the Web graph. Since these graphs are very large, the asymptotical theoretical results obtained for this model are applicable to these graphs. Although the market graph is significantly smaller than the Web and the Call graphs, and one cannot expect the same level of agreement between theoretical and practical results, this graph is continuously growing, since many new instruments appear in the stock market. Does the market graph obey the power-law model? In the next section we present a detailed analysis of the market graph which will give an answer to this question.

2.4   Structure of the Market Graph

As it was pointed out above, the power-law model fairly well describes some of the real-life massive graphs, such as the Web graph and the Call graph. In this section we will find out whether or not the market graphs obey the power-law model.

2.4.1   Constructing the Market Graph

The market graph that we study in this chapter represents the set of financial instruments traded in the US stock markets. More specifically, we consider

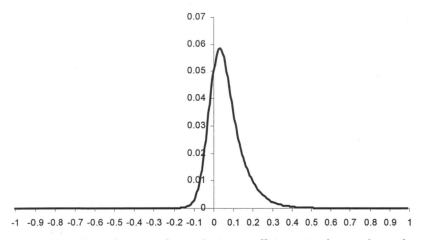

Fig. 2.1. Distribution of correlation coefficients in the stock market

6546 instruments and analyze daily changes of their prices over a period of 500 consecutive trading days in 2000-2002. Based on this information, we calculate the cross-correlations between each pair of stocks using the following formula (Mantegna and Stanley (2000)):

$$C_{ij} = \frac{\langle R_i R_j \rangle - \langle R_i \rangle \langle R_j \rangle}{\sqrt{\langle R_i^2 - \langle R_i \rangle^2 \rangle \langle R_j^2 - \langle R_j \rangle^2 \rangle}},$$

where $R_i(t) = \ln \frac{P_i(t)}{P_i(t-1)}$ defines the return of the stock i for day t. $P_i(t)$ denotes the price of the stock i on day t.

The correlation coefficients C_{ij} can vary from -1 to 1. Figure 2.1 shows the distribution of the correlation coefficients based on the prices data for the years 2000-2002. It can be seen that this plot has a shape similar to the normal distribution with the mean 0.05.

The main idea of constructing a market graph is as follows. Let the set of financial instruments represent the set of vertices of the graph. Also, we specify a certain threshold value $\theta, -1 \le \theta \le 1$ and add an undirected edge connecting the vertices i and j if the corresponding correlation coefficient C_{ij} is greater than or equal to θ. Obviously, different values of θ define the market graphs with the same set of vertices, but different sets of edges.

It is easy to see that the number of edges in the market graph decreases as the threshold value θ increases. In fact, our experiments show that the edge density of the market graph decreases exponentially with respect to θ. The corresponding graph is presented on Figure 2.2.

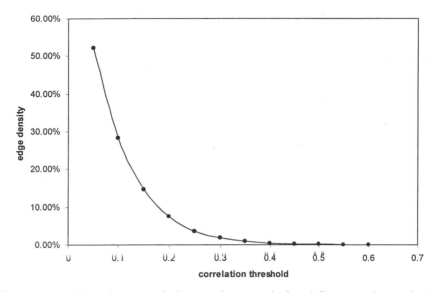

Fig. 2.2. Edge density of the market graph for different values of the correlation threshold

2.4.2   Connectivity of the Market Graph

In Section 2.3 we mentioned connectivity thresholds in random graphs. The main idea of this concept is finding a threshold value of the parameter of the model (p in the case of uniform random graphs, and β in the case of power-law graphs) that will define whether the graph is connected or not. Moreover, if the graph is disconnected, another threshold value can be defined to determine if the graph has a giant connected component or all of its connected components have a small size.

For instance, in the case of the power-law model $\beta = 1$ is a threshold value that determines the connectivity of the power-law graph, i.e. the graph is *a.a.s.* connected if $\beta < 1$, and it is *a.a.s.* disconnected otherwise. Similarly, $\beta \approx 3.47875$ defines the existence of a giant connected component in the power-law graph.

Now a natural question arises: what is the connectivity threshold for the market graph? Since the number of edges in the market graph depends on the chosen correlation threshold θ, we should find a value θ_0 that determines the connectivity of the graph. As was mentioned above, the smaller the value of θ that we choose, the more edges the market graph will have. So, if we decrease θ, after a certain point, the graph will become connected. We have conducted a series of computational experiments for checking the connectivity of the market graph using the breadth-first search technique, and we have obtained a relatively accurate approximation of the connectivity threshold:

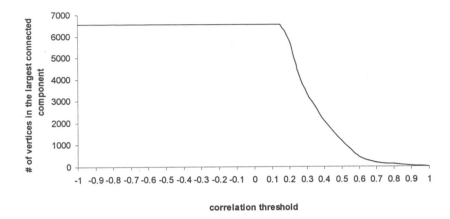

Fig. 2.3. Plot of the size of the largest connected component in the market graph as a function of correlation threshold θ

$\theta_0 \simeq 0.143482$. Moreover, we investigated the dependency of the size of the largest connected component in the market graph with respect to θ. The corresponding plot is shown on Figure 2.3.

2.4.3 Degree Distributions in the Market Graph

As it was shown in the previous section, the power-law model fairly well describes some of the real-life massive graphs, such as the Web graph and the Call graph. In this section, we will show that the market graph also obeys the power-law model.

It should be noted that since we consider a set of market graphs, where each graph corresponds to a certain value of θ, the degree distributions will be different for each θ.

The results of our experiments turned out to be rather interesting.

If we specify a small value of the correlation threshold θ, such as $\theta = 0$, $\theta = 0.05$, $\theta = 0.1$, $\theta = 0.15$, the distribution of the degrees of the vertices is very "noisy" and does not have any well-defined structure. Note that for these values of θ the market graph is connected and has a high edge density. The market graph structure seems to be very difficult to analyze in such cases.

However, the situation changes drastically if a higher correlation threshold is chosen. As the edge density of the graph decreases, the degree distribution more and more resembles a power law. In fact, for $\theta \geq 0.2$ this distribution is approximately a straight line in the log-log scale, which is exactly the power law distribution, as it was shown in Section 2.3. Figure 2.4 demonstrates the degree distributions of the market graphs for some values of the correlation threshold.

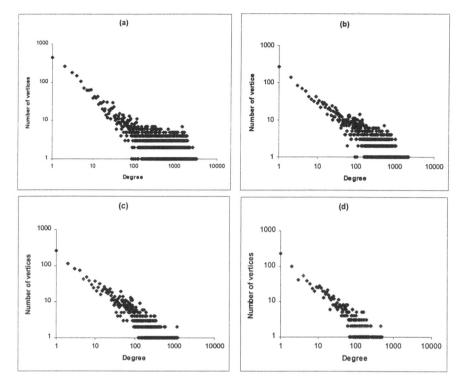

Fig. 2.4. Degree distribution of the market graph for (a) $\theta = 0.2$; (b) $\theta = 0.3$; (c) $\theta = 0.4$; (d) $\theta = 0.5$

An interesting observation is that the slope of the lines (which is equal to the parameter β of the power-law model) is rather small. It can be seen from Formula (2.1) that in this case the graph will contain many vertices with a high degree. This fact is important for the next subject of interest – finding maximum cliques in the market graph. Intuitively, one can expect a large clique in a graph with a small value of the parameter β. As we will see in the next section, this assumption is true for the market graph.

Another combinatorial optimization problem associated with the market graph is finding maximum independent sets in the graphs with a negative correlation threshold θ. Clearly, instruments in an independent set will be negatively correlated with each other, and therefore form a diversified portfolio.

However, we can consider a *complementary graph* for a market graph with a negative value of θ. In this graph, an edge will connect instruments i and j if the correlation between them $C_{ij} < \theta$. Recall that a maximum independent set in the initial graph is a maximum clique in the complementary graph, so the maximum independent set problem can be reduced to the maximum clique problem in the complementary graph.

Table 2.1. Clustering coefficients of the market graph (* – complementary graph)

θ	Clustering coefficient
-0.15^*	2.64×10^{-5}
-0.1^*	0.0012
0.3	0.4885
0.4	0.4458
0.5	0.4522
0.6	0.4872
0.7	0.4886

Therefore, it is also useful to investigate the degree distributions of these complementary graphs. As it can be seen from Figure 2.1, the distribution of the correlation coefficients is almost symmetric around $\theta = 0.05$, so for the values of θ close to 0 the edge density of both the initial and the complementary graph is high enough. Hence, for these values of θ the degree distribution of a complementary graph is also "noisy" as in the case of the corresponding initial graph.

As θ decreases (i.e. increases in the absolute value), the degree distribution of a complementary graph tends to the power law. The corresponding graphs are shown on Figure 2.5. However, in this case, the slope of the line in the log-log scale (the value of the parameter β) is higher than in the case of positive values of θ. It means that there are not many vertices with a high degree in these graphs, so the size of a maximum clique should be significantly smaller than in the case of the market graphs with a positive correlation threshold.

It is also interesting to compare the difference in clustering coefficients of a market graph (with positive values of θ) or its complement (with negative values of θ) (see Table 2.1).

Intuitively, the large clustering coefficients should correspond to graphs with larger cliques; therefore, from Table 2.1 one should expect that the cliques in market graph with positive θ are much larger than the independent sets in market graph with negative θ. This prediction will be confirmed in the next section, where we present the computational results of solving the maximum clique and maximum independent set problems in the market graph.

2.4.4 Cliques and Independent Sets in the Market Graph

As was mentioned above, the maximum clique and the maximum independent set problems are NP-hard. It makes these problems especially challenging in large graphs. The maximum clique problem admits an integer programming

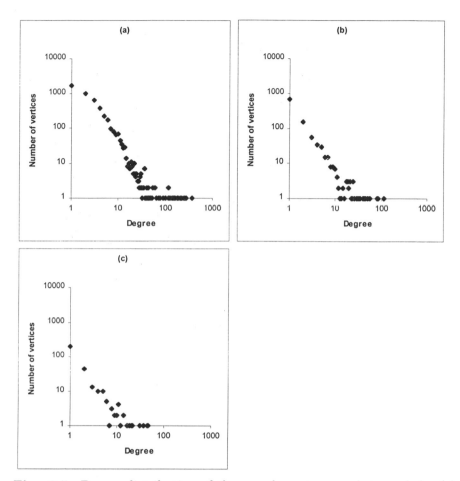

Fig. 2.5. Degree distribution of the complementary market graph for (a) $\theta = -0.15$; (b) $\theta = -0.2$; (c) $\theta = -0.25$

formulation; however, in the case of the graph with 6546 vertices this integer programming problem cannot be solved in a reasonable time. Therefore, we used a greedy heuristic for finding a lower bound of the clique number, and a special preprocessing technique which reduces a problem size.

To find a large clique, we apply the following greedy algorithm. Starting with an empty set, we recursively add to the clique a vertex from the neighborhood of the clique adjacent to the most vertices in the neighborhood of the clique. If we denote by $N(i) = \{j|(i,j) \in E\}$ the set of neighbors of i in $G = (V, E)$, then the neighborhood of a clique C is $\bigcap_{i \in C} N(i)$, and we obtain the following algorithm:

$$C = \emptyset, G_0 = G;$$

do

$$G_0 = \bigcap_{i \in C} N(i) \setminus C;$$

$C = C \bigcup j$, where j is a vertex of largest degree in G_0;

until $G_0 = \emptyset$.

After running this algorithm, we applied the following preprocessing procedure (Abello, Pardalos, and Resende (1999)). We recursively remove from the graph all of the vertices which are not in C and whose degree is less than $|C|$, where C is the clique found by the above algorithm. This simple procedure enabled us to significantly reduce the size of the maximum clique search space. Let us denote by $G'(V', E')$ the graph induced by remaining vertices. Table 2.2 presents the sizes of the cliques found using the greedy algorithm, and sizes of the graphs remaining after applying the preprocessing procedure.

Table 2.2. Sizes of cliques found using the greedy algorithm and sizes of graphs remaining after applying the preprocessing technique

θ	Edge density	Clique size	$|V'|$	Edge density in G'
0.35	0.0090	168	535	0.6494
0.40	0.0047	104	405	0.6142
0.45	0.0024	109	213	0.8162
0.50	0.0013	84	146	0.8436
0.55	0.0007	61	102	0.8701
0.60	0.0004	45	70	0.8758
0.65	0.0002	23	80	0.5231
0.70	0.0001	21	33	0.7557

In order to find the maximum clique of G' (which is also the maximum clique in the original graph G), we used the following integer programming formulation of the maximum clique problem (Bomze et al. (1999)):

$$\text{Maximize } \sum_i x_i$$

subject to:

$$x_i + x_j \leq 1, \quad (i, j) \notin E',$$

$$x_i \in \{0, 1\}, \quad \forall i.$$

We used CPLEX (cf. ILOG (2000)) to solve this integer program for some of the considered instances.

Table 2.3. Sizes of the maximum cliques in the market graph with different values of the correlation threshold

θ	Edge density	Clique size
0.35	0.0090	193
0.40	0.0047	144
0.45	0.0024	109
0.50	0.0013	85
0.55	0.0007	63
0.60	0.0004	45
0.65	0.0002	27
0.70	0.0001	22

Table 2.3 summarizes the sizes of the maximum cliques found in the graph for different values of θ. It turns out that these cliques are rather large. In fact, even for $\theta = 0.6$, which is a very high correlation threshold, the clique of size 45 was found.

These results are in agreement with the discussion in the previous section, where we analyzed the degree distributions of the market graphs with positive values of θ and came to the conclusion that the cliques in these graphs should be large.

The financial interpretation of the clique in the market graph is that it defines the set of stocks whose price fluctuations exhibit a similar behavior. Our results show that in the modern stock market there are large groups of instruments that are correlated with each other.

Next, we consider the maximum independent set problem in the market graphs with nonpositive values of the correlation threshold θ. As described in the previous section, this problem can be easily represented as a maximum clique problem in a complementary graph. Interestingly, the preprocessing procedure that was very helpful for finding maximum cliques in original graphs was absolutely useless in the case with their complements, therefore we conclude that the maximum independent set appears to be more difficult to compute than the maximum clique in the market graph. Table 2.4 presents the results obtained using the greedy algorithm described above.

As one can see, the sizes of the computed independent sets are very small, which coincides with the prediction that was made in the previous section based on the analysis of the degree distributions.

From the financial point of view, the independent set in the market graph represents "the completely diversified" portfolio, where all instruments are negatively correlated with each other. It turns out that choosing such a portfolio is not an easy task, and one cannot expect to easily find a large group of negatively correlated instruments.

Table 2.4. Sizes of independent sets found using the greedy algorithm

θ	Edge density	Independent set size
0.05	0.4794	36
0.00	0.2001	12
−0.05	0.0431	5
−0.10	0.0050	3
−0.15	0.0005	2

2.4.5   Instruments Corresponding to High-Degree Vertices

Up to this point, we have studied the properties of the market graph as one big system, and did not consider the characteristics of every vertex in this graph. However, a very important practical issue is to investigate the degree of each vertex in the market graph and to find the vertices with high degrees, i.e. the instruments that are highly correlated with many other instruments in the market. Clearly, this information will help us to answer a very important question: which instruments most accurately reflect the behavior of the market?

For this purpose, we chose the market graph with a high correlation threshold ($\theta = 0.6$), calculated the degrees of each vertex in this graph and sorted the vertices in the decreasing order of their degrees.

Interestingly, even though the edge density of the considered graph is only 0.04% (only highly correlated instruments are connected by an edge), there are many vertices with degrees greater than 100.

According to our calculations, the vertex with the highest degree in this market graph corresponds to the NASDAQ 100 Index Tracking Stock. The degree of this vertex is 216, which means that there are 216 instruments that are highly correlated with it. An interesting observation is that the degree of this vertex is twice as high than the number of companies whose stock prices the NASDAQ index reflects, which means that these 100 companies greatly influence the market.

In Table 2.5 we present the "top 25" instruments in the US stock market, according to their degrees in the considered market graph. The corresponding symbols definitions can be found on several websites, for example http://www.nasdaq.com. Note that most of them are indices that incorporate a number of different stocks of the companies in different industries. Although this result is not surprising from the financial point of view, it is important as a practical justification of the market graph model.

Table 2.5. Top 25 instruments with highest degrees ($\theta = 0.6$)

Symbol	Vertex degree
QQQ	216
IWF	193
IWO	193
IYW	193
XLK	181
IVV	175
MDY	171
SPY	162
IJH	159
IWV	158
IVW	156
IAH	155
IYY	154
IWB	153
IYV	150
BDH	144
MKH	143
IWM	142
IJR	134
SMH	130
STM	118
IIH	116
IVE	113
DIA	106
IWD	106

2.5   Conclusion

In this chapter, we presented a detailed study of the properties of the market graph. Finding cliques and independent sets in the market graph gives us a new tool for the analysis of the market structure by classifying the stocks into different groups.

As was pointed out above, our experiments show that the distribution of the correlation coefficients between the stocks in the US stock market remains very stable over time. Therefore, the results of the analysis of the market graph can be used for predicting the behavior of the stock market in the future.

Another important result obtained in this paper is that the power-law model, which well describes the massive graphs arising in telecommunications and the Internet, is also applicable in finance. It confirms an amazing observation that many real-life massive graphs have a similar power-law structure.

Although we addressed many issues in our analysis of the market graph, there are still a lot of open problems. For instance, since the independent sets in the market graph turned out to be very small, there is a possibility of considering quasi-cliques instead of cliques in the complementary graph. This will allow us to find larger diversified portfolios which is important from the practical point of view. Also, one can consider another type of market graph based on the data of the liquidity of different instruments, instead of considering the returns. It would be very interesting to study the properties of this graph and compare it with the market graph considered in this paper. Therefore, this research direction is very promising and important for deeper understanding of the market behavior.

Acknowledgments

The authors would like to thank the referees for their comments which helped to improve the quality of presentation.

References

Abello, J., Pardalos, P. M., and Resende, M. G. C. (1999), "On Maximum Clique Problems in Very Large Graphs," *DIMACS Series* **50**, 119-130, American Mathematical Society, Providence, Rhode Island.

Abello, J., Pardalos, P. M., and Resende, M. G. C., editors (2002), *Handbook of Massive Data Sets*, Kluwer Academic Publishers, Boston, Massachusetts.

Aiello, W., Chung, F., and Lu, L. (2001), "A Random Graph Model for Power Law Graphs," *Experimental Mathematics* **10**, 53-66.

Boginski, V., Butenko, S., and Pardalos, P. M. (2003), "Modeling and Optimization in Massive Graphs," in *Novel Approaches to Hard Discrete Optimization*, pp. 17-39, P. M. Pardalos and H. Wolkowicz, editors, American Mathematical Society, Providence, Rhode Island.

Bollobás, B. (1978), *Extremal Graph Theory*, Academic Press, New York.

Bollobás, B. (1985), *Random Graphs*, Academic Press, London, England.

Bomze, I. M., Budinich, M., Pardalos, P. M., and Pelillo, M. (1999), "The Maximum Clique Problem," in *Handbook of Combinatorial Optimization*, pp. 1-74, D.-Z. Du and P. M. Pardalos, editors, Kluwer Academic Publishers, Dordrecht, The Netherlands.

Broder, A., Kumar, R., Maghoul, F., Raghavan, P., Rajagopalan, S., Stata, R., Tomkins, A., and Wiener, J. (2000), "Graph Structure in the Web," *Computer Networks* **33**, 309-320.

Erdös, P., and Rényi, A. (1959), "On Random Graphs," *Publicationes Mathematicae* **6**, 290-297.

Erdös, P., and Rényi, A. (1960), "On the Evolution of Random Graphs," Publication of the Mathematical Institute of the Hungarian Academy of Sciences **5**, 17-61.

Erdös, P., and Rényi, A. (1961), "On the Strength of Connectedness of a Random Graph," *Acta Mathematica Academiae Scientiarum Hungaricae* **12**, 261-267.

Faloutsos, M., Faloutsos, P., and Faloutsos, C. (1999), "On Power-Law Relationships of the Internet Topology," *Proceedings of the ACM SIGCOMM*, pp. 251-262, Cambridge, Massachusetts.

Garey, M. R., and Johnson, D. S. (1979), *Computers and Intractability: A Guide to the Theory of NP-Completeness*, WH Freeman and Company, New York.

Håstad, J. (1999), "Clique is Hard to Approximate Within $n^{1-\epsilon}$," *Acta Mathematica* **182**, 105-142.

ILOG (2000), *CPLEX 7.0 Reference Manual*, Gentilly, France.

Johnson, D. S., and Trick, M. A., editors (1996), *Cliques, Coloring, and Satisfiability: Second DIMACS Implementation Challenge*, DIMACS Series **26**, American Mathematical Society, Providence, Rhode Island.

Mantegna, R. N., and Stanley, H. E. (2000), *An Introduction to Econophysics: Correlations and Complexity in Finance*, Cambridge University Press, Cambridge, England.

Watts, D. (1999), *Small Worlds: The Dynamics of Networks between Order and Randomness*, Princeton University Press, Princeton, New Jersey.

Watts, D., and Strogatz, S. (1998), "Collective Dynamics of 'Small-World' Networks," *Nature* **393**, 440-442.

3 Multistage Stochastic Mean-Variance Portfolio Analysis with Transaction Costs

Nalan Gülpinar, Berç Rustem, and Reuben Settergren

3.1 Introduction

A rational framework for investment decisions is provided by the maximization of return for an acceptable level of risk. A fundamental example is the single-period Markowitz (1952) model in which expected portfolio return is maximized and risk measured by the variance of portfolio return is minimized.

Consider n risky assets with random rates of return $r_1, r_2, \ldots, r_n$. Their expected values are denoted $E(r_i)$, $i = 1, \ldots, n$. A full description of our notation is given in Table 3.1. All quantities in boldface represent vectors in $\mathbb{R}^n$ unless otherwise noted. For example, $\mathbf{r}$ denotes the column vector whose ith element is $E(r_i)$. The transpose of a vector or matrix will be denoted with the symbol $'$.

The single-period model of Markowitz considers a portfolio of n assets defined in terms of a set of weights w^i for $i = 1, \ldots, n$, which sum to unity. Many traditional portfolio analysis models seek only to maximize expected return. This can be achieved with a classical stochastic linear programming formulation which incorporates the mean term. This is a risk-neutral approach which does not take risk-attitudes into account. Stochastic linear programming is mathematical programming (with linear objective function and constraints) under uncertainty where one or more parameters are not known at the time of decision making. For further information on stochastic programming, the reader is referred to Birge and Louveaux (1997), Kall and Wallace (1994), and Prekopa (1995).

Given an expected rate of return $\bar{r}$, the optimal portfolio is defined in terms of the solution of the following quadratic programming problem:

$$\min_{\mathbf{w}} \left\{ < \mathbf{w}, \Lambda \mathbf{w} > \, | \, \mathbf{w}'\mathbf{r} = \bar{r}, \;\; \mathbf{1}'\mathbf{w} = 1, \;\; \mathbf{w} \geq 0 \right\}$$

where Λ is the covariance matrix of asset returns. The quadratic program yields the minimum variance portfolio. Note that the classical stochastic linear programming formulation maximizes the expected return but takes no account of risk.

The single-period mean-variance optimization problem can be extended to multistage programming. In this case, after the initial investment, we can rebalance our portfolio (subject to any desired bounds) to maximize profit at the investment horizon and minimize the risk at discrete time periods and redeem at the end of the period. Uncertainty is represented by the mathematical methods such as mean-variance analysis, utility function analysis and arbitrage analysis, for example see Kallberg and Ziemba (1983) and Pulley (1981). The mean-variance model has some inconsistencies such as the assumption of normal returns, quadratic utility and shifting efficient frontiers as the number of periods in the model changes. While these are serious issues, we believe that a framework that admits a longer term perspective and incorporates transaction costs is important. The issue of normality can be relaxed in due course by using higher order moments. The same is also partially true for the quadratic variance term. Including skewness and kurtosis is possibly an attractive extension of the present work, despite the added computational complexity. The sensitivity of the result to the length of horizon considered, on the other hand, is common to all dynamic optimization problems. It is somewhat alleviated by considering the sensitivity of the first-period decision to differing horizons. A discount factor for future risk is also a relevant option. The purpose of this paper is to discuss the basic tool and its use in view of transaction costs to overcome the well-known suboptimality of the sequential application of single-period optimal decisions.

The multistage decision problems under uncertainty are considered in Becker, Hall, and Rustem (1994), Darlington et al. (1999, 2000), and Rustem (1994) for nonlinear problems. A mean-variance approach is adopted with a static transcription of the dynamic decision model. This utilizes analytical second order approximations to the mean and variance functions. In Frauendorfer (1995) and Steinbach (1998), however, a scenario-based discretization is developed and a stochastic programming model formulated. Gassman and Ireland (1995) present a scenario formulation in an algebraic modeling language. An alternative to the standard mean-variance approach for controlling risk that is based on a concept of wealth accumulation reflecting investor preferences was proposed in Frauendorder and Siede (2000) and Ziemba and MacLean (1999).

In this chapter, we consider the multistage extension of the mean-variance optimization problem. The first distinguishing feature of the mean-variance approach over expected value optimization, formulated as linear stochastic programming, is that the former takes into account the approximate nature of the set of discrete scenarios by considering the variance around each return scenario. The second feature of the variance term is that it does allow for the variability of returns over the scenario tree. Consequently, uncertainty on return values of instruments is represented by a discrete approximation of a multivariate continuous distribution as well as the variability due to the discrete approximation. This is discussed further in Section 3.2.

Another issue considered in the chapter is the adoption of benchmark-relative computations in view of the transaction costs and the use of a powerful interior-point algorithm (Mészáros (1997)) to compute the overall solution. The existence of transaction costs makes it essential that the multistage decision problem is addressed directly. The application of single-period optimization sequentially clearly leads to suboptimal results as overall investment performance depends on these costs. Single period optimization cannot incorporate the effect of future transaction of assets considered for the single period. Multistage optimization thus overcomes the suboptimality of myopic single-period optimization.

A quadratic (linearly constrained) stochastic programming model is developed, and its implementation tested. Data from large-scale problems in the literature (Finance Research Group) are used to examine run-time. Backtesting is performed on historical data to examine the model's ability to compute Markowitz-efficient investment strategies in a multistage context.

The rest of the chapter is organized as follows. In Section 3.2, the problem statement is given. In Section 3.3, we present the multistage stochastic mean-variance portfolio optimization model (based on the scenario tree). In Section 3.4, the computational results are shown and conclusions are presented in Section 3.5.

3.2   Problem Statement

The central problem considered in the chapter is the determination of multiperiod discrete-time optimal portfolio strategies over a given finite investment horizon. Therefore, we start with the definition of returns and uncertainties. Subsequently, we present the model constraints, the expected return and risk formulations based on the scenario tree.

We consider n risky assets and construct a portfolio over an investment horizon T. The portfolio is restructured over a period in terms of both return and risk. After the initial investment ($t = 0$), the portfolio may be restructured at discrete times $t = 1, \ldots, T - 1$, and redeemed at the end of the period ($t = T$).

Scenario Tree

Let $\boldsymbol{\rho}^t \equiv \{\boldsymbol{\rho}_1, \ldots, \boldsymbol{\rho}_t\}$ be stochastic events at $t = 1, \ldots, T$. The decision process is non-anticipative (i.e decision at a given stage does not depend on the future realization of the random events). The decision at t is dependent on $\boldsymbol{\rho}_{t-1}$. Thus, constraints on a decision at each stage involve past observations and decisions.

Table 3.1. Notation

n	number of investment assets.
T	planning horizon. Initial investment is at $t = 0$, the portfolio is restructured at discrete times $t = 1, \ldots, T - 1$, and finally redeemed at $t = T$.
$\boldsymbol{\rho}_t$	vector of stochastic data observed at time t, $t = 0, \ldots, T$.
$\boldsymbol{\rho}^t$	$\equiv \{\boldsymbol{\rho}_0, \ldots, \boldsymbol{\rho}_t\}$ — history of stochastic data up to t.
$\mathcal{N}$	set of all nodes in the scenario tree.
$\mathcal{N}_t$	set of nodes of the scenario tree representing possible events at time t.
$\mathcal{N}_I$	$\equiv \mathcal{N} - (\mathcal{N}_0 \cup \mathcal{N}_T)$, i.e. set of all *interior* nodes of the scenario tree.
s	index denoting a scenario, i.e. path from root to leaf in the scenario tree.
$\mathbf{e} \equiv (s, t)$	index denoting an event (node of the scenario tree), which can be identified by an ordered pair of scenario and time period.
$a(\mathbf{e})$	ancestor of event $\mathbf{e} \in \mathcal{N}$ (parent in the scenario tree).
$p_{\mathbf{e}}$	branching probability of event $\mathbf{e}$: $p_{\mathbf{e}} = \text{Prob}[\mathbf{e}\|a(\mathbf{e})]$.
$P_{\mathbf{e}}$	probability of event $\mathbf{e}$: if $\mathbf{e} = (s, t)$, then $P_{\mathbf{e}} = \prod_{i=1\ldots t} P(s, i)$.
$\text{E}[\cdot]$	expectation with respect to ρ.
$\mathbf{p}$	current portfolio position (i.e. at $t = 0$, before optimization).
$\mathbf{c}_b$	vector of unit transaction costs for buying.
$\mathbf{c}_s$	vector of unit transaction costs for selling.
$\mathbf{b}_*$	decision vector of "buy" transaction volumes.
$\mathbf{s}_*$	decision vector of "sell" transaction volumes.
$\mathbf{r}_t(\boldsymbol{\rho}^t)$	stochastic vector of return values for the n assets, $t = 1, \ldots, T$.
$\Lambda \in \mathbb{R}^{n \times n}$	covariance matrix associated with return values.
$\mathbf{r}_{\mathbf{e}}$	stochastic realization of $\mathbf{r}_t$ in event $\mathbf{e}$: $\mathbf{r}_{\mathbf{e}} \sim N(\mathbf{r}_t(\boldsymbol{\rho}^t), \Lambda)$.
$\hat{\mathbf{r}}_{\mathbf{e}}$	$\equiv \text{E}\left(\mathbf{r}_{\mathbf{e}}(\boldsymbol{\rho}_t\|\boldsymbol{\rho}^{t-1})\right)$ — expectation of $\mathbf{r}_t(\boldsymbol{\rho}^t)$ for event $\mathbf{e}$, conditional on $\boldsymbol{\rho}^{t-1}$.
$\mathbf{w}_*$	decision vector indicating asset balances.
$\overline{\mathbf{w}}_*$	market benchmark.
$*$	Vectors $\mathbf{w}, \overline{\mathbf{w}}, \mathbf{b}$, and $\mathbf{s}$ can be indexed either with $t = 1, \ldots, T$ (in which case they represent stochastic quantities with an implied dependence on $\boldsymbol{\rho}^t$), or $\mathbf{e} \in \mathcal{N}$ (in which case they represent specific realizations of those quantities).
$\mathcal{W}_t$	expected total wealth at time $t = 1, \ldots, T$.
$\mathbf{1}$	$\equiv (1, 1, 1, \ldots, 1)'$
$\mathbf{u} \circ \mathbf{v}$	$\equiv (u_1 v_1, \ u_2 v_2, \ \ldots, u_n v_n)'$

A scenario is defined as a possible realization of the stochastic variables $\{\rho_1, \ldots, \rho_T\}$. Hence, the set of scenarios corresponds to the set of leaves of the scenario tree, $\mathcal{N}_T$, and nodes of the tree at level $t \geq 1$ (the set $\mathcal{N}_t$) correspond to possible realizations of ρ^t. We denote a node of the tree (or event) by $\mathbf{e} = (s, t)$, where s is a scenario (path from root to leaf), and time period t specifies a particular node on that path. The root of the tree is $\mathbf{0} = (s, 0)$ (where s can be any scenario, since the root node is common to all scenarios). The ancestor (parent) of event $\mathbf{e} = (s, t)$ is denoted $a(\mathbf{e}) = (s, t - 1)$, and the branching probability $p_{\mathbf{e}}$ is the conditional probability of event $\mathbf{e}$, given its parent event $a(\mathbf{e})$. The path to event $\mathbf{e}$ is a partial scenario with probability $P_{\mathbf{e}} = \prod p_{\mathbf{e}}$ along that path; since probabilities $p_{\mathbf{e}}$ must sum to one at each individual branching, probabilities $P_{\mathbf{e}}$ will sum up to one across each layer of tree nodes $\mathcal{N}_t; t = 0, 1, \ldots, T$. Each node at a level t corresponds to a decision $\{\mathbf{w}_t, \mathbf{b}_t, \mathbf{s}_t\}$ which must be determined at time t, and depends in general on ρ^t, the initial wealth $\mathbf{w}_0$ and past decisions $\{\mathbf{w}_j, \mathbf{b}_j, \mathbf{s}_j\}, j = 1, \ldots, t-1$. This process is adapted to ρ^t as $\mathbf{w}_t, \mathbf{b}_t, \mathbf{s}_t$ cannot depend on future events $\rho_{t+1}, \ldots, \rho_T$ which are not yet realized. Hence $\mathbf{w}_t = \mathbf{w}_t(\rho^t)$, $\mathbf{b}_t = \mathbf{b}_t(\rho^t)$, and $\mathbf{s}_t = \mathbf{s}_t(\rho^t)$. However, for simplicity, we shall use the terms $\mathbf{w}_t$, $\mathbf{b}_t$ and $\mathbf{s}_t$, and assume their implicit dependence on ρ^t. Notice that ρ_t can take only finitely many values. Thus, the factors driving the risky events are approximated by a discrete set of scenarios or sequence of events. Given the event history up to a time t, ρ^t, the uncertainty in the next period is characterized by finitely many possible outcomes for the next observation ρ_{t+1}. This branching process is represented using a scenario tree. An example of a scenario tree with three time periods and two-two-three branching structure is presented in Figure 3.1. We also model a continuous perturbation in addition to the discretized uncertainty (see also Frauendorfer (1995)), so that the vector of return values at time t has a multivariate normal distribution, with mean $\mathbf{r}_t(\rho^t)$, and specified covariance matrix Λ.

Capital Allocation

As the problem is dynamic in nature, the wealth to be invested varies with time. Hence, the traditional approach used, which is the static formulation, where wealth is normalized to unity, needs to be appropriately extended. At $t = 0$, the initial budget is normalized to 1. If the investor currently has holdings of assets $1, \ldots, n$, then vector $\mathbf{p}$ (scaled so that $\mathbf{1}'\mathbf{p} = 1$) represents his current position. If the investor currently has no holdings (wishing to buy in at time $t = 0$), then $\mathbf{p} = \mathbf{0}$. If the investor wishes to add to a current portfolio for the initial time period, then $\mathbf{p}$ can be scaled so that $\mathbf{1}'\mathbf{p}$ is the appropriate value smaller than 1. Then, the allocation of the initial budget of 1 can be represented with the following constraints:

$$\mathbf{p} + (1 - c_b)\mathbf{b}_0 - (1 + c_s)\mathbf{s}_0 = \mathbf{w}_0 \tag{3.1}$$

$$\mathbf{1}'\mathbf{b}_0 - \mathbf{1}'\mathbf{s}_0 = 1 - \mathbf{1}'\mathbf{p} \tag{3.2}$$

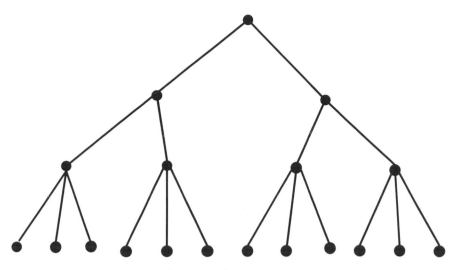

Fig. 3.1. A scenario tree

Note the following consequences of transaction costs c_b and c_s in (3.1) which generalize beyond the initial time period:

- If any assets are initially transacted so that $w_0 \neq p$ (i.e. $b_0 + s_0 \neq 0$) the total value of the resulting initial portfolio will be less than the initial budget of 1, due to loss through transaction costs.

- The fact that transactions have cost ensures that for the same asset $(b_0^j \cdot s_0^j = 0)$; buy and sell variables corresponding to the same asset can never simultaneously be nonzero.

- The incorporation of transaction costs in the model provides essential "friction" (Fragniere (2001)); without this friction, the optimization has complete freedom in reallocating the portfolio every time period, which (if implemented) can result in significantly poorer realized performance than forecast, due to excessive transaction costs. Hakansson (1971, 1974) explains that in the absence of transaction costs, myopic policies are sufficient to achieve optimality.

Constraint (3.2) enforces the initial budget of unity (whether it be new investment or reallocation). The net total amount of buying makes up the shortfall of the original portfolio beneath the budget. It is important to note that our model allows money to be added to the portfolio in this way only in the initial time period.

Transaction Constraints

An investor must pay a commission to the broker when buying or selling a stock. That commission is the transaction cost of the purchase or sale.

The impact of transaction costs on performance of the mean-variance models have been investigated by Perold (1984), Konno and Yamazaki (1991), and Chopra, Hensel, and Turner (1993).

The decision at time $t > 0$ is clearly dependent on ρ^t and yields, after observing ρ^t, the investments in asset j as

$$w_t^j = r_t^j(\rho^t)w_{t-1}^j + (1 - c_b^j)b_t^j - (1 + c_s^j)s_t^j, \quad j = 1, \ldots, n; \ t = 1, \ldots, T-1$$

$$w_T^j = r_T^j(\rho^T)w_{T-1}^j, \quad j = 1, \ldots, n.$$

These last two constraints can be written more concisely in vector form as

$$\mathbf{w}_t = \mathbf{r}_t(\rho^t) \circ \mathbf{w}_{t-1} + (\mathbf{1} - \mathbf{c}_b) \circ \mathbf{b}_t - (\mathbf{1} + \mathbf{c}_s) \circ \mathbf{s}_t, \quad t = 1, \ldots, T-1 \quad (3.3)$$

$$\mathbf{w}_T = \mathbf{r}_T(\rho^T) \circ \mathbf{w}_{T-1}. \quad (3.4)$$

As $\mathbf{w}_t(\rho^t)$ depends on the past and not the future, the policy $\{\mathbf{w}_0, \ldots, \mathbf{w}_t\}$ is non-anticipative. Furthermore, ρ_0 is observed before the initial decision and is thus treated as deterministic information.

Balance Constraints

Assuming that there are no exogenous cash injections, the amount of stock bought at any time needs to be financed by the amount of stock sold in the same period. We also observe that the amount invested at each period is given by the amount inherited from the previous period, less transaction costs. This is reflected by the following equality

$$\mathbf{1}'\mathbf{w}_t = \mathbf{1}'(\mathbf{r}_t \circ \mathbf{w}_{t-1}) - \mathbf{1}'(\mathbf{c}_b \circ \mathbf{b}_t) - \mathbf{1}'(\mathbf{c}_s \circ \mathbf{s}_t). \quad (3.5)$$

In order for (3.5) to be satisfied along with (3.3) it suffices that we require subsequent transactions (buy $= \mathbf{b}_t$, sell $= \mathbf{s}_t$) not to alter the wealth within the period t. Hence, we have the condition

$$\mathbf{1}'\mathbf{b}_t - \mathbf{1}'\mathbf{s}_t = 0, \quad t = 1, \ldots, T-1. \quad (3.6)$$

In order to model additions to or withdrawals from the portfolio, (3.6) could be modified as $\mathbf{1}'\mathbf{b}_t - \mathbf{1}'\mathbf{s}_t = h$.

Benchmarks

A benchmark is a measure of performance for a predetermined set of securities. It is designed to reflect prevailing market conditions. Such sets may be based on published indexes or may be customized to suit an investment strategy. One aspect of this paper is the use of mean-variance optimization in relation to a specified benchmark portfolio. Benchmark tracking may be very important for portfolio management. A risk-averse investor may prefer to remain as close to the benchmark as possible for all return scenarios.

An initial benchmark portfolio is specified as $\overline{\mathbf{w}}_0$ (possibly $= \mathbf{p}$), and benchmarks at later time periods derive from $\overline{\mathbf{w}}_0$ by accruing returns, but not allowing any reallocation:

$$\overline{\mathbf{w}}_t(\boldsymbol{\rho}^t) = \mathbf{r}_t(\boldsymbol{\rho}^t) \circ \overline{\mathbf{w}}_{t-1}(\boldsymbol{\rho}^{t-1}), \quad t = 1, \dots, T. \tag{3.7}$$

Henceforth, $\overline{\mathbf{w}}_t$ will be referred to without its implicit dependence on $\boldsymbol{\rho}^t$.

Expected Wealth

The objective of an investor is to minimize portfolio risk while maximizing expected portfolio return on investment, or achieving a prescribed expected return. The expected wealth at time t, arising from period $[t-1, t]$ is

$$\mathrm{E}\left[\mathbf{r}_t(\boldsymbol{\rho}^t)' \mathbf{w}_{t-1}\right].$$

Note that, due to transaction costs in (3.3), this could be slightly less than $\mathrm{E}\left[\mathbf{1}'\mathbf{w}_t\right]$; this is intended, as we want to measure the expectation and variance of the wealth before the accounts are reallocated with $\mathbf{b}_t$ and $\mathbf{s}_t$. Given the possible events $\mathbf{e} \in \mathcal{N}_t$ (the discretization of $\boldsymbol{\rho}_t$), the expected wealth at time t, relative to benchmark $\overline{\mathbf{w}}_t$, is given by

$$\mathcal{W}_t = \mathrm{E}\left[\mathbf{1}'\left(\mathbf{w}_t - \overline{\mathbf{w}}_t\right)\right]$$

$$= \mathrm{E}\left[\mathbf{r}_t(\boldsymbol{\rho}_t|\boldsymbol{\rho}^{t-1})'\left(\mathbf{w}_{t-1} - \overline{\mathbf{w}}_{t-1}\right)\right]$$

$$= \mathrm{E}\left[\sum_{e \in \mathcal{N}_t} P_e \left(\mathbf{r}_e' \left(\mathbf{w}_{a(e)} - \overline{\mathbf{w}}_{a(e)}\right)\right)\right]$$

$$= \sum_{e \in \mathcal{N}_t} P_e \left(\hat{\mathbf{r}}_e' \left(\mathbf{w}_{a(e)} - \overline{\mathbf{w}}_{a(e)}\right)\right), \tag{3.8}$$

where $\hat{\mathbf{r}}_e$ and $\mathbf{w}_e$ ($e \in \mathcal{N}_t$) are the various realizations of stochastic quantities $\mathbf{r}_t(\boldsymbol{\rho}_t|\boldsymbol{\rho}^{t-1})$ and $\mathbf{w}_{t-1}(\boldsymbol{\rho}^{t-1})$.

Expected Risk

Risk, for any realization of $\boldsymbol{\rho}^t$, is measured as the variance of the portfolio return relative to the benchmark $\overline{\mathbf{w}}$:

$$\mathrm{Var}\left[\mathbf{r}_t(\boldsymbol{\rho}^t|\boldsymbol{\rho}^{t-1})'\left(\mathbf{w}_{t-1} - \overline{\mathbf{w}}_{t-1}\right)\right]$$

$$= \mathrm{E}\left[\left(\mathbf{r}_t(\boldsymbol{\rho}_t|\boldsymbol{\rho}^{t-1})'\left(\mathbf{w}_{t-1} - \overline{\mathbf{w}}_{t-1}\right)\right)^2\right] - \left(\mathrm{E}\left[\mathbf{r}_t(\boldsymbol{\rho}_t|\boldsymbol{\rho}^{t-1})'\left(\mathbf{w}_{t-1} - \overline{\mathbf{w}}_{t-1}\right)\right]\right)^2$$

$$= \mathrm{E}\left[\left(\mathbf{w}_{t-1} - \overline{\mathbf{w}}_{t-1}\right)'(\Lambda + \mathbf{r}_t(\boldsymbol{\rho}^t|\boldsymbol{\rho}^{t-1})\mathbf{r}_t(\boldsymbol{\rho}^t|\boldsymbol{\rho}^{t-1})')(\mathbf{w}_{t-1} - \overline{\mathbf{w}}_{t-1})\right]$$

$$- \left(\mathrm{E}\left[\mathbf{r}_t(\boldsymbol{\rho}^t|\boldsymbol{\rho}^{t-1})'\left(\mathbf{w}_{t-1} - \overline{\mathbf{w}}_{t-1}\right)\right]\right)^2. \tag{3.9}$$

The two components $(\Lambda + \mathbf{r}_t \mathbf{r}'_t)$ in (3.9) reflect risk arising from two types of uncertainty. The term corresponding to the outer product $\mathbf{r}_t \mathbf{r}'_t$ represents the uncertainty due to the discrete distribution of realizations of ρ^t (various paths through the scenario tree, as discussed below). The term corresponding to Λ reflects continuous uncertainty due to the variability of the return at a given realization of ρ.

Once $\mathcal{W}_t$ is known, the variance of the wealth at time t (relative to the benchmark) can be similarly calculated:

$$\text{Var}\left[\mathbf{r}_t(\rho_t|\rho^{t-1})'(\mathbf{w}_{t-1} - \overline{\mathbf{w}}_{t-1})\right] = \text{E}\left[\left(\mathbf{r}_t(\rho_t|\rho^{t-1})'(\mathbf{w}_{t-1} - \overline{\mathbf{w}}_{t-1})\right)^2\right] - (\mathcal{W}_t)^2$$

$$= \text{E}\left[\sum_{e \in \mathcal{N}_t} P_e \left(\mathbf{r}'_e (\mathbf{w}_{a(e)} - \overline{\mathbf{w}}_{a(e)})\right)^2\right] - (\mathcal{W}_t)^2$$

$$= \sum_{e \in \mathcal{N}_t} P_e \left((\mathbf{w}_{a(e)} - \overline{\mathbf{w}}_{a(e)})'(\Lambda + \hat{\mathbf{r}}_e \hat{\mathbf{r}}'_e)(\mathbf{w}_{a(e)} - \overline{\mathbf{w}}_{a(e)})\right) - (\mathcal{W}_t)^2. \quad (3.10)$$

Bounds on Variables: No Short Sale

It is possible to sell an asset that you do not own through the process of short selling, or shorting the asset. In order to do this, the investor borrows the asset, then sells the borrowed asset. At a later date, the investor repays the loan by purchasing the asset and returning it to the lender. The short selling is profitable if the asset price declines. It is quite risky for many investors since potential for loss is unlimited. For this reason, short selling is prohibited within certain financial institutions, and it is purposely avoided as a policy by many individuals and institutions. However, it is not universally forbidden, and there is, in fact a considerable level of short selling of stock market securities. In the mean-variance optimization framework, bounds on decision variables prevent the short sale and enforce further restrictions imposed by the investor.

Let there be box constraints on $\mathbf{w_e}$, $\mathbf{b_e}$, $\mathbf{s_e}$ for each event $\mathbf{e} \in \mathcal{N}$ such that

$$\mathbf{w}_\mathbf{e}^L \leq \mathbf{w_e} \leq \mathbf{w}_\mathbf{e}^U$$

$$0 \leq \mathbf{b_e} \leq \mathbf{b}_\mathbf{e}^U$$

$$0 \leq \mathbf{s_e} \leq \mathbf{s}_\mathbf{e}^U.$$

3.3   Multistage Stochastic Programming Model

Let the expected returns $\hat{\mathbf{r}}_\mathbf{e}$, and covariance matrix $\Lambda_\mathbf{e}$ be given for $\mathbf{e} \in \mathcal{N}$. The multistage portfolio reallocation problem can be expressed as the minimization of risk subject to constraints given in (3.1) − (3.4) (which describe the growth of the portfolio along all the various scenarios), a performance constraint, and bounds on the variables.

The constant parameter W is supplied to constrain final expected wealth to a particular value (due to the minimization of risk, an equality constraint would be equivalent). The optimization will find the lowest-variance (least risky) investment strategy to achieve that specified expected wealth. Varying W and reoptimizing will generate points along the efficient frontier.

$$QP(W)$$

$$\min_{\mathbf{w},\mathbf{b},\mathbf{s}} \sum_{t=1}^{T} \alpha_t \sum_{e \in \mathcal{N}_t} P_e \left[(\mathbf{w}_{a(e)} - \overline{\mathbf{w}}_{a(e)})'(\Lambda_e + \hat{\mathbf{r}}_e \hat{\mathbf{r}}_e')(\mathbf{w}_{a(e)} - \overline{\mathbf{w}}_{a(e)}) \right]$$

subject to :

$$\mathbf{p} + (1 - \mathbf{c}_b)\mathbf{b}_0 - (1 + \mathbf{c}_s)\mathbf{s}_0 \;=\; \mathbf{w}_0$$

$$\mathbf{1}'\mathbf{b}_0 - \mathbf{1}'\mathbf{s}_0 \;=\; 1 - \mathbf{1}'\mathbf{p}$$

$$\hat{\mathbf{r}}_e \circ \mathbf{w}_{a(e)} + (1 - \mathbf{c}_b) \circ \mathbf{b}_e - (1 + \mathbf{c}_s) \circ \mathbf{s}_e \;=\; \mathbf{w}_e \qquad e \in \mathcal{N}_I$$

$$\mathbf{1}'\mathbf{b}_e - \mathbf{1}'\mathbf{s}_e \;=\; 0 \qquad e \in \mathcal{N}_I$$

$$\sum_{e \in \mathcal{N}_T} P_e \left(\hat{\mathbf{r}}_e' (\mathbf{w}_{a(e)} - \overline{\mathbf{w}}_{a(e)}) \right) \;\geq\; W$$

$$\mathbf{w}_e^L \leq \mathbf{w}_e \leq \mathbf{w}_e^U \qquad e \in \mathcal{N}$$

$$0 \leq \mathbf{b}_e \leq \mathbf{b}_e^U \qquad e \in \mathcal{N}_I \cup \mathbf{0}$$

$$0 \leq \mathbf{s}_e \leq \mathbf{s}_e^U \qquad e \in \mathcal{N}_I \cup \mathbf{0}.$$

Note that the classical stochastic linear programming formulation (Dempster (1993), Finance Research Group) has the linear expression for $E[W]$ at the final time period as the objective function, and takes no account of risk. This formulation allows for calculation of efficient investment strategies which are not totally risk-seeking. There also exist stochastic linear programs which take account of risk such as utility models (which can be easily modeled as linear by piecewise approximation) and worst-case outcome (Young (1998)).

3.3.1 Computation of Transaction Costs

The transaction cost computation requires further clarification. It is implicit in the formulation that buy and sell variables for a particular asset in any scenario cannot be both nonzero – otherwise more money is spent on transaction costs than is necessary. In linear programming formulations using the simplex algorithm, this is inherently assured. The problem becomes especially acute nearer the risk-averse computations when portfolio performance is less important than risk. However, in quadratic programming formulations such as the above, it has been observed that common buy and sell variables often are found to be both significantly nonzero. This seems to arise from numerical instabilities due to the near linear dependence of the constraint columns of buy and sell variables. To solve this problem in our quadratic model above, we penalize the quantity $b_{\mathbf{e}}^i s_{\mathbf{e}}^i$ in every instance. This yields the following augmented objective function:

$$\min_{\mathbf{w},\mathbf{b},\mathbf{s}} \sum_{t=1}^{T} \sum_{\mathbf{e}\in\mathcal{N}_t} \left(\alpha_t P_{\mathbf{e}} \left[(\mathbf{w}_{a(\mathbf{e})} - \overline{\mathbf{w}}_{a(\mathbf{e})})'(\Lambda_{\mathbf{e}} + \hat{\mathbf{r}}_{\mathbf{e}}\hat{\mathbf{r}}_{\mathbf{e}}')(\mathbf{w}_{a(\mathbf{e})} - \overline{\mathbf{w}}_{a(\mathbf{e})}) \right] + \gamma \mathbf{b}_{\mathbf{e}} \circ \mathbf{s}_{\mathbf{e}} \right).$$

Too large a penalty $\gamma \geq 0$ can introduce additional numerical instability that severely hinders convergence, but a penalty coefficient of $\gamma = 0.001$ was found empirically to enforce complementarity of buy and sell variables without significant detriment to optimization performance.

3.3.2   Constraining Intermediate Risk/Return

In addition to constraining the final wealth, constraints of the following form

$$\sum_{\mathbf{e}\in\mathcal{N}_t} P_{\mathbf{e}} \left(\hat{\mathbf{r}}_{\mathbf{e}}' (\mathbf{w}_{a(\mathbf{e})} - \overline{\mathbf{w}}_{a(\mathbf{e})}) \right) \geq \mathcal{W}_t \qquad (3.11)$$

for any $t = 1 \ldots, T - 1$ can be added to ensure any desired intermediate (expected) performance.

The objective function of $QP(\mathcal{W})$ is a weighted sum of (3.10) for each time period, with constant terms $\mathcal{W}_t^2$ dropped. If $\alpha_t \equiv 1$, then risk in each time period is weighted equally, but allowing α_t to decrease with t (e.g. $\alpha_t = \gamma^t$, for some $\gamma \in (0,1)$) reflects a discount for risk further in the future. As another alternative, instead using an objective function which minimizes risk for all t, it may be preferable to have bounds on risk in the intermediate periods and just minimize final risk at $t = T$. This is reflected in the objective function by setting

$$\alpha_t = \begin{cases} 0 & t < T \\ 1 & t = T \end{cases} \qquad (3.12)$$

and maximum intermediate risks would be enforced (in conjunction with (3.11)) by additional constraints of the form

$$\sum_{\mathbf{e}\in\mathcal{N}_t} P_{\mathbf{e}} \left[(\mathbf{w}_{a(\mathbf{e})} - \overline{\mathbf{w}}_{a(\mathbf{e})})'(\Lambda_{\mathbf{e}} + \hat{\mathbf{r}}_{\mathbf{e}}\hat{\mathbf{r}}_{\mathbf{e}}')(\mathbf{w}_{a(\mathbf{e})} - \overline{\mathbf{w}}_{a(\mathbf{e})}) \right] - (\mathcal{W}_t)^2 \leq \lambda_t \quad (3.13)$$

(with $\lambda_t \geq 0$) for any $t = 1, \ldots, T - 1$. The intermediate performance (3.11) and intermediate risk (3.13) constraint types may be applied at specific junctures and need not be present for all t.

3.3.3   Implementation Issues: Saving Space

In implementation, the model can be simplified to reduce the number of variables. First, all variables $\mathbf{w}_T$ may be substituted out using (3.4) (as they are in the performance constraint above). As the majority of nodes in any branching tree are nodes, this will result in significant space savings (which any good optimization preprocessor should do as well).

It could be unreasonable or impossible to specify bounds for the decision variables *a priori* as the size of the portfolio at any particular scenario node depends on values of variables in time periods, as well as on the quality of asset returns along the scenario path particular to that node. It is possible to express variable bounds in a percentage, rather than absolute sense; for instance, percentage bounds such as

$$\beta_e^{iL} \leq \frac{w_e^i}{w_e^1 + w_e^2 + \ldots + w_e^n} \leq \beta_e^{iU}$$

can easily be linearized, as

$$(1 - \beta_e^{iL})w_e^i - \sum_{j \neq i} \beta_e^{iL} w_e^j \geq 0$$

$$(1 - \beta_e^{iU})w_e^i - \sum_{j \neq i} \beta_e^{iU} w_e^j \leq 0.$$

These constraints, unfortunately, are not as simple as the original box constraints (which are typically handled as a special case by any optimization algorithm), and could add significantly to the size of the problem, and its solution time. Percentage lower and upper bounds on $\mathbf{w}$, $\mathbf{b}$, and $\mathbf{s}$ variables will require $4n^2 + 2n$ nonzeroes per node of the problem (compared to $6n$ coefficients necessary for transaction and balance constraints).

A significant savings in space can be obtained with the introduction of an auxiliary total variable

$$T_e = \mathbf{1}'\mathbf{w}_e,$$

allowing percentage constraints to be simplified to

$$\mathbf{w}_e^i \geq \beta_e^{iL} T$$

$$\mathbf{w}_e^i \leq \beta_e^{iU} T,$$

for a total of $9n + 1$ nonzeroes spent on percentage bounds. This compares favourably with the previous $4n^2 + 2n$ even with only $n = 2$ assets, and for higher n the move from a quadratic to a linear number of coefficients per node can reduce the problem to a fraction of its original size. In our implementation (using interior point quadratic optimizer BPMPD; Mészáros (1997)), this reduction in space did not correspond to a reduction in solution time. This is presumably because the reduction in size of inequality constraints was offset by the complexity difference of additional equality constraints.

3.4   Performance

3.4.1   Implementation

The model $QP(\mathcal{W})$ was implemented as a software package called *foliage*. *Foliage*, coded in C++, is a financial software developed in the Department of Computing by the authors. It integrates with LP/QP solver BPMPD (Mészáros (1997)) which is based on special interior point algorithm developed for solving QP problems. An alternative solution strategy based on the interior point algorithm has been developed by Blomvall and Lindberg (2002), where a Riccati based primal barrier method is specially fitted to solve large scale multistage stochastic programming with a quadratic objective.

Foliage computes the minimum-variance investment strategy to achieve that expected wealth by solving $QP(\mathcal{W})$ if a value of $\mathcal{W}$ is provided. Otherwise, *foliage* proceeds in the following manner:

- Accumulate the benchmark initial investment allocation through each scenario (from root to leaf), and calculate the expected final wealth generated by the non-active benchmark investment strategy. Call this amount $\mathcal{W}_{min}$.

- Remove the final wealth constraint from $QP(\mathcal{W})$, and use its linear left-hand side to replace the quadratic objective function. Maximize the resulting linear program to obtain $\mathcal{W}_{max}$.

- For a number of equally-spaced points $\mathcal{W} \in [\mathcal{W}_{min}, \mathcal{W}_{max}]$, solve $QP(\mathcal{W})$, and output the resulting points of the efficient frontier.

Foliage has the ability to handle simple box constraints on the decision variables, as well as percentage constraints, as discussed above. The discounts can either be of the form $\alpha_t = \gamma^t$, or (3.12), which would ignore variance in intermediate time periods and optimize only the variance of the final wealth. The scenario trees input to the program can have arbitrary branching structure and depth (limited only by computer memory).

All of the problems were solved on a 500 MHz Pentium III, running Linux with 256Meg of RAM.

3.4.2   WATSON Data

The WATSON family of problems (Finance Research Group) forecast to a horizon of 10 years a portfolio of four asset classes, as well as number of liabilities, and riskless assets (bank deposits or borrowing). There are 24 data sets, ranging in size from 16 to 2688 scenarios. The data sets were generated in two ways, either with Conditional Scenarios (C), or Independent Scenarios (I). The CALM model (Dempster (1993)) underlying the WATSON data sets incorporates more data than was needed by our model (i.e. liabilities in addition to assets, separate returns for the same asset bought at different

Table 3.2. Performance of *foliage* on WATSON data sets

Scenarios	Branching	Nonzeroes	Secs.	(Avg.)	Its.	(Avg.)
16	$(2^4 \cdot 1^6)$	10634	2.42	(1.2)	16	(6.6)
32	$(2^5 \cdot 1^5)$	18378	5.07	(2.4)	19	(7.2)
64	$(2^6 \cdot 1^4)$	30794	9.14	(4.5)	20	(7.9)
128	$(2^7 \cdot 1^3)$	49482	15.7	(8.1)	21	(8.9)
256	$(2^8 \cdot 1^2)$	74570	31.6	(12.9)	28	(9.0)
512	$(2^9 \cdot 1)$	100170	46.8	(20.2)	29	(10.1)
768	$(3 \cdot 2^8 \cdot 1)$	150250	70.2	(34.8)	28	(11.4)
1024	$(4 \cdot 2^8 \cdot 1)$	200330	124.5	(48.7)	38	(11.8)
1152	$(3^2 \cdot 2^7 \cdot 1)$	225226	112.9	(57.0)	30	(12.4)
1536	$(4 \cdot 3 \cdot 2^7 \cdot 1)$	300298	195.0	(85.2)	39	(13.7)
1920	$(5 \cdot 3 \cdot 2^7 \cdot 1)$	375370	239.4	(113.5)	38	(14.7)
2304	$(6 \cdot 3 \cdot 2^7 \cdot 1)$	450442	273.7	(144.5)	35	(15.2)
2688	$(7 \cdot 3 \cdot 2^7 \cdot 1)$	525514	335.1	(178.1)	37	(16.0)

times, etc.). We kept the same scenario tree structure, using return prices between times $t-1$ and t as our $\hat{r}$, incorporated dividends into the returns, and discarded the remainder of the data.

For bounds, we specified that at all times each of the four assets must represent between 10–50% of the total portfolio, and that individual transactions must never be more than 50% of the portfolio (also in percentage). Use of the percentage bounds greatly increases the size of the problems (in these cases, typically threefold), due to the addition of $O(n^2)$ nonzeroes at each scenario node.

In Table 3.2, time and BPMPD iterations (its.) are reported for the solution of each problem, with $\mathcal{W} = 2.0$ (a value typically in the middle of the efficient frontier). In parentheses are the average time and iterations required to solve 20 equally-spaced points of the efficient frontier; the warm-start capabilities of BPMPD allow for significant time savings. Only the problems generated with Conditional Scenarios are provided, since the Independent Scenario problems have identical sizes and the performance of *foliage* was virtually identical.

3.4.3   Backtesting

In order to demonstrate the viability of the investment decisions produced by *foliage*, we did backtesting using historical stock price data, in the following manner:

Initialize the following parameters:

- Past horizon p
- Future horizon f

- Branching b
- Risk level r
- number of Simulations S

Set current time to $t = p$, and initial portfolio value to $V = 1$.

Analyze the past p time periods (from $t - p + 1$ to t). Use logarithmic regression to estimate the growth rate of each stock. Calculate the covariance matrix of the residuals from this regression.

Forecast a scenario tree f time periods into the future, branching b at each time period. The root of the scenario tree incorporates the present data. To determine the branching of any scenario node to its children, simulate a large number S of single time period scenarios using the state of the present scenario and the growth and covariance data; then cluster those simulations into b groups, the "centers" of which will be the child scenario nodes. For more details on the forecasting of scenario trees through simulation, see Gülpinar, Rustem, and Settergren (2003).

Optimize investment decisions by running *foliage* on the generated scenario tree to find the efficient investment strategy for $W = rW_{\max} + (1 - r)W_{\min}$.

Invest portfolio value V among the various assets according to the initial allocation prescribed in the optimal solution.

Accrue balances in each asset according to the change in price from current time t to "tomorrow", the stock prices at $t + 1$. Update V, the total value of the portfolio, and increment t.

Iterate back to step **Analyze** as long as there is more historical data.

Results are depicted in Figures 3.2 and 3.3. The data arise from 10 British stocks (arbitrarily chosen from the FTSE 100), priced monthly from 1988 to early 2000. The "index" in all figures charts the growth of an initially equally-weighted portfolio without rebalancing. Each of the other curves represents a fixed value of risk throughout the time horizon. It is interesting to note that the crash in month 120 reflects the crash of the FTSE in late 1998.

It should also be noted that, as the scenario trees involved in this experiment were generated using randomized procedures, repetition of the experiments can (and indeed do) yield different results. However, this effect was minimized by the use of low-discrepancy quasirandom (but deterministic) Sobol sequences (Sobol (1967), Bratley, Fox, and Niederreiter (1992)), see Gülpinar, Rustem, and Settergren (2003) for comparison of quasirandom vs. pseudorandom numbers in scenario tree generation).

In Figures 3.2 and 3.3 we can see the effect of transaction costs on the model, as well as the importance of an appropriate choice of benchmark.

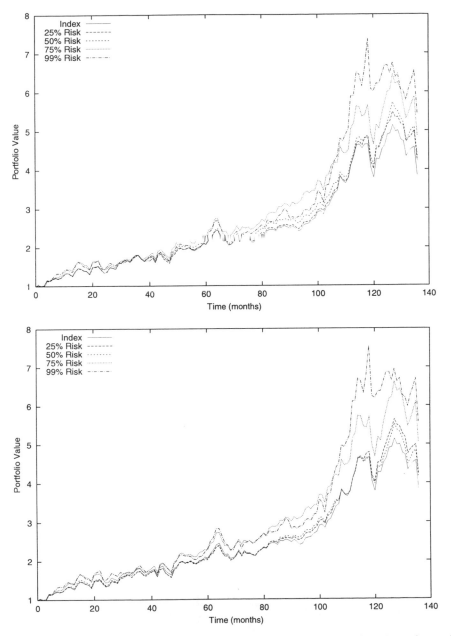

Fig. 3.2. Backtesting results with a fixed, equal-weight benchmark, and 0.2% transaction cost for purchases. In the graph above, the optimizer had no knowledge of the transaction costs

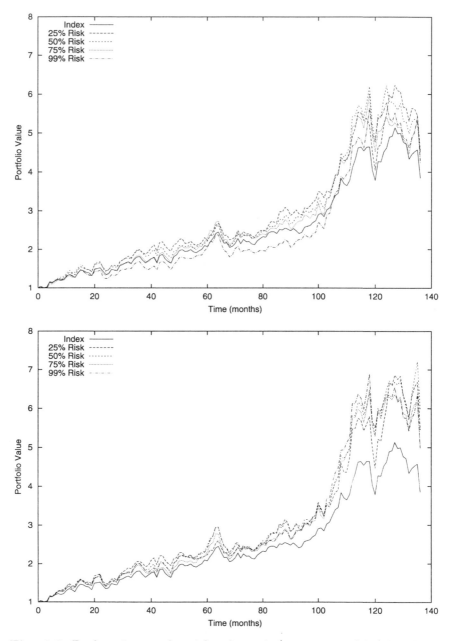

Fig. 3.3. Backtesting results with a dynamic (current portfolio) benchmark, and 0.5% transaction cost for purchases. In the graph above, the optimizer had no knowledge of the transaction costs

For Figure 3.2, every scenario tree generated in the backtesting experiment used a constant benchmark of 1/10 per asset. Beyond being a natural arbitrary choice, we can justify this by noting that the index is based on an initially equally-weighted portfolio. The two graphs display the subtle effect of including transaction costs in the optimization model. In both backtesting experiments, a transaction fee of 0.2% was deducted for all purchases; however, only in the latter experiment was that transaction cost also included in the data input to optimizer *foliage*. The effect is a subtle improvement to the higher risk curves (75% and 99%), and subtle worsening of the lower risk curves (25% and 50%). This is because higher-risk strategies involve more active trading, so the cost of trading cannot be ignored. Lower-risk strategies, however, are already trading less, and inclusion of transaction costs in the optimization model further penalized trading, and prevented or delayed some necessary rebalancing.

Figure 3.3, considers an alternative benchmark selection and alternative transaction cost value. The benchmark supplied as data to each optimization is the same as the current portfolio **p** prior to optimization. This means that the zero-risk (as measured by the model's quadratic objective function) strategy is to maintain the current portfolio. This ensures that a portfolio is never changed radically (unless high performance demands of risk-seeking strategies demand it), but allows the portfolio to migrate to the naturally lowest-risk strategy, instead of always being tied to an equal-weight benchmark (which might not be a particularly low-risk or high-performance strategy). The alternative benchmark is also motivated by an inertia-based approach to investment. The results indicate the clear superiority of taking transaction costs into account during optimization.

3.5   Conclusions

In this chapter, we consider the optimization of the mean and variance of portfolio returns for a multiperiod investment problem with transaction costs. The basic investment model is adopted with the benchmark relative computations in view of the transaction costs. A detailed study of transaction costs as well as computational approaches for addressing the issues arising from them is presented.

The chapter is based on the observation that, in view of the transaction costs, it is essential to consider the multistage decision problem directly. This overcomes the suboptimality of myopic sequential application of single-period optimization and provides a realistic cost conscious strategy.

We provide a general benchmark-relative return framework, and use an interior point optimizer to solve the overall quadratic programming problem. We generate scenario trees using low-discrepancy quasirandom Sobol sequences based on historical information to test the *ex ante* performance of the methodology. We also test the methodology using publicly available large-scale problems based on the CALM model. We report a number of computational backtesting experiments which illustrate the performance of the transaction cost model.

Acknowledgments

This research was supported by EPSRC grant GR/M41124. The authors are grateful to anonymous referees for helpful comments and suggestions.

References

Becker, R., Hall, S., and Rustem, B. (1994), "Robust Optimal Control of Stochastic Nonlinear Economic Systems," *Journal of Economic Dynamics and Control* **18**, 125-148.

Birge, J. R., and Louveaux, F. (1997), *Introduction to Stochastic Programming*, Springer-Verlag, New York.

Blomvall, J., and Lindberg, P. O. (2002), "A Riccati-Based Primal Interior Point Solver for Multistage Stochastic Programming – Extensions," *Optimization Methods and Software* **17**, 383-407.

Bratley, P., Fox, B. L., and Niederreiter, H. (1992), "Implementation and Tests of Low-Discrepancy Sequences," *ACM Transactions on Modeling and Computer Simulation* **2**, 195-213.

Chopra, V. K., Hensel, C. R., and Turner, A. L. (1993), "Massaging Mean-Variance Inputs: Returns from Alternative Global Investment Strategies in the 1980s," *Management Science* **39**, 845-855.

Darlington, J., Pantelides, C. C., Rustem, B., and Tanyi, B. A. (1999), "An Algorithm for Constrained Nonlinear Optimisation Under uncertainty," *Automatica* **35**, 217-228.

Darlington, J., Pantelides, C. C., Rustem, B., and Tanyi, B. A. (2000), "Decreasing the Sensitivity of Open-Loop Optimal Solutions in Decision Making under Uncertainty," *European Journal of Operations Research* **121**, 330-342.

Dempster, M. A. H. (1993), "CALM: A Stochastic MIP Model," Department of Mathematics, University of Essex, Colchester, United Kingdom.

Finance Research Group, Judge Institute of Management Studies, Cambridge, England, Watson Pension Fund Management Problem, http://www-cfr.jims.cam.ac.uk/research/stprog.html.

Fragniere, E. (2001), Private Communication, University of Lausanne, Lausanne, Switzerland.

Frauendorfer, K. (1995), "The Stochastic Programming Extension of the Markowitz Approach," *International Journal of Mass-Parallel Computing and Information Systems* **5**, 449-460.

Frauendorfer, K., and Siede, H. (2000), "Portfolio Selection Using Multistage Stochastic Programming," *Central European Journal of Operations Research* **7**, 277-289.

Gassman, H., and Ireland, A. M. (1995), "Scenario Formulation in an Algebraic Modelling Language," *Annals of Operations Research* **59**, 45-75.

Gülpinar, N., Rustem, B., and Settergren, R. (2003), "Optimisation and Simulation Approaches to Scenario Tree Generation," forthcoming in *Journal of Economic Dynamics and Control*.

Hakansson, N. H. (1971), "On Optimal Myopic Portfolio Policies, with and without Serial Correlations of Yields," *Journal of Business* **44**, 324-334.

Hakansson, N. H. (1974), "Convergence to Isoelastic Utility and Policy in Multiperiod Portfolio Choice," *Journal of Financial Economics* **1**, 201-224.

Kall, P., and Wallace, S. (1994), *Stochastic Programming*, John Wiley & Sons, Chichester, England.

Kallberg, J. G., and Ziemba, W. T. (1983), "Comparison of Alternative Utility Functions in Portfolio Selection Problems," *Management Science* **29**, 1257-1276.

Konno, H., and Yamazaki, H. (1991), "Mean-Absolute Deviation Portfolio Optimization Model and its Applications to Tokyo Stock Market," *Management Science* **37**, 519-531.

Markowitz, H. (1952), "Portfolio Selection," *Journal of Finance* **7**, 77-91.

Mészáros, C. (1997), BPMPD User's Manual Version 2.20, Research Report, Department of Computing, Imperial College, United Kingdom, July.

Perold, A. F. (1984), "Large Scale Portfolio Optimization," *Management Science* **30**, 1143-1160

Prekopa, A. (1995), *Stochastic Programming*, Kluwer Academic Publishers, Dordrecht, The Netherlands.

Pulley, L. B. (1981), "A General Mean-Variance Approximation to Expected Utility for Short Holding Periods," *Journal of Financial and Quantitative Analysis* **16**, 361-373.

Rustem, B. (1994), "Stochastic and Robust Control of Nonlinear Economic Systems," *European Journal of Operations Research* **73**, 304-318.

Sobol, I. M. (1967), "The Distribution of Points in a Cube and the Approximate Evaluation of Integrals," *USSR Computational Mathematics and Mathematical Physics* **7**, 86-112.

Steinbach, M. (1998), "Recursive Direct Optimisation and Successive Refinement in Multistage Stochastic Programs," Preprint SC 98-27, Konrad-Zuse Centrum für Informationstechnik, Berlin, Germany.

Young, M. R. (1998), "A Minimax Portfolio Selection Rule with Linear Programming Solution," *Management Science* **44**, 673-683.

Ziemba, W. T., and MacLean, L. C. (1999), "Growth versus Security Trade-offs in Dynamic Investment Analysis," *Annals of Operations Research* **85**, 193-225.

4 A Stochastic Network Approach for Integrating Pension and Corporate Financial Planning

John M. Mulvey, Koray D. Simsek, and Bill Pauling

4.1 Introduction

This chapter presents a multi-period stochastic network model for integrating corporate financial and pension planning. Pension planning in the United States has gained importance with the population aging and the growth of retirement accounts. In certain cases, the pension plan assets are several times larger than the value of the company itself (e.g. General Motors – Market cap: \$19 billion, Pension plan assets: \$67 billion, Estimated pension fund deficit: \$25 billion – in December 31, 2002; see General Motors Corporation (2003)). Thus, pension investment decisions can have a sizeable impact on a company's long-term financial health. However, pension planning is rarely linked to general corporate planning systems since the domain falls outside traditional corporate budgeting and planning processes.

We develop a consistent framework for combining the pension plan with the corporate financial plan via a stochastic optimization model. The approach can be specialized as a stochastic network, providing possible improvements in computational efficiency and ease of understanding. The goals of the integrated planning model can be readily tailored to the company's environment to be consistent with the existing corporate strategy. For example, there are numerous measures of risks for a large corporation, such as volatility of earnings, downside risks with respect to target earnings, share price, etc. The developed framework can be adapted to these objectives. In any event, we suggest that several risk measures be displayed to the senior managers so that they better understand the inherent tradeoffs, especially regarding temporal issues.

The general topic of pension planning affects several groups. First, the company desires to minimize its contribution to the plan over time while being able to meet its obligations to the retirees. For defined benefit plans, an annual actuarial valuation is conducted in order to assess the so-called pension surplus or deficit – market value of assets minus adjusted discounted value of liability cash-flows:

Surplus = Market value of assets minus Discounted (liabilities).

In most cases, there are two general measures of liabilities: (1) accumulated benefit obligations (ABO), and (2) projected benefit obligations (PBO). Roughly speaking, the former represents current legal obligations (say if the plan were to close today), whereas the latter depicts an estimate of the future liabilities (as the company employees age, change positions, etc.). Generally, the PBO is greater than the ABO. Liabilities are defined by FAS 87 (Financial Accounting Standards Statement No: 87) and reported in the company's financial statements. An important consideration involves the requirement that the company must make contributions when the plan is deemed sufficiently underfunded (as determined by ABO and sometimes PBO). The contribution decision is a major link between the core corporation and the pension plan; we model this as an arc in the stochastic network at each time period, for each scenario (more in the next section). Contributions can also be made voluntarily when the company has sufficient cash and under certain IRS regulations. We will show that this decision can be evaluated in the integrated planning model.

The employees have an important stake in the health of the pension plan. A company falling into bankruptcy will at times turn over the pension plan to the quasi-government agency – the Pension Benefit Guarantee Corporation (PBGC) to administer the plan if the company runs out of funds. This organization protect the employees, but only to a certain degree since the PBGC has limited resources and may not be able to raise benefits, for example, with inflation. Thus, a large surplus is desirable from the employees' perspective. However, most companies would rather keep funds in the core company, all else being equal, since retained earnings are more flexible than pension funds. It is noteworthy that over the long US bull market many companies have been able to generate accounting "profits" by generating returns above the projected target returns. Recent events have shown that companies should evaluate their assets and liabilities together. Unfortunately, many have not. We will show that careful integrated planning could have largely eliminated the large decrease in surplus or the loss of surpluses.

Due to the size of the issue (almost $4 trillion in assets), pension plans impact the health of the US economy. What will happen if a number of large plans are unable to continue? The $8 billion surplus in PBGC at the beginning of 2002 had disappeared by early 2003 due to only a couple of large bankruptcies. Thus, pension plan issues have public policy implications. The area of risk management for these plans can be improved by developing more reliable and comprehensive tools.

A stochastic planning system consists of three elements: (1) a stochastic scenario generator; (2) a corporate simulator; and (3) an optimization module for discovering non-dominated recommended solutions. See Mulvey and Ziemba (1998) for a discussion of the general issues.

The first, and to some degree, the most important element involves the scenario generator. This system of stochastic equations drives the underlying stochastic processes (Mulvey (1996)). A simple representation is shown in Figure 4.1; here, we depict a scenario tree for the evolution of future uncertainties. The planning horizon is divided into T time periods (generally years for pension planning). Most pension plans aim for 5 to 7 or more years at the planning horizon. Actuarial tradition requires that the cash-flows be projected over longer time periods – sometimes up to 50 or 75 years. However, the actual planning model will be designed for shorter periods. At each period, the long-term cash-flows are discounted to define the ABO or the PBO.

Importantly, a scenario is defined as a single branch from the root to any leaf of the tree. Thus, all of the parameter uncertainties are depicted along this branch. We model each scenario as a stochastic network (see Section 4.2). The overall stochastic network requires a set of additional constraints, called non-anticipativity conditions. In most cases, a set of scenarios is selected by employing variance reduction methods. We define the sample as set $\{S\}$.

The next section defines the integrated model and discusses some of the technical aspects of constructing and implementing the planning system. In Section 4.3, we describe a historical analysis of a typical pension plan, as developed by a respected actuarial firm, Towers Perrin. The purpose of these empirical tests is to illustrate several ways to employ the integrated model for corporate planning. Also, we show that the large loss of surplus that many firms experienced over the past three years (2000 to early 2003) could have been largely prevented by careful asset and liability management.

4.2 Multi-Period Investment Model

This section defines the integrated pension and corporate financial planning problem as a multi-stage stochastic program. The basic model is a variant of Mulvey et al. (1997). The major extension is that there is a company entity in the model in addition to the entities that constitute the pension fund. While the company grows through the planning horizon, it has to determine whether to make cash contributions to the pension plan.

First, we define the planning horizon T as $T = \{1, \ldots, \tau, \tau+1\}$. We focus on the pension plan's position and the value of the company at the end of period τ. Investment and contribution decisions occur at the beginning of each time stage.

Asset investment categories are defined by set $A = \{1, 2, \ldots, I\}$, with category 1 representing cash. The remaining categories can include broad int=0 $t = 1$ $t = 2$ $t = 3$

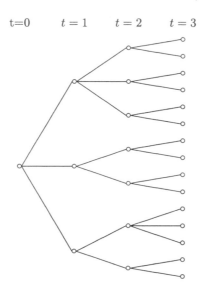

Fig. 4.1. A scenario tree for modeling uncertainties over the planning horizon

vestment groupings such as stocks, long-term government or corporate bonds and foreign equity. The categories should track well-defined market segments. Ideally, the co-movements between pairs of asset returns would be relatively low so that diversification can be done across the asset categories.

As with single-period models, uncertainty is represented by a set of distinct realizations $s \in S$. Scenarios may reveal identical values for the uncertain quantities up to a certain period – i.e., they share common information history up to that period. Scenarios that share common information must yield the same decisions up to that period. We address the representation of the information structure through non-anticipativity conditions. These constraints require that any variables sharing a common history, up to time period t, must be set equal to each other. See equations (4.8).

We assume that the plan portfolio is rebalanced at the beginning of each period. Alternatively, we could simply make no transaction except to reinvest any dividend and interest – a buy and hold strategy. For convenience, we also assume that the cash flows are reinvested in the generating asset category. Another assumption is that we know the current asset allocation of the pension fund. For a variant of this model, where only the initial wealth is known (i.e. initial asset weights are decision variables), see Mulvey and Simsek (2002).

For each $i \in A$, $t \in T$, and $s \in S$, we define the following parameters and decision variables:

Parameters

$r_{i,t}^s$ $= 1 + \rho_{i,t}^s$, where $\rho_{i,t}^s$ is the percentage return for asset i, in time period t, under scenario s (projected by a stochastic scenario generator, for example, see Mulvey et al. (2000)).

g_t^s $= 1 + \gamma_t^s$, where γ_t^s is the percentage growth rate of the company in time period t, under scenario s.

b_t^s Payments to beneficiaries in period t, under scenario s.

π^s Probability that scenario s occurs, $\sum_{s \in S} \pi^s = 1$.

$v_{i,1}^s$ Amount of money in asset category i, at the beginning of period 1, under scenario s, before rebalancing.

z_1 Value of the company at the beginning of time period 1.

$\sigma_{i,t}$ Transaction costs incurred in rebalancing asset i at the beginning of period t (symmetric transaction costs are assumed, i.e. cost of selling equals cost of buying).

Decision Variables

$x_{i,t}^s$ Amount of money in asset category i, at the beginning of period t, under scenario s, after rebalancing.

$v_{i,t}^s$ Amount of money in asset category i, at the beginning of period t, under scenario s, before rebalancing.

$p_{i,t}^s$ Amount of asset i purchased for rebalancing in period t, under scenario s.

$d_{i,t}^s$ Amount of asset i sold for rebalancing in period t, under scenario s.

w_t^s Wealth (pension plan) at the beginning of time period t, under scenario s.

z_t^s Value of the company before a contribution is made in period t, under scenario s.

y_t^s Value of the company after a contribution is made in period t, under scenario s.

c_t^s Amount of cash contributions made in period t, under scenario s.

Given these definitions, we present the deterministic equivalent of the stochastic problem.

Model (SP)

$$\text{Maximize Expected Utility} = \sum_{s \in S} \pi^s U(w_{\tau+1}^s, z_{\tau+1}^s) \tag{4.1}$$

subject to:

$$\sum_{i \in A} v_{i,t}^s = w_t^s \quad \forall s \in S, \ t = 1, \ldots, \tau + 1, \tag{4.2}$$

$$v^s_{i,t+1} = r^s_{i,t} x^s_{i,t} \quad \forall s \in S, \ t = 1, \ldots, \tau, \ i \in A, \tag{4.3}$$

$$z^s_{t+1} = g^s_t y^s_t \quad \forall s \in S, \ t = 1, \ldots, \tau, \tag{4.4}$$

$$y^s_t = z^s_t - c^s_t \quad \forall s \in S, \ t = 1, \ldots, \tau \tag{4.5}$$

$$x^s_{i,t} = v^s_{i,t} + p^s_{i,t}(1 - \sigma_{i,t}) - d^s_{i,t} \quad \forall s \in S, \ i \neq 1, \ t = 1, \ldots, \tau, \tag{4.6}$$

$$x^s_{1,t} = v^s_{1,t} + \sum_{i \neq 1} d^s_{i,t}(1 - \sigma_{i,t}) - \sum_{i \neq 1} p^s_{i,t} - b^s_t + c^s_t, \quad \forall s \in S, \ t = 1, \ldots, \tau, \tag{4.7}$$

$$x^s_{i,t} = x^{s'}_{i,t} \text{ and } \forall s \text{ and } s' \text{ with identical past up to time } t. \tag{4.8}$$

A generalized network investment model is presented in Figure 4.2. This graph depicts the flows across time for each of the asset categories and the company. While all constraints cannot be put into a network model, the graphical form is easy for managers to comprehend. General linear and non-linear programs, the preferred model, are now readily available for solving the resulting problem. However, a network may have computational advantages for extremely large problems, such as security level models.

The objective function (4.1), which we aim to maximize, is the expected value of the firm's utility function at the end of the planning horizon, denoted by $U(w^s_{\tau+1}, z^s_{\tau+1})$. It should be noted that this is a function of both the value of the company and the pension plan surplus at that time. This could very well be a von Neumann-Morgenstern utility function. The function should be defined very carefully because money that goes into pension funds is very difficult to extract. Although the firm will try to avoid a deficit in its pension plan as much as it can, it will also try to avoid transferring money to the plan because the company itself, not the pension fund may have financial troubles. In this chapter, we render several simplifications to illustrate the analysis more clearly. More realistic assumptions will be made for a further study.

The combined utility function is quite flexible, with several possible formulations. For instance, we might maximize a weighted combination of the net value of the pension plan (possibly discounted) and the core company's value. Alternatively, we might constrain the pension plan value at the horizon date to be slightly positive, and then maximize the company's value. The latter objective allows for a variety of strategies to be considered, including the benefits of voluntary contributions today $(t = 1)$.

As in single-period models, the nonlinear objective function (4.1) can take several different forms. If the classical return-risk function is employed, then (4.1) becomes Max η*Mean$[f(w_{t+1}, z_{t+1})]$-$(1 - \eta)$*Risk$[f(w_{\tau+1}, z_{\tau+1})]$, where $f(w_{\tau+1}, z_{\tau+1})$ is a function of values of the pension fund and the company at the end of the planning horizon. The value of this function may be interpreted as the combined wealth. Mean [] and Risk [] are the expected value and the risk of combined final wealth across the scenarios at the end of period τ. Parameter η indicates the relative importance of risk as compared with the

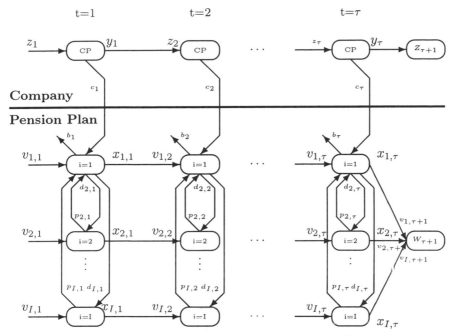

Fig. 4.2. Network representation for each scenario $s \in S$. For the pension plan, money moves between asset classes across time, payments are made to beneficiaries. The company (CP), while growing by itself, may need to make cash contributions to the pension fund. Optimizing the ending values of the company and the pension plan are the main objectives

expected value. This objective leads to an efficient frontier of wealth at the end of period τ by allowing alternative values of η in the range $[0, 1]$. A viable alternative to mean-risk is the von Neumann-Morgenstern expected utility of wealth at the end of period τ. One might consider replacing w_t with the pension plan's surplus, since it is a more important measure than the amount of assets in the pension fund. The surplus definition is discussed in detail towards the end of this section.

Constraint (4.2) represents the total value of assets in the fund in the beginning of period t. This constraint can be modified to include assets, liabilities, and investment goals, in which case, the modified result is called the surplus wealth (Mulvey (1989)). Many investors render investment decisions without reference to their liabilities or investment goals. Mulvey (1989) employs the notion of surplus wealth to the mean-variance and the expected utility models to address liabilities in the context of asset allocation strategies. Constraint (4.3) depicts the wealth accumulated at the beginning of period t before rebalancing in asset i. The growth of the company is depicted in constraint (4.4). Constraint (4.5) represents the balance constraint for the company by subtracting the cash contributions at each period. The

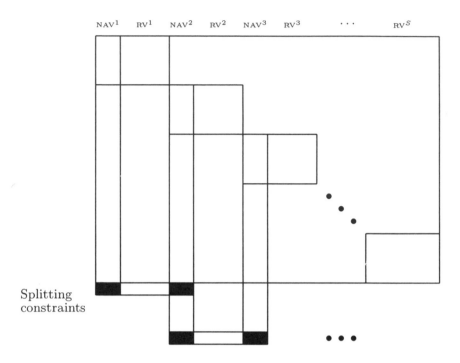

Fig. 4.3. Split variable formulation (NAV – nonanticipativity variables, RV – remaining variables)

flow balance constraint for all assets except cash for all periods is given by constraint (4.6). This constraint guarantees that the amount invested in period t equals the net wealth for the asset. Constraint (4.7) represents the flow balancing constraint for cash. Please note that the benefit payments and the cash contributions are accounted for in this constraint. Non-anticipativity constraints are represented by (4.8). These constraints ensure that the scenarios with the same past will have identical decisions up to that period. While these constraints are numerous, solution algorithms take advantage of their simple structure (Birge and Louveaux (1997), Dantzig and Infanger (1993), Kall and Wallace (1994), Mulvey and Ruszczynski (1995)).

Model (SP) depicts a split variable formulation of the stochastic asset allocation problem. This formulation has proven successful for solving the model using techniques such as the progressive hedging algorithm of Rockafellar and Wets (1991) and the DQA algorithm by Mulvey and Ruszczynski (1995). The split variable formulation can be beneficial for direct solvers that use the interior point method. The constraint structure for this formulation is depicted in Figure 4.3.

By substituting constraint (4.8) back in constraints (4.2) to (4.7), we obtain a standard form of the stochastic allocation problem. Constraints for this formulation exhibit a dual block diagonal structure for two-stage stochastic programs and a nested structure for general multi-stage problems. This formulation may be better for some direct solvers. The standard form of the stochastic program possesses fewer decision variables than the split variable model and is the preferred structure by many researchers in the field. This model can be solved by means of decomposition methods, for example, the L-shaped method (a specialization of Benders algorithm). See Birge and Louveaux (1997), Consigli and Dempster (1998), Dantzig and Infanger (1993), Kouwenberg and Zenios (2001).

The multi-stage model can provide superior performance over single-period models. See Dantzig and Infanger (1993), Mulvey (2000), Mulvey, Gould, and Morgan (2000), Mulvey and Ziemba (1998).

Pension plan administrators must make periodic cash (or in some cases, stock) contributions and pay benefits to the plan's retirees. A pension plan must conduct annual valuations to determine the plan's ability to pay its beneficiaries in the future. To this end, actuaries calculate the plan's surplus or deficit as follows:

$$Sw_t^s = w_t^s - \text{Present value}(b_{t+1}^s, b_{t+2}^s, \ldots, b_{\tau+2}^s) \tag{4.9}$$

where the present value is taken over the nodes in the sub-tree emanating out of the node (s, t).

Generally, a contribution is required when the plan falls into deficit or when obligations exist from previous time periods. The exact amount of the contribution depends upon actuarial rules and the structure under which the plan operates. These rules are complex formulae based on the company's position and the existing economic environment. We define these relationships with the simple functional form as follows:

$$c_t^s = f(Sw_t^s). \tag{4.10}$$

To simplify SP, we develop a model possessing a special policy rule, called fixed mix or dynamically balanced, as a special case of (SP). Define the proportion of wealth to be: $\lambda_{i,t}^s$ for each asset $i \in A$, time period $t \in T$, under scenario $s \in S$. A dynamically balanced portfolio enforces the following condition at each juncture:

$$\lambda_i = \frac{x_{i,t}^s}{\sum_{i \in A} x_{i,t}^s}, \text{ where } \lambda_i = \lambda_{i,t}^s. \tag{4.11}$$

This constraint ensures that the fraction of wealth in each asset category $i \in A$ is equal to λ_i at the beginning of every time period. Ideally, we would maintain the target λ fractions at all time periods and under every scenario. Practical considerations prevent this simple rule from being implemented in a direct fashion. Adding decision rules to model (SP) gives rise to a non-convex optimization model. Thus, the search for the best solution requires specialized algorithms.

4.3   Empirical Analysis

In this section, we highlight the results of a historical analysis for a sample pension plan. This historical study is not an exact implementation of the model presented in the previous section. First of all, it is a backtesting analysis, i.e. there's only one scenario which consists of past data. Furthermore, our goal is to show whether it could have been possible to protect the surplus of a pension fund within the integrated framework. Some of the assumptions we make here are not very realistic due to legal regulations in this area; however, they are necessary for an understandable illustration of the analysis. Most of these simplifications will be relaxed in a further study, in which we will carry out the forward-looking analysis using the scenario structure and the non-anticipativity constraints.

The problem involves strategic asset allocation and contribution decisions for a pension plan. The sample plan's liability data is generated by Towers-Perrin. The present values of the projected benefit obligations (PBO) and actual benefit obligations (ABO) are given in Table 4.1. We use PBO values as the present value of the liabilities in a given year and monthly evaluations are obtained through interpolation. We assume that the pension fund is initially 5% over-funded (i.e. the ratio of assets to the present value of liabilities is 1.05).

It should be noted that the company we choose has an initially over-funded pension plan, which may not always be the case. We also assume that this is a stable company with a constant growth rate (more details later). We assume that the company will try to protect their pension plan against a deficit possibility, i.e. the pension fund is not allowed to be underfunded. In case there's a chance of deficit, the company will bail out the pension fund by making cash contributions equaling the potential deficit amount. This assumption is not very realistic, due to legal standards in this area. First of all, the companies are not required to keep their pension funds over-funded at all times, and besides, the contribution rules are very complicated and a 100% contribution almost never happens. Since our initial goal is to meet the no-deficit plan without making any contributions, we will stick with this simple contribution rule.

For the pension fund, we consider portfolios composed of positions in S&P500, MSCI EAFE index, long-term (20+yr) US T-Bonds, Salomon BIG index, US Corporate AA Long bonds and Cash. The values of these indices were obtained from Datastream (2002). The collected time series involve monthly data for the period from January 1990 through December 2001.

First we analyze the statistical characteristics of these investment instruments. The results are depicted in Table 4.2.

For simplicity, we assume that the company has a constant growth rate of 1% per month and is initially valued at ten times the value of its liabilities. This constant growth assumption is equivalent to discounting the company's value by a constant risk-adjusted discount rate.

Table 4.1. Liability data for the sample pension plan ($)

Year (end of)	PBO	ABO
1989	591,532,524	495,963,198
1990	601,101,106	504,446,255
1991	684,807,026	572,182,478
1992	724,325,694	608,687,836
1993	828,201,120	698,724,056
1994	739,178,438	630,781,498
1995	922,373,874	781,342,986
1996	893,551,753	764,822,375
1997	980,837,350	840,200,500
1998	1,047,130,795	901,380,972
1999	953,045,603	823,637,720
2000	1,048,601,461	899,258,414
2001	1,130,299,827	969,554,542

Table 4.2. Statistical characteristics of asset classes

Asset class	Annualized arithmetic return	Annualized geometric return	Annualized risk (stand. dev.) of return
Cash	5.06%	5.18%	0.40%
S&P 500	13.21%	12.85%	14.55%
MSCI EAFE	4.11%	2.70%	17.03%
US T-Bonds (20 +years)	9.20%	9.20%	8.59%
Salomon BIG	7.91%	8.13%	3.78%
US Corp AA Long Bonds	8.87%	9.02%	6.45%

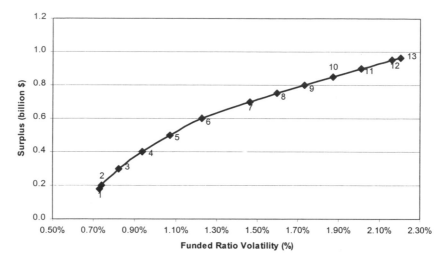

Fig. 4.4. Efficient frontier for the case in which pension fund receives no cash contribution (and still manages to keep a positive surplus across time)

The planning horizon is between January 1990 and December 2001. We employ a monthly rebalanced fixed-mix decision rule, and every month the plan's surplus value is evaluated. For simplicity, the transaction costs are ignored. We try to optimize several objectives such as minimizing discounted sum of contributions, minimizing the volatility of plan surplus, maximizing a weighted sum of plan's ending surplus and company's ending value. This last objective may be interpreted as a combined ending wealth. In our analysis, we assign a unit weight to the company value and a weight of 0.8 to pension plan's ending surplus, considering that company value matters slightly more than the plan's surplus.

Given these assumptions, we note that we are able to meet the no-deficit requirements every month without making any contributions. Therefore, we first set all the contributions to zero level. This eliminates the company sub-tree and results in an asset-liability model for the pension plan. In the absence of transaction costs, we do not need to keep track of amounts before or after rebalancing, which means that the portfolio weights are the only decision variables. There are two conflicting objective functions in this case. The first one is maximizing the ending surplus of the pension fund and the second one is minimizing the funded ratio volatility, which is defined as the standard deviation of the difference vector of the funded ratio. Funded ratio is defined as the ratio of assets to the present value of liabilities.

The efficient frontier corresponding to the no-contribution case is depicted in Figure 4.4. In Table 4.3, the portfolio mixes corresponding to the efficient solutions are presented. The results show that without any contribution, plan

Table 4.3. Asset allocation and objective function values for the points (Pt.) labeled on the frontier. The asset allocations are in percentages. Since there are no contributions, company's final value is constant. Therefore, the combined ending wealth is not a separate objective

Pt.	Cash	S&P 500	MSCI EAFE	US T-Bond 20+ Yr	Salomon BIG	Lehman Corp AA Long	Surplus ($*)	Funded Ratio Volatility	Combined Wealth ($*)
1	58	0	0	0	42	0	0.18	0.73	24.87
2	56	1	0	0	43	0	0.20	0.74	24.88
3	38	4	0	0	58	0	0.30	0.82	24.96
4	21	6	0	0	73	0	0.40	0.94	25.04
5	6	8	0	0	86	0	0.50	1.07	25.12
6	0	14	0	0	86	0	0.60	1.23	25.20
7	0	24	0	0	75	1	0.70	1.46	25.28
8	0	27	0	4	65	4	0.75	1.60	25.32
9	0	30	0	9	54	7	0.80	1.73	25.36
10	0	33	0	13	45	9	0.85	1.87	25.40
11	0	37	0	13	35	15	0.90	2.01	25.44
12	0	41	0	6	26	7	0.95	2.16	25.48
13	0	41	0	0	17	42	0.96	2.20	25.50

Note: * in billions

surplus can reach to the highest possible ending surplus through a portfolio of roughly 40% stocks and 60% bonds. This allocation is exactly the opposite of the typical pension plan asset allocation, which is roughly 60% stocks and 40% bonds.

Next, we assume that the company can make voluntary contributions to the plan, whether there's a surplus or not. However, we set the discounted sum of all contributions to $20 million. In other words, this discounted total should be met, but the decision of making the contribution is not dependent on the funded ratio of the plan at any point. In this case, the objective of maximizing the plan's ending surplus is replaced by maximizing the combined ending wealth, as defined previously. The resulting efficient frontier is plotted on top of the previous one and depicted in Figure 4.5. The attributes of the labeled points are given in Table 4.4. As expected, with the voluntary contribution, at any risk level, the plan's ending surplus is higher than that of the no-contribution case. This time, the high-end of the efficient frontier gives a more typical portfolio. We are able to meet the surplus requirement across time with the help of cash contributions, and maximize the combined ending wealth with an equity-dominating portfolio. In fact, we find that relaxing the $20 million limit to $48 million results in a 100% S&P500 portfolio for

Table 4.4. Asset allocation and objective function values for the points (Pt.) labeled on the frontier. The asset allocations are in percentages. Because there are contributions, the combined wealth replaces the ending surplus as one of the objective.

Pt.	Cash	S&P 500	MSCI EAFE	US T-Bond 20+ Yr	Salomon BIG	Lehman Corp AA Long	Surplus ($*)	Funded Ratio Volatility	Combined Wealth ($*)
1	64	0	0	0	36	0	0.21	0.69	24.81
2	45	2	0	0	53	0	0.32	0.74	24.90
3	25	5	0	0	70	0	0.45	0.87	25.00
4	6	7	0	0	87	0	0.57	1.03	25.10
5	0	17	0	0	83	0	0.70	1.24	25.20
6	0	27	0	0	64	9	0.82	1.55	25.30
7	0	34	0	10	37	19	0.95	1.89	25.40
8	0	38	0	11	25	26	1.01	2.06	25.45
9	0	42	0	17	13	28	1.07	2.24	25.50
10	0	46	0	22	1	31	1.14	2.42	25.55
11	0	52	0	34	0	14	1.20	2.60	25.60
12	0	59	0	17	0	24	1.26	2.82	25.65
13	0	66	0	0	0	34	1.31	3.03	25.69

Note: * in billions

reward-maximization.

After comparing the last two columns of the two data tables; it should be noted that, for lower risk levels, making contributions improves the combined ending wealth (upward improvement in the efficient frontier). However, after a certain point, the no-contribution plan yields higher combined ending wealth values. This dominance continues until you cannot achieve a higher ending value without making any contributions. After that point, for higher-risk levels you can always gain more by making cash contributions. The efficient frontiers for this comparison are not shown, since the chart doesn't reflect the observation very well, due to scaling differences.

Next we analyze how the bonds are distributed as we go along the efficient frontier for the case allowing contributions. In Figure 4.6, each line shows how the weights of respective bonds in the portfolio change as we go from the minimum risk portfolio to the maximum reward portfolio. It is clear that Salomon BIG, which includes shorter term bonds, is more important for a risk-averse portfolio. As maximizing the combined wealth gains more importance the weight is switched to longer term bonds. When reward-maximization is the only goal, corporate long bonds would be the best choice among all bond choices.

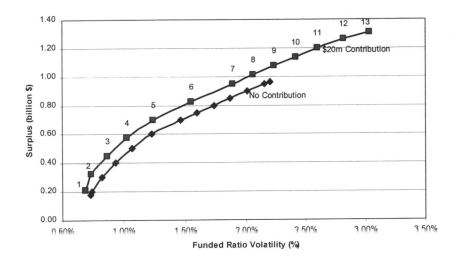

Fig. 4.5. Efficient frontier for the case in which company can make voluntary contributions. Ending surplus is plotted versus the funded ratio volatility

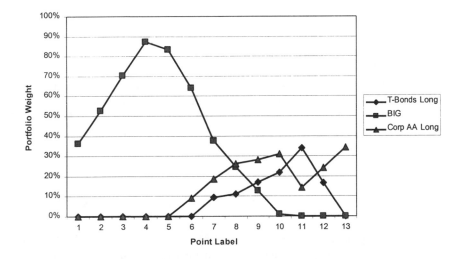

Fig. 4.6. Bonds and their weights in the portfolios corresponding to the labeled points on the efficient frontier (contribution is allowed)

4.4   Conclusions and Future Research

The chapter has defined an integrated pension and financial planning system by means of a stochastic network. For simplicity, we omitted a number of details for the corporate planning system. The sole requirement was to project the company's value, as a function of the scenario set. Large financial companies, especially global insurance companies, perform this task under the title of DFA (dynamic financial analysis). A more comprehensive approach would present further details of the company's operations within the model. The general corporate planning approach is to discount with a single risk-adjusted factor. The integrated model we present improves upon these concepts.

Solving stochastic programming problems has become practical due to the large improvements in computer hardware and software (Birge and Louveaux (1997), Kall and Wallace (1994)). There have been a number of successful implementations of stochastic planning models. The stochastic network model has certain advantages over general nonlinear programs, especially with respect to improving the model's understandability.

The empirical results show that the integration of pension and corporate planning is not only feasible but also it can improve company performance. This improvement is particularly significant when the company's profit is correlated with the business cycle. A large required contribution during an economic downturn can be devastating to certain companies. And in other cases, there are benefits to making voluntary contributions, as shown in the empirical tests. Additional work can be done to refine these concepts, of course. For instance, the model can be extended to address the "optimal" contribution strategy for underfunded plans. Herein, the investment policy rule will not be the fixed-mix rule. In addition, we plan to extend the model to address the problem of decentralized risk management. Many corporations do not have a centralized headquarters with timely and adequate information to carry out the integrated planning system as proposed. A practical decentralized management system is required for these firms.

References

Birge, J. R., and Louveaux, F. (1997), *Introduction to Stochastic Programming*, Springer-Verlag, New York.

Consigli, G., and Dempster, M. A. H. (1998), "Dynamic Stochastic Programming for Asset-Liability Management," *Annals of Operations Research* **81**, 131-161.

Dantzig, G., and Infanger, G. (1993), "Multi-Stage Stochastic Linear Programs for Portfolio Optimization," *Annals of Operations Research* **45**, 59-76.

Datastream International Database [Online], S&PCOMP, MSEAFE$, LHTR20Y, SBBIGBI, LHIGAAL, LHSHT3M (2002), Datastream International Ltd., London, retrieved October 18, 2002.

General Motors Corporation (2003), "Form 10-K," March 13, 2003, Filing Date; Securities and Exchange Commission. Retrieved March 15, 2003: http:// www.sec.gov/Archives/edgar/data/40730/000004073003000054 /complete10k.

Kall, P., and Wallace, S. W. (1994), *Stochastic Programming*, John Wiley & Sons, Chichester, United Kingdom.

Kouwenberg, R., and Zenios, S. A. (2001), "Stochastic Programming Models for Asset Liability Management," Working Paper 01-01, HERMES Center on Computational Finance & Economics, School of Economics and Management, University of Cyprus, April.

Mulvey, J. M. (1989), "A Surplus Optimization Perspective," *Investment Management Review* **3**, 31-39.

Mulvey, J. M. (1996), "Generating Scenarios for the Towers Perrin Investment System," *Interfaces* **26**, 1-15.

Mulvey, J. M. (2000), "Multi-Period Stochastic Optimization Models for Long-Term Investors," in *Quantitative Analysis in Financial Markets* **3**, M. Avellaneda, editor, World Scientific Publishing Co., Singapore.

Mulvey, J. M., Gould, G., and Morgan, C. (2000), "An Asset and Liability Management System for Towers Perrin-Tillinghast," *Interfaces* **30**, 96-114.

Mulvey, J. M., Rosenbaum, D. P., and Shetty, B. (1997), "Strategic Financial Risk Management and Operations Research," *European Journal of Operations Research* **97**, 1-16.

Mulvey, J. M., and Ruszczynski, A. (1995), "A New Scenario Decomposition Method for Large-Scale Stochastic Optimization," *Operations Research* **43**, 477-490.

Mulvey, J. M., and Simsek, K. D. (2002), "Rebalancing Strategies for Long-Term Investors," in *Computational Methods in Decision-Making, Economics and Finance: Optimization Models*, pp. 15-33, E. J. Kontoghiorghes, B. Rustem, and S. Siokos, editors, Kluwer Academic Publishers, Dordrecht, The Netherlands.

Mulvey, J. M., and Ziemba, W. T. (1998), "Asset and Liability Management Systems for Long-Term Investors: Discussion of the Issues," in *Worldwide Asset and Liability Modeling*, pp. 3-38, W. T. Ziemba and J. M. Mulvey, editors, Cambridge University Press, Cambridge, United Kingdom.

Rockafellar, R. T., and Wets, R. J.-B. (1991), "Scenarios and Policy Aggregation in Optimization under Uncertainty," *Mathematics of Operations Research* **16**, 119-147.

5 Variational Inequalities for Evolutionary Financial Equilibrium

Patrizia Daniele

5.1 Introduction

In this chapter, we propose an evolutionary model for the formulation and analysis of multi-sector, multi-instrument financial equilibrium problems. This new framework allows for the variance-covariance matrices associated with risk perception, the financial volumes held by the sectors, the optimal portfolio compositions, as well as the instrument prices, to all be time-dependent.

We note that Nagurney, Dong, and Hughes (1992) were the first to develop a multi-sector, multi-instrument financial equilibrium model using variational inequality theory and recognized the network structure underlying the problem. That contribution was, subsequently, extended by Nagurney (1994) to include more general utility functions and by Nagurney and Siokos (1997a, b) to the international domain. Dong, Zhang, and Nagurney (1996), in turn, formulated a dynamic financial equilibrium model and analyzed it qualitatively using projected dynamical systems theory. Additional dynamic financial models, along with their variational inequality formulations at the equilibrium state (as well as their network structure) can be found in the book by Nagurney and Siokos (1997b).

The model presented in this chapter builds upon the work of Nagurney, Dong, and Hughes (1992) but takes an alternative approach to that noted above in that the dynamics are now modeled not using projected dynamical systems theory (cf. Nagurney and Zhang (1996)) but, rather, *evolutionary variational inequalities*, and these are infinite- rather than finite-dimensional. In addition, the variance-covariance matrices (see also Markowitz (1952, 1959)) which allow for risk minimization are now time-varying as are the sector financial holding volumes.

Infinite-dimensional variational inequalities have been used previously in finance by Jaillet, Lamberton, and Lapeyre (1990) for the pricing of American options, and by Tourin and Zariphopoulou (1994) for single-agent investment modeling and computation. Stochastic variational inequalities, in turn, have been used by McLean (1993) for the nonlinear portfolio choice problem and by Gürkan, Özge, and Robinson (1996) for the pricing of American options. For additional background on finance and variational inequalities, see Nagurney (2001).

In this chapter, we explicitly emphasize the importance of time in the study of financial decision-making and the interactions among financial sectors. Although equilibrium excludes time, time is, nevertheless, central in both the physical-technological world as well as in the socio-economic world. The papers by Daniele and Maugeri (2001) and Daniele, Maugeri, and Oettli (1998, 1999) discuss other time–dependent applications using the approach revealed here for the first time for financial equilibrium problems. Our research in other application settings has led us, in this chapter, to study financial equilibrium problems via an evolutionary model.

This chapter is organized as follows. In Section 5.2, we develop the model, provide the equilibrium conditions, and give the variational inequality formulation. We also identify the underlying network structure of the problem both out of and in the equilibrium state. In Section 5.3, we provide some theoretical results, whereas in Section 5.4 we give the proof of the variational inequality formulation and establish an existence result. In Section 5.5, we propose a computational procedure, based on the subgradient method, which does not require discretization in time. In Section 5.6, we summarize the results of this paper and provide suggestions for future research.

5.2 The Evolutionary Financial Model

In this section, we present the evolutionary financial model and give the variational inequality formulation of the equilibrium conditions. The functional setting in which we study this evolutionary model is the Lebesgue space $L^2([0,T], R^p)$, which appears to be the appropriate setting since it allows us to obtain equilibrium conditions equivalent to a variational inequality involving the L^2-scalar product in $[0,T]$. The time dependence of the model in the $L^2([0,T])$ sense allows the model to follow the financial behavior, even in the presence of possibly very irregular evolution, whereas the equilibrium conditions are required to hold almost everywhere (see Daniele and Maugeri (2001), Daniele, Maugeri, and Oettli (1998), and Daniele, Maugeri, and Oettli (1999) for analogous problems). In this setting, the variance-covariance matrices associated with the sectors' risk perceptions will be required to have $L^\infty([0,T])$ entries.

Analytically, consider a financial economy consisting of m sectors, with a typical sector denoted by i, and with n instruments, with a typical financial instrument denoted by j, in the period $\mathcal{T} = [0,T]$. Examples of sectors include: households, domestic businesses, banks, and other financial institutions, as well as state and local governments. Examples of financial instruments, in turn, are: mortgages, mutual funds, savings deposits, money market funds, etc.

Let $s_i(t)$ denote the total financial volume held by sector i at the time t, which is considered to depend on the time $t \in [0, T]$. We emphasize the fact that in the presence of uncertainty and of risky perspectives, the volume s_i held by each sector cannot be considered stable and may decrease or increase depending on unfavorable or favorable economic conditions. As a consequence, the amounts of the assets and of the liabilities of the sectors will depend on time.

For this reason, at time t, denote the amount of instrument j held as an asset in sector i's portfolio by $x_{ij}(t)$ and the amount of instrument j held as a liability in sector i's portfolio by $y_{ij}(t)$. The assets in sector i's portfolio are grouped into the column vector $x_i(t) = [x_{i1}(t), x_{i2}(t), \ldots, x_{ij}(t), \ldots, x_{in}(t)]^T$ and the liabilities in sector i's portfolio are grouped into the column vector $y_i(t) = [y_{i1}(t), y_{i2}(t), \ldots, y_{ij}(t), \ldots, y_{in}(t)]^T$. Moreover, group the sector asset vectors into the matrix

$$
x(t) = \begin{bmatrix} x_1(t) \\ \ldots \\ x_i(t) \\ \ldots \\ x_n(t) \end{bmatrix} = \begin{bmatrix} x_{11}(t) & \ldots & x_{1j}(t) & \ldots & x_{1n}(t) \\ \ldots & & & & \\ x_{i1}(t) & \ldots & x_{ij}(t) & \ldots & x_{in}(t) \\ \ldots & & & & \\ x_{m1}(t) & \ldots & x_{mj}(t) & \ldots & x_{mn}(t) \end{bmatrix}
$$

and group the sector liability vectors into the matrix

$$
y(t) = \begin{bmatrix} y_1(t) \\ \ldots \\ y_i(t) \\ \ldots \\ y_n(t) \end{bmatrix} = \begin{bmatrix} y_{11}(t) & \ldots & y_{1j}(t) & \ldots & y_{1n}(t) \\ \ldots & & & & \\ y_{i1}(t) & \ldots & y_{ij}(t) & \ldots & y_{in}(t) \\ \ldots & & & & \\ y_{m1}(t) & \ldots & y_{mj}(t) & \ldots & y_{mn}(t) \end{bmatrix}.
$$

In order to determine for each sector i the optimal composition of instruments held as assets and as liabilities, first we consider the influence due to risk-aversion and, following the concept that assessment of risk is based on a variance-covariance matrix denoting the sector's assessment of the standard deviation of prices for each instrument, we use as a measure of this aversion the $2n \times 2n$ variance-covariance matrix $Q^i(t) = \begin{bmatrix} Q^i_{11}(t) & Q^i_{12}(t) \\ Q^i_{21}(t) & Q^i_{22}(t) \end{bmatrix}$ associated with sector i's assets and liabilities, which, in general, will evolve in time as well and which we assume to be symmetric and positive definite and with $L^\infty([0, T])$ entries. Further, denote by $[Q^i_{\alpha\beta}(t)]_j$ the j-th column of $Q^i_{\alpha\beta}(t)$ with $\alpha = 1, 2$ and $\beta = 1, 2$. Then the aversion to the risk at time $t \in [0, T]$ is given by:

$$
\begin{bmatrix} x_i(t) \\ y_i(t) \end{bmatrix}^T Q^i(t) \begin{bmatrix} x_i(t) \\ y_i(t) \end{bmatrix}.
$$

The second component that we have to consider in the process of optimization of each sector in the financial economy is his request to maximize the value of his asset holdings and to minimize the value of his liabilities. These objectives depend on the prices of each instrument, which, in turn, depend on time and appear as variables in our problem. We denote the price of instrument j at the time t by $r_j(t)$ and group the instrument prices into the vector $r(t) = [r_1(t), r_2(t), \ldots, r_i(t), \ldots, r_n(t)]^T$.

Assuming as the functional setting the Lebesgue space $L^2([0,T], R^p)$, the set of feasible assets and liabilities becomes:

$$P_i = \left\{ \begin{bmatrix} x_i(t) \\ y_i(t) \end{bmatrix} \in L^2([0,T], \mathbb{R}^{2n}) : \right.$$

$$\sum_{j=1}^{n} r_{ij}(t) - s_i(t), \quad \sum_{i=1}^{n} y_{ij}(t) - r_i(t) \text{ n n in } [0,T],$$

$$\left. x_{ij}(t) \geq 0, \quad y_{ij}(t) \geq 0, \text{ a.e. in } [0,T] \right\},$$

where a.e. means that the condition holds almost everywhere.

In Figure 5.1, we depict the network structure associated with the above feasible set and the financial economy out of equilibrium. The set of feasible assets and liabilities associated with each sector corresponds to budget constraints.

We now can give the following definition of an equilibrium of the financial model.

Definition 5.1: Financial Equilibrium

A vector of sector assets, liabilities, and instrument prices $(x^*(t), y^*(t),$
$r^*(t)) \in \prod_{i=1}^{m} P_i \times L^2([0,T], R_+^n)$ *is an equilibrium of the evolutionary financial model if and only if it satisfies the system of inequalities*

$$2[Q_{11}^i(t)]_j^T x_i^*(t) + 2[Q_{21}^i(t)]_j^T y_i^*(t) - r_j^*(t) - \mu_i^{(1)}(t) \geq 0, \qquad (5.1)$$

and

$$2[Q_{12}^i(t)]_j^T x_i^*(t) + 2[Q_{22}^i(t)]_j^T y_i^*(t) + r_j^*(t) - \mu_i^{(2)}(t) \geq 0, \qquad (5.2)$$

and equalities

$$x_{ij}^*(t) \left[2[Q_{11}^i(t)]_j^T x_i^*(t) + 2[Q_{21}^i(t)]_j^T y_i^*(t) - r_j^*(t) - \mu_i^{(1)}(t) \right] = 0, \qquad (5.3)$$

$$y_{ij}^*(t) \left[2[Q_{12}^i(t)]_j^T x_i^*(t) + 2[Q_{22}^i(t)]_j^T y_i^*(t) + r_j^*(t) - \mu_i^{(2)}(t) \right] = 0, \qquad (5.4)$$

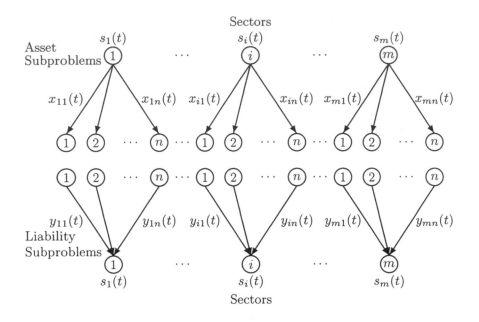

Fig. 5.1. Network structure of the sectors' optimization problems a.e. in $[0, T]$

where $\mu_i^1(t)$, $\mu_i^2(t) \in L^2([0,T])$ are Lagrangean functions, for all sectors i: $i = 1, 2, \ldots, m$, and for all instruments j: $j = 1, 2, \ldots, n$, and the condition

$$
\begin{cases}
\displaystyle\sum_{i=1}^{m} \left(x_{ij}^*(t) - y_{ij}^*(t)\right) \geq 0, & a.e.\ in\ [0,T] \\
\displaystyle\sum_{i=1}^{m} \left(x_{ij}^*(t) - y_{ij}^*(t)\right) r_j^*(t) = 0, & r^*(t) \in L^2([0,T], R_+^n),
\end{cases}
\tag{5.5}
$$

simultaneously.

The meaning of this definition is the following: to each financial volume $s_i(t)$ invested by the sector i, we associate the functions $\mu_i^{(1)}(t)$ and $\mu_i^{(2)}(t)$ related, respectively, to the assets and to the liabilities and which represent the "equilibrium utilities" per unit of the sector i. The financial volume invested in the instrument j as assets $x_{ij}^*(t)$ is greater than or equal to zero if the j-th component

$$
2[Q_{11}^i(t)]_j^T\, x_i^*(t) + 2[Q_{21}^i(t)]_j^T\, y_i^*(t) - r_j^*(t)
$$

of the utility is equal to $\mu_i^{(1)}(t)$, whereas if

$$
2[Q_{11}^i(t)]_j^T\, x_i^*(t) + 2[Q_{21}^i(t)]_j^T\, y_i^*(t) - r_j^*(t) > \mu_i^{(1)}(t),
$$

then $x_{ij}^*(t) = 0$. The same occurs for the liabilities. It is remarkable that the equilibrium definition is, in a sense, the same as that given by the Wardrop (1952) principle which states that in the case of user-optimization on congested transportation networks (see Dafermos and Sparrow (1969)) the user (which is a traveler in that case) rejects the less convenient (or more costly) choice (which, in the context of a transportation network, is a path or route).

The functions $\mu_i^{(1)}(t)$ and $\mu_i^{(2)}(t)$ are Lagrangean functions associated with the constraints $\sum_{j=1}^{n} x_{ij}(t) - s_i(t) = 0$ and $\sum_{j=1}^{n} y_{ij}(t) - s_i(t) = 0$, respectively. The fact that they are unknown has no influence because, as we shall see by means of Theorem 5.1, Definition 5.1 is equivalent to a variational inequality in which $\mu_i^{(1)}$ and $\mu_i^{(2)}$ do not appear. Nevertheless, by the use of Theorem 5.3, they can be obtained.

Conditions (5.5), which represent the equilibrium condition for the prices, express the equilibration of the total assets and the total liabilities of each instrument, namely, If the price of instrument j is positive, then the amount of the assets is equal to amount of liabilities; if there is an excess supply of an instrument in the economy, then its price must be zero.

Moreover, if we consider the group of conditions (5.1)–(5.4) for a fixed $r(t)$, then we realize (see Section 5.3) that they are necessary and sufficient conditions to ensure that (x^*, y^*) is the minimum of the problem:

$$
\min_{P_i} \int_0^T \left\{ \begin{bmatrix} x_i(t) \\ y_i(t) \end{bmatrix}^T Q^i(t) \begin{bmatrix} x_i(t) \\ y_i(t) \end{bmatrix} - r(t) \times [x_i(t) - y_i(t)] \right\} dt,
$$

$$
\forall \begin{bmatrix} x(t) \\ y(t) \end{bmatrix} \in \prod_{i=1}^{m} P_i.
$$

(5.6)

Problem (5.6) means that each sector minimizes his risk while at the same time maximizing the value of his asset holdings and minimizing the value of his liabilities.

Since the feasible set P_i is a bounded, convex, and closed subset of the Hilbert space, then it is also weakly compact and, hence,

$$
\min_{P_i} \int_0^T \left\{ \begin{bmatrix} x_i(t) \\ y_i(t) \end{bmatrix}^T Q^i(t) \begin{bmatrix} x_i(t) \\ y_i(t) \end{bmatrix} - r(t) \times [x_i(t) - y_i(t)] \right\} dt
$$

exists, because the functional

$$
U_i(x_i(t), y_i(t)) = \int_0^T \left\{ \begin{bmatrix} x_i(t) \\ y_i(t) \end{bmatrix}^T Q^i(t) \begin{bmatrix} x_i(t) \\ y_i(t) \end{bmatrix} - r(t) \times [x_i(t) - y_i(t)] \right\} dt
$$

is weakly lower semicontinuous (see Jahn (1996), Lemma 2.11 and Theorem 2.3).

We now state the variational inequality formulation of the governing equilibrium conditions, the proof of which is given in Section 5.4.

Theorem 5.1: Variational Inequality Formulation

A vector $(x^*(t), y^*(t), r^*(t)) \in \prod_{i=1}^{m} P_i \times L^2([0,T], R^n_+)$ is an evolutionary financial equilibrium if and only if it satisfies the following variational inequality:

Find $(x^*(t), y^*(t), r^*(t)) \in \prod_{i=1}^{m} P_i \times L^2([0,T], R^n_+)$:

$$\int_0^T \left\{ \sum_{i=1}^{m} \left[2[Q^i_{11}(t)]^T x^*_i(t) + 2[Q^i_{21}(t)]^T y^*_i(t) - r^*(t) \right] \times [x_i(t) - x^*_i(t)] \right.$$

$$+ \sum_{i=1}^{m} \left[2[Q^i_{12}(t)]^T x^*_i(t) + 2[Q^i_{22}(t)]^T y^*_i(t) + r^*(t) \right] \times [y_i(t) - y^*_i(t)]$$

$$\left. + \sum_{i=1}^{m} (x^*_i(t) - y^*_i(t)) \times [r(t) - r^*(t)] \right\} dt \geq 0,$$

$$\forall (x(t), y(t), r(t)) \in \prod_{i=1}^{m} P_i \times L^2([0,T], R^n_+). \qquad (5.7)$$

In the subsequent section we will prove the equivalence between problem (5.6) and conditions (5.1)–(5.4). In addition, we will establish the equivalence between condition (5.5) and a suitable variational inequality. In Figure 5.2, we depict the network structure of the financial economy in equilibrium. Observe, that due to conditions (5.5), in equilibrium, we have that for each financial instrument, its price times the total amount of the instrument as an asset minus the total amount as a liability is exactly equal to zero. Hence, the network structure of the financial economy, in equilibrium, is as given in Figure 5.2. The model, thus, depicts an evolution of the individual networks, as depicted in Figure 5.1, to the equilibrium network, as given in Figure 5.2. We note that Nagurney, Dong, and Hughes (1992) also identified the network structure of the financial equilibrium in their model which has the structure of the network in Figure 5.2 but that model was not time-dependent. Here, we have also identified the evolution of the networks as depicted in Figure 5.1 through time to the equilibrium network of Figure 5.2.

5.3 Some Theoretical Results

The proof of the equivalence between Definition 5.1 and the variational inequality formulation is obtained by showing that conditions (5.1)–(5.4) are equivalent to problem (5.6), which, in turn, is equivalent to a first variational

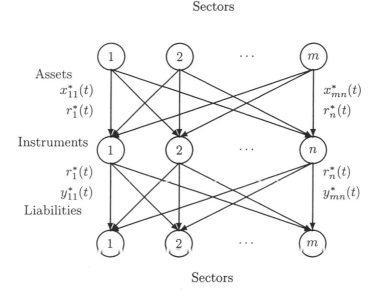

Fig. 5.2. The network structure at equilibrium

inequality and that conditions (5.5) are equivalent to a second variational inequality. From these two variational inequalities, we then derive variational inequality (5.7).

We start by establishing the equivalence between problem (5.6) and a variational inequality. This proof is standard (see Stampacchia (1969) for a similar argument), but we recall it for the reader's convenience.

Theorem 5.2

$\begin{bmatrix} x_i^*(t) \\ y_i^*(t) \end{bmatrix}$ is a solution to (5.6) if and only if $\begin{bmatrix} x_i^*(t) \\ y_i^*(t) \end{bmatrix}$ is a solution to the variational inequality

$$\int_0^T \sum_{i=1}^m \left[2[Q_{11}^i(t)]^T x_i^*(t) + [Q_{21}^i(t)]^T y_i^*(t) - r^*(t) \right] \times [x_i(t) - x_i^*(t)] \, dt$$

$$+ \int_0^T \sum_{i=1}^m \left[2[Q_{22}^i(t)]^T x_i^*(t) + [Q_{12}^i(t)]^T y_i^*(t) + r^*(t) \right] \times [y_i(t) - y_i^*(t)] \, dt \geq 0,$$

$$\forall \begin{bmatrix} x_i(t) \\ y_i(t) \end{bmatrix} \in P_i, \tag{5.8}$$

where $r_j^*(t)$ denotes the price for instrument j at the time $t \in [0, T]$.

Proof: Let us assume that $\begin{bmatrix} x_i^*(t) \\ y_i^*(t) \end{bmatrix}$ is a solution to problem (5.6). Then for all $\begin{bmatrix} x_i(t) \\ y_i(t) \end{bmatrix} \in P_i$ the function

$$F(\lambda) = \int_0^T \sum_{i=1}^m \Big\{ [\lambda x_i^*(t) + (1-\lambda)x_i(t)]^T Q_{11}^i(t) [\lambda x_i^*(t) + (1-\lambda)x_i(t)]$$

$$+ [\lambda y_i^*(t) + (1-\lambda)y_i(t)]^T Q_{21}^i(t) [\lambda x_i^*(t) + (1-\lambda)x_i(t)]$$

$$+ [\lambda x_i^*(t) + (1-\lambda)x_i(t)]^T Q_{12}^i(t) [\lambda y_i^*(t) + (1-\lambda)y_i(t)]$$

$$+ [\lambda y_i^*(t) + (1-\lambda)y_i(t)]^T Q_{22}^i(t) [\lambda y_i^*(t) + (1-\lambda)y_i(t)]$$

$$-r(t) \times [\lambda x_i^*(t) + (1-\lambda)x_i(t) - \lambda y_i^*(t) - (1-\lambda)y_i(t)] \Big\} \, dt, \quad \lambda \in [0,1]$$

admits the minimum solution when $\lambda = 1$ and $F'(1) \leq 0$. It follows then that:

$$F(\lambda) = \lambda^2 \int_0^T \sum_{i=1}^m [x_i^*(t)]^T Q_{11}^i(t) x_i^*(t) \, dt + \lambda(1-\lambda) \int_0^T \sum_{i=1}^m [x_i^*(t)]^T Q_{11}^i(t) x_i(t) \, dt$$

$$+(1-\lambda)\lambda \int_0^T \sum_{i=1}^m [x_i(t)]^T Q_{11}^i(t) x_i^*(t) \, dt + (1-\lambda)^2 \int_0^T \sum_{i=1}^m [x_i(t)]^T Q_{11}^i(t) x_i(t) \, dt$$

$$+\lambda^2 \int_0^T \sum_{i=1}^m [y_i^*(t)]^T Q_{21}^i(t) x_i^*(t) \, dt + \lambda(1-\lambda) \int_0^T \sum_{i=1}^m [y_i^*(t)]^T Q_{21}^i(t) x_i(t) \, dt$$

$$+(1-\lambda)\lambda \int_0^T \sum_{i=1}^m [y_i(t)]^T Q_{21}^i(t) x_i^*(t) \, dt + (1-\lambda)^2 \int_0^T \sum_{i=1}^m [y_i(t)]^T Q_{21}^i(t) x_i(t) \, dt$$

$$+\lambda^2 \int_0^T \sum_{i=1}^m [x_i^*(t)]^T Q_{12}^i(t) y_i^*(t) \, dt + \lambda(1-\lambda) \int_0^T \sum_{i=1}^m [x_i^*(t)]^T Q_{12}^i(t) y_i(t) \, dt$$

$$+(1-\lambda)\lambda \int_0^T \sum_{i=1}^m [x_i(t)]^T Q_{12}^i(t) y_i^*(t) \, dt + (1-\lambda)^2 \int_0^T \sum_{i=1}^m [x_i(t)]^T Q_{12}^i(t) y_i(t) \, dt$$

$$+\lambda^2 \int_0^T \sum_{i=1}^m [y_i^*(t)]^T Q_{22}^i(t) y_i^*(t) \, dt + \lambda(1-\lambda) \int_0^T \sum_{i=1}^m [y_i^*(t)]^T Q_{22}^i(t) y_i(t) \, dt$$

$$+(1-\lambda)\lambda \int_0^T \sum_{i=1}^m [y_i(t)]^T Q_{22}^i(t) y_i^*(t) \, dt + (1-\lambda)^2 \int_0^T \sum_{i=1}^m [y_i(t)]^T Q_{22}^i(t) y_i(t) \, dt$$

$$-\int_0^T \sum_{i=1}^m r(t) \times [\lambda x_i^*(t) + (1-\lambda)x_i(t) - \lambda y_i^*(t) - (1-\lambda)y_i(t)] \, dt.$$

Hence, we can consider the derivative of $F(\lambda)$ with respect to λ and we reach:

$$F'(\lambda) = \int_0^T \sum_{i=1}^m [x_i^*(t) - x_i(t)]^T Q_{11}^i(t) \left[\lambda x_i^*(t) + (1-\lambda)x_i(t)\right] dt$$

$$+ \int_0^T \sum_{i=1}^m [\lambda x_i^*(t) + (1-\lambda)x_i(t)]^T Q_{11}^i(t)[x_i^*(t) - x_i(t)] dt$$

$$+ \int_0^T \sum_{i=1}^m [y_i^*(t) - y_i(t)]^T Q_{21}^i(t) \left[\lambda x_i^*(t) + (1-\lambda)x_i(t)\right] dt$$

$$+ \int_0^T \sum_{i=1}^m [\lambda y_i^*(t) + (1-\lambda)y_i(t)]^T Q_{21}^i(t)[x_i^*(t) - x_i(t))] dt$$

$$+ \int_0^T \sum_{i=1}^m [x_i^*(t) - x_i(t)]^T Q_{12}^i(t) \left[\lambda y_i^*(t) + (1-\lambda)y_i(t)\right] dt$$

$$+ \int_0^T \sum_{i=1}^m [\lambda x_i^*(t) + (1-\lambda)x_i(t)]^T Q_{12}^i(t)[y_i^*(t) - y_i(t)] dt$$

$$+ \int_0^T \sum_{i=1}^m [y_i^*(t) - y_i(t)]^T Q_{22}^i(t) \left[\lambda y_i^*(t) + (1-\lambda)y_i(t)\right] dt$$

$$+ \int_0^T \sum_{i=1}^m [\lambda y_i^*(t) + (1-\lambda)y_i(t)]^T Q_{22}^i(t)[y_i^*(t) - y_i(t)] dt$$

$$- \int_0^T \sum_{i=1}^m r(t) \times [x_i^*(t) - x_i(t) - y_i^*(t) + y_i(t)] \, dt.$$

So we obtain:

$$F'(1)$$

$$= \int_0^T \sum_{i=1}^m [x_i^*(t) - x_i(t)]^T Q_{11}^i(t)x_i^*(t) \, dt + \int_0^T \sum_{i=1}^m [x_i^*(t)]^T Q_{11}^i(t)[x_i^*(t) - x_i(t)] \, dt$$

$$+ \int_0^T \sum_{i=1}^m [y_i^*(t) - y_i(t)]^T Q_{21}^i(t)x_i^*(t) \, dt + \int_0^T \sum_{i=1}^m [y_i^*(t)]^T Q_{21}^i(t)[x_i^*(t) - x_i(t))] \, dt$$

$$+ \int_0^T \sum_{i=1}^m [x_i^*(t) - x_i(t)]^T Q_{12}^i(t)y_i^*(t) \, dt + \int_0^T \sum_{i=1}^m [x_i^*(t)]^T Q_{12}^i(t)[y_i^*(t) - y_i(t)] \, dt$$

$$+ \int_0^T \sum_{i=1}^m [y_i^*(t) - y_i(t)]^T Q_{22}^i(t)y_i^*(t) \, dt + \int_0^T \sum_{i=1}^m [y_i^*(t)]^T Q_{22}^i(t)[y_i^*(t) - y_i(t)] \, dt$$

$$- \int_0^T \sum_{i=1}^m r(t) \times [x_i^*(t) - x_i(t) - y_i^*(t) + y_i(t)] \, dt.$$

Then, taking into account the symmetry of the matrix $Q^i(t)$, we get:

$$F'(1) = \int_0^T \sum_{i=1}^m \left[2[Q_{11}^i(t)]^T x_i^*(t) + 2[Q_{21}^i(t)]^T y_i^*(t) - r^*(t) \right] \times [x_i^*(t) - x_i(t)] \, dt$$

$$+ \int_0^T \sum_{i=1}^m \left[2[Q_{12}^i(t)]^T x_i^*(t) + 2[Q_{22}^i(t)]^T y_i^*(t) + r^*(t) \right] \times [y_i^*(t) - y_i(t)] \, dt \leq 0,$$

namely, the variational inequality (5.8).

Vice versa, let us assume that $\begin{bmatrix} x_i^*(t) \\ y_i^*(t) \end{bmatrix}$ is solution to problem (5.8).

Since the function U_i is convex, then for all $\begin{bmatrix} x_i^*(t) \\ y_i^*(t) \end{bmatrix} \in P_i$ the following estimate holds:

$$U_i \begin{bmatrix} \lambda x_i(t) + (1-\lambda)x_i^*(t) \\ \lambda y_i(t) + (1-\lambda)y_i^*(t) \end{bmatrix} \leq \lambda U_i \begin{bmatrix} x_i(t) \\ y_i(t) \end{bmatrix} + (1-\lambda) U_i \begin{bmatrix} x_i^*(t) \\ y_i^*(t) \end{bmatrix},$$

namely, $\forall \lambda \in (0,1]$:

$$\frac{U_i \begin{bmatrix} x_i^*(t) + \lambda(x_i(t) - x_i^*(t)) \\ y_i^*(t) + \lambda(y_i(t) - y_i^*(t)) \end{bmatrix} - U_i \begin{bmatrix} x_i^*(t) \\ y_i^*(t) \end{bmatrix}}{\lambda}$$

$$\leq U_i \begin{bmatrix} x_i(t) \\ y_i(t) \end{bmatrix} - U_i \begin{bmatrix} x_i^*(t) \\ y_i^*(t) \end{bmatrix}. \tag{5.9}$$

When $\lambda \to 0$, the left-hand side of (5.9) converges to the left-hand side of the variational inequality (5.8), which is ≤ 0 and, hence, $\begin{bmatrix} x_i^*(t) \\ y_i^*(t) \end{bmatrix}$ is solution to the problem (5.6). $\square$

Let $\begin{bmatrix} x_i^*(t) \\ y_i^*(t) \end{bmatrix}$ be the solution to problem (5.6) for a given $r^*(t)$ and, hence, to variational inequality (5.8). Now we can prove the following characterization of the solution.

Theorem 5.3
$\begin{bmatrix} x_i^*(t) \\ y_i^*(t) \end{bmatrix}$ *is a solution to (5.6) or to (5.8) if and only if a.e. in $[0,T]$ it satisfies the conditions:*

$$2[Q_{11}^i(t)]_j^T x_i^*(t) + 2[Q_{21}^i(t)]_j^T y_i^*(t) - r_j^*(t) - \mu_i^{(1)}(t) \geq 0, \tag{5.1}$$

$$2[Q_{12}^i(t)]_j^T x_i^*(t) + 2[Q_{22}^i(t)]_j^T y_i^*(t) + r_j^*(t) - \mu_i^{(2)}(t) \geq 0, \tag{5.2}$$

$$x_{ij}^*(t) \left[2[Q_{11}^i(t)]_j^T x_i^*(t) + 2[Q_{21}^i(t)]_j^T y_i^*(t) - r_j^*(t) - \mu_i^{(1)}(t) \right] = 0, \quad (5.3)$$

$$y_{ij}^*(t) \left[2[Q_{12}^i(t)]_j^T x_i^*(t) + 2[Q_{22}^i(t)]_j^T y_i^*(t) + r_j^*(t) - \mu_i^{(2)}(t) \right] = 0, \quad (5.4)$$

where $\mu_i^1(t)$, $\mu_i^2(t) \in L^2([0,T])$ are Lagrangean functions.

Proof: The proof of this equivalence is based on the infinite-dimensional Lagrangean theory, which has proven to be a powerful tool in determining essential properties of optimization problems (see Jahn (1996), Daniele (1999)). This theory proceeds in the following way.

Let us consider the function

$$\mathcal{L}\left(x_i(t), y_i(t), \lambda_i^{(1)}(t), \lambda_i^{(2)}(t), \mu_i^{(1)}(t), \mu_i^{(2)}(t) \right)$$

$$= \Psi(x_i(t), y_i(t)) - \int_0^T \sum_{j=1}^n \lambda_{ij}^{(1)}(t) x_{ij}(t) \, dt - \int_0^T \sum_{j=1}^n \lambda_{ij}^{(2)}(t) y_{ij}(t) \, dt$$

$$- \int_0^T \mu_i^{(1)}(t) \left(\sum_{j=1}^n x_{ij}(t) - s_i(t) \right) dt - \int_0^T \mu_i^{(2)}(t) \left(\sum_{j=1}^n y_{ij}(t) - s_i(t) \right) dt,$$

where

$$\Psi(x_i(t), y_i(t))$$

$$= \int_0^T \sum_{j=1}^n [2[Q_{11}^i(t)]_j^T x_i^*(t) + [Q_{21}^i(t)]_j^T y_i^*(t) - r_j^*(t)] \times [x_{ij}(t) - x_{ij}^*(t)] \, dt$$

$$+ \int_0^T \sum_{j=1}^n [2[Q_{22}^i(t)]_j^T x_i^*(t) + [Q_{12}^i(t)]_j^T y_i^*(t) + r_j^*(t)] \times [y_{ij}(t) - y_{ij}^*(t)] \, dt,$$

$$\begin{bmatrix} x_i(t) \\ y_i(t) \end{bmatrix} \in L^2([0,T], \mathbb{R}^{2n}) \text{ and } (\lambda_i^1(t), \lambda_i^2(t), \mu_i^1(t), \mu_i^2(t)) \in C$$

$$= \left\{ \lambda_i^{(1)}(t), \lambda_i^{(2)}(t) \in L^2([0,T], R^n), \quad \lambda_i^{(1)}(t), \lambda_i^{(2)}(t) \geq 0, \right.$$

$$\left. \mu_i^{(1)}(t), \mu_i^{(2)}(t) \in L^2([0,T]); \ i = 1,2,\ldots,m \right\}.$$

By means of Lagrangean Theory (cf. Daniele (1999)), it is possible to prove that there exist $\lambda_i^{(1)}(t), \lambda_i^{(2)}(t), \mu_i^{(1)}(t), \mu_i^{(2)}(t)$, such that $\lambda_i^{(1)}(t) \geq 0$, $\lambda_i^{(2)}(t) \geq 0$ and

$$\int_0^T \sum_{j=1}^n \lambda_{ij}^{(1)}(t) x_{ij}^*(t) \, dt = 0 \Rightarrow \lambda_{ij}^{(1)}(t) x_{ij}^*(t) = 0 \text{ a.e. in } [0,T]$$

$$\int_0^T \sum_{j=1}^n \lambda_{ij}^{(2)}(t) y_{ij}^*(t)\, dt = 0 \Rightarrow \lambda_{ij}^{(2)}(t) y_{ij}^*(t) = 0 \text{ a.e. in } [0, T].$$

Moreover, using the characterization of the solution by means of a saddle point (see Daniele (1999)), we obtain:

$$\mathcal{L}\left(x_i(t), y_i(t), \lambda_i^{(1)}(t), \lambda_i^{(2)}(t), \mu_i^{(1)}(t), \mu_i^{(2)}(t)\right)$$

$$= \int_0^T \sum_{j=1}^n \left[2[Q_{11}^i(t)]_j^T\, x_i^*(t) + 2[Q_{21}^i(t)]_j^T\, y_i^*(t) - r_j^*(t) - \lambda_{ij}^{(1)}(t) - \mu_i^{(1)}(t) \right]$$

$$\times [x_{ij}(t) - x_{ij}^*(t)]\, dt$$

$$+ \int_0^T \sum_{j=1}^n \left[2[Q_{12}^i(t)]_j^T\, x_i^*(t) + 2[Q_{22}^i(t)]_j^T\, y_i^*(t) + r_j^*(t) - \lambda_{ij}^{(2)}(t) - \mu_i^{(2)}(t) \right]$$

$$\times [y_{ij}(t) - y_{ij}^*(t)]\, dt \geq 0, \quad \forall \begin{bmatrix} x_i(t) \\ y_i(t) \end{bmatrix} \in L^2([0, T], R^{2n}). \tag{5.10}$$

If we set

$$\varepsilon_1(t) = 2[Q_{11}^i(t)]_j^T\, x_i^*(t) + 2[Q_{21}^i(t)]_j^T\, y_i^*(t) - r_j^*(t) - \lambda_{ij}^{(1)}(t) - \mu_i^{(1)}(t)$$

and

$$\varepsilon_2(t) = 2[Q_{12}^i(t)]_j^T\, x_i^*(t) + 2[Q_{22}^i(t)]_j^T\, y_i^*(t) - r_j^*(t) - \lambda_{ij}^{(1)}(t) - \mu_i^{(1)}(t),$$

by choosing

$$x_i(t) = x_i^*(t) + \varepsilon_1(t),$$

and

$$y_i(t) = y_i^*(t) + \varepsilon_2(t),$$

we get:

$$\int_0^T \sum_{j=1}^n \left[2[Q_{11}^i(t)]_j^T\, x_i^*(t) + 2[Q_{21}^i(t)]_j^T\, y_i^*(t) - r_j^*(t) - \lambda_{ij}^{(1)}(t) - \mu_i^{(1)}(t) \right]^2 dt$$

$$+ \int_0^T \sum_{j=1}^n \left[2[Q_{12}^i(t)]_j^T\, x_i^*(t) + 2[Q_{22}^i(t)]_j^T\, y_i^*(t) + r_j^*(t) - \lambda_{ij}^{(2)}(t) - \mu_i^{(2)}(t) \right]^2 dt$$

$$\geq 0.$$

By choosing

$$x_i(t) = x_i^*(t) - \varepsilon_1(t),$$

and

$$y_i(t) = y_i^*(t) - \varepsilon_2(t),$$

we obtain:

$$-\int_0^T \sum_{j=1}^n \left[2[Q^i_{11}(t)]^T_j \, x^*_i(t) + 2[Q^i_{21}(t)]^T_j \, y^*_i(t) - r^*_j(t) - \lambda^{(1)}_{ij}(t) - \mu^{(1)}_i(t)\right]^2 dt$$

$$-\int_0^T \sum_{j=1}^n \left[2[Q^i_{12}(t)]^T_j \, x^*_i(t) + 2[Q^i_{22}(t)]^T_j \, y^*_i(t) + r^*_j(t) - \lambda^{(2)}_{ij}(t) - \mu^{(2)}_i(t)\right]^2 dt$$

$$\geq 0.$$

Hence,

$$2[Q^i_{11}(t)]^T_j \, x^*_i(t) + 2[Q^i_{21}(t)]^T_j \, y^*_i(t) - r^*_j(t) - \mu^{(1)}_i(t) = \lambda^{(1)}_{ij}(t) \geq 0$$

and

$$2[Q^i_{12}(t)]^T_j \, x^*_i(t) + 2[Q^i_{22}(t)]^T_j \, y^*_i(t) + r^*_j(t) - \mu^{(2)}_i(t) - \lambda^{(2)}_{ij}(t) \geq 0.$$

Moreover, taking into account that $\lambda^{(1)}_i(t)x^*_i(t) = 0$, $\lambda^{(2)}_i(t)y^*_i(t) = 0$, we get:

$$x^*_{ij}(t) \left[2[Q^i_{11}(t)]^T_j \, x^*_i(t) + 2[Q^i_{21}(t)]^T_j \, y^*_i(t) - r^*_j(t) - \mu^{(1)}_i(t)\right] = 0$$

and

$$y^*_{ij}(t) \left[2[Q^i_{12}(t)]^T_j \, x^*_i(t) + 2[Q^i_{22}(t)]^T_j \, y^*_i(t) + r^*_j(t) - \mu^{(2)}_i(t)\right] = 0.$$

Conversely, if estimates (5.1)–(5.4) hold, then we show that the variational inequality (5.8) holds. From (5.1), we obtain:

$$\sum_{j=1}^n \left[2[Q^i_{11}(t)]^T_j \, x^*_i(t) + 2[Q^i_{21}(t)]^T_j \, y^*_i(t) - r^*_j(t) - \mu^{(1)}_i(t)\right] \times [x_{ij}(t) - x^*_{ij}(t)] \geq 0,$$

and taking into account that $\sum_{j=1}^n x_{ij}(t) = s_i(t)$ and $\sum_{j=1}^n x^*_{ij}(t) = s_i(t)$ a.e. in $[0, T]$, we get:

$$\sum_{j=1}^n \left[2[Q^i_{11}(t)]^T_j \, x^*_i(t) + 2[Q^i_{21}(t)]^T_j \, y^*_i(t) - r^*_j(t)\right] \times [x_{ij}(t) - x^*_{ij}(t)] \geq 0,$$

and then

$$\int_0^T \sum_{j=1}^n \left[2[Q^i_{11}(t)]^T_j \, x^*_i(t) + 2[Q^i_{21}(t)]^T_j \, y^*_i(t) - r^*_j(t)\right] \times [x_{ij}(t) - x^*_{ij}(t)] \, dt \geq 0.$$

$$(5.11)$$

Similarly, one obtains:

$$\sum_{j=1}^{n} \left[2[Q_{22}^i(t)]_j^T y_i^*(t) + 2[Q_{12}^i(t)]_j^T x_i^*(t) + r_j^*(t) \right] \times [y_{ij}(t) - y_{ij}^*(t)] \geq 0$$

and, subsequently,

$$\int_0^T \sum_{j=1}^{n} \left[2[Q_{22}^i(t)]_j^T y_i^*(t) + 2[Q_{12}^i(t)]_j^T x_i^*(t) + r_j^*(t) \right] \times [y_{ij}(t) - y_{ij}^*(t)] \, dt \geq 0.$$

(5.12)

Summing now inequalities (5.11) and (5.12) for all i, we conclude that for $(x^*(t), y^*(t)) \in \prod_{i=1}^{n} P_i$:

$$\sum_{i=1}^{m} \int_0^T \sum_{j=1}^{n} \left[2[Q_{11}^i(t)]_j^T x_i^*(t) + 2[Q_{21}^i(t)]_j^T y_i^*(t) - r_j^*(t) \right] \times [x_{ij}(t) - x_{ij}^*(t)] \, dt$$

$$+ \int_0^T \sum_{j=1}^{n} \left[2[Q_{22}^i(t)]_j^T x_i^*(t) + 2[Q_{12}^i(t)]_j^T y_i^*(t) + r_j^*(t) \right] \times [y_{ij}(t) - y_{ij}^*(t)] \, dt \geq 0,$$

$$\forall \begin{bmatrix} x_i(t) \\ y_i(t) \end{bmatrix} \in P_i,$$

and the proof is complete. $\square$

We now describe the variational inequality associated with the instrument prices $r_j(t)$.

The equilibrium condition related to the prices of the instruments is

$$\begin{cases} \sum_{i=1}^{m} \left(x_{ij}^*(t) - y_{ij}^*(t) \right) \geq 0 & \text{a.e. in } [0, T] \\ \sum_{i=1}^{m} \left(x_{ij}^*(t) - y_{ij}^*(t) \right) r_j^*(t) = 0, & r^*(t) \in L^2([0, T], R_+^n). \end{cases}$$

(5.5)

Let us prove the following theorem.

Theorem 5.4

Condition (5.5) is equivalent to

$$\begin{cases} \text{Find } r^*(t) \in L^2([0, T], R_+^n) \text{ such that} \\ \int_0^T \sum_{i=1}^{m} [x_{ij}^*(t) - y_{ij}^*(t)] \times [r_j(t) - r_j^*(t)] \, dt \geq 0, \\ \forall r(t) \in L^2([0, T], R_+^n). \end{cases}$$

(5.13)

Proof: Let us prove that Condition (5.5) implies (5.13). Let us set

$$E_+ = \{t \in [0, T] : r_j^*(t) > 0\},$$

and let us show that in E_+ it follows $\sum_{i=1}^{m} [x_{ij}^*(t) - y_{ij}^*(t)] = 0. \quad \forall r(t) \in$
$L^2([0, T], R_+^n)$, we get:

$$\int_{E_+} \sum_{i=1}^{m} [x_{ij}^*(t) - y_{ij}^*(t)] \times [r_j(t) - r_j^*(t)] \, dt \geq 0.$$

On the other hand, if we consider $E_0 = \{t \in [0, T] : r_j^*(t) = 0\}$, then in E_0 it follows $\sum_{i=1}^{m} [x_{ij}^*(t) - y_{ij}^*(t)] \geq 0$. Hence,

$$\int_0^T \sum_{i=1}^{m} [x_{ij}^*(t) - y_{ij}^*(t)] \times [r_j(t) - r_j^*(t)] \, dt = \int_{E_0} \sum_{i=1}^{m} [x_{ij}^*(t) - y_{ij}^*(t)] \times r_j(t) \, dt$$

$$+ \int_{E_+} \sum_{i=1}^{m} [x_{ij}^*(t) - y_{ij}^*(t)] \times [r_j(t) - r_j^*(t)] \, dt \geq 0,$$

and (5.13) holds.

Let us prove now that (5.13) implies Condition (5.5). From (5.13) follows:

$$\int_{E_0} \sum_{i=1}^{m} [x_{ij}^*(t) - y_{ij}^*(t)] \times r_j(t) \, dt + \int_{E_+} \sum_{i=1}^{m} [x_{ij}^*(t) - y_{ij}^*(t)] \times [r_j(t) - r_j^*(t)] \, dt$$

$$\geq 0.$$

If $\sum_{i=1}^{m} [x_{ij}^*(t) - y_{ij}^*(t)] > 0$ in E_+ (or in a subset of E_+ with positive measure), then we choose

$$r_j(t) = \begin{cases} 0 & \text{in } E_0 \\ r_j^*(t) - \varepsilon(t) & \text{in } E_+, \end{cases}$$

where $0 < \varepsilon(t) < r_j^*(t)$ and we get:

$$\int_0^T \sum_{i=1}^{m} [x_{ij}^*(t) - y_{ij}^*(t)] \times [r_j(t) - r_j^*(t)] \, dt$$

$$= \int_{E_+} \sum_{i=1}^{m} [x_{ij}^*(t) - y_{ij}^*(t)] \times [-\varepsilon(t)] \, dt < 0,$$

which is an absurdity.

On the contrary, if $\sum\limits_{i=1}^{m} \left[x_{ij}^*(t) - y_{ij}^*(t) \right] < 0$ in E_+ (or in a subset of E_+ with positive measure), then we choose

$$r_j(t) = \begin{cases} 0 & \text{in } E_0 \\ r_j^*(t) + \varepsilon(t) & \text{in } E_+, \end{cases}$$

where $\varepsilon(t) > 0$ and we get:

$$\int_0^T \sum_{i=1}^{m} \left[x_{ij}^*(t) - y_{ij}^*(t) \right] \times \left[r_j(t) - r_j^*(t) \right] dt$$

$$= \int_{E_+} \sum_{i=1}^{m} \left[x_{ij}^*(t) - y_{ij}^*(t) \right] \times \varepsilon(t) \, dt < 0,$$

which is also an absurdity.

Further, if we select

$$r_j(t) = \begin{cases} 0 & \text{in } E_+ \\ \varepsilon(t) & \text{in } E_0, \end{cases}$$

where $\varepsilon(t) > 0$, then, if $\sum\limits_{i=1}^{m} \left[x_{ij}^*(t) - y_{ij}^*(t) \right] < 0$ in E_0 (or in a subset of E_0 with positive measure), we get: $\int_{E_0} \sum\limits_{i=1}^{m} \left[x_{ij}^*(t) - y_{ij}^*(t) \right] \varepsilon(t) \, dt < 0$, which is an absurdity. $\square$

5.4 Variational Inequality Formulation Proof and Existence Theorem

Following the proof of Theorem 5.3, we can now prove Theorem 5.1.

Proof of Theorem 5.1: From the results of the preceding section, it immediately follows that if $(x^*(t), y^*(t), r^*(t)) \in \prod\limits_{i=1}^{m} P_i \times L^2([0,T], R_+^n)$ is a financial equilibrium, then it satisfies the variational inequalities (5.8) and (5.13), hence, the variational inequality (5.7) and vice versa. $\square$

We now establish the following existence theorem.

Theorem 5.5: Existence

If $(x^*(t), y^*(t), r^*(t)) \in \prod\limits_{i=1}^{m} P_i \times L^2([0,T], R_+^n)$ is an equilibrium, then the equilibrium asset and liability vector $(x^*(t), y^*(t))$ is a solution to the variational *inequality:*

$$\sum_{i=1}^{m} \int_0^T \left\{ \sum_{j=1}^{n} \left[2[Q_{11}^i(t)]_j^T \, x_i^*(t) + 2[Q_{21}^i(t)]_j^T \, y_i^*(t) \right] \times \left[x_{ij}(t) - x_{ij}^*(t) \right] \right.$$

$$\left. \sum_{j=1}^{n} \left[2[Q_{12}^i(t)]_j^T \, x_i^*(t) + 2[Q_{22}^i(t)]_j^T \, y_i^*(t) \right] \times \left[y_{ij}(t) - y_{ij}^*(t) \right] \right\} dt \geq 0,$$

$$\forall (x(t), y(t)) \in S, \tag{5.14}$$

where

$$S \equiv \left\{ (x(t), y(t)) \in \prod_{i=1}^{m} P_i; \quad \sum_{i=1}^{m} (x_{ij}(t) - y_{ij}(t)) \geq 0, j = 1, 2, \dots, n \right\}.$$

Conversely, if $(x^*(t), y^*(t))$ is a solution to (5.14), then there exists an $r^*(t) \in L^2([0,T], R_+^n)$ such that $(x^*(t), y^*(t), r^*(t))$ is an equilibrium.

Proof: Assume that $(x^*(t), y^*(t), r^*(t)) \in \prod_{i=1}^{m} P_i \times L^2([0,T], R_+^n)$ is an equilibrium. Then $(x^*(t), y^*(t), r^*(t))$ satisfies (5.7). In (5.7) let us set:

$$x_i(t) = x_i^*(t), \quad y_i(t) = y_i^*(t), \quad r(t) = 0, \quad \text{a.e. in } [0, T] \text{ and } \forall i = 1, \dots, m,$$

then we get:

$$-\sum_{i=1}^{m} \int_0^T \sum_{j=1}^{n} \left[x_{ij}^*(t) - y_{ij}^*(t) \right] \times r_j^*(t) \, dt \geq 0. \tag{5.15}$$

Let us now set in (5.7) $r(t) = r^*(t)$ and we obtain:

$$\sum_{i=1}^{m} \int_0^T \left\{ \sum_{j=1}^{n} \left[2[Q_{11}^i(t)]_j^T \, x_i^*(t) + 2[Q_{21}^i(t)]_j^T \, y_i^*(t) \right] \times \left[x_{ij}(t) - x_{ij}^*(t) \right] \right.$$

$$\left. + \sum_{j=1}^{n} \left[2[Q_{12}^i(t)]_j^T \, x_i^*(t) + 2[Q_{22}^i(t)]_j^T \, y_i^*(t) \right] \times \left[y_{ij}(t) - y_{ij}^*(t) \right] \right\} dt$$

$$\geq \int_0^T \sum_{j=1}^{n} r_j^*(t) \left[\sum_{i=1}^{m} (x_{ij}(t) - y_{ij}(t)) - \sum_{i=1}^{m} (x_{ij}^*(t) - y_{ij}^*(t)) \right] dt. \tag{5.16}$$

But the right-hand side of inequality (5.16) is ≥ 0, because of (5.15) and the constraint set S. Thus, we have established that $(x^*(t), y^*(t))$ satisfies (5.14).

Observe that there always exists an asset and liability pattern $(x^*(t), y^*(t))$ satisfying (5.14), because S is weakly compact and for each $(u(t), v(t)) \in S$ the operator

$$(x(t), y(t)) \rightarrow$$

$$\sum_{i=1}^{m} \int_0^T \left\{ \sum_{j=1}^{n} \left[2[Q_{11}^i(t)]_j^T x_i^*(t) + 2[Q_{21}^i(t)]_j^T y_i^*(t) \right] \times [u_{ij}(t) - x_{ij}(t)] \right.$$

$$\left. + \sum_{j=1}^{n} \left[2[Q_{12}^i(t)]_j^T x_i^*(t) + 2[Q_{22}^i(t)]_j^T y_i^*(t) \right] \times [v_{ij}(t) - y_{ij}(t)] \right\} dt$$

is weakly upper semicontinuous (see Daniele, Maugeri, and Oettli (1998, 1999) for more details). Now, in order to prove the existence of $r^*(t) \in L^2([0, T], \mathbb{R}_+^n)$ such that $(x^*(t), y^*(t), r^*(t))$ is an equilibrium, let us apply the Lagrange Multiplier Theorem (see Daniele (1999)) to the function:

$$\mathcal{L}\left(x_i(t), y_i(t), \lambda_i^{(1)}(t), \lambda_i^{(2)}(t), \mu_i^{(1)}(t), \mu_i^{(2)}(t), r(t) \right)$$

$$= \Psi(x_i(t), y_i(t)) - \int_0^T \sum_{j=1}^{n} \lambda_{ij}^{(1)}(t) x_{ij}(t) \, dt - \int_0^T \sum_{j=1}^{n} \lambda_{ij}^{(2)}(t) y_{ij}(t) \, dt$$

$$- \int_0^T \mu_i^{(1)}(t) \left[\sum_{j=1}^{n} x_{ij}(t) - s_i(t) \right] dt - \int_0^T \mu_i^{(2)}(t) \left[\sum_{j=1}^{n} y_{ij}(t) - s_i(t) \right] dt$$

$$- \int_0^T \sum_{j=1}^{n} r_j(t) \left[\sum_{i=1}^{m} (x_{ij}(t) - y_{ij}(t)) \right] dt$$

where

$$(\lambda_i^1(t), \lambda_i^2(t), \mu_i^1(t), \mu_i^2(t), r(t)) \in \overline{C}$$

$$= \left\{ \lambda_i^{(1)}(t), \ \lambda_i^{(2)}(t) \in L^2([0, T], R^n), \quad \lambda_i^{(1)}(t), \ \lambda_i^{(2)}(t) \geq 0, \right.$$

$$\mu_i^{(1)}(t), \ \mu_i^{(2)}(t) \in L^2([0, T]); \ i = 1, 2, \ldots, m;$$

$$\left. r(t) \in L^2([0, T], R^n), \quad r(t) \geq 0 \text{ a.e. in } [0, T] \right\}.$$

We get that, besides $\lambda_i^{(1)}(t)$, $\lambda_i^{(2)}(t)$, $\mu_i^{(1)}(t)$ and $\mu_i^{(2)}(t)$, there exists an $r^*(t) \in L^2([0, T], \mathbb{R}_+^n)$ corresponding to the constraints defining S. For such a pattern $(x^*(t), y^*(t), r^*(t))$ we have:

$$2[Q_{11}^i(t)]_j^T x_i^*(t) + 2[Q_{21}^i(t)]_j^T y_i^*(t) - r_j^*(t) - \mu_i^{(1)}(t) = \lambda_{ij}^{(1)} \geq 0, \qquad (5.1)$$

$$2[Q_{12}^i(t)]_j^T x_i^*(t) + 2[Q_{22}^i(t)]_j^T y_i^*(t) + r_j^*(t) - \mu_i^{(2)}(t) = \lambda_{ij}^{(2)} \geq 0, \quad (5.2)$$

$$x_{ij}^*(t) \left[2[Q_{11}^i(t)]_j^T x_i^*(t) + 2[Q_{21}^i(t)]_j^T y_i^*(t) - r_j^*(t) - \mu_i^{(1)}(t) \right] = 0, \quad (5.3)$$

$$y_{ij}^*(t) \left[2[Q_{12}^i(t)]_j^T x_i^*(t) + 2[Q_{22}^i(t)]_j^T y_i^*(t) + r_j^*(t) - \mu_i^{(2)}(t) \right] = 0, \quad (5.4)$$

and

$$\begin{cases} \displaystyle\sum_{i=1}^m \left(x_{ij}^*(t) - y_{ij}^*(t) \right) \geq 0 & \text{a.e. in } [0, T] \\ \displaystyle\sum_{i=1}^m \left(x_{ij}^*(t) - y_{ij}^*(t) \right) r_j^*(t) = 0, & r^*(t) \in L^2([0, T], R_1^n). \end{cases} \quad (5.5)$$

From Conditions (5.1)–(5.5), a.e. in $[0, T]$, we obtain:

$$\sum_{i=1}^m \sum_{j=1}^n \left[2[Q_{11}^i(t)]_j^T x_i^*(t) + 2[Q_{21}^i(t)]_j^T y_i^*(t) - r_j^*(t) \right] \times \left[x_{ij}(t) - x_{ij}^*(t) \right]$$

$$+ \sum_{i=1}^m \sum_{j=1}^n \left[2[Q_{12}^i(t)]_j^T x_i^*(t) + 2[Q_{22}^i(t)]j^T y_i^*(t) + r_j^*(t) \right] \times \left[y_{ij}(t) - y_{ij}^*(t) \right] \geq 0$$

$$(5.17)$$

and

$$\sum_{i=1}^m \sum_{j=1}^n \left[x_{ij}^*(t) - y_{ij}^*(t) \right] \times \left[r_j(t) - r_j^*(t) \right] \geq 0. \quad (5.18)$$

Summing now (5.17) and (5.18) and integrating the result, we obtain:

$$\sum_{i=1}^m \int_0^T \left\{ \sum_{j=1}^n \left[2[Q_{11}^i(t)]_j^T x_i^*(t) + 2[Q_{21}^i(t)]_j^T y_i^*(t) - r_j^*(t) \right] \times \left[x_{ij}(t) - x_{ij}^*(t) \right] \right.$$

$$+ \sum_{j=1}^n \left[2[Q_{12}^i(t)]_j^T x_i^*(t) + 2[Q_{22}^i(t)]_j^T y_i^*(t) + r_j^*(t) \right] \times \left[y_{ij}(t) - y_{ij}^*(t) \right] +$$

$$\left. + \sum_{j=1}^n \left(x_{ij}^*(t) - y_{ij}^*(t) \right) \times \left[r_j(t) - r_j^*(t) \right] \right\} dt \geq 0,$$

and the proof is complete. $\square$

5.5   Computational Procedure

We now present a computational procedure based on the subgradient method (cf. Polyak (1967)) which does not require a discretization on time.

Let us set, for the sake of brevity, $u(t) = (x(t), y(t), r(t))$ and

$$
U(u) = \begin{bmatrix} 2[Q_{11}^i(t)]_j^T x_i(t) + 2[Q_{21}^i(t)]_j^T y_i(t) - r_j(t) \\ 2[Q_{12}^i(t)]_j^T x_i(t) + 2[Q_{22}^i(t)]_j^T y_i(t) + r_j(t) \\ x_{ij}(t) - y_{ij}(t) \end{bmatrix}_{\substack{i=1,\dots,m \\ j=1,\dots,n}}.
$$

Then

$$
\ll U(u), \tilde{u} - u \gg
$$

$$
= \sum_{i=1}^m \int_0^T \Big\{ \sum_{j=1}^n \Big[2[Q_{11}^i(t)]_j^T x_i(t) + 2[Q_{21}^i(t)]_j^T y_i(t) - r_j(t) \Big] \times (\tilde{x}_{ij}(t) - x_{ij}(t))
$$

$$
+ \sum_{j=1}^n \Big[2[Q_{12}^i(t)]_j^T x_i(t) + 2[Q_{22}^i(t)]_j^T y_i(t) + r_j(t) \Big] \times (\tilde{y}_{ij}(t) - y_{ij}(t))
$$

$$
+ \sum_{j=1}^n (x_{ij}(t) - y_{ij}(t)) \times (\tilde{r}_j(t) - r_j(t)) \Big\} \, dt.
$$

Let

$$
\mathbb{K} = \left\{ \prod_{i=1}^m P_i \times L^2([0,T], \mathbb{R}_+^n) \right\}
$$

and

$$
B = \left\{ u(t) \in \prod_{i=1}^m L^2([0,T], \mathbb{R}_+^{2n}) \times L^2([0,T], \mathbb{R}_+^n) \right\}.
$$

B is easily to handle and projections onto B are readily available. For each $u \in B$ let us set

$$
\psi_1(u) = \max_{\tilde{u} \in \mathbb{K}} \ll U(\tilde{u}), u - \tilde{u} \gg,
$$

$$
\psi_2(u) = \sum_{i=1}^m \int_0^T \left\{ \left(\sum_{j=1}^n x_{ij}(t) - s_i(t) \right)^2 + \left(\sum_{j=1}^n y_{ij}(t) - s_i(t) \right)^2 \right\} dt.
$$

As we observed in Section 5.1, $\psi_1(u)$ is well-defined. Then the real-valued function

$$
\psi(u) = \max \{ \psi_1(u), \psi_2(u) \}
$$

is a gap function for the variational inequality

$$
\ll U(\tilde{u}), \tilde{u} - u \gg \, \geq 0, \quad \forall \tilde{u} \in \mathbb{K} \tag{5.19}
$$

and, being $U(u)$ monotone, also for the variational inequality

$$
\ll U(u), \tilde{u} - u \gg \, \geq 0, \quad \forall u \in \mathbb{K}. \tag{5.20}
$$

In fact, we recall that, if U is monotone, then variational inequalities (5.19) and (5.20) are equivalent.

Note that $\psi(u)$ is a gap function because $\psi(u) \geq 0 \quad \forall u \in \mathbb{K}$ and if $\psi(u) = 0$, then u solves (5.19) and, hence, (5.20).

The function $\psi_1(u)$, being the maximum of a family of continuous and affine functions, is convex and weakly lower semicontinuous. Then $\psi(u)$ is convex and weakly lower semicontinuous, too. The needed convexity of ψ is the main reason for considering (5.19) instead of (5.20).

We shall see below that the subdifferential

$$\partial\psi(u) = \left\{ \quad \tau \in \prod_{i-1}^{m} L^2([0,T], \mathbb{R}^{2n}) \times L^2([0,T], \mathbb{R}^n) : \right.$$
$$\left. \psi(\tilde{u}) - \psi(u) \geq \ll \tau, \tilde{u} - u \gg, \quad \forall \tilde{u} \in B \right\}$$

is nonempty for all $u \in B$. Let us define $\Gamma = \{u \in B : \psi(u) = 0\}$. Because of the equivalence between (5.19) and (5.20), $u \in \prod_{i=1}^{m} L^2([0,T], \mathbb{R}^{2n}) \times L^2([0,T], \mathbb{R}^n)$ is a solution to (5.20) if and only if $u \in \Gamma$.

The subgradient method for finding an element of Γ can now be described as follows. Choose an arbitrary $u^0 \in B$ and given $u^n \in B$, $u^n \notin \Gamma$, let us set

$$u^{n+1} = \text{Proj}_B(u^n - \rho_n \tau_n),$$

where $\tau_n \in \partial\psi(H^n)$, $\rho_n = \dfrac{\psi(H^n)}{\|\tau_n\|^2}$, and Proj_B denotes the projection (cf. Nagurney (1999)) onto the set B.

Using the linearity of U, we shall see below that τ_n can be chosen in such a way that $\|\tau_n\|$ remains bounded. If $\|\tau_n\|$ remains bounded and $u^n \notin \Gamma$ for all n, then we have the following result.

Theorem 5.6: Convergence
There holds that $\psi(u^n) \to 0$. The sequence $\{u^n\}$ has weak cluster points and every weak cluster point is in Γ. If the sequence $\{u^n\}$ has a strong cluster point $\bar{u}$, then $\bar{u}$ is unique and $\{u^n\}$ converges strongly to $\bar{u}$.

Proof: See Daniele, Maugeri, and Oettli (1999). $\square$

We now have to prove the existence of the subdifferential τ. For a given $u \in B$, let us define $\tau^{(1)}(t) = U(\bar{u}(t))$ where $\bar{u}$ is a solution to $\max_{\tilde{u} \in \mathbb{K}} \ll U(\tilde{u}), u - \tilde{u} \gg$. As already observed, $\tilde{u}$ there exists. Then $\tau^{(1)}(t) \in \partial\psi_1(t)$.

Let us define $\tau^{(2)}(t) = 2 \left(\sum_{j=1}^{n} x_{ij}(t) - s_i(t) \right) + 2 \left(\sum_{j=1}^{n} y_{ij}(t) - s_i(t) \right)$. It is easy to prove that $\tau^{(2)}(t) \in \partial\psi_2(t)$, because the estimate

$$\psi_2(\tilde{u}) - \psi_2(u) \geq \ll \tau^{(2)}(t), \tilde{u} - u \gg$$

leads to

$$\left(\sum_{j=1}^{n} \tilde{x}_{ij}(t) - s_i(t)\right)^2 + \left(\sum_{j=1}^{n} \tilde{y}_{ij}(t) - s_i(t)\right)^2$$

$$- \left(\sum_{j=1}^{n} x_{ij}(t) - s_i(t)\right)^2 - \left(\sum_{j=1}^{n} y_{ij}(t) - s_i(t)\right)^2$$

$$\geq 2\left(\sum_{j=1}^{n} x_{ij}(t) - s_i(t)\right)\left(\sum_{j=1}^{n} \tilde{x}_{ij}(t) - s_i(t)\right) - 2\left(\sum_{j=1}^{n} x_{ij}(t) - s_i(t)\right)^2$$

$$+ 2\left(\sum_{j=1}^{n} y_{ij}(t) - s_i(t)\right)\left(\sum_{j=1}^{n} \tilde{y}_{ij}(t) - s_i(t)\right) - 2\left(\sum_{j=1}^{n} y_{ij}(t) - s_i(t)\right)^2,$$

that is,

$$\left(\sum_{j=1}^{n} \tilde{x}_{ij}(t) - s_i(t)\right)^2 - 2\left(\sum_{j=1}^{n} x_{ij}(t) - s_i(t)\right)\left(\sum_{j=1}^{n} \tilde{x}_{ij}(t) - s_i(t)\right)$$

$$+ \left(\sum_{j=1}^{n} x_{ij}(t) - s_i(t)\right)^2 + \left(\sum_{j=1}^{n} \tilde{y}_{ij}(t) - s_i(t)\right)^2$$

$$- 2\left(\sum_{j=1}^{n} y_{ij}(t) - s_i(t)\right)\left(\sum_{j=1}^{n} \tilde{y}_{ij}(t) - s_i(t)\right) + \left(\sum_{j=1}^{n} y_{ij}(t) - s_i(t)\right)^2 \geq 0,$$

which always holds.

Now let us define

$$\tau = \begin{cases} \tau^{(1)} & \text{if} \quad \psi(u) = \psi_1(u) \\ \tau^{(2)} & \text{if} \quad \psi(u) = \psi_2(u). \end{cases}$$

Then $\tau \in \partial\psi(u)$ and it is easy to show that τ remains bounded if u varies in B. $\square$

5.6 Summary and Conclusions

In this chapter, we have proposed a new framework for the modeling, analysis, and computation of financial equilibrium problems through a novel evolutionary model. In contrast to earlier multi-sector, multi-instrument financial equilibrium models, the new model allows for variance-covariance matrices to be time-dependent, as well as the sector financial volumes. We described the behavior of the financial sectors, derived the equilibrium conditions, and then established the equivalent infinite-dimensional variational inequality formulation. We provided the network structure of the problem, both out of and in equilibrium. We also proved the existence of an equilibrium pattern. Finally, we proposed a computational procedure based on the subgradient method.

Another computational procedure can be constructed by discretizing time, but this method, together with other effective computational schemes, will be the aim of future research. Future research will also include exploring a variety of modeling extensions, including, but not limited to, the inclusion of such policy interventions as price bounds and taxes. In addition, it would be interesting to apply the results herein to financial networks with intermediation (cf. Nagurney and Ke (2001)).

Acknowledgments

The author is grateful for the helpful reviews and suggestions provided by the editor.

References

Dafermos, S. C., and Sparrow, F. T. (1969), "The Traffic Assignment Problem for a General Network," *Journal of Research of the National Bureau of Standards* **73B**, 91-118.

Daniele, P. (1999), "Lagrangean Function for Dynamic Variational Inequalities," *Rendiconti del Circolo Matematico di Palermo*, Serie II, Suppl. 58, 101-119.

Daniele, P., and Maugeri, A. (2001), "On Dynamical Equilibrium Problems and Variational Inequalities," in *Equilibrium Problems: Nonsmooth Optimization and Variational Inequality Models*, pp. 59-59, F. Giannessi, A. Maugeri, and P. M. Pardalos, editors, Kluwer Academic Publishers, Dordrecht, The Netherlands.

Daniele, P., Maugeri, A., and Oettli, W. (1998), "Variational Inequalities and Time-Dependent Traffic Equilibria," *Comptes Rendus de l' Académie des Sciences Paris*, T. 326, Serie I, 1059–1062.

Daniele, P., Maugeri, A., and Oettli, W. (1999), "Time-Dependent Traffic Equilibria," *Journal of Optimization Theory and its Applications* **103**, 543-555.

Dong, J., Zhang, D., and Nagurney, A. (1996), "A Projected Dynamical Systems Model of General Financial Equilibrium with Stability Analysis," *Mathematical and Computer Modelling* **24**, 35-44.

Gürkan, G., Özge, A. Y., and Robinson, S. (1996), "Sample-Path Solution of Variational Inequalities with Application to Option Pricing," in *Proceed-

ings 1996 Winter Simulation Conference, pp. 337-344, D. J. Morrice, D. T. Brunner, and J. M. Swain, editors, Coronado, California.

Jahn, J. (1996), *Introduction to the Theory of Nonlinear Optimization*, Springer-Verlag, Berlin, Germany.

Jaillet, P., Lamberton, D., and Lapeyre, B. (1990), "Variational Inequalities and the Pricing of American Options," *Acta Applicanda Mathematicae* **21**, 253-289.

Markowitz, H. M. (1952), "Portfolio Selection," *Journal of Finance* **7**, 77-91.

Markowitz, H. M. (1959), *Portfolio Selection: Efficient Diversification of Investments*, John Wiley & Sons, New York.

McLean, R. P. (1993), "Approximation Theory for Stochastic Variational Inequality and Ky Fan Inequalities in Finite Dimensions," *Annals of Operations Research* **44**, 43-61.

Nagurney, A. (1994), "Variational Inequalities in the Analysis and Computation of Multi-Sector, Multi-Instrument Financial Equilibria," *Journal of Economic Dynamics and Control* **18**, 161-184.

Nagurney, A. (1999), *Network Economics - A Variational Inequality Approach*, second and revised edition, Kluwer Academic Publishers, Dordrecht, The Netherlands.

Nagurney, A. (2001), "Finance and Variational Inequalities," *Quantitative Finance* **1**, 309-317.

Nagurney, A., Dong, J., and Hughes, M. (1992), "Formulation and Computation of General Financial Equilibrium," *Optimization* **26**, 339-354.

Nagurney, A., and Ke, K. (2001), "Financial Networks with Intermediation," *Quantitative Finance* **1**, 441-451.

Nagurney, A., and Siokos, S. (1997a), "Variational Inequalities for International General Financial Equilibrium Modeling and Computation," *Mathematical and Computer Modelling* **25**, 31-49.

Nagurney, A., and Siokos, S. (1997b), *Financial Networks: Statics and Dynamics*, Springer-Verlag, Heidelberg, Germany.

Nagurney, A., and Zhang, D. (1996), *Projected Dynamical Systems and Variational Inequalities with Applications*, Kluwer Academic Publishers, Boston, Massachusetts.

Polyak, B. T. (1967), "A General Method for Solving Extremum Problems," *Doklady Akademii Nauk SSR* **174**, 33-36.

Stampacchia, G. (1969), "Variational Inequalities, Theory and Applications of Monotone Operators," *Proceedings of a NATO Advanced Study Institute (Venice, 1968)*, pp. 101-192, Oderisi, Gubbio, Italy.

Tourin, A., and Zariphopoulou, T. (1994), "Numerical Schemes for Investment Models with Singular Transactions," *Computational Economics* **7**, 287-307.

Wardrop, J. G. (1952), "Some Theoretical Aspects of Road Traffic Research," *Proceedings of the Institute of Civil Engineers*, Part II, London, pp. 325-378.

6 The Growing Importance of Networks in Finance and its Effects on Competition

Stijn Claessens, Gergely Dobos, Daniela Klingebiel, and Luc Laeven

6.1 Introduction

Financial services industries around the world have been undergoing rapid changes fostered by globalization and technological advances, including the emergence of electronic finance and resulting in an increase in the importance of networks in the production and distribution of financial services. Banking systems are consolidating in many markets and banks are extending their presence across borders. Financial conglomerates are increasing in importance. New financial services providers are emerging, including online-only banks and brokerages, and companies that allow consumers to compare financial services more easily as to price and quality. Nonfinancial entities, including telecommunication and utility companies and supermarket chains, are entering financial services markets. In asset markets, trading systems – for equities, fixed income, and foreign exchange – are consolidating globally and moving toward electronic platforms. As a result of these changes, financial services are becoming less special, making policies to preserve the franchise value of financial institutions less necessary while making the application of competition policy more feasible. Financial services also heavily, and increasingly so, depend on networks for their production and distribution, which makes competition policy the more necessary. The two developments mean that the competition policy paradigm for financial services industries will have to be revisited and will increasingly need to resemble that used in other network industries. To investigate the growing importance of networks in the delivery of financial services and its effect on competition, this chapter will address the following issues. What changes have taken place in the financial services industries? What implications have the changes had on competition in financial services? What are the economic characteristics of networks as they apply to financial services? How can network industries, and financial services specifically, best be regulated? Is there a need to change the competition paradigm in the financial sector? Given the complexity of the issues, the chapter will not be able to address all the questions raised above in great detail. The objective of the chapter is to lay out a number of specific issues on the competition policy side and provide some initial answers as to how competition policy could be adjusted by looking at solutions that were adopted in other network industries. Section 6.2 will review the changes that have taken place in the financial services industries over the past few years with advances in electronic finance and the increasing importance of networks. Section 6.3 will review the economic characteristics of networks and the effects of competition, also as they apply to financial services industries. Section 6.4 will review the impact of changes on the competition policy paradigm in the financial sector and suggest approaches for applying lessons from network economics to financial services industries. Section 6.5 will conclude.

6.2   The Increasing Importance of Networks in Finance

The following section will review recent changes in the financial services industry and analyze the impact of these changes on competition policy.

6.2.1   Changes in the Financial Services Industry

Financial services are being reshaped by the globalization of financial markets, technological advances, and structural changes, including the lowering of regulatory barriers. The globalization of financial services has involved increased financial integration, increased cross-border mergers and acquisitions of financial institutions, and lower barriers between markets (see G-10 (2001)). Cross-border capital flows have been the most important form of increased financial integration, but bank consolidation and mergers and acquisitions across borders have increased as well. As the costs of establishing a physical presence have declined, cross-border entry of financial institutions has increased, further spurred by governments that have removed entry barriers. The dismantling of regulatory barriers separating banking, insurance, and securities activities is also driving consolidation. Boundaries between different financial intermediaries are being blurred, and universal (or integrated) banking is becoming the norm, as shown most clearly by the repeal of the Glass-Steagall act in the United States (see Claessens (2003)).

Technological Advances

While there has been a recent retrenchment, developments in information technology, particularly the Internet, have been an important force in reshaping the financial services industries (see Claessens, Glaessner, and Klingebiel (2000) for a review). Given its information intensity, financial services greatly benefit from advances in technology, enabling financial services providers to conduct business more cheaply and more efficiently. These gains include direct as well are indirect cost reductions. For example, the Internet functions as a new, low cost distribution channel, but also facilitates personalized pricing structures and more cost-effective customer stratification. Technological advances are also lowering the costs of entry. Many new types of specialized financial service providers have entered the marketplace. Aggregators allow consumers to comparison shop and have access to all their financial accounts in one place. Online brokers allow easy retail investing and e-payment providers facilitate financial transactions over the Internet. Financial portals meanwhile expose the customer to a whole range of financial services providers, allowing them to compare prices and quality. Many of these entrants have been non-banks, such as telecom companies and utilities, and ties between financial and non-financial institutions have become more extensive. Banks, for example, have entered alliances with retail chains to distribute financial services. These links have been motivated by desires to consolidate around recognized brand names and financial services providers seeking access to the wide distribution networks of telecom, portals, and other merchants. In the securities markets, developments are rapid as well. Exchanges are demutualizing and many new trading systems have been started. Through enhanced communications capability, trading remotely has become much easier and trading services are no longer restricted to any physical exchange.

Changing Industrial Structures

The new industrial structure emerging is becoming more partitioned in the production and distribution of financial services, in the process redefining the nature of financial intermediation. The functions of production and distribution of financial services tended to be vertically integrated in the form of banks, financial conglomerates, or stock and other financial exchanges. Now some of these functions are being separated. On the production side, electronic enablers and other third parties provide software and hardware support to financial service providers. Financial services themselves are being produced in distinct markets where financial institutions and other institutions participate, in the process commoditizing their characteristics. Commercial loans, for example, may be generated by banks, but will then be quickly sold off in markets where other banks and institutional investors participate. The range of financial services is expanding and now includes – besides traditional banking products, such as checking, mortgages, brokerage, insurance, and credit card – e-wallets, electronic bill presentment and payment, and many electronic business services. In securities markets, listing, trading, clearing and settlement services are becoming separately provided services. Financial institutions themselves are either becoming specialized in the production of certain services or diversified entities which add value by tailoring and combining financial products for their clients, without necessarily producing all the inputs themselves. Aggregators help distribute the final services, provide price comparison, and undertake functions such as preprocessing of loan applications, but do not produce financial services themselves. Other companies function mainly as distribution channels, or portals. Today, financial services – besides the brick and mortar branches – can be accessed through phones, kiosks, wireless devices, PCs with modems, and private networks. Advances in technology further facilitate the delivery of a broad array of financial services through one provider that need not be a financial service producer itself. A telecommunications company can well be the first contact for many customers to financial services. These trends have varied by the type of financial service, depending on the existence of entry barriers, and the ease and degree of commoditization. Entry has been particularly strong in financial services that can easily be unbundled and commoditized and that offer attractive initial margins. These include many non-banking financial services including brokerage, trading systems, and some retail banking services. For new services that are subject to less regulation, such as bill presentation or payment gateways for business-to-business (B2B) commerce, new entrants could easily innovate. Although deposit-taking and many traditional payment services exhibit large potential for commoditization – through online banks, payment services using pre-paid and "smart" cards – entry has been limited, in part because of regulatory barriers. However, these services can easily be commoditized. In principle, telecommunications companies can provide small payments services using the balances many mobile phone users carry on their pre-paid calling card. Or supermarket chains can easily provide payment services to their customers in their discount stores, as Wal-Mart in the US, Carrefour in France and others elsewhere are trying to do. At the same time, payment services exhibit network characteristics which are becoming of growing importance in financial services industries.

The Increasing Importance of Networks in Financial Services

Technological advances, including the emergence of electronic finance, have increased the importance of networks in the production and distribution of financial services. For instance, there has been a rapid increase in Internet banking access over the last couple of years (Table 6.1). By now, the majority of banks in Western Europe and the US as well as a number of developing countries (notably Korea) offer online banking services to their clients (see also Claessens, Glaessner, and Klingebiel (2000)).

The developments reviewed suggest that the model for financial services provision has already changed significantly and is likely to change even further in the future with technological advances. Declining economies of scale, increasing standardization and commoditization, and falling up-front costs will typically lead to more competition, better services and lower costs for consumer. This need not be the case, however, for services that exhibit net-

Table 6.1. Increasing access to online banking services

	Region	May 1995	Dec. 2002
Financial institutions offering Internet banking services	Worldwide	1	6,000
Financial institutions with Internet sites	Worldwide	50	14,000
Number of households using online banking	Worldwide	5 million*	100 million
Number of households using online banking	United States	300,000	28 million
Monthly Internet-based bank and credit card traffic	United States	100,000	50 million
Monthly loan applications submitted via the Internet	United States	0	1.5 million

Note: * Using dial-up services such as Prodigy or CitiDirect in the US and Minitel in France.
Source: Online Banking by the Numbers (2003).

work externalities and increasingly a number of financial services display the properties of a network good. In fact, adoption of new technologies in financial services industries has often been inhibited by the fact that they display network properties. A key example is information, one of the main inputs for financial services. In an electronic age, there is less need for specialized financial services providers as any non-bank financial institution or corporation can provide financing for working capital and investment to corporations or consumer credit to households. This trend is already underway in many developed countries where information is easily available and used by a variety of corporations to provide lending and other services. But, information can be a network good, especially when it is provided by credit bureaus that can be controlled by incumbent commercial banks. As such, the functioning of existing networks can inhibit further progress. As such, an existing network can be used as a tool to create additional entry barriers in the credit market as has happened in Mexico (Jappelli and Pagano (2000)) and other countries. Similarly, payment services have experienced decreasing economies of scale, lower up-front costs, and easier commoditization. Payments services need no longer be provided just by banks but could be provided by a range of corporations that have access to the payment network and infrastructure. But incumbents have often controlled access to the payments system. Furthermore, payment services are also subject to large network externalities, because the scope for electronic payment services largely depends on the degree to which users adopt a common standard. The financial service provider that manages to achieve this common standard may end up with a large share of the market, decreasing competition. These concerns also apply to trading systems and exchanges, to financial portals, and to a lesser extent to e-enablers. Against this background of changing financial services industries and increased importance of networks a thorough evaluation of the network properties of financial services and the effects on competition and competition policy is warranted.

6.3 Economic Characteristics of Networks and their Effects

In this section, we describe the general characteristics of network goods as they refer to financial services, using examples as they apply, and outline problems that can emerge in terms of efficiency (market failures) and competition policy. We review separately the economies of scale and scope of network goods on the supply side, and the positive feedback and economies of scale of network goods on the demand side. We also give some specific examples of competition issues in the financial services industries and policy responses carried out by regulatory and competition authorities. As an overall introduction, Table 6.2 provides an overview of the main economic characteristics of networks and public policy issues and responses, as well as some specific examples, both in finance and other industries.

6.3.1   Economies of Scale on the Supply Side

The basic characteristics of network goods on the production side are: economies of scale in the physical infrastructure of the network and in the creation of information goods; the prevalence and importance of vertical relationships; the importance of technological gains; and the threats to competition from other services or providers. In the following section we go through these characteristics, outlining problems that can emerge also in financial services and describing possible policy responses.

Physical Network Infrastructure and Information Goods

Traditionally, industries based on a physical network were thought of as natural monopolies because of economies of scale coming from large fixed costs of construction and operation of the network. While increasing returns to scale arise in most network industries, there are sectoral differences. Building a telecommunications network, gas pipeline carriers, electricity grids and water systems, highways and railway networks or air transportation, for example, are highly capital intensive, whereas postal services and urban transport are less so (see further European Commission (1999)). To avoid duplicating costly network infrastructure, governments often license one company per re-

Table 6.2. Main characteristics of networks and related public policy issues

Network property	Market failure and competition issues	Public policy responses	Examples and cases
Economies of scale on the supply side			
Building and operating a physical network infrastructure typically involves *large fixed costs* and is most efficiently provided by one entity as duplication would be inefficient.	An unregulated vertically integrated monopolist can *foreclose, deter entry*, or harm competitors by *denying access* to the *bottleneck infrastructure assets* which are *essential facilities* to compete on the final market.	Vertical separation and line-of-business restriction together with non-discriminatory access to the infrastructure. Antitrust oversight of (mutual) access prices. Access regulation.	Access to local loop in fixed-line telecom; "common carriers" in utility industries; access to clearing networks in banking.
Economies of scope on the supply side			
Dominant firm on a market for a network product gains benefits from being active on a *complementary* or *adjacent* product market.	Gaining dominance on a related market through *leveraging* market power by anticompetitive *tying*.	Antitrust action against illegal tying.	Software industry; the MAC ATM network illegally tied membership to complementary services; the merger of NYCE and Yankee 24.
Economies of scale on the demand side			
Positive network externality results in *positive feedback* on the demand side. *Critical mass* is needed to become sustainable.	If network externalities are not internalized, private incentives may be insufficient to sustain the new technology and there may be *under-adoption* or from a dynamic point of view, adoption will be *too slow*. The need for *coordination*.	Adoption by the government among the first to make critical mass easier to achieve and help coordination. Caveat: government may be uninformed and choose the wrong technology.	Historical examples: telephone, faxmachines, Internet and e-mail; recently PayPal payment service. The role of the government: Internet, HDTV in Japan, color TV standard in the US, checkpayment.
	Coordination on *compatibility* based on a common *standard* in order to avoid under-adoption. *Interconnection* expands overall network size and increases demand.	Standard setting is a horizontal cooperation and hence may have antitrust dimensions. Public policy may also help or impose standardization.	The failure of Stereo AM radio. Checkpayment; Payment and ATM systems.
Network size translates to competitive advantage: market tipping in favour of one network is possible ("the winner takes all"). However, several differentiated network products can also coexist.	A compatibility standard mitigates tipping but makes *competition more symmetric*; therefore, a large network has *less incentives for compatibility* than small ones. Competition is more *fragile* under incompatibility. Examples of high *barriers* to entry: fixed costs, *large scale* for critical mass, unfavorable consumer *expectations*, product preannouncement of the incumbent, and individual *switching costs*.	1. The government can promote competition by directly *imposing* compatibility, or allowing for *unilateral compatibility* by entrants. 2. The antitrust bureau can block large horizontal *mergers* leading to a dominant network having incentives to incompatibility.	Entry. Examples of 1: The Sega vs. Accolade case; Lotus vs. Borland case; The dominant Canadian ATM network, Interac. Examples of 2: Merger of MCI & WorldCom in 1999; Merger of Plus (Visa) & Cirrus (MCard) with Entree turned down.
	Enforcing full compatibility (or open standards) may lead to *free riding* on the investment of large market players, destroying their incentives to develop their network.	Charging for *interconnection* is a way to make network size matter while keeping compatibility.	Interconnection charges in mobile telecommunication, ATM network surcharges.
	A network owner may go further than incompatibility by imposing *exclusive agreements* to its members.	Competition offices mostly render exclusivity agreements illegal, either explicit or implicit agreements.	Networks with *indirect* network externalities are the most prominent examples: Nintendo; MAC regional ATM network; Visa; Microsoft (implicitly exclusionary agreement).
With heterogeneous preferences or income differences the diffusion of a technology may be lower than optimal.	Some consumer groups may not adopt even if *all* others do so. It may be socially beneficial to attach those consumers to the network.	The government can *subsidize* technology adoption for those consumers. Universal Service Obligation is mostly based on these arguments.	Universal Service Obligation in basic telecommunication services, check payment in the US, UK and other countries. How costs of USO are allocated?

gion or entire country to allow for efficiency gains of scale and protect large investments in the infrastructure.

In the case of financial services industries, the natural monopoly has been applied to stock exchanges, payments systems, clearing and settlement systems, credit bureaus and many other infrastructural inputs necessary to produce financial services. Once the network infrastructure is established and the costs are sunk, services can be provided at nearly zero marginal cost on the network. Since this gives rise to regional or country-level monopolies and can lead to monopoly pricing, governments have established specific regulatory bodies with the power to regulate final prices, taking into account costs from network operation (building, maintenance, operation) and transmission, or have allowed for self-regulation. Whereas economies of scale have mostly been associated with physical infrastructure, the production of information goods, including financial services, is often also subject to economies of scale. Furthermore, although the network may be virtual, many such products are network goods (about information goods and the relevance of network economics, see Shapiro and Varian (1999)). An information good producer typically incurs fixed production (development) costs, while serving an additional user has only negligible marginal cost. Like many other information goods, financial services have these properties. Developing and debugging a payments or trading system is very costly while it may be reproduced at nearly zero marginal cost. Credit information and risk management systems or databases have the same economies of scale characteristics.

Vertical Relationships

The elements of a network (links and nodes) are often complementary to each other. Services delivered through a network can be seen as goods that are composites of complementary components. For example, making a call using a cellphone is the composite of call dispatching, administering and digital voice transmission through the networks of the mobile and fixed line operators. Examples of the complementary nature in financial services industries include card payments, where the inputs include networks of Automatic Teller Machines (ATMs) or Point-of-Sales (POS) readers, the use of electronic networks to transmit the payment instructions, and the use of interbank clearing systems. Also in trading and financial markets, complementarities between inputs (trading, clearing, settlement, payment) are large. Most network industries are therefore still vertically integrated entities: telecommunication network operators are also service providers, and in gas and electricity industries long distance transmission companies are integrated into production and distribution. Railway companies and air transportation with booking services are other examples. This is true in financial services industries as well. Stock exchanges, for example, often not only provide trading services, but also back-office, clearing and settlement services, in addition to setting listing standards and monitoring insider trading. Furthermore, vertically integrated national or regional monopolies will often be controlled by the industry itself. In financial services, self-regulatory agencies control or oversee many activities or even own essential elements, like the mutual ownership structures prevalent until recently for stock exchanges.

Technological Progress

Factors that have reduced the extent of natural monopolies and which have changed the thinking about regulation in network industries have included pressures from potential competitors (like cable companies in telecommunication or from other financial markets). Governments also have sought ways to reduce expenditures on subsidies and raise revenue from the privatization of public enterprises, thereby spurring needs for new regulation. The main factor, however, has been technological progress. Technology has made it possible for some components in network industries to be efficiently produced at a smaller scale.[1] In finance, the scale at which one can efficiently provide services has greatly declined. Trading systems can now, as a manner of speaking, be bought off the shelf and an on-line-only bank or brokerage service can relatively easily be established (although not necessarily be made competitive or profitable). Technology has also made the usage of the existing network infrastructure more efficient by introducing new forms of transmission and by allowing the administering and accounting for the traffic on the network such that it can be used by more service providers in parallel. Many financial services can be provided over a common infrastructure as well as over public networks, although the marginal costs cannot always be easily identified and allocated.

Threats to Competition

When market power arises in some element essential for the operation of the network, bottlenecks can occur in the whole provision of a service. An unregulated, vertically integrated monopolist can extend its market power through limiting competitors' access to the monopolized segment. Denying access to infrastructure assets essential to compete on the final market and the duplication of which is very costly and inefficient, can foreclose competitors from the competitive segment(s). The payments system, for example, can be such an essential element affecting the production of many types of financial services. The larger banks may form a club in the payments system and keep competition limited by charging high access fees for small banks, as has happened in South Africa and elsewhere.[2]

Besides these so-called one-way access problems, two-way access problems can arise in an oligopoly situation (see Economides and White (1996)). An

---

[1] Digital switching and intelligent networking were a breakthrough in telecommunications. In the public utility sector (gas, electricity) generation became more efficient and possible at a smaller scale, as is the case in postal services (automated mail sorting).

[2] The Cruickshank (2000) report found such problems in the UK. It stated *there are real problems with the way banks control networks which allow money to flow around the economy, whether it be cheques, credit and debit cards, or electronic transfers, big and small.*

example is the mobile telecommunications industry where physical networks are by and large duplicated since the market allows for more operators. Because of positive externalities (and as subscribers behind physical networks cannot be multiplicated), networks have to be interconnected to provide quality services to consumers (about interconnection and competition see Laffont and Tirole (1996)). In financial services, interconnections between ATM networks are examples of these two-way access issues (McAndrews (1997)).

Regulatory Responses

Although for many services, vertically integrated monopoly structures have been unbundled, often the former monopolist remains vertically integrated, i.e., active in both the monopolistic and the competitive segments. To promote effective competition, regulation is thus often needed. To prevent foreclosure of competitors, access to the bottleneck infrastructure can be regulated. Rules may stipulate, for example, that no discrimination is allowed among external buyers and between external buyers (competitors) and the monopolist's own division. The former vertical structure may be subject to structural remedies, including divestiture of assets with line-of-business restrictions and obligations to share the monopoly asset. The 1984 break-up of AT&T in the US and the gas and electricity industries in the US and the UK are examples of such vertical break-ups. Examples of public policy intervention in financial services are the pressures in many countries on stock exchanges to give other trading systems access to parts of their network(s), or at least harmonize the information flows with other networks (Steil (2002)). Another example is the reform of pension markets in many countries around the world where private market participants have gained access to market segments and now offer retirement products that were previously offered only by the government. In the banking industry, market pressures have led to an increasing presence of portals offering a wide range of products that were previously offered only by banks.

6.3.2   Economies of Scope on the Supply Side

Vertical integration between firms can have several possible benefits: scope economies may be realized in terms of innovation, cost advantages, and learning-by-doing spillovers. It may also solve coordination problems, in quality of products or advertising. Integration may also alleviate moral hazard and mitigate hold-up problems by replacing incomplete long-term contracts between separate entities (vertical integration is nicely treated in Tirole (1988) and see Williamson (1981) and Grossman and Hart (1986) about contractual incompleteness). Quality of (intermediate) products is sometimes hard to ascertain due to information asymmetries. Reputation, for example, is generally very important in financial services and vertical integration can internalize this. But, vertical integration creates some of its own problems, including the leveraging of market power.

Leveraging of Market Power

A dominant firm on a market for a (real or virtual) network product (A) may benefit from being active on a complementary or adjacent product market (B) also exhibiting network externalities (see Rey, Seabright, and Tirole (2001) and Shapiro (1996) for further details). One example in the financial services industries is the ATM card that was introduced before the debit cards used for point-of-sale (POS) payments. A bank active in the payment business clearly has economies of scope as it does not need to issue any new cards and convince people to use this card, rather it can add a new function to its existing cards (see Allen, McAndrews, and Strahan (2002)). The bank thus has an advantage on market B from a distribution and reputation point of view. In addition, banks will often have some gains through tying formally or informally products (i.e., from consumer experience, reputation and favorable consumer expectations, better interoperability of A and B, or being the focal choice for its clients on market A). Banking products from the same financial institution, for example, may gain reputation spillovers from each other. Or insurance products may be tailored to a consumer's financing needs, e.g., a car insurance may be offered when a car loan has just been obtained. In the extreme, a financial firm can make the sales of one good conditional on the purchase of the other (i.e., engage in tying).

Policy Responses

As a policy response, antitrust authorities' task is to remedy those cases when competition is harmed through leveraging market power or tying. Examples are the responses to the strategy of Sony and Philips, who attempted to leverage their key role in the CD standard to the DVD standard, as DVD players are backward compatible with CDs. Another example where antitrust authorities took actions is Microsoft when it embedded a browser (Internet Explorer) and the protocol to its ISP into its operation system. In the financial sector, the MAC ATM network in the US explicitly tied membership for banks (network access) to complementary services (processing), which was declared illegal. Controlling the processing service, for which there was no alternative for a member, it refused to connect to rival regional ATM networks. This was brought out in the open through a merger between NYCE and Yankee 24 ATM-networks that contained a clause assuring the freedom of members to choose independent providers to ascertain competitively priced services to small banks. Another, ongoing case relates to credit cards. Visa is thought to have become successful because of pursuing an anticompetitive tying strategy by requiring its members to accept also debit cards whenever accepting credit cards (the "accept all cards" rule). These and other cases are discussed in Shapiro and Varian (1999) and Balto (2000).

6.3.3 Economies of Scale on the Demand Side

The basic characteristics of network goods on the demand side are: network externalities resulting from direct and indirect effects leading to positive feedback on the demand side; compatibility of networks; and the possibility of market tipping or coexistence of differentiated network products depending on consumer preferences. Related are issues of incentives to innovate and exclusivity arrangements. These characteristics have in turn triggered various policy responses.

Network Externalities

A positive network externality means that network users' utility increases when more users use the same or compatible product: adopters' utility is thus interdependent and their consumption of the network good is complementary. Accordingly, the value of a network increases if its size increases: additional adoption both makes existing users better off and increases the incentive to adopt (a marginal effect). Therefore customer decisions about which product or technology to adopt, i.e., which network to join, may be strongly affected by network size, besides quality and price (network externalities are described in Liebowitz and Margolis (1998)).

Direct and Indirect Network Externalities

In the telecommunications industry, network externalities are of direct nature: subscribers are directly affected by an increase in the size of their network since then new users can be immediately reached by the service. Conversely, all else equal, a new user is willing to join the largest network if there is a choice and assuming networks are not interconnected. Indirect network effects, also called market mediated effects, arise because a larger network makes members better off because it stimulates supply, leading to higher satisfaction for consumers. On the market for computers cum operating system, for example, a buyer won't have any immediate benefits if other consumers also buy computers. However, more computers means higher demand for software, leading to more entry and product differentiation (more variety), and generally prices closer to marginal cost. In this case and cases like video consoles, broadcasting, dating services, etc., indirect network externalities come from the fact that the two markets are complementary: software developers are interested in hardware owners and vice versa as sales on each market raise the other market's demand. Rochet and Tirole (2001b) and Jullien (2001) describe the sophisticated pricing practices in these industries. Rochet and Tirole (2001a) apply this framework specifically to payment card associations. Direct and indirect network effects are not mutually exclusive: for example, in mobile telecommunications direct effects are primary but indirect effects may also be present. As there are more subscribers, the market for handsets or mobile related services (wireless banking, WAP pages, information services, etc.) grows, allowing for more entrants providing such services and related equipment at lower prices, meaning indirect network effects. These direct and indirect network effects also exist for many financial services, such as stock markets, where existing liquidity can attract more liquidity as it increases the chances for order matching. More active stock markets can also increase the ability of firms to raise new financing as it stimulates the investment banking industry. It would also be true for payment cards if it were possible to make person-to-person payments using cards. This is not (yet) possible using regular cards but PayPal functioning as an intermediary is implementing it on the Internet. Another form of person-to-person payments being explored in some emerging markets is to transfer balances electronically between two pre-paid cellular phones. Both are examples of indirect and direct network externalities.

Positive Feedback

Production economies of scale and network effects (either direct or indirect) can both lead to positive feedback on the demand side. A firm having larger sales can produce at lower unit cost and therefore more consumers may choose its product. In addition, a product purchased by many consumers (a large network) is more attractive to consumers in case of positive network externalities. In turn, this means that in a market with strong positive feedback, a critical mass of adopters needs to exist in order for a new product or technology to be taken up and become sustainable (after reaching the critical mass more adoption will follow; for more details and further references see Economides (1996) and Farrell and Klemperer (2001). Claessens, Glaessner, and Klingebiel (2000) apply this critical mass property to the market for e-finance service (banking and brokerage) in a number of countries and show how network markets are inherently dynamic in their growth paths.

Compatibility

Complementarities – and hence network externalities – cannot be realized without compatibility. At the extreme, members of the same network have to be compatible with each other: two users have to use the same format for payment instructions in order to make payments and realize network gains. Software applications and an operation system or, in financial services industries, payment cards and card readers, have to be compatible (there are many examples where this is not the case). At the network level, compatibility means interconnection, enlarging the overall network size and hence network value, thereby also increasing demand for the network good or service. Since a large dominant network has fewer incentives for compatibility than a small network, policymakers may need to act. Compatibility is mostly based on standards. Standards can also help avoid coordination problems in firms' technology choice, and can help consumers forecast whether the specific technology will be widespread, leading to reduced uncertainty and less risk of consumer lock-in, and thereby avoid non-adoption (waiting). In several cases after the industry agreed on a common standard, the adoption of the good or service increased sharply. In financial services, one example has been the Society for Worldwide Interbank Financial Telecommunication (SWIFT) protocol for transacting international payments introduced in 1977 (see further Katz and Shapiro (1985), Farrell and Saloner (1985, 1992), and Shy (2001)). Besides increasing demand, compatibility can level the playing field between large and small suppliers, i.e., make competition more symmetrical in this dimension.

Market Tipping

Positive feedback may be strong enough to lead to market tipping. Most consumers may choose to belong to the same network, which itself may depend on initial first mover advantages, and the market may tip in favor of one network incompatible with other networks. The battle of the two 56K modem technologies, VHS (vs. Betamax) or DVD (vs. DIVX) are other examples (Gandal (2002) and especially Dranove and Gandal (2001) provide more analysis of critical mass and tipping). Tipping in financial services occurs, for example, in trading systems where there are agglomeration advantages of concentration in liquidity. Some stock exchanges maintain large market shares despite having outdated trading systems (e.g., the New York stock exchange). In credit card markets, the VISA and MasterCard networks are able to maintain an 85 percent market share, despite fierce competition from others. The important policy aspect is that it is not necessarily the firm, service or product providing the highest quality that becomes dominant. Of course, if preferences are sufficiently heterogeneous and if there is sufficient demand for the diversity, several differentiated network products can coexist provided that all of them can eventually achieve critical mass. There are, for example, different types of trading systems for stocks: in the US, besides NYSE and AMEX, there exist ECNs like Archipelago, Instinet, and Tradepoint. These trading systems vary not only in prices offered, but also in other service dimensions, such as transparency, speed, reliability, etc. (see further Steil (2002)). With heterogeneous consumers, these multiple and somewhat incompatible trading systems can coexist. Incompatible networks do not necessarily cause antitrust problems. If the demand for variety is strong enough, or network externalities are weak and/or product differentiation is high, more than one network may coexist and compete. Nevertheless, both market tipping and too many networks can lead to economically inefficient outcomes. Establishing compatibility standards in some dimensions can mitigate these. For trading systems, for example, concerns about fragmentation of order flows and reduced price discovery has led policymakers to require some forms of price disclosure and transparency across trading systems.

Incentives to Innovate

Imposing full compatibility (or open standards) can increase demand, facilitate entry and may increase competition between products on a more symmetrical basis. There can be a trade-off, however, between compatibility and incentives to innovate and invest in networks. Compatibility may result in free-riding on investments in R&D and innovation, destroying incentives to invest in and develop networks. As a result, too little investment or innovation will take place. This lack of new investment and innovation has been a concern in some securities markets. Many stock exchanges used to be mutually owned by commercial and investment banks and brokers. This mutual structure helped in setting standards and rules, thus achieving compatibility, but also led to national monopolies. The conversion of mutually owned stock exchanges for profit exchanges in many countries has, in part, been considered a way to stimulate innovation as it enhances competition and allows more scope and incentives to innovate.

Exclusivity Agreements

If a network has some advantage over competing networks, a network operator may enter into exclusivity contracts. Network members are then forced to make a choice since joining more than one network is ruled out by contract. Exclusivity arrangements can lead to the predominance of a large network, even when more, differentiated networks could proliferate. At the extreme, a rival may have to leave the market if it fails to maintain critical mass. Exclusivity arrangements, however, can limit product diversity. In the payment card case, for example, a bank may want to be a member of networks of differentiated cards motivated by the willingness to increase product diversity (card types) for consumers or card acquisition for merchants. Although there is business for more networks, exclusivity arrangements of the dominant networks may limit this.

Public Policy Responses

The various demand-side issues arising with networks have triggered some policy responses. We describe the possible policy responses to the different market failures and competition problems enumerated above.

Enhancing Coordination in Adoption

If a critical mass is achieved and the product (maybe standardized) is adopted, then a network may proliferate. Since network externalities are not internalized, however, private incentives to adopt a new technology can be lower than socially desirable. Differences in income and preferences may further slow adoption as some consumers find it privately optimal not to adopt the technology even if others do so. The under-adoption or dynamically too slow adoption will be costly if the marginal social value rises when the network is closer to full coverage, such as with access to basic telephone services or banking services. Full coverage may also be necessary to introduce new services, like public communications using the Internet (see further Crémer (2000)). As a public policy response to under-adoption, the government may adopt the technology first, contributing to the achievement of critical mass and perhaps strengthening expectations of the feasibility of the technology.

There is of course no guarantee that the government evaluates the technology the same way the market does, leading to the risk of promoting an inferior technology. In the 1950s the US Federal Communication Commission (FCC) adopted a color television system that was incompatible with the existing black and white program diffusion. The market rejected the standard and the FCC then accepted a rival compatible standard. An example of trying to reach a critical mass in financial services industries are pre-paid cards, which in many countries have been stimulated by converting parking meters and other coin-operated vending machines and telephones to accept only those cards (as on university campuses or office headquarters). Shapiro and Varian (1999) provide several other examples of successful and unsuccessful cases. One other way to avoid under-adoption is through coordination on standards. Cooperation on standards setting is generally tolerated by competition authorities as long as it does not go beyond coordination on technology: price (or quantity) agreements remain illegal. Public policy can help standardization, for example, by establishing an indicative standard as a starting point for negotiations. Examples in financial services include listing and disclosure standards and even some prudential standards. Again, governments will face many trade-offs here, including between stimulating competition, not favoring incumbents, and achieving critical mass with the best technology.

Alleviating Market Tipping

A government can promote competition by directly imposing compatibility or giving the rights to entrants to unilaterally establish compatibility. Often access to or being able to use an established standard may be of key importance to competition. In such cases, the competition law may overrule copyright protection, for example, by allowing for reverse engineering the incumbent's software code that is patented as intellectual property and not given out to entrants (incompatibility). In financial services, the interconnections among Automatic Teller Machine (ATM) networks provide an interesting example. After the first installation in 1969 in the US, ATM networks began to proliferate in the 1970s as proprietary networks (McAndrews (1991)). Banks soon realized that sharing their ATM networks was advantageous as it provided better quality services to customers, which further increased demand for ATM services, and as fixed costs were spread over more transactions per machine. Successful regional networks were started as proprietary networks, some of which became national, like Plus, Cirrus and Southeast Switch. The national expansion was helped by a 1984 legal decision that considered ATM machines as non-branch facilities, avoiding cross-state branching restrictions. Over this period, interconnection in the US mainly took place through private sharing agreements and no actions by a central authority were needed. Besides the increase in demand, ATM network operators were also exposed to fiercer price competition that may have helped spur interconnection. But the private solution to network interconnectivity does not always occur. Interac, the dominant Canadian ATM network refused to interconnect with competing network members. The court forced Interac to let nonmember banks interconnect with its network. Nor are the policy prescriptions to achieve interconnection obvious. Some states in the US required networks to let in any bank seeking membership, but this can be insufficient for full compatibility and does not necessarily lead to full sharing. And while mandatory-sharing rules can lead to full compatibility, they may lessen incentives to develop networks. Laderman (1990) provides some evidence that mandatory sharing delayed the introduction of ATM services and decreased ATM card proliferation. Moreover, neither access nor sharing legislation removes the possibility of incumbents deterring future entry. Nor is fierce competition necessarily good for interconnectivity. In some countries in Europe (Netherlands, France, Belgium), full interconnection of competing banks occurred under what appeared to be collusive banking systems (see Matutes and Padilla (1994)). As sharing agreements imply fiercer competition, banks may also engage in efforts to avoid sharing. Anticompetitive practices in payments system include predatory pricing below marginal cost, too high surcharges and interconnection fees leading to de facto incompatibility, discriminatory access against specific institution-types and exclusive access to potential members, including forbidding simultaneous membership. This can give rise to antitrust challenges, as happened in the case of the ATM-networks Cirrus and Plus (McAndrews (1991) and Balto (2000)). Antitrust actions can also involve the blocking of large horizontal mergers that would create a dominant network operator (see the rejection of the MCI-WorldCom merger by the competition authority in the EU, and Crémer, Rey, and Tirole (2000) for the underlying theory).

Restoring Incentives to Innovate

Often there will be a trade-off between interconnectivity and incentives to innovate and invest. While compatible and large ATMs networks, for example, allow for better services, they can reduce incentives to invest. In strongly asymmetric ATM networks, for example, discrimination between networks through interconnection charges can be a way to keep interconnection but still allow for incentives to invest in networks (McAndrews (1997)). Evidence regarding ATM network surcharges in the US shows that in those states where interchange fees are not allowed or compulsory sharing legislation is in place, the ATM business developed slower. At the same time, too high interchange fees means incompatibility, leading to non-price competition and possibly over-deployment. In other situations, a properly chosen interconnection fee may act as a collusion device (e.g., wireless networks; see Laffont, Rey, and Tirole (1998)). Hence, not only the access rules, but also the terms of interconnection (e.g., level and structure of interchange fees) can fall under antitrust scrutiny, especially for large networks in dominant positions, to balance the trade-offs.

Dealing with Exclusivity Agreements

Networks with indirect network externalities, such as ATM networks, video game systems or software, are prominent examples of industries with exclusivity agreements. The MAC regional ATM network prohibited its members from participating in rival networks, which contributed to its success since rival networks (e.g., NYCE) could not enter where MAC was a dominant network. Competition offices mostly consider exclusivity agreements, either explicit or implicit, illegal. The FTC indeed required MAC to drop this rule. MAC then, however, practiced exclusivity through tying. Another example is payment cards. The payment card industry includes credit cards, debit cards and charge (or stored value) cards (see Bank of International Settlements (1999) for definitions). While different in terms of underlying technology, pricing schemes and services, these cards are similar in their cash substitute function. Alternatively, payment cards can be seen as bundles of different services like ATM cash withdrawal and payment service at point-of-sale (POS) terminals. Network effects have given rise to the formation of payment cards associations. Larger POS networks are more valuable to both cardholders and merchants. This leads to some competition policy issues, for which in the financial services industries credit cards provide an interesting example. Credit cards come in two forms: under a common brand name, mainly Visa and Mastercard (85% of the market), or from closed, proprietary systems, such as AmEx, and Diners' Club. Payment card associations are self-regulating organizations, providing the necessary infrastructure for transactions and interconnection (servers and (international) backbone clearance network, identification and authorization with agreed upon technology standards). Associations have agreed upon operation rules. Both Visa and MasterCard require exclusivity, i.e., members cannot join rival networks, which hinders competition. This rule was challenged and declared illegal in the EU. Additionally, unlike in proprietary systems, Visa and MasterCard require that the interchange fee is paid by the acquirer bank to the issuer bank, that all branded payment cards must be accepted (the "honor all cards" rule, which is a form of tying), and that card and cash payers pay the same price for the good (the "no surcharge" rule). These additional requirements can also have competitive effects that are widely being debated (see Rochet and Tirole (2001a, 2001b), Balto (2000), and the debates over the recent regulation of associations in Australia).

Universal Service Obligation (USO)

For a number of reasons, including the adoption of technology, access to some consumers may be required, and thus subsidized, through USO. Examples are universal service in basic telecommunication and postal services that are in place in almost every country. An example in financial services is the subsidized check payment system in the US, UK and other countries, and the Community Reinvestment Act in the US, requiring banks to establish branches in disadvantaged areas. The risk of USO is possible lock-in to a technology that may soon become obsolete and monopoly rents in exchange for providing universal service (as has happened in telecommunication where incumbent fixed-line providers often still have large privileges). In many developing countries, (state-owned) banks derive some political values from having large networks of branches. Furthermore, and especially with liberalization and new technology being introduced, it is not trivial to implement these objectives: who provides universal services and how costs are allocated are difficult questions to answer (see Laffont and Tirole (1993)).

6.4 Implications for Competition Policy in the Financial Sector

The removal of barriers between markets and products and the technological gains have generally led to more competition in financial services. As a result, the financial services industry has become much more competitive in many segments, both through new entrants and from already existing entities operating more efficiently. At the same time, the increasing importance of network effects in financial services may hamper competition. This calls for a review of the competition policy approach in financial services industries which, due to the perceived special nature of banks, has not been well articulated.

The Existing Competition Paradigm in Financial Services

The limited development of competition policy for financial services arises largely from the so-called "special" character of banks, and the associated argued need for a safety net and prudential regulation. The domination of prudential regulation and supervision over competition in the policy agenda has led many countries, for example, to restrict entry to preserve franchise value for incumbents; or the payments system may not be open to all types of financial and non-financial institutions. The link between competition and prudential regulation can even be institutionalized, such as when competition policy is explicitly delegated to the supervisory agency. More generally, entry as well as exit has often been influenced by the systemic aspects of banking. This is starting to change. The changes in the financial services industries and advances in technology are eroding the special nature of banks. Many substitutes for bank deposit and loan products are emerging and the proprietary information that banks had on their borrowers is becoming cheaper and more widely available. As banks as deposit-taking and lending institutions are becoming less important to financial intermediation and financial sector stability, the arguments in favor of measures to preserve the franchise value of existing financial institutions are losing validity, creating a window of opportunity for reviewing competition policy. Not only will competition policy for financial services become more feasible with a decreasing need to preserve the franchise value of incumbents for stability, but competition policy will also become more necessary given the increasing importance of network effects in financial services. As a consequence, the current paradigm for financial sector regulation needs to be reviewed to allow competition policy to be applied more effectively to financial services. Even with a revision in the regulation paradigm, however, it will not be easy to implement competition policy in the financial sector. Currently, countries mostly use a mixture of an institutional and functional approach for competition policy in financial services. In what follows, we will review these existing approaches and argue that a third approach, the production approach, will become of increasing importance in light of the growing importance of network aspects in financial services.

Institutional Approach to Competition Policy

The institutional approach to competition means that the entry and exit regime for different types of financial institutions should be pro-competitive, or at least as contestable as possible given stability issues. This approach is generally accepted. Evidence also suggests that more contestable financial systems have better performance, are more efficient, have better quality financial services and can lead to a wider extension of and greater access to financial services (Claessens and Jansen (2000)). More competitive systems can also be more stable, provided entry involves a diversified set of institutions. As in other sectors, the institutional approach in the financial sector involves, among others, a review of mergers, investigations of market power and dominance of institutions, and review of entry barriers on a market, regional, country, or global level. There are both conceptual issues (e.g., what is the exact need to balance competition with preserving a certain franchise value for some types of financial institutions to invest in information acquisition), and many implementation problems (e.g., how to balance free cross-border provision with adequate enforcement and consumer protection) with this approach, but it is the most common approach used.

Functional Approach to Competition Policy

The functional approach uses the same concept of contestable markets, except it applies it to the services, rather than to the institutions. There is general evidence that the functions of finance rather than the exact institutional form through which services are being delivered (e.g., banks versus stock markets) are the most important for access, growth and stability (Demirgüç-Kunt and Levine (2001)). The functional approach implies a need to level the playing field across providers for each financial service and across similar types of financial services. It means a proper entry and exit regime for each financial service and avoiding differences in the regulatory treatment of similar financial services.

Few countries have adopted this approach. Even when tried in earnest, however, the principle of a level playing field across functions is difficult to put into practice. One reason is that the substitutability between specific financial services can be high in many dimensions, but involves subtle differences in some dimensions, such as credit risks or access to the safety net. Whether remaining differences are distortionary will often be difficult to establish. Furthermore, historical differences can be difficult to correct. For example, differences in the tax treatment between pension and other forms of savings can be large, although they are in many ways equivalent.

Even when attempts have been made to level the playing field for financial service providers and across financial services, regulatory and other differences may continue to create barriers to full competition. Standards may conflict, for example, such as the need to require capital for local branches of foreign banks, but not for branches of domestic banks. Information requirements may differ by product, although otherwise similar, securities markets products may require more information disclosure than pension products.

Even when distortions in treatment across products have been minimized, however, it will be difficult to assess whether markets for specific financial products are fully competitive. One reason is that financial institutions typically bundle financial services together and/or cross-subsidize services. This can be because financial institutions derive their comparative advantage from the bundle of services they provide, rather than from any specific individual service. But, it may also be because regulatory or other advantages allow the financial institution to provide the bundle of services in a way more advantageous than a single service provider. The leveraging of regulatory power is very important for banks. Differences in access to the safety net or different supervisory approaches may, for example, lead to differences in the net regulatory burden in one service, which are then spread over other services. Open entry in one market segment may as a consequence not guarantee a competitive market for that specific product. Or it can be that predatory cross-subsidization in the presence of natural entry barriers gives existing institutions an unfair advantage, allowing them to build up a market share. More generally, given the network properties analyzed, it is difficult to ascertain that there are no anti-competitive barriers remaining. It may therefore be necessary to go beyond the institutional and functional approaches with a more production-based approach.

Production Approach to Competition Policy

The production approach means that the various inputs, including network services, required for the production and distribution of financial services need to be available to all interested in using them, be fairly priced and efficiently provided. For no part of a specific financial service production and distribution chain, should there be any barriers or unfair pricing. For most inputs (labor, services, etc.), this in turn requires simply competitive supply markets. Since the production and distribution of financial services rely much on common infrastructure with network properties, however, this approach requires more. Specifically, it requires an "efficient" market infrastructure, which itself is not an easily defined concept, in part because many elements of financial infrastructure have been subject to changes recently. As noted, the market infrastructure for financial services involves many parts, such as trading systems, payment and clearing systems, ATM systems, and information systems. Differences are many, but competition policy centers around access, ownership (public versus private), and forms of control, oversight, and corporate governance. The commonly shared infrastructure of payments systems, for example, can be run by central banks, by banks themselves, or by a third party. Choices further vary between for-profit versus not-for-profit organizations, and related, mutual versus demutualized structures. Stock exchanges, for example, can be organized as mutual, not-for-profit organizations or as for-profit corporations. The design and balance of various oversight structures (self-regulatory, government or purely private arrangements) can correspondingly vary by setup, explicit design or consequence. For example, the incentive structures of participants for self-regulation will vary by market structure. The trend recently has been towards the privatization and separation of the various parts of the financial market infrastructure, e.g., the demutualization of stock exchanges, and the separation and privatization of central counterpart, clearing and settlement functions. Parallel to this trend, oversight functions have tended to be placed more with government agencies. Technology has also altered the definition of the elements of a marketplace and the infrastructure supporting financial services provision. The Internet, for example, allows for the rapid construction of electronic-based infrastructure, either closed or open, including front-end trading systems and back-end settlement systems. With it has come its own set of governance issues, including who has control over whom is granted access to some private marketplace. For many of the new trading systems, there is no obvious regulatory authority which has jurisdiction over any restrictive practices, besides possibly a general competition policy agency at a national level. The dimensions according to which one can evaluate the various arrangements for the provision of market infrastructure services and the recent changes, are multiple, with competition being only one of them. The efficiency of providing relevant (supportive) services, risk dimensions, integrity, incentives to innovate and upgrade, are relevant as well. The general assessment is that the trend toward demutualization and privatization of stock markets, for example, has led to efficiency gains in the delivery of these services, without necessarily compromising (and often even enhancing) the objectives of proper risk management, integrity, and stability. But whether they are also always pro-competitive is not clear, at least not as yet. Similar lack of clarity exists with respect to the new alternative trading systems. More generally, the competition policies applicable to the new forms of financial services are not yet clear.

6.5   Concluding Remarks

Financial services industries around the world have been undergoing rapid changes fostered by globalization and technological advances, including the emergence of e-finance and resulting in increased importance of networks in the production and distribution of financial services. As part of these changes, financial services are becoming less special, making policies to preserve the franchise value of financial institutions less necessary while competition policy becomes more feasible. As financial services heavily and increasingly depend on networks for their production and distribution, competition policy for financial services becomes more necessary and will need to resemble that used in other network industries, such as telecommunications. This means the institutional and functional approaches to competition need to be complemented with more production-based approaches to competition in the financial sector. This means that the various inputs, including network services required for the production and distribution chain need to be available to all parties interested in using them, be fairly priced and efficiently provided. This approach also requires an efficient financial market infrastructure. As of yet, there is no consensus on what are the optimal arrangements for the provision of market infrastructure services. More generally, while this chapter made some initial suggestions as to how competition policy could be changed in the financial sector, more work is needed to improve our understanding of how to better implement competition policy in the financial sector. As we have argued in this chapter, such a revision is feasible given the recent changes in the financial services industry and important given the increasing use of networks in this industry. This window of opportunity should not be missed by researchers and policymakers.

Acknowledgments

We would like to thank Jerry Caprio and the reviewer for useful comments. Opinions do not represent necessarily official World Bank policy.

References

Allen, F., McAndrews, J., and Strahan, P. (2002), "E-finance: An Introduction," *Journal of Financial Services Research* **22**, 5-27.

Balto, D. A. (2000), "Creating a Payment System Network: The Tie that Binds or an Honorable Peace?" *The Business Lawyer* **55**, 1391-1408.

Bank of International Settlements (1999), "Retail Payments in Selected Countries: A Comparative Study," BIS – Committee on Payment and Settlement Systems.

Claessens, S. (2003), "Benefits and Costs of Integrated Financial Services Provision," forthcoming in R. E. Litan and R. Herring, editors, Brookings-Wharton Papers on Financial Services 2002, The Brookings Institution, Washington DC.

Claessens, S., Glaessner, T., and Klingebiel, D. (2000), "Electronic Finance: Reshaping the Financial Landscape around the World," Financial Sector Discussion Paper No. 4, The World Bank, Washington DC.

Claessens, S., and Jansen, M., editors (2000), *Internationalization of Financial Services*, Kluwer Publishers, The Hague and Boston, Massachusetts.

Crémer, J. (2000), "Network Externalities and Universal Service Obligation in the Internet," *European Economic Review* **44**, 1021-1031.

Crémer, J., Rey, P., and Tirole, J. (2000), "Connectivity in the Commercial Internet," *Journal of Industrial Economics* **48**, 433-472.

Cruickshank, D. (2000), "Competition in UK Banking: A Report to the Chancellor of the Exchequer," March 20 England

Demirgüç-Kunt, A., and Levine, R., editors (2001), *Financial Structure and Economic Growth: A Cross-Country Comparison of Banks, Markets, and Development*, MIT Press, Cambridge, Massachusetts.

Dranove, D., and Gandal, N. (2001), "The DVD vs. DIVX Standard War. Network Effects and Empirical Evidence of Preannouncement Effects," forthcoming in *The Journal of Economics & Management Strategy*.

Economides, N. (1996), "The Economics of Networks," *International Journal of Industrial Organization* **14**, 673-699.

Economides, N., and White, L. J. (1996), "One-Way Networks, Two-Way Networks, Compatibility and Antitrust," in *Opening Networks to Competition: The Regulation and Pricing of Access*, D. Gabel and D. Weiman, editors, Kluwer Academic Press, Dordrecht, The Netherlands.

European Commission (1999), "Liberalization of Network Industries: Economic Implications and Main Policy Issues," Directorate General for Economic and Financial Affairs – Reports and Studies No. **4**.

Farrell, J., and Klemperer, P. (2001), "Coordination and Lock-In: Competition with Switching Costs and Network Effects," preliminary draft chapter for *The Handbook of Industrial Organization*, Volume **3**.

Farrell, J., and Saloner, G. (1985), "Standardization, Compatibility and Innovation," *RAND Journal of Economics* **16**, 70-83.

Farrell, J., and Saloner, G. (1992), "Converters, Compatibility, and the Control of Interfaces," *Journal of Industrial Economics* **40**, 9-35.

G-10 (2001), "Report on Consolidation in Financial Sector," Bank for International Settlements: Basel, Switzerland, January.

Gandal, N. (2002), "Compatibility, Standardization, and Network Effects: Some Policy Implications," *Oxford Review of Economic Policy* **18**, 80-91.

Grossman, S., and Hart, O. (1986), "The Costs and Benefits of Ownership: A Theory of Lateral and Vertical Integration," *Journal of Political Economy* **94**, 691-719.

Jappelli, T., and Pagano, M. (2000), "Information Sharing in Credit Markets: A Survey," Centre for Studies in Economics and Finance (CSEF) Working Paper, No. 36, University of Salerno, Italy.

Jullien, B. (2001), "Competing in Network Industries: Divide and Conquer," Institut d'Economie Industrielle (IDEI), Université de Toulouse 1 Sciences Sociales, France.

Katz, M., and Shapiro, C. (1985), "Network Externalities, Competition and Compatibility," *American Economic Review* **75**, 424-440.

Laderman, E. (1990), "The Public Policy Implications of State Laws Pertaining to Automated Teller Machines," *Federal Reserve Bank of San Francisco Economic Review* **1**, 43-58.

Laffont, J.-J., Rey, P., and Tirole, J. (1998), "Network Competition: I. Overview and Non-Discriminatory Pricing," *RAND Journal of Economics* **29**, 1-37.

Laffont, J.-J., and Tirole, J. (1993), *A Theory of Incentives in Procurement and Regulation*, MIT Press, Cambridge, Massachusetts.

Laffont, J.-J., and Tirole, J. (1996), "Creating Competition through Interconnection: Theory and Practice," *Journal of Regulatory Economics* **10**, 227-256.

Liebowitz, S. J., and Margolis, S. E. (1998), "Network Externalities," in *The New Palgrave Dictionary of Economics and the Law*, Palgrave/St Martin's Press, London, England.

Matutes, C., and Padilla, J. (1994), "Shared ATM Networks and Banking Competition," *European Economic Review* **38**, 1113-1138.

McAndrews, J. (1991), "The Evolution of Shared ATM Networks," *Federal Reserve Bank of Philadelphia Business Review*, 3-16.

McAndrews, J. J. (1997), "Network Issues and Payment Systems," *Federal Reserve Bank of Philadelphia Business Review*, 15-25.

Online Banking Report (2002), "Online Banking by the Numbers 2003," Online Banking Report, Seattle, Washington.

Rey, P., Seabright, P., and Tirole, J. (2001), "The Activities of a Monopoly Firm in Adjacent Competitive Markets: Economic Consequences and Implications to Competition Policy," Institute d'Economie Industrielle (IDEI), Université de Toulouse 1 Sciences Sociales, France.

Rochet, J.-C., and Tirole, J. (2001a), "Cooperation among Competitors: Some Economics of Payment Card Networks," Institut d'Economie Industrielle (IDEI), Université de Toulouse 1, France.

Rochet, J.-C., and Tirole, J. (2001b), "Platform Competition in Two-Sided Markets," Institut d'Economie Industrielle (IDEI), Université de Toulouse 1, France.

Shapiro, C. (1996), "Antitrust in Network Industries," Department of Justice, Stouffer Stanford Court Hotel, San Francisco, California;
http://www.usdoj.gov/atr/public/speeches/shapir.mar.htm.

Shapiro, C., and Varian, H. R. (1999), *Information Rules*, Harvard Business School Press, Boston, Massachusetts.

Shy, O. (2001), "The Economics of Network Industries," Cambridge University Press, Cambridge, England.

Steil, B. (2002), "Changes in the Ownership and Governance of Securities Exchanges: Causes and Consequences," in Brookings-Wharton Papers on Financial Services, R. E. Litan and R. Herring, editors, Brookings Institution Press, Washington DC.

Tirole, J. (1988), *The Theory of Industrial Organization*, MIT Press, Cambridge, Massachusetts.

Williamson, O. E. (1981), "The Modern Corporation: Origins, Evolution, Attributes," *Journal of Economic Literature* **19**, 1537-1568.

7 International Financial Networks with Electronic Transactions

Anna Nagurney and Jose Cruz

7.1 Introduction

The landscape for financial decision-making has been transformed through advances in telecommunications and, in particular, the Internet. Indeed, the adoption of the Internet by businesses, consumers, as well as financial institutions from brokerages to banks has had an immense effect on financial services and the options as well as the means of transaction. New types of products and services have been introduced, new distribution channels made available, and the role of financial intermediaries altered in this new networked economy.

Importantly, the growth of technology has allowed consumers and businesses to explore and conduct their financial transactions not only within the confines of national boundaries but outside as well. In addition, new currencies such as the euro have been introduced, and new financial products in different currencies and countries. The wealth of choices available for financial transactions in the international arena plus the number of different decision-makers involved, be they sources of financial funds, intermediaries, and/or, ultimately, the consumers of the various financial products, raise major challenges and opportunities for modeling, analysis, and computation.

In this chapter, we focus on *financial networks* and develop an international financial network model which includes intermediaries and also allows for the decision-makers to transact either physically or electronically. The framework that we propose predicts the equilibrium financial flows between tiers of the international financial network as well as the equilibrium prices associated with the different tiers. It is sufficiently general to be able to handle as many countries, sources of funds, currencies, and financial products as mandated by the particular application. Although the topic of electronic finance, in general, has received much attention lately (cf. McAndrews and Stefanidis (2000), Claessens, Glaessner, and Klingebiel (2000, 2001), Economides (2001), Allen, Hawkins, and Sato (2001), Sato and Hawkins (2001), Banks (2001), Claessens et al. (2003), and the references therein), there has been very little work in the modeling, analysis, and solution of such problems, except for that due to Nagurney and Ke (2003) who focused, however, on single country modeling. Fan, Stallaert, and Whinston (2000) have recognized and argued for the necessity of including financial intermediaries in any formal study of electronic finance.

Financial networks date to the work of Quesnay (1758) who introduced a graph to formulate the circular flow of financial funds in the economy. Since that conceptualization, financial flow of funds accounts (cf. Board of Governors (1980), Cohen (1987), and Nagurney and Hughes (1992)) have been utilized to statistically describe the flows of money and credit in an economy, albeit in matrix form. Thore (1980) recognized some of the shortcomings of such accounts and developed network models of linked portfolios with intermediation and proposed their solution using decentralization/decomposition theory. Nagurney, Dong, and Hughes (1992), in turn, developed a multisector, multi-instrument financial equilibrium model and recognized the network structure in both the formulation and computation of the equilibrium flows. Their approach was based on finite-dimensional variational inequality theory. Since that contribution both single and international financial network equilibrium models have been proposed (cf. Nagurney and Siokos (1997) and the references therein).

More recently, financial networks have been utilized to develop general models with multiple tiers of decision-makers by Nagurney and Ke (2001, 2003) and Nagurney and Cruz (2002). These models differ from the financial network models described in Nagurney and Siokos (1997) in that the behavior of the individual decision-makers associated with the distinct tiers of the network is explicitly captured and modeled. In particular, source agents as well as intermediaries are assumed to be both risk minimizers as well as net revenue maximizers. Consumers, on the other hand, seek to minimize costs, with all decision-makers being subject to transaction costs. Moreover, unlike the framework considered in Thore (1980), more general, including nonlinear and asymmetric functions can be handled.

This chapter is organized as follows. In Section 7.2, we develop the international financial network model. It extends the network model of Nagurney and Cruz (2002) through the explicit incorporation of electronic transactions and that of Nagurney and Ke (2003) by considering an international economy. We describe the various decision-makers and their behaviors, and construct the equilibrium conditions, along with the variational inequality formulation. In Section 7.3, we derive, under appropriate assumptions, qualitative properties of the equilibrium pattern, notably, the existence and uniqueness of a solution to the governing variational inequality. We also establish properties of the function that enters the variational inequality needed for proving convergence of the algorithmic scheme. In Section 7.4, we present the algorithm, which is then applied in Section 7.5 to several international financial network examples. We conclude the chapter with a summary and discussion in Section 7.6.

7.2   The International Financial Network Model

In this section, we develop the international financial network model with electronic transactions. The model consists of L countries, with a typical country denoted by l or $\hat{l}$; I "source" agents in each country with sources of funds, with a typical source agent denoted by i, and J financial intermediaries with a typical financial intermediary denoted by j. Examples of source agents include households and businesses, whereas examples of financial intermediaries include banks, insurance companies, investment companies, brokers, including electronic brokers, etc.

We assume that each source agent can transact directly electronically with the consumers through the Internet and can also conduct his financial transactions with the intermediaries either physically or electronically in different currencies. There are H currencies in the international economy, with a typical currency being denoted by h. Also, we assume that there are K financial products which can be in distinct currencies and in different countries with a typical financial product (and associated with a demand market) being denoted by k. Hence, the financial intermediaries in the model, in addition to transacting with the source agents, also determine how to allocate the incoming financial resources among distinct uses, which are represented by the demand markets with a demand market corresponding to, for example, the market for real estate loans, household loans, or business loans, etc., which, as mentioned, can be associated with a distinct country and a distinct currency combination. We let m refer to a mode of transaction with $m = 1$ denoting a physical transaction and $m = 2$ denoting an electronic transaction via the Internet.

The international financial network with electronic transactions is now described and depicted graphically in Figure 7.1. The top tier of nodes consists of the agents in the different countries with sources of funds, with agent i in country l being referred to as agent il and associated with node il. There are, hence, IL top-tiered nodes in the network. The middle tier of nodes consists of the financial intermediaries (which need not be country-specific), with a typical intermediary j associated with node j in this (second) tier of nodes in the network. The bottom tier of nodes consists of the demand markets, with a typical demand market for product k in currency h and country $\hat{l}$ associated with node $kh\hat{l}$. There are, as depicted in Figure 7.1, J middle (or second) tiered nodes corresponding to the intermediaries and KHL bottom (or third) tiered nodes in the financial network. In addition, we add a node $J + 1$ to the middle tier of nodes in order to represent the possible non-investment (of a portion or all of the funds) by one or more of

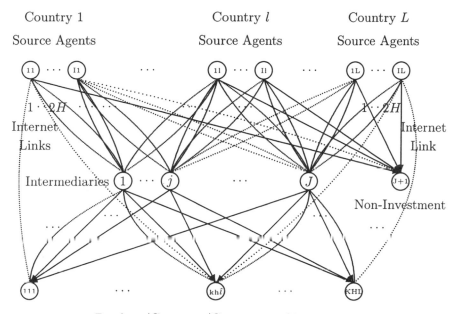

Product/Currency/Country combination

Fig. 7.1. International financial network with intermediaries and with electronic transactions (non-investment allowed)

the source agents.

Now that we have identified the nodes in the international financial network we turn to the identification of the links joining the nodes in a given tier with those in the next tier. We also associate the financial flows with the appropriate links. We assume that each agent i in country l has an amount of funds S^{il} available in a base currency. Since there are assumed to be H currencies and 2 modes of transaction (physical or electronic), there are $2H$ links joining each top tier node il with each middle tier node j; $j = 1, \ldots, J$, with the first H links representing physical transactions between a source and intermediary, and with corresponding flow on such a link given, respectively, by x^{il}_{jh1}, and the subsequent H links representing electronic transactions with the corresponding flow given, respectively, by x^{il}_{jh2}. Hence, x^{il}_{jh1} denotes the nonnegative amount invested (across all financial instruments) by source agent i in country l in currency h transacted through intermediary j using the physical mode whereas x^{il}_{jh2} denotes the analogue but for an electronic transaction. We group the financial flows for all source agents/intermediaries/modes into the column vector $x^1 \in R^{2ILJH}_+$. In addition, a source agent i in country l may transact directly with the consumers at demand market k in currency h and country $\hat{l}$ via an Internet link. The nonnegative flow on such a link joining node il with node $kh\hat{l}$ is denoted by $x^{il}_{kh\hat{l}}$. We group all such financial flows, in turn, into the column vector $x^2 \in R^{ILKHL}_+$. Also, we let x^{il} denote the $(2JH + KHL)$-dimensional column vector associated with source agent il with components:$\{x^{il}_{jhm}, x^{il}_{kh\hat{l}}; j = 1, \ldots, J; h = 1, \ldots, H; m = 1, 2; k = 1, \ldots, K; \hat{l} = 1, \ldots, L\}$. Furthermore, we construct a link from each top tiered node to the second tiered node $J + 1$ and associate a flow s^{il} on such a link emanating from node il to represent the possible nonnegative amount not invested by agent i in country l.

Each intermediary node j; $j = 1, \ldots, J$, may transact with a demand market via a physical link, and/or electronically via an Internet link. Hence, from each intermediary node j, we construct two links to each node $kh\hat{l}$, with the first such link denoting a physical transaction and the second such link - an electronic transaction. The corresponding flow, in turn, which is nonnegative, is denoted by $y^{j}_{kh\hat{l}m}$; $m = 1, 2$, and corresponds to the amount of the financial product k in currency h and country l transacted from intermediary j via mode m. We group the financial flows between node j and the bottom tier nodes into the column vector $y^j \in R^{2KHL}_+$. All such financial flows for all the intermediaries are then further grouped into the column vector $y \in R^{2JKHL}_+$.

The notation for the prices is now given. There will be prices associated with each of the tiers of nodes in the international financial network. The prices are assumed to be in the base currency. Let ρ^{il}_{1jhm} denote a price (in the base currency) associated with the financial instrument in currency h transacted via mode m as quoted by intermediary j to agent il and group the top tier prices into the column vector $\rho_1 \in R^{2ILJH}_+$. In addition, let $\rho^{il}_{1kh\hat{l}}$ denote a price, also in the base currency, associated with the financial instrument as quoted by demand market $kh\hat{l}$ to agent il and group these top tier prices into the column vector $\rho_{12} \in R^{ILKHL}_+$. Let $\rho^{j}_{2kh\hat{l}m}$, in turn, denote the price associated with intermediary j for product k in currency h and country $\hat{l}$ transacted via mode m and group all such prices into the column vector $\rho_2 \in R^{2JKHL}_+$. Also, let $\rho_{3kh\hat{l}}$ denote the price of the financial product k in currency h and in country $\hat{l}$, and defined in the base currency, and group all such prices into the column vector $\rho_3 \in R^{KHL}_+$. Finally, let e_h denote the rate of appreciation of currency h against the base currency, which can be interpreted as the rate of return earned due to exchange rate fluctuations (see Nagurney and Siokos (1997)). These "exchange" rates are grouped into the column vector $e \in R^H_+$.

We now turn to describing the behavior of the various decision-makers represented by the three tiers of nodes in Figure 7.1. We first focus on the top-tier decision-makers. We then turn to the intermediaries and, subsequently, to the consumers at the demand markets.

The Behavior of the Agents with Sources of Funds and their Optimality Conditions

We denote the transaction cost associated with source agent il transacting with intermediary j for the instrument in currency h via mode m by c_{jhm}^{il} (and measured in the base currency) and assume that:

$$c_{jhm}^{il} = c_{jhm}^{il}(x_{jhm}^{il}), \quad \forall i, l, j, h, m, \qquad (7.1a)$$

that is, the cost associated with source agent i in country l transacting with intermediary j for the instrument in currency h depends on the volume of the transaction. We denote the transaction cost associated with source agent il transacting with demand market k in country $\hat{l}$ for the instrument in currency h via the Internet link by $c_{kh\hat{l}}^{il}$ (and also measured in the base currency) and assume that:

$$c_{kh\hat{l}}^{il} = c_{kh\hat{l}}^{il}(x_{kh\hat{l}}^{il}), \quad \forall i, l, k, h, \hat{l}, \qquad (7.1b)$$

that is, the cost associated with source agent i in country l transacting with the consumers for product k in currency h and country $\hat{l}$. The transaction cost functions are assumed to be convex and continuously differentiable and depend on the volume of flow of the transaction.

The total transaction costs incurred by source agent il are equal to the sum of all of his transaction costs associated with dealing with the distinct intermediaries and demand markets in the different currencies. His revenue, in turn, is equal to the sum of the price (rate of return plus the rate of appreciation) that the agent can obtain for the financial instrument times the total quantity obtained/purchased of that instrument. Let now ρ_{1jhm}^{il*} denote the actual price charged agent il for the instrument in currency h by intermediary j by transacting via mode m and let $\rho_{1kh\hat{l}}^{il*}$, in turn, denote the price associated with source agent il transacting electronically with demand market $kh\hat{l}$. Similarly, let e_h^* denote the actual rate of appreciation in currency h. We later discuss how such prices are recovered.

We assume that each such source agent seeks to maximize his net return while, simultaneously, minimizing his risk, with source agent il's objective function denoted by U^{il}. In particular, we assume, as given, a risk function for sector il and denoted by r^{il}, such that

$$r^{il} = r^{il}(x^{il}), \quad \forall i, l, \qquad (7.2)$$

where r^{il} is assumed to be strictly convex and continuously differentiable. Clearly, a possible risk function could be constructed as follows. Assume a variance-covariance matrix Q^{il} associated with agent il, which is of dimension $(2JH + KHL) \times (2JH + KHL)$, symmetric, and positive definite. Then a possible risk function for source agent i in country l would be given by:

$$r^{il}(x^{il}) = x^{il^T} Q^{il} x^{il}, \quad \forall i, l. \qquad (7.3)$$

In such a case, one assumes that each source agent's uncertainty, or assessment of risk, is based on a variance-covariance matrix representing the source agent's assessment of the standard deviation of the prices of the financial instruments in the distinct currencies (see also Markowitz (1959)).

The optimization problem facing sector i in country l is, thus, given by:

$$
\text{Maximize} \quad U^{il}(x^{il}) = \sum_{j=1}^{J} \sum_{h=1}^{H} \sum_{m=1}^{2} (\rho_{1jhm}^{il*} + e_h^*) x_{jhm}^{il}
$$

$$
+ \sum_{k=1}^{K} \sum_{h=1}^{H} \sum_{\hat{l}=1}^{L} (\rho_{1kh\hat{l}}^{il*} + e_h^*) x_{kh\hat{l}}^{il}
$$

$$
- \sum_{j=1}^{J} \sum_{h=1}^{H} \sum_{m=1}^{2} c_{jhm}^{il}(x_{jhm}^{il}) - \sum_{k=1}^{K} \sum_{h=1}^{H} \sum_{\hat{l}=1}^{L} c_{kh\hat{l}}^{il}(x_{kh\hat{l}}^{il}) - r^{il}(x^{il}), \tag{7.4}
$$

subject to $x_{jhm}^{il} \geq 0$, $x_{kh\hat{l}}^{il} \geq 0$ for all $j, h, m, k, \hat{l}$, and to the constraint:

$$
\sum_{j=1}^{J} \sum_{h=1}^{H} \sum_{m=1}^{2} x_{jhm}^{il} + \sum_{k=1}^{K} \sum_{h=1}^{H} \sum_{\hat{l}=1}^{L} x_{kh\hat{l}}^{il} \leq S^{il}, \tag{7.5}
$$

that is, the allocations of source agent il's funds among those available from the different intermediaries in distinct currencies and demand markets cannot exceed his holdings. The first two terms in the objective function (7.4) denote the revenue whereas the third and fourth terms denotes the transaction costs and the last term denotes the risk. Note that the objective function given in (7.4) is strictly concave in the x^{il} variables. Note also that constraint (7.5) allows a source agent not to invest a portion (or all) of his funds, with the "slack," that is, the funds not invested by agent i in country l being given by s^{il}.

Optimality Conditions for All Source Agents

The optimality conditions of all source agents i; $i = 1, \ldots, I$; in all countries: l; $l = 1, \ldots, L$ (see also Bazaraa, Sherali, and Shetty (1993) and Bertsekas and Tsitsiklis (1989)), under the above stated assumptions on the underlying functions, can be expressed as: determine $(x^{1*}, x^{2*}) \in \mathcal{K}^1$, satisfying

$$
\sum_{i=1}^{I} \sum_{l=1}^{L} \sum_{j=1}^{J} \sum_{h=1}^{H} \sum_{m=1}^{2} \left[\frac{\partial r^{il}(x^{il*})}{\partial x_{jhm}^{il}} + \frac{\partial c_{jhm}^{il}(x_{jhm}^{il*})}{\partial x_{jhm}^{il}} - \rho_{1jhm}^{il*} - e_h^* \right]
$$

$$
\times \left[x_{jhm}^{il} - x_{jhm}^{il*} \right]
$$

$$
+ \sum_{i=1}^{I} \sum_{l=1}^{L} \sum_{k=1}^{K} \sum_{h=1}^{H} \sum_{\hat{l}=1}^{L} \left[\frac{\partial r^{il}(x^{il*})}{\partial x_{kh\hat{l}}^{il}} + \frac{\partial c_{kh\hat{l}}^{il}(x_{kh\hat{l}}^{il*})}{\partial x_{kh\hat{l}}^{il}} - \rho_{1kh\hat{l}}^{il*} - e_h^* \right]
$$

$$\times \left[x_{kh\hat{l}}^{il} - x_{kh\hat{l}}^{il*} \right] \geq 0, \quad \forall (x^1, x^2) \in \mathcal{K}^1, \tag{7.6}$$

where $\mathcal{K}^1 \equiv \{(x^1, x^2)|(x^1, x^2) \in R_+^{IL(2JH+KHL)}$ and satisfies $(7.5), \forall i, l\}$.

The Behavior of the Intermediaries and their Optimality Conditions

The intermediaries (cf. Figure 7.1), in turn, are involved in transactions both with the source agents in the different countries, as well as with the users of the funds, that is, with the ultimate consumers associated with the markets for the distinct types of loans/products in different currencies and countries and represented by the bottom tier of nodes of the network. Thus, an intermediary conducts transactions via a physical link, and/or electronically via an Internet link both with the "source" agents as well as with the consumers at the demand markets.

An intermediary j is faced with what we term a *handling/conversion* cost, which may include, for example, the cost of converting the incoming financial flows into the financial loans/products associated with the demand markets. We denote such a cost faced by intermediary j by c_j and, in the simplest case, c_j would be a function of $\sum_{i=1}^{I} \sum_{l=1}^{L} \sum_{h=1}^{H} \sum_{m=1}^{2} x_{jhm}^{il}$, that is, the holding/conversion cost of an intermediary is a function of how much he has obtained in the different currencies from the various source agents in the different countries. For the sake of generality, however, we allow the function to depend also on the amounts held by other intermediaries and, therefore, we may write:

$$c_j = c_j(x^1), \quad \forall j. \tag{7.7}$$

The intermediaries also have associated transaction costs in regards to transacting with the source agents, which can depend on the type of currency as well as the source agent. We denote the transaction cost associated with intermediary j transacting with agent il associated with currency h via mode m by $\hat{c}_{jhm}^{il}$ and we assume that it is of the form

$$\hat{c}_{jhm}^{il} = \hat{c}_{jhm}^{il}(x_{jhm}^{il}), \quad \forall i, l, j, h, m, \tag{7.8}$$

that is, such a transaction cost is allowed to depend on the amount allocated by the particular agent to the financial instrument in a currency and transacted with the particular intermediary via the particular mode. In addition, we assume that an intermediary j also incurs a transaction cost $c_{kh\hat{l}m}^{j}$ associated with transacting with demand market $kh\hat{l}$, where

$$c_{kh\hat{l}m}^{j} = c_{kh\hat{l}m}^{j}(y_{kh\hat{l}m}^{j}), \quad \forall j, k, h, \hat{l}, m. \tag{7.9}$$

Hence, the transaction costs given in (7.9) can vary according to the intermediary/product/currency/country combination and are a function of the volume of the product transacted. We assume that the cost functions (7.7) –

(7.9) are convex and continuously differentiable and that the costs are measured in the base currency.

The actual price charged for the financial products by the intermediaries is denoted by $\rho_{2kh\hat{l}m}^{j*}$, for intermediary j and associated with transacting with consumers for product k via mode m in currency h and country $\hat{l}$. Subsequently, we discuss how such prices are arrived at. We assume that the intermediaries are also objective function optimizers with the objective functions for each being comprised of net revenue maximization as well as risk minimization.

We assume that the intermediaries have risk associated both with transacting with the various source agents in the different countries and with the consumers for the products in the different currencies and countries, and which can also depend on the mode of transaction. Hence, we assume for each intermediary j a risk function r^j, which is strictly convex in its variables and continuously differentiable, and of the form:

$$r^j = r^j(x^1, y), \quad \forall j. \tag{7.10}$$

For example, the risk for intermediary j could be represented by a variance-covariance matrix denoted by Q^j with this matrix being positive definite and of dimensions $(2IL + 2KHL) \times (2IL + 2KHL)$ for each intermediary j. Such a matrix would reflect the risk associated with transacting with the various source agents in the different countries and with the consumers at the demand markets for the products in different currencies and in different countries. If we let x_j, without any loss in generality, denote the $2ILH$-dimensional column vector with the $ilhm$-th component given by x_{jhm}^{il}. Indeed, then a possible risk function for intermediary j could be represented by the function:

$$r^j(x^1, y) = \begin{bmatrix} x_j \\ y^j \end{bmatrix}^T Q^j \begin{bmatrix} x_j \\ y^j \end{bmatrix}. \tag{7.11}$$

Note that, for the sake of modeling generality and flexibility, we allow the risk function for an intermediary to depend not only on the financial flows flowing "into" and "out of" that intermediary but on the other financial flows as well. The risk function given by (7.11) is actually a special case of the one in (7.10) in that it depends only on the financial volumes that the particular intermediary actually deals with.

The optimization problem for intermediary j, with his objective function expressed by U^j, and assuming net revenue maximization and risk minimization can, hence, be expressed as:

$$\text{Maximize} \quad U^j(x_j, y^j) = \sum_{k=1}^{K} \sum_{h=1}^{H} \sum_{\hat{l}=1}^{L} \sum_{m=1}^{2} (\rho_{2kh\hat{l}m}^{j*} + e_h^*) y_{kh\hat{l}m}^j - c_j(x^1)$$

$$- \sum_{i=1}^{I} \sum_{l=1}^{L} \sum_{h=1}^{H} \sum_{m=1}^{2} \hat{c}_{jhm}^{il}(x_{jhm}^{il}) - \sum_{k=1}^{K} \sum_{h=1}^{H} \sum_{\hat{l}=1}^{L} \sum_{m=1}^{2} c_{kh\hat{l}m}^j(y_{kh\hat{l}m}^j)$$

$$-\sum_{i=1}^{I}\sum_{l=1}^{L}\sum_{h=1}^{H}\sum_{m=1}^{2}(\rho_{1jhm}^{il*}+e_h^*)x_{jhm}^{il}-r^j(x^1,y)\tag{7.12}$$

subject to: the nonnegativity constraints: $x_{jhm}^{il}\geq 0$, $y_{kh\hat{l}m}^{j}\geq 0$, for all $i,l,h,m,k,\hat{l}$, and

$$\sum_{k=1}^{K}\sum_{h=1}^{H}\sum_{\hat{l}=1}^{L}\sum_{m=1}^{2}y_{kh\hat{l}m}^{j}\leq\sum_{i=1}^{I}\sum_{l=1}^{L}\sum_{h=1}^{H}\sum_{m=1}^{2}x_{jhm}^{il}.\tag{7.13}$$

Objective function (7.12) expresses that the difference between the revenues (given by the first term) minus the handling cost, the two sets of transaction costs, and the payout to the source agents (given by the subsequent four terms, respectively) should be maximized, whereas the risk (see the last term in (7.12)) should be minimized. The objective function in (7.12) is concave in its variables under the above imposed assumptions.

Here we assume that the financial intermediaries can compete, with the governing optimality/equilibrium concept underlying noncooperative behavior being that of Nash (1950, 1951), which states that each decision-maker (intermediary) will determine his optimal strategies, given the optimal ones of his competitors. The optimality conditions for all financial intermediaries simultaneously, under the above stated assumptions, can be compactly expressed as (cf. Gabay and Moulin (1980), Dafermos and Nagurney (1987), and Nagurney and Ke (2001)): determine $(x^{1*},y^*,\gamma^*)\in R_+^{2ILJH+2JKHL+J}$, such that

$$\sum_{j=1}^{J}\sum_{i=1}^{I}\sum_{l=1}^{L}\sum_{h=1}^{H}\sum_{m=1}^{2}\left[\frac{\partial r^j(x^{1*},y^*)}{\partial x_{jhm}^{il}}+\frac{\partial c_j(x^{1*})}{\partial x_{jhm}^{il}}+\rho_{1jhm}^{il*}+e_h^*+\frac{\partial\hat{c}_{jhm}^{il}(x_{jhm}^{il*})}{\partial x_{jhm}^{il}}\right.$$

$$\left.-\gamma_j^*\right]\times\left[x_{jhm}^{il}-x_{jhm}^{il*}\right]$$

$$+\sum_{j=1}^{J}\sum_{k=1}^{K}\sum_{h=1}^{H}\sum_{\hat{l}=1}^{L}\sum_{m=1}^{2}\left[\frac{\partial r^j(x^{1*},y^*)}{\partial y_{kh\hat{l}m}^{j}}+\frac{\partial c_{kh\hat{l}m}^{j}(y_{kh\hat{l}m}^{j*})}{\partial y_{kh\hat{l}m}^{j}}-\rho_{2kh\hat{l}m}^{j*}-e_h^*+\gamma_j^*\right]$$

$$\times\left[y_{kh\hat{l}m}^{j}-y_{kh\hat{l}m}^{j*}\right]$$

$$+\sum_{j=1}^{J}\left[\sum_{i=1}^{I}\sum_{l=1}^{L}\sum_{h=1}^{H}\sum_{m=1}^{2}x_{jhm}^{il*}-\sum_{k=1}^{K}\sum_{h=1}^{H}\sum_{\hat{l}=1}^{L}\sum_{m=1}^{2}y_{kh\hat{l}m}^{j*}\right]\times\left[\gamma_j-\gamma_j^*\right]\geq 0,$$

$$\forall(x^1,y,\gamma)\in R_+^{2ILJH+2JKHL+J},\tag{7.14}$$

where γ_j is the Lagrange multiplier associated with constraint (7.9) (see Bazaraa, Sherali, and Shetty (1993)), and γ is the J-dimensional column vector of Lagrange multiplers of all the intermediaries with γ^* denoting the vector of optimal multipliers.

The Consumers at the Demand Markets and the Equilibrium Conditions

We now describe the consumers located at the demand markets. The consumers take into account in making their consumption decisions not only the price charged for the financial product by the agents with source of funds and intermediaries but also their transaction costs associated with obtaining the product.

Let $\hat{c}^{j}_{kh\hat{l}m}$ denote the transaction cost associated with obtaining product k in currency h in country $\hat{l}$ via mode m from intermediary j and recall that $y^{j}_{kh\hat{l}m}$ is the amount of the financial product k in currency h flowing between intermediary j and consumers in country $\hat{l}$ via mode m. We assume that the transaction cost is measured in the base currency, is continuous, and of the general form:

$$\hat{c}^{j}_{kh\hat{l}m} = \hat{c}^{j}_{kh\hat{l}m}(y), \quad \forall j, k, h, \hat{l}, m. \tag{7.15a}$$

Furthermore, let $\hat{c}^{il}_{kh\hat{l}}$ denote the transaction cost associated with obtaining the financial product k in currency h in country $\hat{l}$ electronically from source agent il, where we assume that the transaction cost is continuous and of the general form:

$$\hat{c}^{il}_{kh\hat{l}} = \hat{c}^{il}_{kh\hat{l}}(x^2), \quad \forall i, l, k, h, \hat{l}. \tag{7.15b}$$

Hence, the transaction cost associated with transacting directly with source agents is of a form of the same level of generality as the transaction costs associated with transacting with the financial intermediaries.

Denote the demand for product k in currency h in country $\hat{l}$ by $d_{kh\hat{l}}$ and assume, as given, the continuous demand functions:

$$d_{kh\hat{l}} = d_{kh\hat{l}}(\rho_3), \quad \forall k, h, \hat{l}. \tag{7.16}$$

Thus, according to (7.16), the demand of consumers for the financial product in a currency and country depends, in general, not only on the price of the product at that demand market (and currency and country) but also on the prices of the other products at the other demand markets (and in other countries and currencies). Consequently, consumers at a demand market, in a sense, also compete with consumers at other demand markets.

The consumers take the price charged by the intermediary, which was denoted by $\rho^{j*}_{2kh\hat{l}m}$ for intermediary j, product k, currency h, and country $\hat{l}$ via mode m, the price charged by source agent il, which was denoted by $\rho^{il*}_{1kh\hat{l}}$, and the rate of appreciation in the currency, plus the transaction costs, in making their consumption decisions. The equilibrium conditions for the consumers at demand market $kh\hat{l}$, thus, take the form: for all intermediaries: $j = 1, \ldots, J$ and all mode m; $m = 1, 2$:

$$\rho^{j*}_{2kh\hat{l}m} + e^{*}_{h} + \hat{c}^{j}_{kh\hat{l}m}(y^*) \begin{cases} = \rho^{*}_{3kh\hat{l}}, & \text{if} \quad y^{j*}_{kh\hat{l}m} > 0 \\ \geq \rho^{*}_{3kh\hat{l}}, & \text{if} \quad y^{j*}_{kh\hat{l}m} = 0, \end{cases} \tag{7.17}$$

and for all source agents il; $i = 1, \ldots, I$ and $l = 1, \ldots, L$:

$$\rho_{1kh\hat{\imath}}^{il*} + e_h^* + \hat{c}_{kh\hat{\imath}}^{il}(x^{2*}) \begin{cases} = \rho_{3kh\hat{\imath}}^*, & \text{if} \quad x_{kh\hat{\imath}}^{il*} > 0 \\ \geq \rho_{3kh\hat{\imath}}^*, & \text{if} \quad x_{kh\hat{\imath}}^{il*} = 0, \end{cases} \tag{7.18}$$

In addition, we must have that

$$d_{kh\hat{\imath}}(\rho_3^*) \begin{cases} = \displaystyle\sum_{j=1}^{J}\sum_{m=1}^{2} y_{kh\hat{\imath}m}^{j*} + \sum_{i=1}^{I}\sum_{l=1}^{L} x_{kh\hat{\imath}}^{il*}, & \text{if} \quad \rho_{3kh\hat{\imath}}^* > 0 \\ \leq \displaystyle\sum_{j=1}^{J}\sum_{m=1}^{2} y_{kh\hat{\imath}m}^{j*} + \sum_{i=1}^{I}\sum_{l=1}^{L} x_{kh\hat{\imath}}^{il*}, & \text{if} \quad \rho_{3kh\hat{\imath}}^* = 0. \end{cases} \tag{7.19}$$

Conditions (7.17) state that consumers at demand market $kh\hat{\imath}$ will purchase the product from intermediary j, if the price charged by the intermediary for the product and the appreciation rate for the currency plus the transaction cost (from the perspective of the consumer) does not exceed the price that the consumers are willing to pay for the product in that currency and country, i.e., $\rho_{3kh\hat{\imath}}^*$. Note that, according to (7.17), if the transaction costs are identically equal to zero, then the price faced by the consumers for a given product is the price charged by the intermediary for the particular product and currency in the country plus the rate of appreciation in the currency. Condition (7.18) states the analog, but for the case of electronic transactions with the source agents.

Condition (7.19), on the other hand, states that, if the price the consumers are willing to pay for the financial product at a demand market is positive, then the quantity of the product at the demand market is precisely equal to the demand.

In equilibrium, conditions (7.17), (7.18), and (7.19) will have to hold for all demand markets and these, in turn, can be expressed also as an inequality analogous to those in (7.6) and (7.14) and given by: determine $(x^{2*}, y^*, \rho_3^*) \in R_+^{(IL+2J+1)KHL}$, such that

$$\sum_{j=1}^{J}\sum_{k=1}^{K}\sum_{h=1}^{H}\sum_{\hat{\imath}=1}^{L}\sum_{m=1}^{2} \left[\rho_{2kh\hat{\imath}m}^{j*} + e_h^* + \hat{c}_{kh\hat{\imath}m}^{j}(y^*) - \rho_{3kh\hat{\imath}}^* \right] \times \left[y_{kh\hat{\imath}m}^{j} - y_{kh\hat{\imath}m}^{j*} \right]$$

$$+ \sum_{i=1}^{I}\sum_{l=1}^{L}\sum_{k=1}^{K}\sum_{h=1}^{H}\sum_{\hat{\imath}=1}^{L} \left[\rho_{1kh\hat{\imath}}^{il*} + e_h^* + \hat{c}_{kh\hat{\imath}}^{il}(x^{2*}) - \rho_{3kh\hat{\imath}}^* \right] \times \left[x_{kh\hat{\imath}}^{il} - x_{kh\hat{\imath}}^{il*} \right]$$

$$+ \sum_{k=1}^{K}\sum_{h=1}^{H}\sum_{\hat{\imath}=1}^{L} \left[\sum_{j=1}^{J}\sum_{m=1}^{2} y_{kh\hat{\imath}m}^{j*} + \sum_{i=1}^{I}\sum_{l=1}^{L} x_{kh\hat{\imath}}^{il*} - d_{kh\hat{\imath}}(\rho_3^*) \right] \times \left[\rho_{3kh\hat{\imath}} - \rho_{3kh\hat{\imath}}^* \right]$$

$$\geq 0, \quad \forall (x^2, y, \rho_3) \in R_+^{(IL+2J+1)KHL}. \tag{7.20}$$

The Equilibrium Conditions for the International Financial Economy with Electronic Transactions

In equilibrium, the financial flows that the source agents in different countries transact with the intermediaries must coincide with those that the intermediaries actually accept from them. In addition, the amounts of the financial products that are obtained by the consumers in the different countries and currencies must be equal to the amounts that both the source agents and the intermediaries actually provide. Hence, although there may be competition between decision-makers at the same level of tier of nodes of the financial network there must be, in a sense, cooperation between decision-makers associated with pairs of nodes (through positive flows on the links joining them). Thus, in equilibrium, the prices and financial flows must satisfy the sum of the optimality conditions (7.6) and (7.14) and the equilibrium conditions (7.20). We make these relationships rigorous through the subsequent definition and variational inequality derivation below.

Definition 7.1: International Financial Network Equilibrium with Electronic Transactions
The equilibrium state of the international financial network with electronic transactions is one where the financial flows between the tiers of the network coincide and the financial flows and prices satisfy the sum of conditions (7.6), (7.14), and (7.20).

The equilibrium state is equivalent to the following:

Theorem 7.1: Variational Inequality Formulation
The equilibrium conditions governing the international financial network with electronic transactions according to Definition 7.1 are equivalent to the solution of the variational inequality given by: determine $(x^{1*}, x^{2*}, y^*, \gamma^*, \rho_3^*)$ $\in \mathcal{K}$, satisfying:

$$\sum_{i=1}^{I}\sum_{l=1}^{L}\sum_{j=1}^{J}\sum_{h=1}^{H}\sum_{m=1}^{2}\left[\frac{\partial r^{il}(x^{il*})}{\partial x^{il}_{jhm}} + \frac{\partial c^{il}_{jhm}(x^{il*}_{jhm})}{\partial x^{il}_{jhm}} + \frac{\partial r^{j}(x^{1*}, y^*)}{\partial x^{il}_{jhm}} + \frac{\partial c_j(x^{1*})}{\partial x^{il}_{jhm}}\right.$$

$$\left.+\frac{\partial \hat{c}^{il}_{jhm}(x^{il*}_{jhm})}{\partial x^{il}_{jhm}} - \gamma_j^*\right] \times \left[x^{il}_{jhm} - x^{il*}_{jhm}\right]$$

$$+\sum_{i=1}^{I}\sum_{l=1}^{L}\sum_{k=1}^{K}\sum_{h=1}^{H}\sum_{\hat{l}=1}^{L}\left[\frac{\partial r^{il}(x^{il*})}{\partial x^{il}_{kh\hat{l}}} + \frac{\partial c^{il}_{kh\hat{l}}(x^{il*}_{kh\hat{l}})}{\partial x^{il}_{kh\hat{l}}} + \hat{c}^{il}_{kh\hat{l}}(x^{2*}) - \rho^*_{3kh\hat{l}}\right]$$

$$\times \left[x^{il}_{kh\hat{l}} - x^{il*}_{kh\hat{l}}\right]$$

$$+\sum_{j=1}^{J}\sum_{k=1}^{K}\sum_{h=1}^{H}\sum_{\hat{l}=1}^{L}\sum_{m=1}^{2}\left[\frac{\partial r^{j}(x^{1*}, y^*)}{\partial y^{j}_{kh\hat{l}m}} + \frac{\partial c^{j}_{kh\hat{l}m}(y^{j*}_{kh\hat{l}m})}{\partial y^{j}_{kh\hat{l}m}} + \hat{c}^{j}_{kh\hat{l}m}(y^*) - \rho^*_{3kh\hat{l}}\right]$$

$$+\gamma_j^*\Big] \times \Big[y_{kh\hat{\imath}m}^j - y_{kh\hat{\imath}m}^{j*}\Big]$$

$$+\sum_{j=1}^{J}\left[\sum_{i=1}^{I}\sum_{l=1}^{L}\sum_{h=1}^{H}\sum_{m=1}^{2}x_{jhm}^{il*} - \sum_{k=1}^{K}\sum_{h=1}^{H}\sum_{\hat{\imath}=1}^{L}\sum_{m=1}^{2}y_{kh\hat{\imath}m}^{j*}\right] \times \Big[\gamma_j - \gamma_j^*\Big]$$

$$+\sum_{k=1}^{K}\sum_{h=1}^{H}\sum_{\hat{\imath}=1}^{L}\left[\sum_{j=1}^{J}\sum_{m=1}^{2}y_{kh\hat{\imath}m}^{j*} + \sum_{i=1}^{I}\sum_{l=1}^{L}x_{kh\hat{\imath}}^{il*} - d_{kh\hat{\imath}}(\rho_3^*)\right] \times \Big[\rho_{3kh\hat{\imath}} - \rho_{3kh\hat{\imath}}^*\Big]$$

$$\geq 0, \quad \forall(x^1, x^2, y, \gamma, \rho_3) \in \mathcal{K}, \tag{7.21}$$

where $\mathcal{K} \equiv \{\mathcal{K}^1 \times \mathcal{K}^2\}$, *and* $\mathcal{K}^2 \equiv \{(y, \gamma, \rho_3)|(y, \gamma, \rho_3) \in R_+^{2JKHL+J+KHL}\}$.

Proof: We first establish that the equilibrium conditions imply variational inequality (7.21). Indeed, summation of inequalities (7.6), (7.14), and (7.20), after algebraic simplifications, yields variational inequality (7.21). We now establish the converse, that is, that a solution to variational inequality (7.21) satisfies the sum of conditions (7.6), (7.14), and (7.20), and is, hence, an equilibrium.

To inequality (7.21), add the term: $-\rho_{1jhm}^{il*} - e_h^* + \rho_{1jhm}^{il*} + e_h^*$ to the term in the first set of brackets (preceding the first multiplication sign). Similarly, add the terms: $-\rho_{1kh\hat{\imath}}^{il*} - e_h^* + \rho_{1kh\hat{\imath}}^{il*} + e_h^*$ to the term in brackets preceding the second multiplication sign and $-\rho_{2kh\hat{\imath}m}^{j*} - e_h^* + \rho_{2kh\hat{\imath}m}^{j*} + e_h^*$ to the term in brackets preceding the third multiplication sign in (7.21). The addition of such terms does not change (7.21) since the value of these terms is zero and yields:

$$\sum_{i=1}^{I}\sum_{l=1}^{L}\sum_{j=1}^{J}\sum_{h=1}^{H}\sum_{m=1}^{2}\left[\frac{\partial r^{il}(x^{il*})}{\partial x_{jhm}^{il}} + \frac{\partial c_{jhm}^{il}(x_{jhm}^{il*})}{\partial x_{jhm}^{il}} + \frac{\partial r^j(x^{1*}, y^*)}{\partial x_{jhm}^{il}} + \frac{\partial c_j(x^*)}{\partial x_{jhm}^{il}}\right.$$

$$\left.+\frac{\partial \hat{c}_{jhm}^{il}(x_{jhm}^{il*})}{\partial x_{jhm}^{il}} - \gamma_j^* - \rho_{1jhm}^{il*} - e_h^* + \rho_{1jhm}^{il*} + e_h^*\right] \times \Big[x_{jhm}^{il} - x_{jhm}^{il*}\Big]$$

$$+\sum_{i=1}^{I}\sum_{l=1}^{L}\sum_{k=1}^{K}\sum_{h=1}^{H}\sum_{\hat{\imath}=1}^{L}\left[\frac{\partial r^{il}(x^{il*})}{\partial x_{kh\hat{\imath}}^{il}} + \frac{\partial c_{kh\hat{\imath}}^{il}(x_{kh\hat{\imath}}^{il*})}{\partial x_{kh\hat{\imath}}^{il}} + \hat{c}_{kh\hat{\imath}}^{il}(x^{2*}) - \rho_{3kh\hat{\imath}}^*\right.$$

$$\left.-\rho_{1kh\hat{\imath}}^{il*} - e_h^* + \rho_{1kh\hat{\imath}}^{il*} + e_h^*\right] \times \Big[x_{kh\hat{\imath}}^{il} - x_{kh\hat{\imath}}^{il*}\Big]$$

$$+\sum_{j=1}^{J}\sum_{k=1}^{K}\sum_{h=1}^{H}\sum_{\hat{\imath}=1}^{L}\sum_{m=1}^{2}\left[\frac{\partial r^j(x^{1*}, y^*)}{\partial y_{kh\hat{\imath}m}^j} + \frac{\partial c_{kh\hat{\imath}m}^j(y_{kh\hat{\imath}m}^{j*})}{\partial y_{kh\hat{\imath}m}^j} + \hat{c}_{kh\hat{\imath}m}^j(y^*) - \rho_{3kh\hat{\imath}}^*\right.$$

$$\left.+\gamma_j^* - \rho_{2kh\hat{\imath}m}^{j*} - e_h^* + \rho_{2kh\hat{\imath}m}^{j*} + e_h^*\right] \times \Big[y_{kh\hat{\imath}m}^j - y_{kh\hat{\imath}m}^{j*}\Big]$$

$$+\sum_{j=1}^{J}\left[\sum_{i=1}^{I}\sum_{l=1}^{L}\sum_{h=1}^{H}\sum_{m=1}^{2}x_{jhm}^{il*}-\sum_{k=1}^{K}\sum_{h=1}^{H}\sum_{\hat{l}=1}^{L}\sum_{m=1}^{2}y_{kh\hat{l}m}^{j*}\right]\times\left[\gamma_{j}-\gamma_{j}^{*}\right]$$

$$+\sum_{k=1}^{K}\sum_{h=1}^{H}\sum_{\hat{l}=1}^{L}\left[\sum_{j=1}^{J}\sum_{m=1}^{2}y_{kh\hat{l}m}^{j*}+\sum_{i=1}^{I}\sum_{l=1}^{L}x_{kh\hat{l}}^{il*}-d_{kh\hat{l}}(\rho_{3}^{*})\right]\times\left[\rho_{3kh\hat{l}}-\rho_{3kh\hat{l}}^{*}\right]$$

$$\geq 0, \quad \forall(x^{1},x^{2},y,\gamma,\rho_{3})\in\mathcal{K}, \tag{7.22}$$

which, in turn, can be rewritten as:

$$\sum_{i=1}^{I}\sum_{l=1}^{L}\sum_{j=1}^{J}\sum_{h=1}^{H}\sum_{m=1}^{2}\left[\frac{\partial r^{il}(x^{il*})}{\partial x_{jhm}^{il}}+\frac{\partial c_{jhm}^{il}(x_{jhm}^{il*})}{\partial x_{jhm}^{il}}-\rho_{1jhm}^{il*}-e_{h}^{*}\right]$$

$$\times\left[x_{jhm}^{il}-x_{jhm}^{il*}\right]$$

$$+\sum_{j=1}^{J}\sum_{i=1}^{I}\sum_{l=}^{L}\sum_{h=1}^{H}\sum_{m=1}^{2}\left[\frac{\partial r^{j}(x^{1*},y^{*})}{\partial x_{jhm}^{il}}+\frac{\partial c_{j}(x^{*})}{\partial x_{jhm}^{il}}+\rho_{1jhm}^{il*}+e_{h}^{*}\right.$$

$$\left.+\frac{\partial\hat{c}_{jhm}^{il}(x_{jhm}^{il*})}{\partial x_{jhm}^{il}}-\gamma_{j}^{*}\right]\times\left[x_{jhm}^{il}-x_{jhm}^{il*}\right]$$

$$+\sum_{i=1}^{I}\sum_{l=1}^{L}\sum_{k=1}^{K}\sum_{h=1}^{H}\sum_{\hat{l}=1}^{L}\left[\frac{\partial r^{il}(x^{il*})}{\partial x_{kh\hat{l}}^{il}}+\frac{\partial c_{kh\hat{l}}^{il}(x_{kh\hat{l}}^{il*})}{\partial x_{kh\hat{l}}^{il}}-\rho_{1kh\hat{l}}^{il*}-e_{h}^{*}\right]$$

$$\times\left[x_{kh\hat{l}}^{il}-x_{kh\hat{l}}^{il*}\right]$$

$$+\sum_{i=1}^{I}\sum_{l=1}^{L}\sum_{k=1}^{K}\sum_{h=1}^{H}\sum_{\hat{l}=1}^{L}\left[\rho_{1kh\hat{l}}^{il*}+e_{h}^{*}+\hat{c}_{kh\hat{l}}^{il}(x^{2*})-\rho_{3kh\hat{l}}^{*}\right]\times\left[x_{kh\hat{l}}^{il}-x_{kh\hat{l}}^{il*}\right]$$

$$+\sum_{j=1}^{J}\sum_{k=1}^{K}\sum_{h=1}^{H}\sum_{\hat{l}=1}^{L}\sum_{m=1}^{2}\left[\frac{\partial r^{j}(x^{1*},y^{*})}{\partial y_{kh\hat{l}m}^{j}}+\frac{\partial c_{kh\hat{l}m}^{j}(y_{kh\hat{l}m}^{j*})}{\partial y_{kh\hat{l}m}^{j}}-\rho_{2kh\hat{l}m}^{j*}-e_{h}^{*}+\gamma_{j}^{*}\right]$$

$$\times\left[y_{kh\hat{l}m}^{j}-y_{kh\hat{l}m}^{j*}\right]$$

$$+\sum_{j=1}^{J}\sum_{k=1}^{K}\sum_{h=1}^{H}\sum_{\hat{l}=1}^{L}\sum_{m=1}^{2}\left[\rho_{2kh\hat{l}m}^{j*}+e_{h}^{*}+\hat{c}_{kh\hat{l}m}^{j}(y^{*})-\rho_{3kh\hat{l}}^{*}\right]\times\left[y_{kh\hat{l}m}^{j}-y_{kh\hat{l}m}^{j*}\right]$$

$$+\sum_{j=1}^{J}\left[\sum_{i=1}^{I}\sum_{l=1}^{L}\sum_{h=1}^{H}\sum_{m=1}^{2}x_{jhm}^{il*}-\sum_{k=1}^{K}\sum_{h=1}^{H}\sum_{\hat{l}=1}^{L}\sum_{m=1}^{2}y_{kh\hat{l}m}^{j*}\right]\times\left[\gamma_{j}-\gamma_{j}^{*}\right]$$

$$+\sum_{k=1}^{K}\sum_{h=1}^{H}\sum_{\hat{l}=1}^{L}\left[\sum_{j=1}^{J}\sum_{m=1}^{2}y_{kh\hat{l}m}^{j*}+\sum_{i=1}^{I}\sum_{l=1}^{L}x_{kh\hat{l}}^{il*}-d_{kh\hat{l}}(\rho_{3}^{*})\right]\times\left[\rho_{3kh\hat{l}}-\rho_{3kh\hat{l}}^{*}\right]$$

$$\geq 0. \tag{7.23}$$

But inequality (7.23) is equivalent to the sum of conditions (7.6), (7.14), and (7.20), and hence the financial flow and price pattern is an equilibrium according to Definition 7.1. $\square$

We now put variational inequality (7.21) into standard form which will be utilized in the subsequent sections. For additional background on variational inequalities and their applications, see the book by Nagurney (1999). In particular, we have that variational inequality (7.21) can be expressed as:

$$\langle F(X^*), X - X^* \rangle \geq 0, \quad \forall X \in \mathcal{K}, \tag{7.24}$$

where $X \equiv (x^1, x^2, y, \gamma, \rho_3)$ and $F(X) \equiv (F_{iljhm}, F_{ilkh\hat{l}}, F_{jkh\hat{l}m}, F_j, F_{kh\hat{l}})$ for indices: $i = 1, \ldots, I; \hat{l}, l = 1, \ldots, L; j = 1, \ldots, J; h = 1, \ldots, H; m = 1, 2$, and the specific components of F are given by the functional terms preceding the multiplication signs in (7.21), respectively. The term $\langle \cdot, \cdot \rangle$ denotes the inner product in N-dimensional Euclidean space.

We now describe how to recover the prices associated with the first two tiers of nodes in the international financial network. Clearly, the components of the vector ρ_3^* are obtained directly from the solution of variational inequality (7.21) as will be demonstrated explicitly through several numerical examples in Section 7.5. In order to recover the second tier prices associated with the intermediaries and the exchange rates one can (after solving variational inequality (7.21) for the particular numerical problem) *either* (cf. (7.17)) set $\rho_{2kh\hat{l}m}^{j*} + e_h^* = \rho_{3kh\hat{l}}^* - \hat{c}_{kh\hat{l}m}(y^*)$, for any $j, k, h, \hat{l}, m$ such that $y_{kh\hat{l}m}^{j*} > 0$, *or* (cf. (7.14)) for any $y_{kh\hat{l}m}^{j*} > 0$, set $\rho_{2kh\hat{l}m}^{j*} + e_h^* = \frac{\partial r^j(x^{1*}, y^*)}{\partial y_{kh\hat{l}m}^j} + \frac{\partial c_{kh\hat{l}m}^j(y_{kh\hat{l}m}^{j*})}{\partial y_{kh\hat{l}m}^j} + \gamma_j^*$.

Similarly, from (7.14) we can infer that the top tier prices comprising the vector ρ_1^* can be recovered (once the variational inequality (7.21) is solved with particular data) thus: for any i, l, j, h, m, such that $x_{jhm}^{il*} > 0$, set $\rho_{1jhm}^{il*} + e_h^* = \gamma_j^* - \frac{\partial r^j(x^{1*}, y^*)}{\partial x_{jhm}^{il}} - \frac{\partial c_j(x^{1*})}{\partial x_{jhm}^{il}} - \frac{\partial \hat{c}_{jhm}^{il}(x_{jhm}^{il*})}{\partial x_{jhm}^{il}}$.

In addition, in order to recover the first tier prices associated with the demand market and the exchange rates one can (after solving variational inequality (7.21) for the particular numerical problem) *either* (cf. (7.18)) set $\rho_{1kh\hat{l}}^{il*} + e_h^* = \rho_{3kh\hat{l}}^* - \hat{c}_{kh\hat{l}}^{il}(x^{2*})$, for any $i, l, k, h, \hat{l}$ such that $x_{kh\hat{l}}^{il*} > 0$, *or* (cf. (7.6)) for any $x_{kh\hat{l}}^{il*} > 0$, set $\rho_{1kh\hat{l}}^{il*} + e_h^* = \frac{\partial r^{il}(x^{il*})}{\partial x_{kh\hat{l}}^{il}} + \frac{\partial c_{kh\hat{l}}^{il}(x_{kh\hat{l}}^{il*})}{\partial x_{kh\hat{l}}^{il}}$.

Note that in the absence of electronic transactions the above model collapses to the model developed by Nagurney and Cruz (2002).

7.3 Qualitative Properties

In this section, we provide some qualitative properties of the solution to variational inequality (7.21). In particular, we derive existence and uniqueness results. We also investigate properties of the function F (cf. (7.24)) that enters the variational inequality of interest here.

Since the feasible set is not compact we cannot derive existence simply from the assumption of continuity of the functions. Nevertheless, we can impose a rather weak condition to guarantee existence of a solution pattern. Let

$$\mathcal{K}_b \equiv \{(x^1, x^2, y, \gamma, \rho_3) | 0 \le x^1 \le b_1; \ 0 \le x^2 \le b_1; 0 \le y \le b_3; 0 \le \gamma \le b_4;$$

$$0 \le \rho_3 \le b_5\}, \tag{7.25}$$

where $b = (b_1, b_2, b_3, b_4, b_5) \ge 0$ and $x^1 \le b_1; x^2 \le b_2; y \le b_3; \gamma \le b_4; \rho_3 \le b_5$ means that $x^{il}_{jhm} \le b_1; x^{il}_{kh\hat{l}} \le b_2; \ y^j_{kh\hat{l}m} \le b_3; \ \gamma_j \le b_4; \ and \ \rho_{3kh\hat{l}} \le b_5$ for all $i, l, j, k, h, \hat{l}, m$. Then $\mathcal{K}_b$ is a bounded closed convex subset of $R^{2ILJH+ILKHL+2JKHL+J+KHL}$. Thus, the following variational inequality

$$\langle F(X^b), X - X^b \rangle \ge 0, \quad \forall X^b \in \mathcal{K}_b, \tag{7.26}$$

admits at least one solution $X^b \in \mathcal{K}_b$, from the standard theory of variational inequalities, since $\mathcal{K}_b$ is compact and F is continuous. Following Kinderlehrer and Stampacchia (1980) (see also Theorem 1.5 in Nagurney (1999)), we then have:

Theorem 7.2
Variational inequality (7.21) admits a solution if and only if there exists a $b > 0$, such that variational inequality (7.26) admits a solution in $\mathcal{K}_b$ with

$$x^{1b} < b_1, \quad x^{2b} < b_2, \quad y^b < b_3, \quad \gamma^b < b_4, \quad \rho_3^b < b_5. \tag{7.27}$$

Theorem 7.3: Existence
Suppose that there exist positive constants M, N, R, with $R > 0$, such that:

$$\frac{\partial r^{il}(x^{il})}{\partial x^{il}_{jhm}} + \frac{\partial c^{il}_{jhm}(x^{il}_{jhm})}{\partial x^{il}_{jhm}} + \frac{\partial r^j(x^1, y)}{\partial x^{il}_{jhm}} + \frac{\partial c_j(x^1)}{\partial x^{il}_{jhm}} + \frac{\partial \hat{c}^{il}_{jhm}(x^{il}_{jhm})}{\partial x^{il}_{jhm}} \ge M,$$

$$\forall x^1 \ with \ x^{il}_{jhm} \ge N, \quad \forall i, l, j, h, m, \tag{7.28}$$

$$\frac{\partial r^{il}(x^{il})}{\partial x^{il}_{kh\hat{l}}} + \frac{\partial c^{il}_{kh\hat{l}}(x^{il}_{kh\hat{l}})}{\partial x^{il}_{kh\hat{l}}} + \hat{c}^{il}_{kh\hat{l}}(x^2) \ge M, \forall x^2 \ with \ x^{il}_{kh\hat{l}} \ge N, \ \forall i, l, k, h, \hat{l},$$

$$\tag{7.29}$$

$$\frac{\partial r^j(x^1, y)}{\partial y^j_{kh\hat{l}m}} + \frac{\partial c^j_{kh\hat{l}m}(y^j_{kh\hat{l}m})}{\partial y^j_{kh\hat{l}m}} + \hat{c}^j_{kh\hat{l}m}(y) \ge M,$$

$$\forall y \ with \ y^j_{kh\hat{l}m} \ge N, \quad \forall j, k, h, \hat{l}, m, \tag{7.30}$$

$$d_{kh\hat{l}}(\rho_3) \leq N, \quad \forall \rho_3 \text{ with } \rho_{3kh\hat{l}} > R, \quad \forall k, h, \hat{l}. \tag{7.31}$$

Then variational inequality (7.21); equivalently, variational inequality (7.24), admits at least one solution.

Proof: Follows using analogous arguments as the proof of existence for Proposition 1 in Nagurney and Zhao (1993) (see also the existence proof in Nagurney and Ke (2001)). $\square$

Assumptions (7.28), (7.29), and (7.30) are reasonable from an economics perspective, since when the financial flow between a source agent and intermediary or demand market or between an intermediary and demand market is large, we can expect the corresponding sum of the associated marginal risks and marginal costs of transaction and handling to exceed a positive lower bound. Moreover, in the case where the demand price of the financial product in a currency and country as perceived by consumers at a demand market is high, we can expect the demand for the financial product at the demand market to not exceed a positive bound.

We now establish additional qualitative properties both of the function F that enters the variational inequality problem (cf. (7.21) and (7.24)), as well as uniqueness of the equilibrium pattern. Monotonicity and Lipschitz continuity of F will be utilized in Section 7.4 to establish convergence of the proposed algorithmic scheme. Since the proofs of Theorems 7.4 and 7.5 below are similar to the analogous proofs in Nagurney and Ke (2001) they are omitted here. Additional background on the properties establish below can be found in the books by Nagurney and Siokos (1997) and Nagurney (1999).

Theorem 7.4: Monotonicity
Suppose that the risk functions r^{il}; $i = 1, \ldots, I$; $l = 1, \ldots, L$, and r^j; $j = 1, \ldots, J$, are strictly convex and that the c^{il}_{jhm}, $c^{il}_{kh\hat{l}}$, c_j, $\hat{c}^{il}_{jhm}$, and $c^j_{kh\hat{l}m}$ functions are convex; the $\hat{c}^j_{kh\hat{l}m}$ and $\hat{c}^{il}_{kh\hat{l}}$ functions are monotone increasing, and the $d_{kh\hat{l}}$ functions are monotone decreasing functions, for $i = 1, \ldots, I$; $l = 1, \ldots, L$; $j = 1, \ldots, J$; $h = 1, \ldots, H$; $k = 1, \ldots, K$, $\hat{l} = 1, \ldots, L$, and $m = 1, 2$. Then the vector function F that enters the variational inequality (7.21) is monotone, that is,

$$\langle F(X') - F(X''), X' - X'' \rangle \geq 0, \quad \forall X', X'' \in \mathcal{K}. \tag{7.32}$$

Monotonicity plays a role in the qualitative analysis of variational inequality problems similar to that played by convexity in the context of optimization problems.

Theorem 7.5: Strict Monotonicity
Assume all the conditions of Theorem 7.4. In addition, suppose that one of the families of convex functions c^{il}_{jhm}; $i = 1, \ldots, I$; $l = 1, \ldots, L$; $j = 1, \ldots, J$;

$h = 1, \ldots, H$; $m = 1, 2$; $c^{il}_{kh\hat{l}}$; $i = 1, \ldots, I$; $l = 1, \ldots, L$; $k = 1, \ldots, K$; $h = 1, \ldots, H$; $\hat{l} = 1, \ldots, L$; c_j; $j = 1, \ldots, J$; $\hat{c}^{il}_{jhm}$; $i = 1, \ldots, I$; $l = 1, \ldots, L$; $j = 1, \ldots, J$; $h = 1, \ldots, H$; $m = 1, 2$, and $c^j_{kh\hat{l}m}$; $j = 1, \ldots, J$; $k = 1, \ldots, K$; $h = 1, \ldots, H$, $\hat{l} = 1, \ldots, L$, and $m = 1, 2$ is a family of strictly convex functions. Suppose also that $\hat{c}^j_{kh\hat{l}m}$; $j = 1, \ldots, J$; $k = 1, \ldots, K$; $h = 1, \ldots, H$; $\hat{l} = 1, \ldots, L$; $m = 1, 2$; $\hat{c}^{il}_{kh\hat{l}}$; $i = 1, \ldots, I$; $l = 1, \ldots, L$; $k = 1, \ldots, K$; $h = 1, \ldots, H$; $\hat{l} = 1, \ldots, L$, and $-d_{kh\hat{l}}$; $k = 1, \ldots, K$; $h = 1, \ldots, H$; $\hat{l} = 1, \ldots, L$, are strictly monotone. Then, the vector function F that enters the variational inequality (7.21) is strictly monotone, with respect to (x^1, x^2, y, ρ_3), that is, for any two X', X'' with $(x^{1'}, x^{2'}, y', \rho_3') \neq (x^{1''}, x^{2''}, y'', \rho_3'')$

$$\langle F(X') - F(X''), X' - X'' \rangle > 0. \tag{7.33}$$

Theorem 7.6: Uniqueness
Assuming the conditions of Theorem 7.5, there must be a unique financial flow pattern (x^{1*}, x^{2*}, y^*), and a unique demand price price vector ρ_3^* satisfying the equilibrium conditions of the international financial network with intermediation. In other words, if the variational inequality (7.21) admits a solution, then that is the only solution in (x^1, x^2, y, ρ_3).

Proof: Under the strict monotonicity result of Theorem 7.5, uniqueness follows from the standard variational inequality theory (cf. Kinderlehrer and Stampacchia (1980)) □

Theorem 7.7: Lipschitz Continuity
The function that enters the variational inequality problem (7.21) is Lipschitz continuous, that is,

$$\|F(X') - F(X'')\| \leq \mathcal{L}\|X' - X''\|, \quad \forall X', X'' \in \mathcal{K}, \text{ where } \mathcal{L} > 0, \tag{7.34}$$

under the following conditions:
(i). the functions: r^{il}, r^j, c^{il}_{jhm}, $c^{il}_{kh\hat{l}}$, c_j, $\hat{c}^{il}_{jhm}$, and $c^j_{kh\hat{l}m}$ have bounded second-order derivatives, for all $i, l, j, h, k, \hat{l}, m$;
(ii). the functions: $\hat{c}^j_{kh\hat{l}m}$, $\hat{c}^{il}_{kh\hat{l}}$, and $d_{kh\hat{l}}$ have bounded first-order derivatives for all $i, l, j, k, h, \hat{l}, m$.

Proof: The result is direct by applying a mid-value theorem from calculus to the vector function F that enters the variational inequality problem (7.21). □

It is worth noting that the risk functions of the form (7.3) and (7.11) have bounded second-order derivatives.

In the next section, we will utilize the conditions of monotonicity and Lipschitz continuity in order to establish the convergence of the algorithm for the solution of the equilibrium financial flows and prices satisfying variational inequality (7.21).

7.4   The Algorithm

In this section, we consider the computation of solutions to variational inequality (7.21). The algorithm that we propose is the modified projection method of Korpelevich (1977), which is guaranteed to solve any variational inequality problem in standard form (see (7.24)) provided that certain conditions are satisfied by the function F that enters the variational inequality problem and that a solution exists. The realization of the modified projection method for the variational inequality (7.21) (for further details see also Nagurney and Siokos (1997)) is as follows, where $\mathcal{T}$ denotes an iteration counter:

Modified Projection Method for the Solution of the Variational Inequality

Step 0: Initialization

Set $(x^{10}, x^{20}, y^0, \gamma^0, \rho_3^0) \in \mathcal{K}$. Let $\mathcal{T} = 1$ and set α such that $0 < \alpha \leq \frac{1}{L}$, where L is the Lipschitz constant for the problem (cf. (7.34)).

Step 1: Computation

Compute $(\bar{x}^{1T}, \bar{x}^{2T}, \bar{y}^T, \bar{\gamma}^T, \bar{\rho}_3^T) \in \mathcal{K}$ by solving the variational inequality subproblem:

$$
\sum_{i=1}^{I}\sum_{l=1}^{L}\sum_{j=1}^{J}\sum_{h=1}^{H}\sum_{m=1}^{2} \left[\bar{x}_{jhm}^{ilT} + \alpha\left(\frac{\partial r^{il}(\bar{x}^{ilT-1})}{\partial x_{jhm}^{il}} + \frac{\partial r^j(\bar{x}^{1T-1}, \bar{y}^{T-1})}{\partial x_{jhm}^{il}} \right. \right.
$$

$$
\left. + \frac{\partial c_{jhm}^{il}(\bar{x}_{jhm}^{ilT-1})}{\partial x_{jhm}^{il}} + \frac{\partial c_j(\bar{x}^{1T-1})}{\partial x_{jhm}^{il}} + \frac{\partial \hat{c}_{jhm}^{il}(\bar{x}_{jhm}^{ilT-1})}{\partial x_{jhm}^{il}} - \bar{\gamma}_j^{T-1} \right) - \bar{x}_{jhm}^{ilT-1} \right]
$$

$$
\times \left[x_{jhm}^{il} - \bar{x}_{jhm}^{ilT} \right]
$$

$$
+ \sum_{i=1}^{I}\sum_{l=1}^{L}\sum_{k=1}^{K}\sum_{h=1}^{H}\sum_{\hat{l}=1}^{L} \left[\bar{x}_{kh\hat{l}}^{ilT} + \alpha\left(\frac{\partial r^{il}(\bar{x}^{ilT-1})}{\partial x_{kh\hat{l}}^{il}} + \frac{\partial c_{kh\hat{l}}^{il}(\bar{x}_{kh\hat{l}}^{ilT-1})}{\partial x_{kh\hat{l}}^{il}} \right. \right.
$$

$$
\left. \left. + \hat{c}_{kh\hat{l}}^{il}(\bar{x}^{2T-1}) - \bar{\rho}_{3kh\hat{l}}^{T-1} \right) - \bar{x}_{kh\hat{l}}^{ilT-1} \right] \times \left[x_{kh\hat{l}}^{il} - \bar{x}_{kh\hat{l}}^{ilT} \right]
$$

$$
+ \sum_{j=1}^{J}\sum_{k=1}^{K}\sum_{h=1}^{H}\sum_{\hat{l}=1}^{L}\sum_{m=1}^{2} \left[\bar{y}_{kh\hat{l}m}^{jT} + \alpha\left(\frac{\partial r^j(\bar{x}^{1T-1}, \bar{y}^{T-1})}{\partial y_{kh\hat{l}m}^{j}} + \frac{\partial c_{kh\hat{l}m}^{j}(\bar{y}_{kh\hat{l}m}^{jT-1})}{\partial y_{kh\hat{l}m}^{j}} \right. \right.
$$

$$
\left. \left. + \hat{c}_{kh\hat{l}m}^{j}(\bar{y}^{T-1}) - \bar{\rho}_{3kh\hat{l}}^{T-1} + \bar{\gamma}_j^{T-1} \right) - \bar{y}_{kh\hat{l}m}^{jT-1} \right] \times \left[y_{kh\hat{l}m}^{j} - \bar{y}_{kh\hat{l}m}^{jT} \right]
$$

$$
+ \sum_{j=1}^{J} \left[\bar{\gamma}_j^T + \alpha\left(\sum_{m=1}^{2} \left[\sum_{i=1}^{I}\sum_{l=1}^{L}\sum_{h=1}^{H} \bar{x}_{jhm}^{ilT-1} - \sum_{k=1}^{K}\sum_{h=1}^{H}\sum_{\hat{l}=1}^{L} \bar{y}_{kh\hat{l}m}^{jT-1} \right] \right) - \bar{\gamma}_j^{T-1} \right]
$$

$$
\times \left[\gamma_j - \bar{\gamma}_j^T \right]
$$

$$+\sum_{k=1}^{K}\sum_{h=1}^{H}\sum_{\hat{l}=1}^{L}\left[\bar{\rho}_{3kh\hat{l}}^{T}+\alpha(\sum_{j=1}^{J}\sum_{m=1}^{2}\bar{y}_{kh\hat{l}m}^{jT-1}+\sum_{i=1}^{I}\sum_{\hat{l}=1}^{L}\bar{x}_{kh\hat{l}}^{ilT-1}-d_{kh\hat{l}}(\bar{\rho}_{3}^{T-1}))\right.$$

$$\left.-\bar{\rho}_{3kh\hat{l}}^{T-1}\right]\times\left[\rho_{3kh\hat{l}}-\bar{\rho}_{3kh\hat{l}}^{T}\right]\geq 0,\quad\forall(x^{1},x^{2},y,\gamma,\rho_{3})\in\mathcal{K}.\qquad(7.35)$$

Step 2: Adaptation

Compute $(x^{1T},x^{2T},y^{T},\gamma^{T},\rho_{3}^{T})\in\mathcal{K}$ by solving the variational inequality subproblem:

$$\sum_{i=1}^{I}\sum_{l=1}^{L}\sum_{j=1}^{J}\sum_{h=1}^{H}\sum_{m=1}^{2}\left[x_{jhm}^{ilT}+\alpha(\frac{\partial r^{il}(\bar{x}^{ilT})}{\partial x_{jhm}^{il}}+\frac{\partial r^{j}(\bar{x}^{1T},\bar{y}^{T})}{\partial x_{jhm}^{il}}+\frac{\partial c_{jhm}^{il}(\bar{x}_{jhm}^{ilT})}{\partial x_{jhm}^{il}}\right.$$

$$\left.+\frac{\partial c_{j}(\bar{x}^{1T})}{\partial x_{jhm}^{il}}+\frac{\partial \hat{c}_{jhm}^{il}(\bar{x}_{jhm}^{ilT})}{\partial x_{jhm}^{il}}-\bar{\gamma}_{j}^{T})-x_{jhm}^{ilT-1}\right]\times\left[x_{jhm}^{il}-x_{jhm}^{ilT}\right]$$

$$+\sum_{i=1}^{I}\sum_{l=1}^{L}\sum_{k=1}^{K}\sum_{h=1}^{H}\sum_{\hat{l}=1}^{L}\left[x_{kh\hat{l}}^{ilT}+\alpha(\frac{\partial r^{il}(\bar{x}^{ilT})}{\partial x_{kh\hat{l}}^{il}}+\frac{\partial c_{kh\hat{l}}^{il}(\bar{x}_{kh\hat{l}}^{ilT})}{\partial x_{kh\hat{l}}^{il}}+\hat{c}_{kh\hat{l}}^{il}(\bar{x}^{2T})\right.$$

$$\left.-\bar{\rho}_{3kh\hat{l}}^{T})-x_{kh\hat{l}}^{ilT-1}\right]\times\left[x_{kh\hat{l}}^{il}-x_{kh\hat{l}}^{ilT}\right]$$

$$+\sum_{j=1}^{J}\sum_{k=1}^{K}\sum_{h=1}^{H}\sum_{\hat{l}=1}^{L}\sum_{m=1}^{2}\left[y_{kh\hat{l}m}^{jT}+\alpha(\frac{\partial r^{j}(\bar{x}^{1T},\bar{y}^{T})}{\partial y_{kh\hat{l}m}^{j}}+\frac{\partial c_{kh\hat{l}m}^{j}(\bar{y}_{kh\hat{l}m}^{jT})}{\partial y_{kh\hat{l}m}^{j}}\right.$$

$$\left.+\hat{c}_{kh\hat{l}m}^{j}(\bar{y}^{T})-\bar{\rho}_{3kh\hat{l}}^{T}+\bar{\gamma}_{j}^{T})-y_{kh\hat{l}m}^{jT-1}\right]\times\left[y_{kh\hat{l}m}^{j}-y_{kh\hat{l}m}^{jT}\right]$$

$$+\sum_{j=1}^{J}\left[\gamma_{j}^{T}+\alpha(\sum_{m=1}^{2}\left[\sum_{i=1}^{I}\sum_{l=1}^{L}\sum_{h=1}^{H}\bar{x}_{jhm}^{ilT}-\sum_{k=1}^{K}\sum_{h=1}^{H}\sum_{\hat{l}=1}^{L}\bar{y}_{kh\hat{l}m}^{jT}\right])-\gamma_{j}^{T-1}\right]$$

$$\times\left[\gamma_{j}-\gamma_{j}^{T}\right]$$

$$+\sum_{k=1}^{K}\sum_{h=1}^{H}\sum_{\hat{l}=1}^{L}\left[\rho_{3kh\hat{l}}^{T}+\alpha(\sum_{j=1}^{J}\sum_{m=1}^{2}\bar{y}_{kh\hat{l}m}^{jT}+\sum_{i=1}^{I}\sum_{\hat{l}=1}^{L}\bar{x}_{kh\hat{l}}^{ilT}-d_{kh\hat{l}}(\bar{\rho}_{3}^{T-1}))\right.$$

$$\left.-\rho_{3kh\hat{l}}^{T-1}\right]\times\left[\rho_{3kh\hat{l}}-\bar{\rho}_{3kh\hat{l}}^{T}\right]\geq 0,\quad\forall(x^{1},x^{2},y,\gamma,\rho_{3})\in\mathcal{K}.\qquad(7.36)$$

Step 3: Convergence Verification

If $|x_{jhm}^{ilT}-x_{jhm}^{ilT-1}|\leq\epsilon,|x_{kh\hat{l}}^{ilT}-x_{kh\hat{l}}^{ilT-1}|\leq\epsilon,|y_{kh\hat{l}m}^{jT}-y_{kh\hat{l}m}^{jT-1}|\leq\epsilon,|\gamma_{j}^{T}-\gamma_{j}^{T-1}|\leq\epsilon,$ $|\rho_{3kh\hat{l}}^{T}-\rho_{3kh\hat{l}}^{T-1}|\leq\epsilon$, for all $i=1,\cdots,I;\ l=1,\ldots,L;\ \hat{l};\hat{l}=1,\ldots,L;\ m=1,2;\ j=1,\cdots,J;\ h=1,\ldots,H;\ k=1,\cdots,K$, with $\epsilon>0$, a pre-specified tolerance, then stop; otherwise, set $T:=T+1$, and go to Step 1.

Both variational inequality subproblems (7.35) and (7.36) can be solved explicitly and in closed form since they are actually quadratic programming problems and the feasible set is a Cartesian product consisting of the product of $\mathcal{K}^1$ and $\mathcal{K}^2$ The former has a simple network structure, whereas the latter consists of the cross product of the nonnegative orthants: R_+^{2ILJH}, R_+^J, and R_+^{KHL}, and corresponding to the variables y, γ, and ρ_3, respectively. In fact, the subproblems in (7.35) and (7.36) corresponding to the x variables can be solved using exact equilibration (cf. Dafermos and Sparrow (1969) and Nagurney (1999)), whereas the remainder of the variables in (7.35) and (7.36) can be obtained by explicit formulae.

We now, for completeness, and also to illustrate the simplicity of the proposed computational procedure in the context of the international financial network model with electronic transactions, state the explicit formulae for the computation of the $\bar{y}^T$, the $\bar{\gamma}^T$, and the $\bar{\rho}_3^T$ (cf. (7.35)). The y^T, γ^T, and ρ_3^T can then be computed for (36) in an analogous fashion.

Computation of the Financial Products from the Intermediaries

In particular, compute, at iteration T, the $\bar{y}_{kh\hat{l}m}^{jT}$s, according to:

$$\bar{y}_{kh\hat{l}m}^{jT} = \max\{0, \bar{y}_{kh\hat{l}m}^{jT-1} - \alpha(\frac{\partial r^j(\bar{x}^{1T-1}, \bar{y}^{T-1})}{\partial y_{kh\hat{l}m}^j} + \frac{\partial c_{kh\hat{l}m}^j(\bar{y}_{kh\hat{l}m}^{jT-1})}{\partial y_{kh\hat{l}m}^j} + \hat{c}_{kh\hat{l}m}^j(\bar{y}^{T-1})$$

$$-\bar{\rho}_{3kh\hat{l}}^{T-1} + \bar{\gamma}_j^{T-1})\}, \quad \forall j, k, h, \hat{l}, m. \tag{7.37}$$

Computation of the Prices

At iteration T, compute the $\bar{\gamma}_j^T$s according to:

$$\bar{\gamma}_j^T = \max\{0, \bar{\gamma}_j^{T-1} - \alpha(\sum_{m=1}^{2}\left[\sum_{i=1}^{I}\sum_{l=1}^{L}\sum_{h=1}^{H}\bar{x}_{jhm}^{ilT-1} - \sum_{k=1}^{K}\sum_{h=1}^{H}\sum_{\hat{l}=1}^{\hat{L}}\bar{y}_{kh\hat{l}m}^{jT-1}\right])\}, \forall j, \tag{7.38}$$

whereas the $\bar{\rho}_{3kh\hat{l}}^T$s are computed explicitly and in closed form according to:

$$\bar{\rho}_{3kh\hat{l}}^T = \max\{0, \bar{\rho}_{3kh\hat{l}}^{T-1} - \alpha(\sum_{j=1}^{J}\sum_{m=1}^{2}\bar{y}_{kh\hat{l}m}^{jT-1} + \sum_{i=1}^{I}\sum_{l=1}^{L}\bar{x}_{kh\hat{l}}^{ilT-1} - d_{kh\hat{l}}(\bar{\rho}_3^{T-1}))\},$$

$$\forall k, h, \hat{l}. \tag{7.39}$$

In the next section, we apply the modified projection method to solve several international financial network examples.

We now state the convergence result for the modified projection method for this model.

Theorem 7.8: Convergence
Assume that the function that enters the variational inequality (7.21) (or (7.24)) has at least one solution and satisfies the conditions in Theorem 7.4 and in Theorem 7.7. Then the modified projection method described above converges to the solution of the variational inequality (7.21) or (7.24).

Proof: According to Korpelevich (1977), the modified projection method converges to the solution of the variational inequality problem of the form (7.21), provided that the function F that enters the variational inequality is monotone and Lipschitz continuous and that a solution exists. Existence of a solution follows from Theorem 7.3, monotonicity follows Theorem 7.4, and Lipschitz continuity, in turn, follows from Theorem 7.7. The proof is complete. □

Of course, the algorithm may converge even if the conditions in Theorems 7.4 and 7.7 do not hold in which case the algorithm, nevertheless, converges to the equilibrium solution.

7.5   Numerical Examples

In this section, we apply the modified projection method to several international financial network examples. The modified projection method was implemented in FORTRAN and the computer system used was a DEC Alpha system located at the University of Massachusetts at Amherst. For the solution of the induced network subproblems in the (x^1, x^2) variables we utilized the exact equilibration algorithm (see Dafermos and Sparrow (1969), Nagurney (1999), and the references therein). The other variables were determined in the computation and adaptation steps of the modified projection method explicitly and in closed form as described in the preceding section.

The convergence criterion used was that the absolute value of the flows and prices between two successive iterations differed by no more than 10^{-4}. The parameter α was set to .1 in the algorithm for all the examples. We assumed in all the examples that the risk functions were of the form (7.3) and (7.11), that is, that risk was represented through variance-covariance matrices for both the source agents in the countries and for the intermediaries. We initialized the modified projection method as follows: we set $x_{jh1}^{il} = \frac{S^{il}}{JH}$ for each source agent i and country l and for all j and h. All the other variables were initialized to zero.

We solved two sets of numerical examples, with two examples each. Detailed descriptions are given below. The first example in each set was an international financial network with no electronic transactions in order to create a baseline. Additional numerical examples for international financial networks without electronic transactions can be found in Nagurney and Cruz (2002).

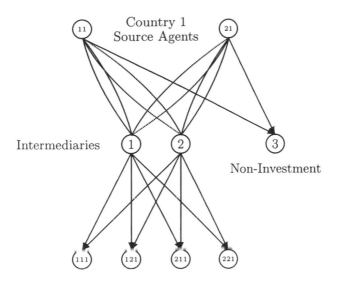

Product/Currency/Country combination

Fig. 7.2. International financial network for Example 7.1

Example 7.1

The first set of numerical examples consisted of one country, two source agents, two currencies, two intermediaries, and two financial products. Hence, $L = 1$, $I = 2$, $H = 2$, $J = 2$, and $K = 2$, for this and the subsequent two numerical examples. The international financial network for the first example is depicted in Figure 7.2. Note that in the first example no electronic transactions are allowed.

The data for the first example were constructed for easy interpretation purposes. The financial holdings of the two source agents were: $S^{11} = 20$ and $S^{21} = 20$. The variance-covariance matrices Q^{il} and Q^j were equal to the identity matrices (appropriately dimensioned) for all source agents and all intermediaries, respectively. Note that since only physical transactions are allowed, we have that only mode $m = 1$ can be used.

The transaction cost functions faced by the source agents associated with transacting with the intermediaries (cf. (7.1a)) were given by:

$$c_{jhm}^{il}(x_{jhm}^{il}) = .5(x_{jhm}^{il})^2 + 3.5x_{jhm}^{il}; i = 1, 2; l = 1; j = 1, 2; h = 1, 2; m = 1.$$

The handling costs of the intermediaries, in turn (see (7.7)), were given by:

$$c_j(x^1) = .5(\sum_{i=1}^{2}\sum_{h=1}^{2} x_{jh1}^{i1})^2; j = 1, 2.$$

The transaction costs of the intermediaries associated with transacting with the source agents were (cf. (7.8)) given by:

$$\hat{c}_{jhm}^{il}(x_{jhm}^{il}) = 1.5x_{jhm}^{il2} + 3x_{jhm}^{il}; \quad i = 1,2; l = 1; j = 1,2; h = 1,2; m = 1.$$

The demand functions at the demand markets (refer to (7.16)) were:

$$d_{111}(\rho_3) = -2\rho_{3111} - 1.5\rho_{3121} + 1000, \quad d_{121}(\rho_3) = -2\rho_{3121} - 1.5\rho_{3111} + 1000,$$

$$d_{211}(\rho_3) = -2\rho_{3211} - 1.5\rho_{3221} + 1000, \quad d_{221}(\rho_3) = -2\rho_{3221} - 1.5\rho_{3211} + 1000.$$

and the transaction costs between the intermediaries and the consumers at the demand markets (see (7.15a)) were given by:

$$\hat{c}_{kh\hat{l}m}^{j}(y) = y_{kh\hat{l}m}^{j} + 5; \quad j = 1,2; k = 1,2; h = 1,2; \hat{l} = 1; m = 1.$$

We assumed for this and the subsequent examples that the transaction costs as perceived by the intermediaries and associated with transacting with the demand markets (cf. (7.9)) were all zero, that is, $c_{kh\hat{l}m}^{j}(y_{kh\hat{l}m}^{j}) = 0$; $j, k, h, \hat{l}, m$.

The modified projection method converged in 94 iterations and yielded the following equilibrium financial flow pattern:

$$x^{1*} := x_{111}^{11*} = x_{121}^{11*} = x_{211}^{11*} = x_{221}^{11*} = x_{111}^{21*} = x_{121}^{21*} = x_{211}^{21*} = x_{221}^{21*} = 5.0000;$$

$$y^{*} := y_{1111}^{1*} = y_{1211}^{1*} = y_{2111}^{1*} = y_{2211}^{1*} = y_{1111}^{2*} = y_{1211}^{2*} = y_{2111}^{2*} = y_{2211}^{2*} = 5.0000.$$

The vector γ^{*} had components: $\gamma_{1}^{*} = \gamma_{2}^{*} = 262.8566$, and the computed demand prices at the demand markets were: $\rho_{3111}^{*} = \rho_{3121}^{*} = \rho_{3211}^{*} = \rho_{3221}^{*} = 282.856$.

We also, for completeness, recover the equilibrium prices associated with the source agents according to the discussion following (7.24). In particular, we had that all components of the vector ρ_{1}^{*} were identically equal to 214.8566.

It is easy to verify that the optimality/equilibrium conditions were satisfied with good accuracy. Note that in this example, constraint (7.5) was tight for both source agents, that is, there was zero flow on the links connecting node 3 with top tier nodes. Thus, it was optimal for both source agents to invest their entire financial holdings in the instrument made available by each of the two intermediaries in each of the two currencies. Clearly, due to the input data in this highly stylized example, the equilibrium financial flow pattern could have been "predicted" even without any computations; however, the same does not hold (even in this quite "symmetric" example) for the prices.

Example 7.2

In the second example, we kept the data as in Example 7.1 except that now we allowed for electronic transactions between the source agents and

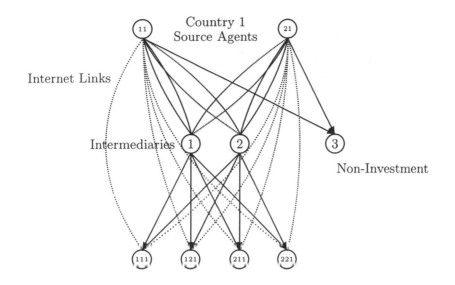

Product/Currency/Country combination

Fig. 7.3. International financial network for Example 7.2

the consumers at the demand markets. Hence, the international financial network was now as depicted in Figure 7.3.

The additional data were as follows. The transaction costs (cf. (7.1b)) were given by:

$$c_{kh\hat{l}}^{il}(x_{kh\hat{l}}^{il}) = .5(x_{kh\hat{l}}^{il})^2 + x_{kh\hat{l}}^{il}; \quad i = 1,2; l = 1; k = 1,2; h = 1,2; \hat{l} = 1,$$

whereas the transaction costs (cf. (7.15b)) were given by:

$$\hat{c}_{kh\hat{l}}^{il}(x^2) = .1x_{kh\hat{l}}^{il} + 1; \quad i = 1,2; l = 1; k = 1,2; h = 1,2; \hat{l} = 1.$$

The variance-covariance matrices were redimensioned and, again, were equal to the identity matrices.

The modified projection method converged in 88 iterations and yielded the following equilibrium financial flow pattern:

$$x^{1*} := x_{111}^{11*} = x_{121}^{11*} = x_{211}^{11*} = x_{221}^{11*} = x_{111}^{21*} = x_{121}^{21*} = x_{211}^{21*} = x_{221}^{21*} = .372;$$

$$x^{2*} := x_{111}^{11*} = x_{121}^{11*} = x_{211}^{11*} = x_{221}^{11*} = x_{111}^{21*} = x_{121}^{21*} = x_{211}^{21*} = x_{221}^{21*} = 4.627;$$

$$y^* := y_{1111}^{1*} = y_{1211}^{1*} = y_{2111}^{1*} = y_{2211}^{1*} = y_{1111}^{2*} = y_{1211}^{2*} = y_{2111}^{2*} = y_{2211}^{2*} = .372.$$

As was the case in Example 7.1, both source agents allocated the entirety of their funds to the instrument in the two currencies; thus, there was no non-investment.

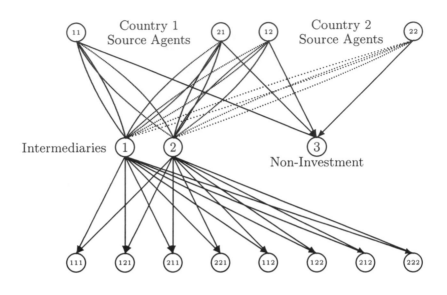

Product/Currency/Country combination

Fig. 7.4. International financial network for Example 7.3

The vector γ^* had components: $\gamma_1^* = \gamma_2^* = 276.738$, and the computed demand prices at the demand markets were: $\rho_{3111}^* = \rho_{3121}^* = \rho_{3211}^* = \rho_{3221}^* = 282.857$.

We also computed (as discussed in Example 7.1 and following (7.24)) the new equilibrium prices associated with the top tier of nodes in the international financial network and now the new equilibrium vector ρ_1^* had all of its components equal to 270.385.

Note that due to the lower transaction costs associated with electronic transactions directly between the source agents and the demand markets a sizeable portion of the financial funds vis-á-vis those in Example 7.1 were transacted in this manner.

Example 7.3

In the first example in the second set, the international financial network was as given in Figure 7.4. The two examples in this set consisted of two countries with two source agents in each country; two currencies, two intermediaries, and two financial products. Hence, $L = 2$, $I = 2$, $H = 2$, $J = 2$, and $K = 2$. In the first example, however, we assumed that there were no electronic transactions and, hence, the only mode for transacting was given by $m = 1$.

The data for the first example in this set was constructed for easy interpretation purposes and to create a baseline from which the simulations could be conducted. In fact, we essentially "replicated" the data for the first country as it appeared in Example 7.1 in order to construct the data for the second country.

Specifically, the financial holdings of the source agents were: $S^{11} = 20$, $S^{21} = 20$, $S^{12} = 20$, and $S^{22} = 20$. The variance-covariance matrices Q^{il} and Q^j were equal to the identity matrices (appropriately dimensioned) for all source agents in each country and for all intermediaries, respectively.

The transaction cost functions faced by the source agents associated with transacting with the intermediaries were given by:

$$c_{jhm}^{il}(x_{jhm}^{il}) = .5(x_{jhm}^{il})^2 + 3.5x_{jhm}^{il}; \quad i = 1, 2; l = 1, 2; j = 1, 2; h = 1, 2; m = 1.$$

The handling costs of the intermediaries (since the number of intermediaries in this set is still equal to two) remained as in Example 7.1, that is, they were given by:

$$c_j(r^1) = 5(\sum_{i=1}^{2}\sum_{h=1}^{2} r_{jhi}^{il})^2; \quad j = 1, 2.$$

The transaction costs of the intermediaries associated with transacting with the source agents in the two countries were given by:

$$\hat{c}_{jhm}^{il}(x_{jhm}^{il}) = 1.5(x_{jhm}^{il})^2 + 3x_{jhm}^{il}; \quad i = 1, 2; l = 1, 2; j = 1, 2; h = 1, 2; m = 1.$$

The demand functions at the demand markets were:

$$d_{111}(\rho_3) = -2\rho_{3111} - 1.5\rho_{3121} + 1000, \quad d_{121}(\rho_3) = -2\rho_{3121} - 1.5\rho_{3111} + 1000,$$

$$d_{211}(\rho_3) = -2\rho_{3211} - 1.5\rho_{3221} + 1000, \quad d_{221}(\rho_3) = -2\rho_{3221} - 1.5\rho_{3211} + 1000,$$

$$d_{112}(\rho_3) = -2\rho_{3112} - 1.5\rho_{3122} + 1000, \quad d_{122}(\rho_3) = -2\rho_{3122} - 1.5\rho_{3112} + 1000,$$

$$d_{212}(\rho_3) = -2\rho_{3212} - 1.5\rho_{3222} + 1000, \quad d_{222}(\rho_3) = -2\rho_{3222} - 1.5\rho_{3212} + 1000,$$

and the transaction costs between the intermediaries and the consumers at the demand markets were given by:

$$\hat{c}_{kh\hat{l}m}^j(y) = y_{kh\hat{l}m}^j + 5; \quad j = 1, 2; k = 1, 2; h = 1, 2; \hat{l} = 1, 2; m = 1.$$

The modified projection method converged in 64 iterations and yielded the following equilibrium financial flow pattern:

$$x^{1*} := x_{111}^{11*} = x_{121}^{11*} = x_{211}^{11*} = x_{221}^{11*} = x_{111}^{21*} = x_{121}^{21*} = x_{211}^{21*} = x_{221}^{21*} = 5.0000,$$

$$x_{111}^{12*} = x_{121}^{12*} = x_{211}^{12*} = x_{221}^{12*} = x_{111}^{22*} = x_{121}^{22*} = x_{211}^{22*} = x_{221}^{22*} = 5.0000;$$

$$y^* := y_{1111}^{1*} = y_{1211}^{1*} = y_{2111}^{1*} = y_{2211}^{1*} = y_{1111}^{2*} = y_{1211}^{2*} = y_{2111}^{2*} = y_{2211}^{2*} = 5.0000,$$

$$y_{1121}^{1*} = y_{1221}^{1*} = y_{2121}^{1*} = y_{2221}^{1*} = y_{1121}^{2*} = y_{1221}^{2*} = y_{2121}^{2*} = y_{2221}^{2*} = 5.0000.$$

The vector γ^* had components: $\gamma_1^* = \gamma_2^* = 262.8486$, and the computed demand prices at the demand markets were: $\rho_{3111}^* = \rho_{3121}^* = \rho_{3211}^* = \rho_{3221}^*$

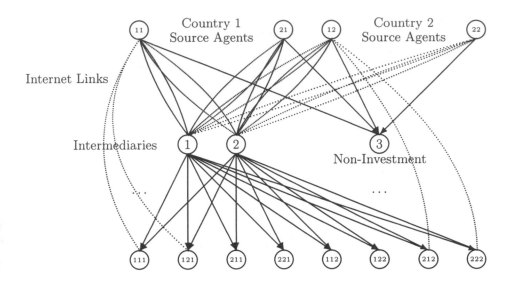

Product/Currency/Country combination

Fig. 7.5. International financial network for Example 7.4

$\rho^*_{3112} = \rho^*_{3122} = \rho^*_{3212} = \rho^*_{3222} = 282.8591$. The components of the vector ρ^*_1 were identically equal to 194.8486.

Example 7.4

Example 7.4 was constructed from the preceding example as follows. We kept the data as in Example 7.3 except that now we added links from the source agents to the demand markets to represent electronic transactions as depicted in Figure 7.5. The additional data for the Internet links were replications of the analogous functions in Example 7.2.

The variance-covariance matrices were redimensioned and were equal to the identity matrices.

The modified projection method converged in 59 iterations and yielded the following equilibrium financial flow pattern: only the electronic links had positive flows with all other flows being identically equal to 0.000. In particular, the financial holdings of the source agents in the different countries were equally allocated via electronic transactions directly to the demand markets with $x^{il*}_{khl̂} = 2.5000$ for all $i, l, k, h, l̂$.

The vector γ^* had components: $\gamma^*_1 = \gamma^*_2 = 278.0899$, and the computed demand prices at the demand markets were: $\rho^*_{3khl̂} = 282.8568$, $\forall k, h, l̂$. Note that the demand market prices were essentially unchanged from those in Example 7.3 whereas the γ^* vector components did change. In this example, all the financial transactions were conducted electronically.

These examples have been presented to show both the model and the computational procedure. Obviously, different input data and dimensions of the problems solved will affect the equilibrium financial flow and price patterns. One now has a powerful tool with which to explore the effects of perturbations to the data as well as the effects of changes in the number of source agents, countries, currencies, and/or products, as well as the effects of the introduction of electronic transactions.

7.6 Summary and Conclusions

In this chapter, we developed a framework for the modeling, analysis, and computation of solutions to international financial problems with intermediaries in the presence of electronic transactions. We proposed an international financial network model consisting of three tiers of decision-makers: the source agents, the financial intermediaries, and the consumers associated with the demand markets for distinct financial products in distinct currencies and countries. We modeled the behavior of the decision makers, derived the optimality conditions as well as the governing equilibrium conditions which reflect (possible) competition among decision-makers at the same tier of nodes but cooperation between tiers of nodes. The framework allows for the handling of as many countries, as many source agents in each country, as many currencies in which the financial products can be obtained, and as many financial intermediaries, as mandated by the specific application. Moreover, it incorporates the possibility of electronic transactions between distinct tiers of the international financial network.

The formulation of the equilibrium conditions was shown to be equivalent to a finite-dimensional variational inequality problem. The variational inequality problem was then utilized to obtain qualitative properties of the equilibrium financial flow and price pattern as well as to propose a computational procedure for the numerical determination of the equilibrium flows in particular examples. The algorithm was subsequently applied to several international financial network examples to illustrate both the model as well as the computational procedure.

This framework generalizes the recent work of Nagurney and Cruz (2002) in international financial networks with intermediation to include explicit electronic transactions. Further research will focus on the exploration of the dynamics of international financial networks (see, e.g., Nagurney and Dong (2002) for a single country dynamic model) as well as the incorporation of policy instruments such as taxes.

Acknowledgments

This research was supported, in part, by NSF Grant No.: IIS-0002647 and, in part, by an AT&T Industrial Ecology Fellowship. This support is gratefully acknowledged. The authors acknowledge the helpful suggestions of the reviewer.

References

Allen, H., Hawkins, J., and Sato, S. (2001), "Electronic Trading and its Implications for Financial Systems," Bank of International Settlements Papers No. 7, November, Bern, Switzerland.

Banks, E. (2001), *E-Finance: The Electronic Revolution*, John Wiley & Sons, New York.

Bazaraa, M. S., Sherali, H. D., and Shetty, C. M. (1993), *Nonlinear Programming: Theory and Algorithms*, John Wiley & Sons, New York.

Bertsekas, D. P., and Tsitsiklis, J. N. (1989), *Parallel and Distributed Computation – Numerical Methods*, Prentice Hall, Englewood Cliffs, New Jersey.

Board of Governors (1980), *Introduction to Flow of Funds*, Flow of Funds Section, Division of Research and Statistics, Federal Reserve System, Washington, DC, June.

Claessens, S., Glaessner, T., and Klingebiel, D. (2000), "Electronic Finance: Reshaping the Financial Landscape around the World," Financial Sector Discussion Paper No. 4, The World Bank, Washington DC.

Claessens, S., Glaessner, T., and Klingebiel, D. (2001), "E-Finance in Emerging Markets: Is Leapfrogging Possible?" Financial Sector Discussion Paper No. 7, The World Bank, Washington DC.

Claessens, S., Dobos, G., Klingebiel, D., and Laeven, L. (2003), "The Growing Importance of Networks in Finance and their Effects on Competition," in *Innovations in Financial and Economic Networks*, pp. 110-135, A. Nagurney, editor, Edward Elgar Publishers, Cheltenham, England.

Cohen, J. (1987), *The Flow of Funds in Theory and Practice, Financial and Monetary Studies* **15**, Kluwer Academic Publishers, Dordrecht, The Netherlands.

Dafermos, S., and Nagurney, A. (1987), "Oligopolistic and Competitive Behavior of Spatially Separated Markets," *Regional Science and Urban Economics* **17**, 245-254.

Dafermos, S., and Sparrow, F. T. (1969), "The Traffic Assignment Problem for a General Network," *Journal of Research of the National Bureau of Standards* **73B**, 91-118.

Economides, N. (2001), "The Impact of the Internet on Financial Markets," *Journal of Financial Transformation* **1**, 8-13.

Fan, M., Staellert, J., and Whinston, A. B. (2000), "The Internet and the Future of Financial Markets," *Communications of the ACM* **43**, 83-88.

Gabay, D., and Moulin, H. (1980), "On the Uniqueness and Stability of Nash Equilibria in Noncooperative Games," in *Applied Stochastic Control of Econometrics and Management Science*, pp. 271-294, A. Bensoussan, P. Kleindorfer, and C. S. Tapiero, editors, North-Holland, Amsterdam, The Netherlands.

Kinderlehrer, D., and Stampacchia, G. (1980), *An Introduction to Variational Inequalities and their Application*, Academic Press, New York.

Korpelevich, G. M. (1977), "The Extragradient Method for Finding Saddle Points and Other Problems," *Matekon* **13**, 35-49.

Markowitz, H. M. (1959), *Portfolio Selection: Efficient Diversification of Investments*, John Wiley & Sons, Inc., New York.

McAndrews, J., and Stefanidis, C. (2000), "The Emergence of Electronic Communications Networks in US Equity Markets," *Current Issues in Economics and Finance* **6**, 1 6, Federal Reserve Bank of New York.

Nagurney, A. (1999), *Network Economics: A Variational Inequality Approach*, second and revised edition, Kluwer Academic Publishers, Dordrecht, The Netherlands.

Nagurney, A. and Cruz, J. (2002), "International Financial Networks with Intermediation: Modeling, Analysis, and Computations," to appear in *Computational Management Science*.

Nagurney, A., and Dong, J. (2002), *Supernetworks: Decision-Making for the Information Age*, Edward Elgar Publishers, Cheltenham, England.

Nagurney, A., Dong, J., and Hughes, M. (1992), "Formulation and Computation of General Financial Equilibrium," *Optimization* **26**, 339-354.

Nagurney, A., and Hughes, M. (1992), "Financial Flow of Funds Networks," *Networks* **2**, 145-161.

Nagurney, A., and Ke, K. (2001), "Financial Networks with Intermediation," *Quantitative Finance* **1**, 441-451.

Nagurney, A., and Ke, K. (2003), "Financial Networks with Electronic Transactions: Modeling, Analysis, and Computations," *Quantitative Finance* **3**, 71-87.

Nagurney, A., and Siokos, S. (1997), *Financial Networks: Statics and Dynamics*, Springer-Verlag, Heidelberg, Germany.

Nagurney, A., and Zhao, L. (1993), "Networks and Variational Inequalities in the Formulation and Computation of Market Disequilibria: The Case of Direct Demand Functions," *Transportation Science* **27**, 4-15.

Nash, J. F. (1950), "Equilibrium Points in N-Person Games," in *Proceedings of the National Academy of Sciences, USA* **36**, 48-49.

Nash, J. F. (1951), "Noncooperative Games," *Annals of Mathematics* **54**, 286-298.

Quesnay, F. (1758), *Tableau Economique*, reproduced in facsimile with an introduction by H. Higgs by the British Economic Society, 1895.

Sato, S., and Hawkins, J. (2001), "Electronic Finance: An Overview of the Issues," Bank of International Settlements Paper No. 7, November, Bern, Switzerland.

Thore, S. (1980), *Programming the Network of Financial Intermediation*, Universitetsforslaget, Oslo, Norway.

8 Using Financial Options to Hedge Transportation Capacity in a Deregulated Rail Industry

Stephen M. Law, Alexandra E. MacKay, and James F. Nolan

8.1 Introduction

The rail industry in the United States and Canada is in the midst of a major restructuring. Mergers and shipper concerns about the exercise of market power by railways in many lucrative shipping markets have produced calls for improving competition in the rail industry (see, e.g., Larson and Spraggins (2000)). Conversely, railways maintain that they operate in a competitive, multi-modal transportation environment (Gallamore (1999)). Nevertheless, it is clear that the rail industry in the US and Canada has become extremely concentrated. When the US rail market was first liberalized in 1980, there were 39 large (Class I) carriers in operation (Kwoka and White (1999)). Presently, there are only four Class I carriers; in effect, the US rail shipping market has been partitioned into roughly four quadrants, with little inter-rail contact between major carriers in vast portions of the country. Since the Canadian rail industry was liberalized in 1987, it has followed a similar path to the American industry (cf. Bonsor (1995)). Especially since regulations were modified in 1996, the two Canadian Class I carriers have streamlined their network operations and consolidated their respective operational areas.

In our view, the evolution of rail merger policy in the recently lifted moratorium on rail mergers in the US and the serious consideration in Canada of policies recommending increased infrastructure access in the rail industry are indicative that the entry-protected rail industry will be forced to adapt to increased inter-rail competition at some point in the future. Indeed, the Surface Transportation Board (STB) has enacted stricter criteria for its approval of mergers, the need for which has been publicly acknowledged by the railways themselves. The Canadian government, in turn, has issued a transportation policy blueprint for the immediate future of transportation policy, which seriously considers the infrastructure access issue (cf. Transport Canada (2003)).

This chapter gazes into a crystal ball and maps out some intriguing perspectives on the evolution of rail provision in the US and Canada. In particular, we describe the potential formation of new markets to manage freight transportation risk, with emphasis on the demand for, creation of, and use of derivative securities for which the underlying asset is rail car capacity.

This chapter is organized as follows. Section 8.2 describes the rail industry in Canada and the US, drawing distinctions between the existing market structures. An interesting feature of the current market situation in Canada and the US is the existence of car capacity auction contracts that resemble the type of derivative on rail capacity that we envision existing on a more widespread and potentially standardized basis as the future unfolds. The rail market of today is outlined in Section 8.3. We sketch the features of the rail car capacity market that we expect to evolve if there is entry deregulation in this industry, noting both the characteristics of the existing capacity allocation mechanisms that will be retained and those that will be entirely new.

Section 8.4 more fully describes a market for derivative securities on rail car capacity within a completely deregulated rail industry. We draw links between the possible future for the rail industry and the path that has been followed by other network industries that have deregulated in recent years. We also describe the risks faced by players in this market. This leads to the conclusion that, under certain conditions, the market for derivative contracts written on rail car capacity will exist, and that there will be sufficient liquidity in this market. This section also provides a description of possible losses for both providers and users of rail car capacity if the market fails. The cost of these failures indicates that there is a potential market for hedging instruments that mitigate or eliminate the risk of such losses from the viewpoint of individual players in this market.

Section 8.5 describes the derivatives written on rail car capacity and outlines pricing arguments for such derivatives. We find the underlying asset can be sufficiently well-defined and that it is feasible to employ usual arbitrage pricing arguments. We utilize US rail rate data to construct hypothetical call options for coal movements by rail from 1997-1999. The nature of coal movement and the existing regulatory structure of that industry means that the calculated prices of the hypothetical options are not high. These results are discussed in the context of future potential changes to rail transportation that may change the price characteristics of the asset underlying the option to increase its value.

Section 8.6 concludes this chapter, summarizes the findings, and provides direction for the application of the results to other network industries.

8.2   Historical Rail Transportation Markets

After almost 70 years of government oversight, the US rail industry was partially deregulated with the passage of the Staggers Act (cf. United States Government (1980)). While the original reason for regulating the rail industry was to protect shippers from the potential of railways to abuse market power, it was recognized through the 1970s that economic regulation was hampering the ability of railways to compete with the growing trucking industry. In addition, the bankruptcy of several major US railways led regulators to concede that regulation was ruining the industry (Gallamore (1999)).

Since the Staggers Act, the US railways have thrived and continue to serve an important role in the North American economy. For instance, as of 1999, US railroads carried more than 40 percent of the nation's intercity freight, over 60 percent of the nation's coal, and over 40 percent of the nation's grain. In addition, from 1981 to 1998, railroads invested over $75 billion in capital expenditures (American Association of Railroads (2000)).

Railway economics have changed since the lifting of rate regulations. Railways have always known that they could minimize operating costs by moving larger and larger trains between high density origins and destinations. Through the era of rate deregulation, US railways have sought various methods to improve productivity and profitability in this manner. The clearest example of this is the abandonment of thousands of miles of low-density rail lines throughout the United States. Given the large economies of scale and scope that exist in rail, efforts at cost reduction through mergers between mid-sized to large rail firms have also been commonplace. While mergers have had a notable impact on the organization of the industry, efficiency problems with recent mergers are indicative that this method of cost reduction has likely run its course. Minimizing logistics costs are clearly an important factor behind these cost-reducing policies, and somewhat less attention has been given to developing specific business strategies and incentives to streamline the interaction between railway and shipper.

Traditionally, rail cars were allocated to shippers on a first-come, first-served basis. This method, apparently equitable and, therefore, favored by many shippers, does not allow either the railway or the shipper to forecast logistics and capital usage requirements accurately. Until recently, railways were not perceived to be capable of useful reliability in delivery when compared to other modes such as trucking.

Intermodal competition has had a strong impact on the development of the rail industry. The deregulation of interstate trucking in 1980 brought trucks into many transportation markets that were traditionally thought to be the domain of rail. Empirical work has shown that trucking deregulation decreased costs in the trucking industry (McMullen and Lee (1993)). This decline in trucking costs has increased the modal switch point (the point at which the least transportation cost mode shifts from trucking to rail). This distance has been estimated to be somewhere in the range of 800 to

1100 kilometers (Wood and Johnson (1996)), and is sufficient to ensure that trucking handles a substantial proportion of intercity, interstate, and inter-provincial traffic. Increasingly, these movements represent a valuable part of the transportation market that railways do not want to lose. Combine these shifts with increasing inventory costs and the evolution of just-in-time delivery systems for many industries, and it is not surprising that process changes in rail markets are underway in North America.

From this just-in-time business environment have come railway and ship-per transactions designed to minimize costs by ensuring delivery reliability. From the perspective of the railway, the more reliable the forecasts of capital usage, the more efficiently will capital be utilized. From the perspective of the shipper, demurrage (storage) and delivery penalties mean that reliability of delivery at the destination is paramount. In particular, the bulk handling system is a growing concern for railways because of the large amount of railway resources needed to move commodities such as grain or coal and the increasing need for reliable port delivery of these products. For example, most US and Canadian railways obtain well over 20 percent of their net revenues from grain movement.

8.3   The Rail Market of Today

In order to transport a commodity by rail in the US and Canada, shippers must negotiate contract conditions with a railway specifying the parameters of the transportation transaction. The most important among these parameters include when and where the railway will pick up the shipment, along with the shippers' preferred destination. To expedite this process, some industries own rail cars, but this is not common practice and most industries rely on railways to control and provide access to cars or freight capacity. Thus, for most shippers that use rail, securing access to the appropriate type of rail car is critical. In order to simplify the analysis in this chapter, the example that we present uses a specific kind of rail car as the unit of freight capacity to be transacted. Due to its importance and potential, we will revisit the issue of pricing trackage rights in Sections 8.4.2 and 8.5.3.

The need for dependable rail traffic forecasts to further simplify logistics planning has already generated some innovative solutions from within the rail industry. In 1988, Burlington Northern Railway was the first to move away from the longstanding first-come, first-served car allocation process and to develop a more controlled car allocation system for grain movement. This process became known as the Certificate of Transportation, or COT. Interestingly, COT bears a strong resemblance to a forward contract for rail cars.

Under COT, shippers purchase the right to access grain hopper cars by electronically conducted, sealed bid auctions. Bids are submitted directly to the railway, and bids can now also be made on-line. The access rights to the hopper cars are offered for sale up to five months in advance and are grouped by specific origins and destinations and by commodity. Successful bidders are scheduled to receive hopper cars within a specified two-week window (Drew and Rosher (1999)). In addition, if a shipper decides, after winning a car bid, that the car is not needed, the shipper can re-sell the car space in a secondary market. One restriction on this secondary market is that a decision to sell car availability on the secondary car market must occur before the two-week delivery window has opened.

Financial penalties are imposed upon the shipper if the car is not used or re-sold, or if there is a need to change the origin or destination from the original bid specification. The penalty is extracted primarily from the funds put on deposit at the time the bid is successful. Conversely, financial penalties are imposed upon BNSF if a COT car does not arrive within a 15-day delivery window. Regulatory oversight also dictates that only a portion of BNSF's hopper car fleet (roughly 50 percent) can be used for COT allocations. The remaining cars are still allocated on a first come, first served basis. A lottery is used in those cases where car demand exceeds car supply for a given time period.

The implementation of COT generated considerable opposition among shippers. Various shipper representatives felt that such programs were worse for shippers than the traditional first-come, first-served order systems because they permitted more discriminatory pricing in those markets (such as bulk movement) where rail already enjoys considerable market power in transportation services. However, after some debate, a favorable 1992 regulatory decision by the Interstate Commerce Commission cleared the way for other US railways to develop their own car allocation programs (cf. Surface Transportation Board (1992)).

The Soo line (owned by Canadian Pacific Railways) introduced an allocation system known as PERX into grain transportation. Union Pacific updated its ACOS (Advanced Car Order System) program with a more comprehensive car allocation system based on the issuance of vouchers for guarantees of future shipments. This first wave of bid-car systems for grain movement has been so successful for the railways that almost all US Class I carriers have adopted some kind of auction-based car allocation program for bulk agricultural commodity movements (Wilson, Priewe, and Dahl (1998); see Table 8.1). We note that the ranges of all the contracts in Table 8.1 lie in the range $(0, \infty)$ for the different railways and that all are sold on secondary markets.

In Canada, the removal of freight rate regulation for grain movement in 1999 allowed Canadian Pacific Railways (CPR) to introduce a car allocation and logistics program for grain called MaxTrax (Canadian Pacific (2001)). While it does not rely on a bidding mechanism for car allocations, MaxTrax offers considerable rate discounts for shippers who can assemble large trains for movement on CPR lines. One of the CPR programs known as Advance-

Table 8.1. Comparison of US car bidding programs (Vachal (2001))

Railway	# Auctions	Minimum # of cars per certificate	When sold	Prepayment
BNSF (COT)	Weekly	1, 26, or 72	4 months in advance	$300 + premium ($400 cancellation)
Soo Line/ Canadian Pacific (PERX)	Monthly*	5	4 months in advance	$250 + premium
Union Pacific (Vouchers)	Weekly	1, 25, or 75	6 months in advance	$300 + premium

Note: *Bi-weekly during grain harvest

Railway	Late penalty	Charge for change of origin	Max # of cars per certificate	Guaranteed rates?
BNSF (COT)	$300	$30/car if order $300/car if corridor changed	Siding capacity, existing service levels	Buyer's option to lock rates
Soo Line/ Canadian Pacific (PERX)	$50/car per day, $250 max	$50/car if within shipping period	Siding capacity	Not in terminals, no flax or edible beans
Union Pacific (Vouchers)	$50/car per day, $400 max	$25/car, $250/car if corridor changed	Siding capacity, existing service levels	Up to 90 days in advance

Max uses an offer system for penalty payment. As part of an AdvanceMax order, a shipper must offer an amount per car that he would be willing to pay as a penalty for not meeting the order. In the event that a car shortage exists, the amount of this offer is used to determine car allocations (Canadian Pacific (2001)). Mostly, the set of MaxTrax programs relies on a penalty system for missed orders to ensure that commitment to a pre-ordered service is met.

The rail car bidding mechanism and penalty system apportion transaction risk between the railway and the shipper by minimizing the occurrence of so-called "phantom car orders." Phantom orders were a byproduct of the first-come, first-served allocation procedure; historically, to ensure that enough cars were available for a given transaction, shippers frequently over-ordered railcars. The major cost to the railway of phantom orders is poor fleet utilization, which results in reduced or lost freight business. By charging the shipper for poor order forecasts, railways reduced the likelihood of phantom orders. In essence, the railways developed a system for sharing with shippers the *risk* and the *opportunity cost* of not using a rail car that has been allocated space in the rail system.

As an allocation mechanism, the sealed bid system appears to be profitable for the railways. The rapid adoption of similar systems by other railways is a strong indication of this. The benefits to shippers from improved rail logistics must also be significant, but are harder to quantify. Nevertheless, there are concerns, especially from smaller shippers, about the fairness of the auction system in a transportation market with little or no inter- or intra-modal competition, as is the case with many bulk movements (Drew and Rosher (1999)).

This last point leads us to offer that if the rail industry in North America were to become competitive via the implementation of third-party rail access policies, then capacity pricing mechanisms based upon railway controlled auction markets as used today will need to change. Entry deregulation means that shippers will necessarily gain more control over the car allocation process than they presently possess with the car auctions described here. Consequently, car allocation and pricing mechanisms will need to evolve to better fit with a regime of full economic deregulation in rail. One capacity pricing mechanism that offers the potential to benefit both railways and shippers is a car allocation system founded on the theory of financial derivatives. The next sections of the chapter explore this idea in detail.

8.4 The Demand for Hedging Instruments in the Rail Industry

The development of a market for derivative instruments written on rail car capacity hinges on the future need for the ability to hedge transportation risk. Accordingly, we now describe the risks in this industry.

The railways, as suppliers of rail transportation capacity, enjoy market power for this good. They manipulate the supply of rail transportation capacity in an uncompetitive environment. Without a fundamental change in the industry resulting in a reduction or elimination of this market power, the future for derivatives for which rail car capacity is the underlying asset is bleak.

Currently, there is not much scope to envisage possible risk mitigation to the railways. With control over the network asset, they are in full control of the risks faced and the risks hedged. The car auction systems (a type of derivative contract with the sealed car auction mechanism being a type of forward contract) thrive because railways enjoy market power in the transportation markets being served by car auctions. Railways extract the majority of economic rent derived from managing transportation risk and shippers are left to deal with greater than optimal amounts of this risk. The development of a market for unregulated hedging instruments applied to rail capacity would represent a significant welfare change over the present situation.

The clearest example for which one can identify a possible demand for hedging instruments is that of transportation within peak periods of activity. It might be the case that for individual shippers using rail, the cost associated with the failure to obtain car or freight capacity justifies a mechanism for hedging that risk. A derivative contract for which freight capacity is the underlying asset would facilitate this hedging.

Such derivative contracts will not be written as long as the railroads continue to enjoy market power in the market for car capacity. Our vision of the future of risk management in rail requires changes in the regulatory structure of the rail industry as a precursor. In particular, these changes must result in the reduction of market power in the provision of rail transportation capacity.

Under what circumstances will changes in the market for rail transportation result in conditions that are favorable to the creation of an associated market for derivatives? We conjecture that the erosion of price stability when an industry fully de-regulates is integral to the evolutionary process. To illustrate this concept, we now examine the process of deregulation in natural gas and then electricity, along with the evolution of associated derivative contracts. Where appropriate, we draw analogies that are relevant to a potential market in rail capacity, recognizing that the deregulation processes in different network industries will not be identical.

8.4.1   The Development of Hedging Instruments in Other Industries

There has been dramatic growth in the exchange of financial instruments in some other network-type industries, such as natural gas. This process started with the exchange of long-term fixed-price supply contracts in the 1970s and moved to the market exchange of futures contracts. The first natural gas futures contracts were traded on the New York Mercantile Exchange (NYMEX) in April 1990. As natural gas industry supply was gradually deregulated, volumes grew to the point where 19 million futures contracts were traded on the NYMEX in 1999. Toward the end of the 1990s, the US annual retail natural gas market of $60 billion was accompanied by the exchange of $300 billion in natural gas futures and a further $300 billion in over-the-counter derivatives (Spiewak (1998)).

However, this level of growth has not been observed in all deregulated or partially deregulated network industries. Although there were predictions of strong growth in the trading of electricity futures, this market has not seen a comparable expansion. NYMEX launched electricity futures (California-Oregon Border and Palo Verde) in March of 1996, introduced more in 1998 (Cinergy and Entergy), and another (PJM) in March of 1999. Trading volume in 1999 on NYMEX was less than 200,000 electricity futures. Some contracts have fewer than 200 trades per day (e.g., PJM at 13 contracts per day) (cf. *Electricity Daily* (2000)).

There are a number of possible explanations for these differences. Foremost, electricity markets and trades can be extremely complex, primarily as a result of institutional design problems (Stoft (2002)). If rates are set or capped by a regulator, neither electric utilities nor their customers would have an incentive to hedge output price movements. More generally, in the current less-regulated environment, utilities are reluctant to enter into hedging markets to manage risk, either because of a threat of re-regulation or due to a perception of financial derivatives as risky instruments. Finally, the underlying commodity of electricity future contracts is unusual in that it cannot be stored, leading to greater uncertainty in pricing of the contracts (see Bessembinder and Lemmon (2002)).

In fact, the highly time-sensitive nature of electricity is a characteristic partially shared by rail services. Ultimately, it may be that the period since the introduction of electricity futures has not been long enough for the full development of the necessary institutional capability (personnel, familiarity, contacts, training, controls, etc.). It is worth noting that if the same ratio of contract trading volume to commodity sales were observed in electricity as in natural gas, the resulting market would be very large. Annual revenues in the electricity supply industry in the United States in 1998 were $270 billion (see Borenstein, Bushnell, and Wolak (2000)). Derivatives markets in electricity would be on the order of $2.7 trillion, if a similar "ten-times-sales" ratio held for electricity as in natural gas.

We expect that the prospect for trading in rail derivatives is likely to lie between the extensive market for natural gas derivatives and the disappointing situation in electricity. While natural gas markets are unnaturally large – the 19 million contracts traded on NYMEX in 1999 exceeds even the 8.7 million unleaded gasoline futures traded – electricity options markets remain small despite optimistic predictions. However, some of the unusual pricing issues in electricity derivatives would not present themselves for rail derivatives. The learning curve to develop similar pricing institutions should not be as steep for rail, nor should the possibility of expensive mistakes while on the learning curve be as great.

8.4.2   The Incentive to Participate in a Hedging Market in Rail Transportation Capacity

In a standard forward contract, two parties (on their own or through an intermediary) negotiate the delivery of a particular asset for an agreed-upon price on a specified date at a specified location. No funds beyond margin requirements exchange until the delivery date. Each party is obligated to honor its side of the contract, unless it can find an alternative party who is willing to "step into its shoes" and assume all aspects of the obligation.

While confidential contracting with various kinds of shippers in the rail industry is now commonplace, little is publicly known about the structure of these contracts. More importantly, since they are specific to certain shippers, these contracts cannot be traded readily among shippers in any meaningful sense. For the tradable shipping contracts we do know about, the bid car allocation systems discussed in Section 8.3 have many of the hallmarks of a forward contract.

Under BN's COT system, a shipper has an obligation to pay for the capacity that has been successfully bid upon unless it can be re-sold in a secondary market. If a shipper wishes to extract himself from paying the entire agreed-upon price for freight capacity that will not be used and he cannot re-sell the capacity, the shipper can turn it back to the railway. The railway will then try to re-sell the capacity, but, in turn, extracts a penalty from the shipper who won the initial auction. In contrast, if this were a full-fledged forward contract, the penalty would be exactly 100 percent of the agreed-upon price. In this case, the shipper would be obligated to accept delivery of the asset (freight cars), and would be obligated to pay the full price. As can be seen in Table 8.1, the present program prices for defaulting are considerably less than 100 percent. We conclude that the bid car allocation systems now in place are more generous than a standard forward contract would be to a shipper who would wish to cancel the transaction.

If the railways have market power in many of the car auction markets, why are these programs more generous than a standard forward contract? The reason is likely due to the relative inflexibility that the shipper has with respect to negotiating most aspects of the bid contract. When setting up the car bidding, the railway offers a set amount of car volume for particular origins and destinations, along with an offer of timing for car arrival. The shipper has very little ability to set these key contract factors. Therefore, in order to induce the shippers to participate in the market, the railways need to offer additional financial incentives to shippers. This is intended to compensate them for their relative lack of flexibility in designing transportation transactions.

There is also a direct cost to the railway of not meeting auction contract conditions in the form of the 15-day car delivery window. This cost (about $400 for COT at present) is just a small fraction of the average total value of freight capacity. The cost to the railway of not "hedging" by selling forward under the present auction systems is uncertain revenue and uncertain plans for allocation of rail capacity with different origin-destination routings. The cost is reduced through auctioned contracts, but it cannot be eliminated entirely. The remaining costs to the railway are similar to those that would exist in a forward contract – the inability to fully participate in an upward price movement of the commodity being sold by the railway – as well as the cost associated with the generous nature of the penalties imposed by the present systems on the shippers.

The cost to the shipper of not "hedging" by bidding for rail capacity can also be characterized as uncertainty regarding both the price and availability of rail capacity at the time required. The cost of a forward hedge in which the prices moved the wrong way (i.e. the hedger would have been better off in a revenue sense had he not hedged) is the same as the cost to the shipper given similar price movements. However, unlike in the case of a pure forward contract, the shipper can extract himself without being sued for default and without paying 100 percent of the agreed-upon price.

There are other costs to a shipper associated with not being able to rely on timely transportation capacity at stable prices. If a product cannot be shipped to its destination as agreed, many shippers incur pre-contracted penalties and demurrage fees if volumes, type and timing of good delivery are not met. Timely transportation capacity will be particularly important when the shipped goods are perishable, storage costs are particularly high, contract penalties for late delivery are high, or opportunity costs of foregone sales are high (lost sales from delays may be costly if demand for the shipped goods is cyclical or unstable or otherwise time-sensitive).

Rail is still used predominantly by shippers of bulk goods over long distances. Traditionally, bulk commodity hauls were not strongly affected by strict on-time delivery needs. More recently, for certain bulk movements, shippers are demanding more reliability in delivery in order to avoid demurrage fees either at intermediate port or final destination (Wood and Johnson (1996)). There are also substantial transaction costs in moving freight between different firms and between modes, and these supply chain considerations dictate that modern shippers increasingly desire "seamless" and reliable transportation services between origin and destination.

A key question arises regarding whether the central risk to shippers is priced in the provision of rail transportation capacity. The chief risk may not be the price of rail transportation capacity, but rather its supply in a timely fashion. Though the shipper is not insensitive to the cost of transportation, the failure to achieve shipment may impose costs that shift the source of the primary risk to reliability of capacity supplied rather than its cost.

Turning to the railway, there are considerable costs incurred if cars are supplied but not demanded. The rapid action by US railways to put in place mechanisms to avoid phantom orders is an indication of the magnitude of the logistics and operations costs associated with unused rail capacity and assets. Further development of transparent mechanisms to reduce imbalances between temporal and spatial transportation supply and demand will be looked upon favorably by major railways.

At present, the essential elements of railway car capacity allocation systems are controlled almost completely by the railway. In advance of the actual auction, the railway determines most of the important features of the final contract to be bid upon (see Table 8.1). In particular, the bulkiness of a commodity such as grain and the transportation captivity of many grain shippers make auction control of capacity useful. If this were not the case, then a capacity auction might not generate any bids in situations where the railway did not offer origin/destination pairings and routings that were favorable to most shippers. Control over the routings and capital utilization combined with the need for many bulk shippers to bid on virtually any type of transportation transaction offered by a railway makes the existing bidding mechanisms very effective.

We refer to existing rail car allocation mechanisms as being *asymmetric* or one-sided in a bargaining sense. In the markets served by these mechanisms, the bidder (shipper) is frequently obliged to bid on whatever cars/capacity is made available by the railway, whether it efficiently serves shipper needs or not. Transportation capacity derivatives are unlikely to prosper in the current regulatory environment. A change toward more open access and a more competitive supply of rail capacity is needed for the development of these derivatives and to ensure a more equitable division between rail capacity supplier and demander. In addition, it is probable that the railways would want to realize more benefits under a forward contracting system than they obtain now under bid-car allocations systems.

As alluded to in the previous section, to facilitate the use of financial derivatives for pricing capacity in this industry, railways will need to be permitted to charge for the full cost of default in a forward shipping contract market. If this is allowed, shippers, in turn, will need leverage on derivative contracts offered by railways because of the existence of market power in transportation. One possible solution to this problem is for the rail regulator to fully enforce the existing laws regarding common carrier obligations.[1] This simple action would allow most shippers to have more input into the process of setting parameters of transportation contracts than exists in the present car/capacity allocation process.

---

[1] A common carrier obligation for a railway means that it has a legal obligation to serve all customers who request services. Furthermore, a common carrier as defined also assumes the following basic obligations to shippers for all transactions: (1) delivery, (2) service, (3) reasonable rates, and (4) avoidance of price discrimination (Wood and Johnson (1996)).

A simple solution to the asymmetric bargaining power problem between railways and shippers would be a change in regulatory policy towards improved infrastructure access for third-party rail providers (DeVany and Walls (1997)).[2] It is clear that the rail industry will need to consider more advanced car capacity pricing mechanisms in order to adapt to what appears to be an evolving and favorable regulatory environment.

Under transportation car capacity hedging, railways would assume responsibility for the risk that cars will run from origin to destination with only partial capacity bought and filled. This may mean that empty cars are moved, or that an engine moves fewer full cars than physically optimal. Even the presence of advance contracting systems, such as COT, cannot completely eliminate this risk. Similarly, in a situation where more than one supplier of rail capacity operates in the same corridor, the risk becomes either that the train will run under-filled or that the train will run with capacity purchased at prices below costs. We conclude that given the market power currently held by the railways, and their ability to manipulate the supply of rail transportation capacity, it is unlikely that a market for derivative contracts on rail capacity will evolve within the existing regulatory framework.

With potential future alterations to the regulation of railways, our view of the future may include derivatives on rail capacity. In the next section, we apply a simple model of rail car option pricing to data derived from the STB Rail Waybill sample on coal movements.

8.5 The Existence of Derivatives for Rail Freight Car Capacity

The previous section outlined those conditions under which one would reasonably expect a well-functioning and liquid market for derivative contracts on rail capacity to develop together with the new market for the underlying asset itself. Changes that reduce the market power of the railways are necessary. If these changes result in price instability in the market for rail capacity, then there could well emerge substantial demand for and supply of "derivative-type contracts" for rail capacity under deregulation, since these contracts can solve logistics problems, providing cost-savings and potentially significant profit opportunities.

---

[2]Early work by Tye (1991) discusses the issues of deregulation and contestability in rail, as well as the need to consider open infrastructure access as an alternative to existing rate regulation. Research on access fee structure has been done for other industries (e.g. Laffont, Rey, and Tirole (1998), Armstrong (2002)); other research examines the nature of institutions that will allocate track capacity (Nilsson (1999)). While conceptually similar to the pricing mechanism developed here, the merits of the latter institutions derive from the assumption that track and rail operations are vertically separated. This is not the case at present in North America. Rail access policies with a vertically separated rail system have been implemented in Australia, Sweden, and Great Britain. Gibson, Cooper, and Ball (2002) provide a preliminary assessment of the evolution of rail capacity charges in the UK.

Here, we construct a derivative pricing model for rail car capacity. For another perspective on the use of financial contracts in rail transportation, see Kober and Baumel (1990). The exercise is conducted to show that it is relatively straightforward to compute call options for transportation under our assumptions. We acknowledge that the data do not permit prices on actual track capacity to be computed, and, hence, the example is not necessarily complete. Nevertheless, the results do provide a good illustration of the dampening effect of entry regulation, manifested through low rate volatility, on the rail industry. We postulate that one of the immediate consequences of entry deregulation in rail will be an increase in price volatility and the subsequent development of advanced pricing mechanisms to help manage traffic coordination along with other forms of transportation risk.

8.5.1 A Hypothetical Derivatives Contract for Coal Transportation

We use the standard binomial option pricing model (cf. Cox, Ross, and Rubinstein (1979)) to calculate prices of hypothetical call options on the cost of transporting coal by rail. Coal transportation is chosen for this study because of its frequency in the US rate sample. The asset underlying the option is a unit of rail car capacity, where the rail car in question is suitable for the transportation of coal. In this way, the asset is homogeneous but for origin and destination specifications. We assume that this underlying asset can be readily traded among market participants. We also assume that the stochastic process for the price of coal transportation is not mean-reverting or subject to seasonal fluctuations so that the model is appropriate.

Here, for completeness, we describe the model. The binomial option pricing model assumes that there exist no arbitrage opportunities in the market. The underlying asset can be traded, and written options on that asset are also readily tradable. The multi-step binomial model is a collection of one-period binomial trees.

In the one-period binomial model, the price evolution of the underlying asset is known with certainty to the extent that there are only are only two possible prices for the underlying asset on the maturity date of the option. These two prices determine the two possible future payoffs from the option. At maturity, T, the call option will pay off the (positive) difference between the spot price on the underlying asset at maturity of the option, S_T, and the exercise price of the option, X, if it is *in-the-money*, and will pay off nothing if the spot asset price is below the exercise price of the call option. The payoff from the call option can, therefore, be written as $\max(S_T - X, 0)$. Let $S_{T,1}$ and $S_{T,2}$ denote, respectively, the two possible prices for the underlying asset at time T, and let $c_{T,1} = \max(S_{T,1} - X, 0)$ and $c_{T,2} = \max(S_{T,2} - X, 0)$ denote the associated two possible call option payoffs at maturity.

We form a perfectly hedged portfolio, one for which the future payoff is known with certainty, regardless of which of the two prices materializes for the underlying asset at time T. This portfolio is constructed by taking a short position in the option and a long position in Δ units of the underlying asset. To ensure that the portfolio payoff at the maturity of the call option is identical no matter which price path is taken by the underlying asset, Δ is chosen such that $S_{T,1}\Delta - c_{T,1} = S_{T,2}\Delta - c_{T,2}$. The portfolio payoff is known with certainty, and, hence, it is appropriate to use a risk-free rate of interest to discount its cash flows from time T to time zero. The cost of entering this portfolio must be equal to the present value of its expected future payoff, $e^{-rT}(S_{T,1}\Delta - c_{T,1})$, where r denotes the continuously compounded riskless rate of interest. The spot price of one unit of the underlying asset at time zero, S_0, is also known at time zero. The option price is calculated as $c = S_0\Delta - e^{-rT}(S_{T,1}\Delta - c_{T,1})$, where c denotes the price of a (European) call option.

Applying the binomial model in more realistic settings requires some enhancement. This is necessary in order to overcome the problematic requirement of precisely narrowing future uncertainty to only two possible future prices for the underlying asset on the option's expiration date. In order to accomplish this, a series of one-step binomial models are joined together to form a binomial tree. The last nodes of the binomial tree correspond to the maturity date of the option. The length of each binomial piece is a fraction of the total time between the present and the expiration of the option, and each branch of the multi-step tree is of equal length. (The total remaining life of the option is divided into smaller units of time, each identical.) As the tree branches and fans out, the final nodes of the tree portray a multitude of possible prices for the underlying asset over the life of the option. The prices for the underlying asset corresponding to the final nodes of a multi-step binomial tree determine the possible payoffs from the option.

Empirical application of the binomial tree methodology requires a decision regarding the number of time steps into which the maturity length of the option is divided. The amount by which the price of the underlying asset can move up or down in each time step is related to the volatility of the price of the underlying asset, and to the length of each time step. Choosing a higher number of steps will increase the accuracy of the option price (given the accuracy of the parameter assumptions input to the model), but will also increase the computational complexity and size of the tree. In the limit, the option price from the binomial model with many time steps will approach the well-known Black-Scholes option price (see Hull (2000)).

In this example, the distinctions between the evolution of derivatives in this network industry and existing derivatives in other network industries are already becoming apparent. Consider, for example, the natural gas industry. The cost of transportation, the capacity to transport natural gas, and the risks associated with those costs or the unavailability or untimely delivery of natural gas are all subsumed in the price of natural gas itself. The underlying asset for contracts in natural gas is the delivery of natural gas to a specific location. In the example, the underlying asset is not the commodity coal or the price of coal. Rather, our focus is on the transportation capacity itself – its cost and its timely availability for a given origin-destination pair. To ensure homogeneity, we focus on a particular commodity and on a particular type of rail car as the unit of capacity for this example.

As stated earlier, the underlying asset for our derivatives is a unit of rail capacity suitable for the transport of coal (i.e. a coal hopper car). The relevant price is the market price paid by the shipper to transport coal along the given route on the specified date. We conduct our hypothetical investigation of rail capacity derivatives by examining waybill data available on rail shipments within the continental US. We collect these prices for each route and calculate each of the relevant input parameters to the option pricing model.

The US rail waybill data is a collection of public-use files on rail transportation movement made available by the US rail regulator since the mid-1980s. Transportation waybills are filed with the Surface Transportation Board for every rail movement within the continental US, but the waybill data available to the public comprises approximately a 2 percent sample of all waybills filed (American Association of Railroads (1998)). The individual data records include such items as origin and destination codes, type of commodity, number of cars, shipment tons, length of haul, and interchange locations. The sampled data contain information on various commodity movements, including grain, coal and industrial chemicals. There have been some reporting problems with the waybill data in the past (cf. Schmidt (2001) and American Association of Railroads (1998)). Nevertheless, we regard the 1997-1999 coal data used here as adequate for our purposes, and demonstrate with an illustrative example that option prices can be easily computed using the proper spot market data on freight rates.

While the majority of existing rail car bidding programs in place are used with respect to grain movements, it is difficult to specifically identify grain movements in the existing waybill data. Since coal and coal shippers share many similarities with grain[3], we felt that coal was a useful and identifiable substitute to illustrate the basic options pricing model discussed below. The most commonly sampled and easily identifiable transported good is coal. Goods are identified by a three-digit SIC code for the United States. As used in this study, commodity code #112 represents bituminous coal or lignite. The waybill sample contains extensive records for this commodity; the raw data on coal alone contains almost 2 million records over five years.

The waybill sample uses official US Bureau of Economic Analysis (BEA) codes to identify shipment origins and destinations. For the purposes of demonstrating the binomial option pricing model applied to rail capacity,

---

[3]While similar in many ways, grain movement is more peaked (due to harvest conditions) than coal. This implies that coal transportation prices will be less volatile than grain transportation prices, which is clear from our results. But the extremely low volatility of these rates is unusual, and is certainly due to entry barriers and residual rate regulation in rail.

Table 8.2. Sample descriptive statistics (coal movements)

Rate series ($/ton)	Number of observations	Mean	Standard deviation
West Virginia to New York	278	18.79	2.94
Nebraska to Texas	1337	17.01	2.02

we collected a series of unregulated daily mill rates paid by shippers for transporting coal in selected rail corridors. While appropriate data were not necessarily available for each day, the sample was quite consistent over the chosen interval. The two transportation corridors chosen for this analysis represent coal movements from Lincoln, Nebraska to Corpus Christi, Texas and data from a busy corridor through lower West Virginia to New York state. The sample covers the time period from January 1997 through December 1998. In addition, each of these corridors not only contained enough data to compute the option pricing model, but we also confirmed that each origin was served by more than one railway; implying that some degree of rail competition was present for these movements.

The data allows us to estimate the historical price volatility associated with shipping coal in different time periods. Considering these calculations, along with a comparison to historical rates on Treasury bills of differing maturities, we were able to set prices on hypothetical call options on coal transportation by rail within these corridors. A summary of the input data for each of the two corridors is shown in Table 8.3, Panels A and B. Note that typical values of stock volatility are in the range of 20 to 40 percent (see, e.g., Hull (2000)).

It is well-understood that the option value depends crucially on the volatility of the price or return from the asset underlying the option. Indeed, hedgers are particularly interested in hedging when the price uncertainty or volatility is high.

For comparative purposes, we have defined several hypothetical call options for rail transportation of coal. Each contract is defined by a standardized amount of coal to be transported (a full coal hopper car) from a defined origin to a defined destination, along with an exercise price for the contract and a time frame for the contract. These resultant option prices are illustrated in Table 8.4, Panels A and B. These prices were calculated using the binomial model with the time until option maturity divided into 50 sub-intervals.

Table 8.3. Inputs to the option pricing model

Panel A: Lower West Virginia to New York

Date	Maturity	Corresponding T-Bill rate	Volatility
July 1997	September 97	5.000	0.03939
	December 97	5.095	0.07252
January 1998	March 98	4.940	0.06317
	June 98	4.980	0.10984
April 1998	June 98	4.957	0.06684
	September 98	4.039	0.09073
January 1999	March 99	4.382	0.08024
	June 99	4.420	0.09734

Panel B: Lincoln, Nebraska to Corpus Christi, Texas

Date	Maturity	Corresponding T-Bill rate	Volatility
July 1997	September 97	5.000	0.06704
	December 97	5.095	0.08374
January 1998	March 98	4.940	0.06845
	June 98	4.980	0.09610
April 1998	June 98	4.957	0.07962
	September 98	4.039	0.10466
January 1999	March 99	4.382	0.07221
	June 99	4.420	0.10067

Table 8.4 can be interpreted as follows: the September 1997 contract on coal from lower West Virginia (origin) to New York (destination) with an exercise price of $16 priced on July 1, 1997 would permit the option holder to purchase coal transportation from origin to destination at the end of September 1997 for $16. To purchase such flexibility, i.e. to buy the option, the shipper would pay $1.119 on July 1, 1997. If the hypothetical market price for transporting coal in September exceeded $16, the shipper would exercise his option and purchase coal hopper car capacity along this corridor using the option. If the market price were below the exercise price of the option, the option would expire as worthless. In this case, the shipper would need to purchase coal hopper car capacity in some other manner (presumably in some form of spot market).

8.5.2   Interpreting the Results

One noteworthy feature of the (hypothetical) option price table is the number of options for which the calculated price is low or zero. This is not surprising given the very low volatility of the price of the asset underlying these options. The value of an option at any moment in time depends on the current price of the asset underlying the option, the option's strike price and time to maturity, the current interest rate over the remaining life of the option, and the price volatility of the underlying asset. The option values recorded in Panels A and B of Table 8.4 display characteristics that reflect these influences. The option prices are decreasing with increasing strike prices, and increasing with longer time to maturity or higher spot prices for the underlying asset. Finally, the option value is very sensitive to the last variable, volatility, and options on assets with low price volatility are not valuable.

When considering the merits of a market for coal hopper car capacity, one needs to also consider the regulatory environment of the industry from which this data is taken. The coal freight rate data comes from a period of rate stability characterized by rate liberalization coupled with continued entry regulation in the industry. That there is low freight rate volatility during this period is not surprising. If the market for rail car capacity were to completely deregulate in the fashion described earlier in this paper, we would expect to see increased uncertainty in rail freight transportation rates, similar to what occurred in the natural gas industry. It is this increased uncertainty that players in the market would like to hedge. Derivative instruments that facilitate hedging activity become very valuable to those who would like to hedge when it becomes financially attractive. If one can reasonably expect price volatility for rail shipping to increase, one can reasonably expect options, if written, to have positive value.

Table 8.4. Call option prices

Panel A: Lower West Virginia to New York

	Option maturity date	Exercise price of call option				Spot price of underlying ($/ton)
		16	17	18	19	
Jul. 1997	Sep. 97	1.119	0.205	0.000	0.000	16.92
	Dec. 97	1.351	0.518	0.084	0.000	
Jan. 1998	Mar. 98	2.084	1.089	0.276	0.000	17.89
	Jun. 98	2.281	1.451	0.687	0.336	
Apr. 1998	Jun. 98	2.345	1.357	0.465	0.010	18.15
	Sep. 98	2.546	1.628	0.788	0.336	
Jan. 1999	Mar. 99	0.373	0.000	0.000	0.000	16.06
	Jun. 99	0.632	0.249	0.000	0.000	

Panel B: Lincoln, Nebraska to Corpus Christi, Texas

	Option maturity date	Exercise price of call option				Spot price of underlying ($/ton)
		15	16	17	18	
Jul. 1997	Sep. 97	1.789	0.825	0.158	0.000	16.603
	Dec. 97	1.980	1.096	0.424	0.021	
Jan. 1998	Mar. 98	2.744	1.756	0.807	0.165	17.560
	Jun. 98	2.929	1.960	1.127	0.496	
Apr. 1998	Jun. 98	0.000	0.000	0.000	0.000	13.929
	Sep. 98	0.168	0.000	0.000	0.000	
Jan. 1999	Mar. 99	0.000	0.000	0.000	0.000	13.832
	Jun. 99	0.104	0.000	0.000	0.000	

8.5.3   Additional Key Features

Derivative contracts that are readily traded and thus inexpensive and relatively easy to obtain will not evolve on each and every rail route in the United States and Canada. How then can hedging be accomplished for the routes on which derivatives are not written?

Two alternatives for a rail capacity derivatives market are offered. The first is the suggestion that, as in so many other cases where a perfect hedge does not exist, the hedger can employ one or a series of imperfect hedges. The hedger can choose derivative instruments for those routes for which the price movements are most highly correlated with the routes at risk.

For the second alternative, we note the use of the Baltic Freight Index (BFI) and the futures contract written on that index, in the ocean shipping industry. The Baltic International Financial Futures Exchange was born in 1985 with the intent of providing a mechanism to hedge freight rate risk in the dry bulk sector of the shipping industry (Kvussanos and Nomikos (2000)). The BFI is a weighted-average dry cargo freight rate index, compiled from actual freight rates on 11 shipping routes. These routes are not similar in terms of commodities shipped or transportation vessels employed.

Finally, we note that the idea of implementing derivative contracts that improve efficiency and allocation mechanisms in the rail industry is not entirely novel. In a submission to the Surface Transportation Board, Enron Corporation (cf. Enron Corporation (2000)) promoted the evolution of a "system of tradable capacity rights, which will allow customers to build an infinite number of 'virtual railroads'." The idea is that arbitrageurs, shippers, and railways would buy and sell physical track capacity and, in so doing, the rail network itself would be used more efficiently. The submission emphasized the legitimate logistical improvements that trading of capacity rights could bring about.

8.6   Conclusions and Future Research

This chapter has described a hypothetical derivatives market for rail car capacity pricing that could define an exciting new future for the rail industry. The eventual development of such a market in rail capacity is quite likely since current car allocation systems (COTS, PERX, ACOS, MaxTrax, etc.) already resemble more advanced forms of financial pricing instruments. However, if entry deregulation in rail is enacted, we predict both car and track capacity pricing mechanisms will evolve into the kind of contracts commonly traded on forward/futures exchanges. These contracts, standardized, and traded in a market with enough liquidity, would form the basis for the capacity options markets we envisage.

We developed an example to help illustrate how such a market might function. During the random sample period chosen for illustration, there appears to have been insufficient price volatility to render such contracts desirable in sufficient volume to generate the kind of market we predict will eventually develop. Greater price volatility in the future, along with greater experience with the trading of such contracts, and the potential for future changes in regulation, would generate demand for these trades. This has already occurred in other industries where the characteristics of the underlying asset are sufficiently tractable (with electricity being an example of a less tractable underlying asset).

We acknowledge the limitations of our example due to restrictions on data availability. Nevertheless, the exercise remains useful because it serves to highlight the features of the existing marketplace for rail transportation capacity that make a thriving derivatives market unlikely. Moreover, it sets the stage for modeling how the market for rail capacity might look with deregulated access. A vision of that market would permit a more detailed model of an associated derivatives market, and with it, one could define contract specifications as well as the interactions between market participants. Of particular interest would be the role of speculators and the design of the market to facilitate their efficient involvement in writing contracts and holding a multiplicity of market positions.

The necessary precursor to such derivatives is a change in the supply side of the rail transportation market. With price transparency and price volatility, we believe that hedging instruments would develop. These instruments need not be exchange-traded. One end of the spectrum is tailor-made contracting arrangements. The other extreme is highly standardized exchange-traded instruments. In between, there exists a host of relatively standardized over-the-counter products. Where the rail capacity derivatives of the future will fall along this spectrum cannot be forecast. We contend only that such derivatives are very likely to be born when the rail industry is deregulated, and not before, and that they will be born because of their usefulness in such a new marketplace.

The creation of a capacity derivatives market as defined in this chapter would better serve the interests of the industry. In addition, we believe that information from such a market could provide regulators with a better foundation from which to evaluate proposed mergers among the network operators. In summary, our analysis suggests that the growth of such a market will accelerate and that this growth is a favorable outcome.

Acknowledgments

The authors acknowledge the reviewer for careful reading of an earlier version of this chapter and many helpful comments and suggestions.

References

American Association of Railroads (Railinc Business Services Division) (1998), "User Guide for the 1997 Surface Transportation Board Waybill Sample," Washington DC.

American Association of Railroads (2000), "Economic Impact of Railroads," http://www.aar.org.

Armstrong, M. (2002), "The Theory of Access Pricing and Interconnection," in *Handbook of Telecommunications Economics* 1, pp. 297-384, M. E. Cave, S. K. Majumdar, and I. Vogelsang, editors, Elsevier Science, Amsterdam, The Netherlands.

Bessembinder, H. and Lemmon, M. (2002), "Equilibrium Pricing and Optimal Hedging in Electricity Forward Markets," *Journal of Finance* 3, 1347-1382.

Bonsor, N. (1995), "Competition, Regulation and Efficiency in the Canadian Railway and Highway Industries," in *Essays in Canadian Surface Transportation*, pp. 53-92, F. Palda, editor, The Fraser Institute, Vancouver, British Columbia.

Borenstein, S., Bushnell, J., and Wolak, F. (2000), "Diagnosing Market Power in California's Restructured Wholesale Electricity Market," National Bureau of Economic Research, Working Paper 7868, September.

Canadian Pacific (2001), "MaxTrax Home Page," http://www.cpr.ca/Internet/Content/BusinessLines/Grain/../MaxTrax/MaxTrax.asp.

Cox, J., Ross, S., and Rubinstein, M. (1979), "Option Pricing: A Simplified Approach," *Journal of Financial Economics* 7, 229-264.

De Vany, A., and Walls, D. (1997), "Open Access to Rail Networks," *Transportation Quarterly* 51, 73-78.

Drew, W., and Rosher, P. (1999), "US-Canadian System Comparison: A Grain Shipper's Perspective," in *Going Beyond: Moving into the New Millenium. Proceedings of the 34th Annual Conference, Canadian Transportation Research Forum*, pp. 569-584.

Electricity Daily (2000), 4, Elsevier Science, Amsterdam, The Netherlands.

Enron Corporation (2000), "Ex Parte No. 582, Public Views on Major Rail Consolidations," Submission to the United States of America Department of Transportation Surface Transportation Board, February 29.

Gallamore, R. (1999), "Regulation and Innovation: Lessons from the American Railroad Industry," in *Essays in Transportation Economics and Policy*, pp. 493-529, J. A. Gomez-Ibanez, W. B. Tye, and C. Winston, editors, Brookings Institution Press, Washington DC.

Gibson, S., Cooper, G., and Ball, B. (2002), "Developments in Transport Policy: The Evolution of Capacity Charges on the UK Rail Network," *Journal of Transport Economics and Policy* 36, 341-354.

Hull, J. C. (2000), *Options, Futures & Other Derivatives*, fourth edition, Prentice Hall, Upper Saddle River, New Jersey.

Kober, R., and Baumel, C. P. (1990), "Transportation Forward Contracting or Options: A Description and Analysis of an Application to Railroads," *Transportation Practitioners Journal* **58**, 51-63.

Kvussanos, M. G., and Nomikos, N. K. (2000), "Hedging in the Freight Futures Market," *Journal of Derivatives*, 41-58.

Kwoka, J. E., and White, L. J. (1999), "Manifest Destiny? The Union Pacific-Southern Pacific Merger (1996)," in *The Antitrust Revolution: Economics, Competition, and Policy*, third edition, pp. 64-88, J. E. Kwoka and L. J. White, editors, Oxford University Press, New York.

Laffont, J.-J., Rey, P., and Tirole, J. (1998), "Network Competition: I. Overview and Nondiscriminatory Pricing," *RAND Journal of Economics* **29**, 1-37.

Larson, P. D., and Spraggins, H. B. (2000), "The American Railroad Industry: Twenty Years After Staggers," *Transportation Quarterly* **54**, 31-45.

McMullen, B. S., and Lee, M-K. (1993), "Assessing the Impact of Regulatory Reform on Motor Carrier Cost Efficiency," *Journal of the Transportation Research Forum* **33**, 1-9.

Nilsson, J. E. (1999), "Allocation of Track Capacity: Experimental Evidence on the Use of Priority Auctioning in the Railway Industry," *International Journal of Industrial Organization* **17**, 1139-1162.

Schmidt, S. (2001), "Market Structure and Market Outcomes in Deregulated Rail Freight Markets," *International Journal of Industrial Organization* **19**, 99-131.

Spiewak, S. (1998), "Power Marketing: Price Creation in Electricity Markets," Power Marketing Association and The Edison Electric Institute, Washington DC.

Stoft, S. (2002), *Power System Economics: Designing Markets for Electricity*, IEEE/Wiley Press, Piscataway, New Jersey.

Surface Transportation Board (1992), Docket No. 40169, National Grainand Feed Association vs. Burlington Northern Railroad Company, April 20.

Transport Canada (2003), "Straight Ahead – A Vision for Transportation in Canada," Ottawa, Canada.

Tye, W. B. (1991), *The Transition to Deregulation Developing Economic Standards For Public Policies*, Quorum Books, Westport, Connecticut.

United States Government (1980), Staggers Rail Act, Publication L. No. 96-448, 94, Stat. 1895.

Vachal, K. (2001), "Comparison of Guaranteed Equipment Programs," Upper Great Plains Transportation Institute, North Dakota State University, Fargo, North Dakota.

Wilson, W. W., Priewe, S. R., and Dahl, B. (1998), "Forward Shipping Options for Grain by Rail," *Journal of Agricultural and Resource Economics* **23**, 526-544.

Wood, D. F., and Johnson, J. C. (1996), *Contemporary Transportation*, fifth edition, Prentice-Hall, Upper Saddle River, New Jersey.

Part II Economic Networks

9 A Supply Chain Network Economy: Modeling and Qualitative Analysis

Ding Zhang, June Dong, and Anna Nagurney

0.1 Introduction

This chapter proposes a modeling intitiative that is network-based to formalize both intra-supply chain cooperation and inter-supply chain competition. In particular, we propose a general network model for a supply chain economy since it is now recognized that when it comes to production, distribution, and consumption today, it is no longer simply firms that compete with one another, but, rather, it is *supply chains*, consisting of economic decision-makers and their spectrum of activities. The supply chain network economic model that we develop in this chapter aims to answer such fundamental questions as: How do economic decision-makers form coalitions in a competitive environment? How do supply chains compete with one another, and how does one identify the *winning* supply chain?

We note that, to-date, the major emphasis in the study of supply chains in the literature has been the optimization of a supply chain that is owned (and controlled) by a single entity with various issues explored such as the distribution network design, coordination, and inventory management (see, e.g., Chen (1998) and the reviews by Geoffrion and Power (1995) and Beamon (1998)). More recently, competition among supply chain agents has been addressed using game theoretic formulations as in the inventory-capacity game models of Cachon and Zipkin (1999) and Cachon and Lariviere (1999a, b) who studied two-stage serial supply chains. Corbett and Karmarkar (2001), on the other hand, investigated a supply chain network consisting of several tiers of decision-makers who compete within a tier. Under the assumption of identical linear production cost functions, they determined the number of entrants under Nash equilibrium.

Nagurney, Dong, and Zhang (2002), in turn, developed a three tiered supply chain network equilibrium model consisting of manufacturers, retailers, and consumers, who may compete within a tier but cooperate between tiers.

Using a variational inequality formulation, the equilibrium production outputs, shipments, and consumption quantities, along with the prices of the
product associated with the different tiers could then be determined with an
iterative computational procedure. Nagurney et al. (2002a) further extended
the basic framework to incorporate electronic commerce whereas Nagurney et
al. (2002b) focused on the dynamics of supply chain networks. Subsequently,
Dong, Zhang, and Nagurney (2002) developed a supply chain network equilibrium model with random demands associated with the product at different
retail outlets and formulated and solved the model as a variational inequality
problem. Our work is similar in spirit, although derived from an entirely different perspective and application setting, to that of Dafermos and Nagurney
(1984), who constructed a general network model of production, along with
its variational inequality formulation.

This chapter is organized as follows. In Section 9.2, we introduce the
concept of a supply chain economy and develop the general network model.
In particular, we consider an economy with multiple profit-driven decision-
makers or "agents," who represent distinct supply chain entities such as raw
material suppliers, manufacturers, logistic firms, wholesalers, and/or retailers. The supply chain economy is, hence, a network of agents and their
activities, which can include, for example, the production, distribution, sale,
and consumption of one or more products. Hence, a supply chain network
economy may consist of several supply chains which interact in their procurement, production, logistic, and retailing activities.

The notable features of the network model include:

1. The model is not limited to a fixed number of tiers with similar func-
tions/operations associated with a given tier as in the work of Cachon and
Zipkin (1999), Cachon and Lariviere (1999a, 1999b), Nagurney, Dong, and
Zhang (2002), Nagurney et al. (2002a, b), Dong, Zhang, and Nagurney
(2002). For an example of a supply chain network with a fixed number of
tiers and similar functions associated with a given tier, see Figure 9.1. The
model developed in this chapter, in contrast, allows for an entirely *general
structure* of the supply chains. In addition, the model allows for the study of
inter-chain competition as well as coordination and integration of *intra*-chain
activities with appropriately defined variables, network topology, and costs
associated with the links.

2. The model addresses inter-supply chain competition at multiple markets
and does not assume homogeneity of the product throughout the chain but,
rather, captures also the costs associated with the subcomponents as the
"product" proceeds down the chain.

3. The network model includes operation links as well as interface links with
the former corresponding to such possible business operations as manufacturing, storage, and transportation and with the latter acting as a bridge
between businesses.

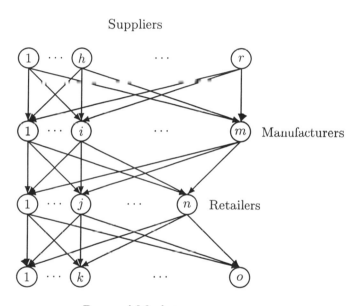

Fig. 9.1. An example of a four-tiered supply chain network with suppliers, manufacturers, retailers, and demand markets and with similar functions associated with a given tier

The cost on a specific interface link, in turn, can measure the effectiveness of the coordination and the integration of the network agents. Moreover, we impose no artificial conditions on the cost functions associated with the various links.

In Section 9.3, we derive the equilibrium conditions, which are based on the identification of those chains in the network with minimal marginal chain cost and positive flow. The concept, which is based on the ideas of Wardrop (1952), and which has had wide application in traffic networks as well as other application settings (see Nagurney (1999), Nagurney and Dong (2002), and the references therein), is here generalized to apply to network chains, rather than paths, and to material flows, rather than identical types of network flows (such as travelers). We establish the variational inequality formulation of the equilibrium conditions governing the supply chain network economy. It is noteworthy that the model enables us to bring potential supply chain structures into our study. Moreover, the solution of the model identifies potential supply chain structures with minimum marginal costs and, hence, predicts what supply chain may prevail in the future. Consequently, the model can suggest effective supply chain formations.

In Section 9.4, we then turn to the examination of the qualitative properties of the equilibrium flow pattern and provide both existence and uniqueness results. Section 9.5 summarizes the results of this chapter and presents suggestions for future research.

9.2   A Network Model of the Supply Chain Economy

It is clear that, in today's business environment, multiple supply chains co-exist and many of them compete in similar businesses such as Wal-Mart, Target, and Sears. The interaction among different supply chains, however, is not solely one of competition, but may involve other dimensions, such as cooperation. In this section, we propose a new concept – that of a *Supply Chain Network Economy* – to address the multi-dimensional interaction among supply chains. We first present the definition and then develop the model.

Definition 9.1: A Supply Chain Network Economy
A supply chain economy is a network of interrelated activities of procurement, production, distribution, sale, and consumption of one or more products, conducted by coalitions of business entities who act collectively within a coalition. Given the definition of a supply chain, we state that a supply chain network economy is a network of interrelated supply chains.

A supply chain network economy describes the environment (competitive and cooperative, in parts) of all the market-related and operation-related activities of business firms who belong to many supply chains and these supply chains compete in several related markets.

In this chapter, we consider a supply chain network economy associated with a particular product with multiple markets. We assume that there are n markets that are spatially separated, with a typical one denoted by j.

Let $G = [N, L]$ denote the network of the supply chain economy, where N denotes the set of nodes and L the set of oriented links in the network. The orientation of a link indicates the flow of material. The supply chain network economy may consist of several supply chains with each one being a subnetwork (connected subgraph) of G.

There are three different types of nodes in the network model: the origin nodes, the intermediate nodes, and the destination nodes. An origin node corresponds to the "beginning" or origin of a supply chain or supply chains and usually indicates the source of raw material or other resource. A destination node corresponds to the destination of a supply chain material flow and usually indicates a market for the end product. An intermediate node, in turn, lies in between the other nodes, including other intermediate ones, and serves as a connection for the supply chain links.

We consider two basic types of links in the network model: an operation link and an interface link. An operation link represents a business function performed by a firm in a supply chain network, and can reflect a manufacturing, transportation, storage, or, even, service operation. A firm may have several operation links in the supply chain network economy with distinct links corresponding to the firm's distinct business functions. An interface link, in turn, serves as a business-to-business bridge and lies, typically, between operation links in the network model. If we denote the set of operation links by A and the set of interface links by B, then we have that $L = A \cup B$.

We now distinguish between potential and active supply chains, with the latter playing an especially important role in terms of competitiveness of the supply chain network economy. A potential supply chain is represented by a connected subgraph of the network characterized by a destination node corresponding to its pertinent market. It is recognized in the model that a possible supply chain structure may not necessarily be prevailing at a particular time. However, a potential chain can evolve to prevail in the supply chain economy if it possesses a competitive structure. A potential supply chain becomes active in our model if it carries positive flow of material; hence, a potential supply chain is active if and only if its chain flow of material is positive. Later, we provide conditions that allow us to explicitly identify such chains and chain flows.

Let S_j denote the set of all potential supply chains pertaining to market j. S denotes the set of all potential supply chains in the network representing the supply chain economy.

The *chain flow* of a supply chain is defined to be the volume of the final or end product that the supply chain delivers to its pertinent market, that is, it is the output of the supply chain. Let X_s denote the chain flow of chain s and let X be the vector of all the chain flows of all the supply chains in the supply chain economy. The volume of the end product of a supply chain determines the amount of "work" processed at each stage of the material flow stream. For example, by tracking back the flow of material from the end product and exploding the series of bills of materials, one can determine the amount of work (and information) processed or resources (such as labor hours, machine hours, storage space, etc.) utilized in each participator link of a supply chain. To make such a measure rigorous, we define the process rate below.

Definition 9.2: Process Rate

For a supply chain s and its participant operation link a, the process rate of a with respect to s, denoted by λ_{as}, is the amount of resource utilized (work conducted or information processed) by link a necessary to make one unit of end product of the supply chain s.

Consider, for example, an automobile supply chain, in which a participating tire manufacturer would have a process rate of four since each car requires four tires. Hence, an output of two hundred cars from such a chain would imply eight hundred tires to be manufactured by the participating tire manufacturer. Consequently, the actual material flow down the supply chain varies in substance as well as in quantity. It is distinct from a transportation network in that the actual amount of flow in a supply chain does not always equal its chain flow but is, in fact, λ_{as} *times* the chain flow on the link a. Here, for the sake of technical simplicity, we adopt the convention that the value of any particular λ_{as} is not less than one. In practice, a processing rate can always be scaled to an appropriate unit so that this assumption is satisfied.

We assume, for simplicity, that no link is shared by two different supply chains. However, this assumption may be ultimately relaxed. Therefore, the operation links and interface links can be partitioned into their supply chain families, A_s and B_s, that is,

$$A = \sum_{s \in S} A_s, \quad B = \sum_{s \in S} B_s. \tag{9.1}$$

In Figure 9.2, we depict an example of two supply chains competing at a demand market. Supply chain 1 is comprised of four operation links: a_{11}, a_{12}, a_{13}, and a_{14}, and three interface links: b_{11}, b_{12}, and b_{13}. Supply chain 2, on the other hand, is comprised of three operation links: a_{21}, a_{22}, and a_{23}, and one interface link b_{21}.

For any link $a \in L$, we let x_a denote the flow on the link. In the case of an operation link, x_a is the total amount of work processed on the link. Units for measuring the flow on an operation link can vary from application to application and should be appropriately selected. Examples of appropriate units, based on the nature of the operation, can correspond to the number of subassemblies, the parts determined by the bill of materials, the number of

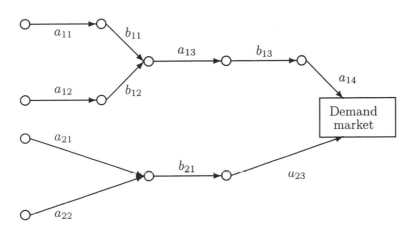

Fig. 9.2. An example of two supply chains competing at a demand market

machine hours, the hours of labor of the production operations, the number of truckloads required for transportation, or even the square footage in the warehouse used for storage purposes.

Recall that X_s denotes the chain flow of chain s. Then, one has the following relationship between an operation link flow and a chain flow:

$$x_a = \lambda_{as} X_s, \quad \forall a \in A_s, \quad \forall s \in S. \tag{9.2}$$

For an interface link b, on the other hand, the link flow x_b indicates the amount of integration work, coordination effort, and/or information processed on this link. Therefore, the link flow of an interface link is determined by the chain flow of its governing supply chain, that is,

$$x_b = x_b(X_s), \quad \forall b \in B_s, \quad \forall s \in S. \tag{9.3a}$$

It is reasonable to assume that the chain-link flow relationship given in (9.3a) is a strictly monotone increasing function, although it can be nonlinear; that is, the greater the volume of the supply chain output, the greater the integration work required on all the interface links. Hence, the inverse function of (9.3a) exists, that is,

$$X_s = X_s^{-1}(x_b), \quad \forall b \in B_s, \quad \forall s \in S. \tag{9.3b}$$

The link cost of an operation link is defined to be the total cost incurred by the firm in performing the corresponding task function, which is in concert with the definition of an operation link being a business function performed by a firm. Therefore, the link cost $\bar{c}_a$ of link a is a function of its flow x_a, and can be expressed as

$$\bar{c}_a = \bar{c}_a(x_a), \quad \forall a \in A; \tag{9.4}$$

in other words, the cost of carrying out a task function depends on the amount of work processed in the task. Depending upon the nature of the operation corresponding to the link, the link cost function can be nonlinear, with consolidation and congestion being the two primary factors that determine the cost structure. For example, if a batch or lot size is required for a production operation or if a truckload or shipload is applicable, a consolidation effect can be expected to be present and, thus, the greater the volume, the cheaper the rate. On the other hand, if the link represents a bottleneck operation, then one can expect a congestion effect, with the function increasing as the volume of "traffic" increases.

The cost of an interface link, since such a link is an *inter-link*, reflects the effectiveness of coordination and integration of the two operation links that it bridges. The geographic distance, the experience of past cooperation, and/or the sophistication of the information system integrated in the two joined operations, as well as the compatibility of the two, represent several factors that could account for the cost of an interface link. Since effective coordination of two successive operation links of a supply chain may depend upon other joints of this chain as well, we assume that the cost of an interface link may, in general, depend on the flows of all the interface links belonging to the same supply chain. However, in light of (9.3a), it can be determined by the chain flow of its governing supply chain, and according to (9.3b), it also uniquely depends on the link flow of the interface link, that is,

$$\bar{c}_b = \bar{c}_b(X_s) = \bar{c}_b(x_b), \quad \forall b \in B_s, \quad \forall s \in S. \tag{9.5}$$

The cost of a supply chain s is then the sum of the link costs of its operation and interface links, which can be expressed as

$$\bar{C}_s = \sum_{a \in A_s} \bar{c}_a + \sum_{b \in B_s} \bar{c}_b. \tag{9.6}$$

We assume that the demand for the product at a marketplace is elastic and can be characterized by its market value. Let q_j and v_j denote, respectively, the supply and the market value of the product at market j. Further, let q, and v be, respectively, the corresponding n-dimensional vectors of supplies and prices. By definition, the supply at a market is equal to the sum of the chain flows of all the supply chains that are driven by that market, that is,

$$q_j = \sum_{s \in S_j} X_s, \quad j = 1, \ldots, n. \tag{9.7}$$

In general, we assume that the market value of the product at a market may depend on the vector of supplies of the products at all the markets, that is,

$$v_j = v_j(q), \quad j = 1, \ldots, n, \tag{9.8}$$

or, in vector form,

$$v = v(q) = (v_j(q)); \quad j = 1, \ldots, n). \tag{9.9}$$

It is reasonable to assume, from an economic perspective, that, in (9.8) and (9.9), the market value is a decreasing function of the supply.

9.3 Equilibrium Conditions

In this section, we present the equilibrium conditions, the mathematical formulation of which can be utilized to determine the answers to the central questions of this chapter. These are: Who, among the multiple agents will enter this economy? Which potential chains will win through competition and become active chains? What outputs do the active chains deliver to the end markets?

We first, however, need to introduce the concepts of *link marginal cost* and *chain marginal cost*.

Definition 9.3: Link Marginal Cost

For any operation link, $a \in A_s$, the link marginal cost, c_a, is defined to be the unit link processing cost, if the flow on link a is no less than the processing rate, λ_{as}, for its governing supply chain, s; otherwise, it is defined to be the unit link cost for the processing rate, λ_{as}, namely,

$$c_a(x_a) = \begin{cases} \bar{c}_a(x_a)/x_a, & \text{if } x_a \geq \lambda_{as} \\ \bar{c}_a(\lambda_{as})/\lambda_{as}, & \text{if } x_a \leq 1. \end{cases} \tag{9.10}$$

For any interface link, $b \in B_s$, the link marginal cost, c_b, is defined to be the unit link cost, if the chain flow of its governing supply chain is no less than the one unit; otherwise, it is defined to be the link cost for one unit of the chain flow, namely,

$$c_b(X_s) = \begin{cases} \bar{c}_b(X_s)/X_s, & \text{if } X_s \geq 1 \\ \bar{c}_b(1), & \text{if } X_s \leq 1. \end{cases} \tag{9.11}$$

Since any active operation link in a supply chain s must process a minimum of one unit of the chain flow, and, consequently, the amount of λ_{as} link flow; in practice, the link marginal cost (9.10) is the unit processing cost for an active link. On the other hand, if the link flow turns out to be less than λ_{as}, then it would imply that the link is not on an active supply chain. In this case, the link marginal cost in (9.10) can be interpreted as the *triggering cost*, that is, the marginal cost necessary to activate this link. The link marginal cost for an interface link is similarly defined, except that it is based on the chain flow of the governing supply chain.

In line with the above definitions of operation and interface link marginal costs, we state the definition of the chain marginal cost as follows.

Definition 9.4: Chain Marginal Cost
The chain marginal cost of a supply chain s is defined to be the unit chain processing cost of chain s, if the chain flow X_s is no less than one unit; otherwise, it is the chain cost for one unit of flow.

$$C_s = \begin{cases} \bar{C}_s(X_s)/X_s, & \text{if } X_s \geq 1 \\ \bar{C}(1), & \text{if } X_s \leq 1. \end{cases} \tag{9.12}$$

It is clear that the above-defined link marginal costs and chain marginal cost are continuous when the link costs are continuous, and are differentiable when the link costs are differentiable. Furthermore, in view of (9.6), we can spell out the chain marginal cost in terms of link marginal costs in a uniform expression regardless of the value of X_s:

$$C_s = \sum_{a \in A_s} \lambda_{as} c_a(x_a) + \sum_{b \in B_s} c_b(X_s). \tag{9.13}$$

An end market can be viewed as the *destination* of the product, which, in turn, "pulls" the flow of materials through all its pertinent supply chains. The supply chains, as alternative "paths" to the destination are "racing" to deliver the product. In line with the perspective that the firms' goal in terms of cooperation in the supply chain is to make the final product overall at less cost than competing supply chain firms (see Cavinato (1992)), the winning chains in this race or competition are, in effect, the "shortest paths," that is, those that can deliver the product at the least marginal cost.

There is an interesting analogy between this interpretation and that occurring in the context of traffic networks in which travelers seek to determine the shortest paths from their origins to their destinations. In a congested urban transportation network, travelers are assumed to select shortest paths (minimal cost paths) from their origins to their destinations with Wardrop (1952) being credited with the following (first) principle:

Wardrop's First Principle
The travel costs of all paths actually used are equal and less than those which would be experienced by a single traveler on any unused path.

One should realize that the network structure of a supply chain can be any connected subgraph, with the simplest topology being that of a tree and, hence, it is more complex than a path in a transportation network from an origin to a destination. Also, unlike travelers (in vehicles), who arrive at their destinations in the same form as they leave their origins, the flow of material in a supply chain network economy evolves from raw materials, through fabricated parts, subassemblies, to finished products, compounded at various stages of a supply chain process.

Nevertheless, the economic rationale that an inferior or less cost-effective supply chain will lose to its rivals is in the same spirit as Wardrop's first principle.

We now formally state the definition of an equilibrium in this framework.

Definition 9.5: Equilibrium of a Supply Chain Network Economy
In a supply chain network equilibrium, the active supply chains are those whose marginal cost is equal to the market value of the product at the pertinent market, and the inactive supply chains are those whose marginal cost is greater than or equal to the market value of the product at the pertinent market. Mathematically, a feasible supply chain network economy with flows X^*, with induced q^* through (9.7), constitutes a supply chain network equilibrium if and only if the following system of equalities and inequalities holds true:

$$C_s(X) \begin{cases} = v_j(q^*), & if \quad X_s^* > 0 \\ \geq v_j(q^*), & if \quad X_s^* = 0, \end{cases} \quad \forall s \in S_j, \qquad (9.14)$$

for all end markets j; $j = 1, \ldots, n$.

With this definition, we now have the answers to the aforementioned questions. The winning (active) chains are those supply chains with least marginal cost for their pertinent markets, and they are the only ones that carry positive flow of materials.

Before deriving the variational inequality formulation of the governing equilibrium conditions, we introduce link capacities. Recall that since an operation link may represent a manufacturing process, transport, and/or storage, it may face such constraints as limited machine hours, a fixed number of trucks available, and/or limited storage space in a warehouse. Denote the link capacity of an operation link by h_a. Then, we have that

$$\lambda_{as} X_s = x_a \leq h_a, \quad \forall a \in A_s, \quad \forall s \in S. \qquad (9.15)$$

The feasible set underlying the supply chain economy in terms of the chain variables' accounting operational capacities is expressed as

$$\Omega_X = \{X \geq 0 : (9.15) \text{ holds for all } a \in A_s, \, s \in S\}. \qquad (9.16)$$

This set is equivalent to the feasible set in chain variables and supply patterns, defined as

$$\Omega_{Xq} = \{X \geq 0, \, q \geq 0 : (9.7), (9.15) \text{ hold for all } a \in A_s, \, s \in S; \, j = 1, \ldots, n\}. \qquad (9.17)$$

The following theorem gives a mathematical formulation for the supply chain network equilibrium in chain variables.

Theorem 9.1: Variational Inequality Formulation
X^* with induced q^* through (9.7) is a supply chain network equilibrium if and only if (X^*, q^*) solves the following variational inequality problem: determine $(X^*, q^*) \in \Omega_{Xq}$ such that

$$\sum_{j=1}^{n} \left[\sum_{s \in S_j} C_s(X^*)(X_s - X_s^*) - v_j(q^*)(q_j - q_j^*) \right] \geq 0, \quad (X, q) \in \Omega_{Xq}. \quad (9.18)$$

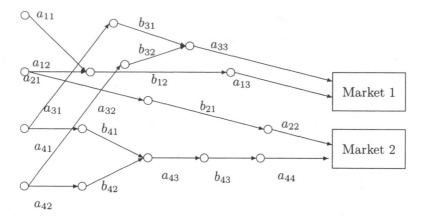

Fig. 9.3. An example of a supply chain network economy

Proof: The proof is standard (see, e.g., Nagurney (1999)). □

9.3.1   An Example

In this subsection, we present a numerical example.

Example

Consider a supply chain network example as depicted in Figure 9.3. There are two demand markets, Market 1 and Market 2. There are four supply chains, denoted, respectively, by S_1, S_2, S_3, and S_4 and also referred to, without loss of generality, as Supply Chains 1, 2, 3, and 4. Supply chain S_1 is comprised of operation links a_{11}, a_{12}, a_{13} and interface link b_{12}. S_2 is comprised of operation links a_{21} and a_{22} and interface link b_{21}. S_3, in turn, is comprised of operation links a_{31}, a_{32}, and a_{33} and interface links b_{31} and b_{32}. Supply chain S_4 consists of operation links a_{41}, a_{42}, a_{43}, and a_{44} and interface links b_{41}, b_{42}, and b_{43}. Supply Chain 1 and Supply Chain 3 are competing for Market 1, while Supply Chain 2 and Supply Chain 4 are competing for Market 2.

The process rates for the operation links are given by:

$$\lambda_{11} = 2, \quad \lambda_{12} = 3, \quad \lambda_{13} = 1,$$

$$\lambda_{21} = 4, \quad \lambda_{22} = 1,$$

$$\lambda_{31} = 2, \quad \lambda_{32} = 2, \quad \lambda_{33} = 1,$$

$$\lambda_{41} = 2, \quad \lambda_{42} = 4, \quad \lambda_{43} = 2, \quad \lambda_{44} = 1.$$

The link marginal cost functions of the operation and the interface links, for each supply chain, are as given below.

$$c_{a11} = 0.5x_{a11} + 1, \quad c_{a12} = 0.1x_{a12},$$

$$c_{b11} = 2.1x_{b11} + 1, \quad c_{a13} = 5x_{a13} + 3,$$

$$c_{a21} = 0.5x_{a21} + 0.5, \quad c_{b21} = X_2, \quad c_{a22} = x_{a22} + 2,$$

$$c_{a31} = x_{a31} + 4, \quad c_{a32} = x_{a32} + 4, \quad c_{b31} = X_3 + 4,$$

$$c_{b32} = X_3 + 4, \quad c_{a33} = x_{a33} + 4,$$

$$c_{a41} = c_{a42} = c_{a43} = 0.5,$$

$$c_{a44} = 2x_{a44} + 1, \quad c_{b41} = c_{b42} = c_{b43} = X_4.$$

The chain marginal costs can be computed according to (9.13) by using the link marginal costs. They are as follows:

$$C_{S_1} = 10X_1 + 6, \quad C_{S_2} = 10X_2 + 4, \quad C_{S_3} = 11X_3 + 28, \quad C_{S_4} = 5X_4 + 5.$$

Suppose now that the two demand markets are interrelated and that their market value functions are:

$$v_1(q) = 40 - 5q_1 - q_2, \quad v_2(q) = 60 - q_1 - 10q_2.$$

The supply chain network equilibrium in this example is given by

$$X^* = (X_1^*, X_2^*, X_3^*, X_4^*) = (2, 1.4, 0, 2.6),$$

which generates the equilibrium supply pattern

$$q^* = (q_1^*, q_2^*) = (2, 4).$$

The market value at Market 1 at equilibrium is 26, whereas the market value at Market 2 at equilibrium is 18.

Examining the two competing supply chains for Market 1 at the equilibrium, one see that the marginal chain cost of Supply Chain 1 is 26 and the marginal chain cost of Supply Chain 3 is 28. This verifies the equilibrium condition that the market value is equal to the marginal chain cost for the active (winning) supply chain, Supply Chain 1, and that the inactive chain (the loser), Supply Chain 3, has a marginal cost that is higher than the market value. The equilibrium condition also holds for Market 2. In this case, the two competing supply chains, Supply Chain 2 and Supply Chain 4, are both active, and have the same marginal chain cost, 18, which is equal to the market value at Market 2 in equilibrium.

9.4 Qualitative Properties

This section provides the fundamental qualitative properties of the mathematical formulation of the equilibrium of the supply chain network economy presented in the previous section. First, we establish the existence of an equilibrium and then turn to its uniqueness.

Theorem 9.2: Existence
Suppose that the link cost functions for all the operation and interface links are continuous. Then, there exists an equilibrium of the supply chain network economy.

Proof: We claim that the feasible set Ω_{Xq} is compact. It is easy to see that Ω_{Xq} is closed. To show that it is bounded, one has, in view of (9.15), for every supply chain s

$$X_s \leq \lambda_{as}^{-1} h_a, \quad \forall a \in A_s, \tag{9.19}$$

which yields

$$X_s \leq \min_{a \in A_s} \{\lambda_{as}^{-1} h_a\}, \quad \forall s \in S. \tag{9.20}$$

(9.20) suggests that in (9.7),

$$q_j \leq \sum_{s \in S_j} \min_{a \in A_s} \{\lambda_{as}^{-1} h_a\}, \quad j = 1, \ldots, n. \tag{9.21}$$

Expressions (9.20) and (9.21) imply that all the variables are, indeed, bounded from above, and, hence, Ω_{Xq} is bounded.

As noted before, the continuity of the link cost functions guarantees the continuity of the link marginal cost functions, which further implies the continuity of the chain marginal cost functions through (9.13). Therefore, the variational inequality (9.18) is a continuous mapping over a compact set. It, thus, according to the standard theory of variational inequalities (see Kinderlehrer and Stampacchia (1980)) has at least one solution. $\square$

The uniqueness of the supply chain network equilibrium pattern can, in general, be ensured under an assumption of strict monotonicity (cf. Nagurney (1999) and the references therein) of the marginal link cost functions and the market value functions as given by the following theorem.

Theorem 9.3: Uniqueness
Suppose that the marginal link cost functions are strictly monotone increasing, and the market value functions are strictly monotone decreasing, with respect to their arguments. Then, there exists a unique equilibrium of the supply chain network economy.

Proof: The monotonicity assumption on link marginal cost functions implies that the chain marginal cost function is monotone increasing, in view of (9.13). Therefore, under the condition of the theorem, the vector function of the variational inequality problem (9.18) is monotone. The conclusion of the theorem follows from Theorem 9.2 and the standard theory of variational inequality problem (see, e.g., Nagurney (1999)). $\square$

Let $J_q v$ denote the Jacobian matrix of the market value function with respect to the supply vector q. It is well-known (see, e.g., Nagurney (1999)) that if $J_q v$ is symmetric, then there is a real-valued function $\bar{v}$ whose gradient is v, namely,

$$v = \nabla_q \bar{v}. \tag{9.22}$$

A special case of v being a gradient of a real-valued function is that the market value function is separable; namely, in this case, the market value of the product at market j depends only on the supply at market j. In this case, the Jacobian matrix of v is a diagonal matrix with the diagonal entries being the derivative of the market value with respect to their own supply.

Under certain conditions, the supply chain network equilibrium can also be formulated as the following optimization problem:

$$\min_{(X,q) \in \Omega_{Xq}} \sum_{j=1}^{n} \sum_{s \in S_j} \int_0^{X_s} C_s(u)du - \bar{v}(q). \tag{9.23}$$

Theorem 9.4: Sufficient Condition

Suppose that the Jacobian matrix of the market value function is symmetric. Then, a sufficient condition for (X^*, q^*) to be an equilibrium of a supply chain network economy is that it solves the optimization problem (9.23).

Proof: According to Theorem 9.1, it suffices to show that any solution to optimization problem (9.23) is a solution to (9.18). However, the variational inequality problem (9.18) is simply a restatement of the first-order necessary condition of the optimization problem (9.23) by noticing that the vector function entering into (9.18) is the gradient of the objective function in (9.23). □

Theorem 9.5: Necessary and Sufficient Condition

Suppose that the marginal link cost functions are monotone increasing, and the Jacobian matrix of the market value function is symmetric and negative semi-definite. Then, (X^*, q^*) is an equilibrium of the supply chain network economy if and only if it solves the optimization problem (9.23).

Proof: The vector function entering (9.18) is the gradient of the objective function in (9.23). Hence, the assumption of monotone marginal link costs, together with negative semi-definiteness of the Jacobian matrix of the market value function, implies that the objective function of (9.23) is convex. According to Bazaraa, Sherali, and Shetty (1993), the variational inequality problem (9.23) is the necessary and sufficient condition of the solution to the convex programming (9.23). □

9.5   Summary and Conclusions

In this chapter, we proposed a new framework, that is network-based, to formalize the modeling and analysis of supply chains. The framework allows for the simultaneous study of both intra-supply chain cooperation as well as inter-supply chain competition. Moreover, it has the notable feature that unlike many of the supply chain models in the literature, the underlying network topological structure is general. In addition, the model allows for the transformation of material flows as they proceed through the network.

We developed the supply chain network economic model, derived the governing equilibrium conditions, and then provided the variational inequality formulation. We established existence of an equilibrium pattern, and also gave conditions under which uniqueness is guaranteed.

Acknowledgments

The research of the second and third authors was supported, in part, by NSF Grant No.: IIS-0002647. The research of the third author was also supported by an AT&T Industrial Ecology Fellowship. The support is gratefully acknowledged. The authors are grateful to the anonymous reviewers for their comments and suggestions on an earlier version of this manuscript.

References

Bazaraa, M. S., Sherali, H. D., and Shetty, C. M. (1993), *Nonlinear Programming: Theory and Algorithms*, John Wiley & Sons, New York.

Beamon, B. M. (1998), "Supply Chain Design and Analysis: Models and Methods," *International Journal of Production Economics* **52**, 281-294.

Cachon, G. P., and Lariviere, M. A. (1999a), "Capacity Choice and Allocation: Strategic Behavior and Supply Chain Performance," *Management Science* **45**, 685-703.

Cachon, G. P., and Lariviere, M. A. (1999b), "Capacity Allocation Using Past Sales: When to Turn and Earn," *Management Science* **45**, 1091-1108.

Cachon, G. P., and Zipkin, P. H. (1999), "Competitive and Cooperative Inventory Policies in a Two-Stage Supply Chain," *Management Science* **45**, 936-953.

Cavinato, J. L. (1992), "A Total Cost/Value for Supply Chain Competitiveness," *Journal of Business Logistics* **13**, 285-301.

Chen, F. (1998), "Echelon Reorder Points, Installation Reorder Points, and the Value of Centralized Demand Information," *Management Science* **44**, 221-234.

Corbett, C. J., and Karmarkar, U. S. (2001), "Competition and Structure in Serial Supply Chains with Deterministic Demand," *Management Science* **47**, 966-978.

Dafermos, S., and Nagurney, A. (1984), "A Network Formalism of Market Equilibrium Problems and Variational Inequalities," *Operations Research Letters* **3**, 247-250.

Dong, J., Zhang, D., and Nagurney, A. (2002), "A Supply Chain Network Equilibrium Model with Random Demands," *European Journal of Operational Research*, in press.

Geoffrion, A. M., and Power, R. F. (1995), "Twenty Years of Strategic Distribution System Design: An Evolution Perspective," *Interface* **25**, 105-127.

Kinderlehrer, D., and Stampacchia, G. (1980), *An Introduction to Variational Inequalities and their Application*, Academic Press, New York.

Nagurney, A. (1999), *Network Economics: A Variational Inequality Approach*, Second and Revised Edition, Kluwer Academic Publishers, Dordrecht, The Netherlands.

Nagurney, A., and Dong, J. (2002), *Supernetworks: Decision-Making for the Information Age*, Edward Elgar Publishers, Cheltenham, England.

Nagurney, A., Dong, J., and Zhang, D. (2002), "A Supply Chain Network Equilibrium Model," *Transportation Research E* **38**, 281-303.

Nagurney, A., Ke, K., Cruz, J., Hancock, K., and Southworth, F. (2002a), "Dynamics of Supply Chains: A Multilevel (Logistical/Informational/Financial) Network Perspective," *Environment & Planning B* **29**, 795-818.

Nagurney, A., Loo, J., Dong, J., and Zhang, D. (2002b), "Supply Chain Networks and Electronic Commerce: A Theoretical Perspective," *Netnomics* **4**, 187-220.

Wardrop, J. G. (1952), "Some Theoretical Aspects of Road Traffic Research," *Proceedings of the Institute of Civil Engineers*, Part II, London, pp. 325-378.

10 Applications of Fluid Modeling in Distribution Systems

Soulaymane Kachani and Georgia Perakis

10.1 Introduction

The efficient management of a supply chain system is one of the central problems in operations management. As a result, it has been the focus of extensive research in the past decade. Apart from the attention the topic has received from the academic world, its rapid growth is also reflected in the development of several software companies. This seems to indicate that the business world considers the development of supply chain management significant. A thorough review of supply chain management can be found in Stadtler and Kilger (2000), Tayur, Ganeshan, and Magazine (1998) as well as in Tomlin (2002) and the references therein. Furthermore, the book by Zipkin (1999) and the references therein provide an extensive overview of recent advances in inventory theory and examine its relation to supply chain systems.

In particular, a supply chain can be described as a network of "entities" interacting to transform raw material into finished products for customers. A supply chain system typically refers to a manufacturing system. Nevertheless, it can also arise in other systems such as service systems. In this chapter we consider a particular type of supply chain system, namely, a distribution system. The literature on distribution systems is rich. The papers by Axsater (1993), Muckstadt and Roundy (1993), and the references therein contain a comprehensive review of the literature in this area. Some examples include the work of Roundy (1985), as well as Maxwell and Muckstadt (1985) who were among the first to consider a deterministic model for distribution systems with special structure and to derive policies for the model. Furthermore, Graves (1985, 1996) and Sherbrooke (1986) addressed a multi-echelon inventory system with stochastic demand, while Rosling (1989) addressed the stochastic demand case for assembly systems. Bernstein and Federgruen (1999) analyzed distribution systems under competition. Nagurney, Dong, and Zhang (2002) introduced and analyzed a model for a competitive supply chain system through the theory of variational inequalities.

In this chapter, we introduce a model that addresses the joint problems of pricing, production, and inventory control in a distribution system. Dynamic pricing has become very important in recent years due to its wide range of applicability in a variety of industries. The rapid development of information technology, the Internet, and electronic commerce as well as the success of the Direct-to-Customer (DTC) business model, have had a strong influence on the development of dynamic pricing, as they provide a company with the flexibility of dynamically changing the prices of its products. Dynamic pricing is particularly relevant in industries such as supply chain and manufacturing, as well as in information technology enabled industries such as electronic supply chains and online retailing. Examples of companies where dynamic pricing has had an impact, include, among others, Dell Computers and Amazon.com. Nevertheless, the efficient implementation and coordination of dynamic pricing with production and inventory decisions is still in its infancy. Companies increasingly believe that the efficient implementation of such decisions has the potential to significantly improve their supply chain efficiency.

Furthermore, a study by McKinsey and Company (cf. Baker et al. (2001)) on the cost structure of Fortune 1000 companies in the year 2000 shows that pricing is a more powerful lever than variable cost, fixed cost, or sales volume improvements. An improvement of 1% in pricing yields an average of 8.6% in operating margin improvement (see Figure 10.1). Therefore, companies' ability to survive in this very competitive environment depends on the development of efficient pricing models.

Dynamic pricing has been extensively studied by researchers from a variety of fields. These fields include, among others, economics (see, for example, Wilson (1993)), marketing (cf. Lilien, Kotler, and Moorthy (1992)), telecommunications (see, e.g., Kelly (1994) and Kelly, Maulloo, and Tan (1998)), revenue management and supply chain management (see, e.g., Bitran and Mondschein (1997), Federgruen and Heching (1999), Gallego and Van Ryzin (1993), and Zipkin (1999)). The papers by McGill and Van Ryzin (1999) and by Elmaghraby and Keskinocak (1997) provide a thorough review of, respectively, revenue management and dynamic pricing models.

The previous discussion suggests that it is important for the supply chain industry to design optimal pricing and inventory management strategies that maximize profits, reduce inventory levels, and effectively manage the delays that goods incur before being sold. In particular, we will take a fluid dynamics approach. Fluid dynamics models provide a powerful tool for understanding the behavior of systems in which the dynamic aspect is important. Such systems include routing and communication systems as well as queueing, supply chain, and transportation systems. It is important to notice that in all these systems there is an underlying network structure as well as the

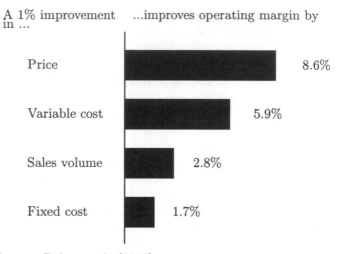

Source: Baker et al. (2000)

Fig. 10.1. Price as a powerful lever to improve profitability

notion of a fluid flowing in the system. This analogy plays a key role in the analysis. Another motivation for using fluid models is that they provide good policies in a variety of settings. Furthermore, these models approximate well the underlying stochasticity of problems in a deterministic way (see Avram, Bertsimas, and Ricard (1995), Bertsimas and Paschalidis (2001), and Meyn (1996)). Fluid models have also been used in the context of transportation, in particular, through the Dynamic Network Loading Model (cf. Bernstein and Friesz (1997, 2001), Friesz et al. (1993), Kachani (2000), Wu, Chen, and Florian (1995), and Xu et al. (1999)). In Section 10.2 we describe this model in further detail.

In the case of a general distribution system, most of the existing models in the literature, while considering the inventory aspect of the problem, do not address the pricing aspect. This chapter introduces a fluid model that combines both aspects by generalizing the model by Kachani and Perakis (2002a) from a single retailer to a distribution system with several wholesalers, intermediate distributors, and retailers.

This chapter makes the following contributions.

- It studies a distribution system by introducing a model of dynamic pricing and inventory control. The model is a general nonlinear continuous-time fluid dynamics model in a network environment.

- This chapter identifies reasonable conditions under which determining optimal policies is possible. In particular, the solution of the model provides the central decision-maker as well as the entities in the distribution system with dynamic policies that best coordinate their sales and production.

- The model considers price-inventory relationships for the entities in the system, where the pricing parameters are not fixed but rather are an output of the model.

- This chapter takes a delay approach that does not require estimating the demand-price relationship. Nevertheless, this approach directly connects with a traditional demand approach.

In the remainder of the chapter we consider a distribution system. In particular, we consider the case of n wholesalers, each producing a single different product, D intermediate distributors, and M retailers each selling some (or all) of these n products to consumers. Wholesalers, intermediate distributors, and retailers are subsidiaries of the same company. This assumption allows us to consider a distribution system that is centralized and controlled by a single decision maker.

We assume that the system is operating under a make-to-stock regime (see, for example, Bertsimas and Paschalidis (2001), Ha (1997), and Wein (1992) for more details on make-to-stock systems). As a result, each entity (wholesaler, intermediate distributor or retailer) in the system first builds some stock (inventory) in anticipation of future sales.

The model we introduce is a fluid model that encompasses the following features:

1. A general distribution system with several wholesalers, various types of intermediate distributors.

2. A dynamic, multi-product environment.

3. The company under study, at the wholesaler level, has a shared dynamic production capacity for all products.

4. There are transportation times (or lead times) elapsing during the transaction between the entities in the system.

5. Each entity in the system faces joint dynamic pricing, production, and inventory decisions. In the case of intermediate distributors and retailers, the production decisions signify the purchase of the products.

6. The objective of the central controller is to maximize the overall profit in the distribution system. This includes maximizing the revenues minus the production, transportation and holding costs faced by each entity in the system.

Our overall approach to this problem is different from the traditional literature in distribution systems. In particular, we do not consider an a priori demand price relationship. Our approach relies on the idea that each newly produced (or purchased) unit of a product by an entity in the distribution system (a wholesaler, an intermediate distributor, or a retailer) incurs a delay before being sold to the next entity in the chain. This delay depends on the inventory level accumulated by the entity as well as the unit price of the product. By taking this approach we do not need to account explicitly for how price affects demand. The estimation of this relationship is often inaccurate for example, due to lack of data. Some advantages to estimating sojourn (delay) times instead are the following:

(i) Delay data are internal and, therefore, are directly observable by the manufacturer.

(ii) If price does not vary a lot with time, then the demand-price relationship estimation may be inaccurate. On the other hand, since inventories always demonstrate moderate to high variability with time, the sojourn time-inventory relationship estimation is more accurate.

(iii) Finally, the recording of entrance and exit times of products by barcode readers in distribution systems is widespread and therefore, estimating sojourn times is not difficult. In Subsection 10.3.3, we discuss further the estimation process of sojourn times in practice. In Section 10.5, we connect our approach with the traditional demand-based approach. Our analysis in this chapter is based on the theory of variational inequalities. The book by Nagurney (1999) provides a thorough review of variational inequalities and several of its applications.

The structure of this chapter is as follows. In Section 10.2, we review the Dynamic Network Loading (DNL) fluid model, as it is the building block for the model we will introduce in this chapter. To enable the formulation of the model, in Subsection 10.3.1, we discuss our modeling assumptions, whereas in Subsection 10.3.2, we discuss the notation we will be using throughout the paper, and, finally, in Subsection 10.3.3, we discuss how the sojourn times we will be using in the model can be estimated in practice. In Section 10.4, we build a model of dynamic pricing and inventory management for distribution systems. Its key characteristic is the concept of a sojourn time of a product in the system. This describes the delay of a product in inventory before being sold and how this is affected by the pricing and the level of inventory. In Section 10.5, we discuss how this delay-based model connects with the traditional demand-based model. In Section 10.6, we discuss when the model we introduce is reasonable by discussing conditions that guarantee that the model indeed has a solution. Finally, in Section 10.7, we present some conclusions and open questions.

10.2   The Dynamic Network Loading Fluid Model

In this section, we review the Dynamic Network Loading fluid model that is often used in a variety of settings including transportation and, more recently, in dynamic pricing (see Kachani and Perakis (2002a)). This model will be the building block in this chapter and has been studied in the context of transportation by Bernstein and Friesz (1997, 2001), Friesz et al. (1993), Kachani (2000), and Wu, Chen, and Florian (1995). A variation of this model has also been studied by Avram, Bertsimas, and Ricard (1995) and Bertsimas and Paschalidis (2001) in the context of inventory control and queueing systems.

The discussion of this section assumes a single pipe where fluid flows. The dynamics equation expresses the relationship between the flow variables. Hence, the change of the total fluid $X(t)$ that exists in the pipe at time t is the entering flow rate $u(t)$ minus the exiting flow rate $v(t)$; that is,

$$\frac{dX(t)}{dt} = u(t) - v(t). \tag{10.1}$$

A flow entering the pipe at time t will exit the pipe at time $s(t)$. Therefore, by time t, the cumulative exit flow $V(t)$, must be equal to the integral of the inflow rate which would have entered at some earlier time ω and exited by time t. This relationship is expressed by $V(t) = \int_{\omega \in W} u(\omega)d\omega$, where $W = \{\omega : s(\omega) \leq t\}$. Finally, for presentation simplicity, we assume that the pipe is empty at $t = 0$, that is, $U(0) = 0$, $V(0) = 0$, $X(0) = 0$.

The previous equations do not specify how the delay $\tau(t)$ (and as a result $s(t) = t + \tau(t)$) can be obtained. We assume that $\tau(t)$ can be obtained by a travel time model that would depend on current and possibly past values of $(X(\omega)|\omega \leq t)$ such as $\tau(t) = D(X(t))$, where $D(\cdot)$ is a given function (see Kachani and Perakis (2001) for such a model and analysis).

The following definition describes the First-In-First-Out (FIFO) properties. The FIFO property plays a key role in the analysis of this model.

Definition 10.1: FIFO Property
The FIFO property holds if and only if:

$$\forall (t_1, t_2) \in [0, T]^2, \ if \ t_1 \leq t_2, \ then: \ s_i(t_1) \leq s_i(t_2). \tag{10.2}$$

The above property expresses that for example, a vehicle (or alternatively a newly produced unit of product) cannot exit (or alternatively be sold) before its predecessors. Similarly, the strict FIFO property holds if and only if the exit time function is strictly increasing.

Notice that if the strict FIFO property is satisfied, and if the exit time $s(.)$ is continuous, then the flow propagation equation can be equivalently rewritten as

$$V(t) = \int_0^{s^{-1}(t)} u(\omega)d\omega. \tag{10.3}$$

Nevertheless, it is important to notice that the model we described holds even if the FIFO property is not necessarily verified.

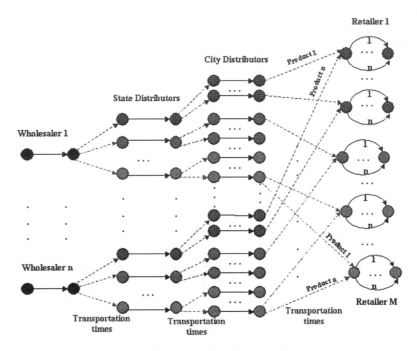

Fig. 10.2. An example of a distribution system

Alternatively, one can consider a demand model by assuming instead of (10.3) that the exiting flow rate $v(t)$ is the demand rate $d(t)$ at time t. In the context of dynamic pricing this may be a function of the price.

10.3 Assumptions and Notation

In this section, we outline the assumptions underlying our framework and also provide the necessary notation for the model development and analysis.

10.3.1 Modeling Assumptions

We consider a multi-product distribution system that we represent through a directed network. This distribution system is composed of wholesalers, intermediate distributors, and retailers. We assume that this distribution system belongs to a single company, the profit of which we wish to maximize. The wholesalers could correspond to national distributors while intermediate distributors could correspond to regional, state, and local distributors, as depicted in Figure 10.2.

We consider n products. The network of Figure 10.2 represents a tree.

The units of each product follow a path in the tree from the moment that they are produced at a wholesaler to the moment that they arrive at the retailers. In this representation, wholesalers and intermediate distributors correspond to a single product and are each represented in the network by an arc. As a result, there are n wholesalers. Furthermore, a wholesaler or an intermediate distributor who deals with multiple products will be represented with copies of an arc in the tree each corresponding to each one of these products. We denote by W the set of wholesalers and by D the set of intermediate distributors. Each element of W and D is an arc in the network.

We further assume that retailers sell a subset of the n products. We denote by R the set of retailers. Each retailer is represented by an origin destination pair linked by n arcs. Each arc corresponds to a product. If a retailer does not sell a specific product, we can either add a constraint to the model imposing that the purchase rate of this product is always zero, or we can assume that the transportation cost of this product to the retailer is very large or infinity. Each product-retailer pair (i, r), where $i \subset [1, ..., n]$ and $r \in R$, is represented through an arc in the network. Note that in what follows, an arc a can denote either a wholesaler, an intermediate distributor, or a product-retailer pair $a = (i, r)$.

Moreover, we assume that each intermediate distributor or retailer of the company under study gets its supply for each product from a unique wholesaler or intermediate distributor of the company. Therefore, each arc in the network can have multiple successors, but has a unique predecessor. For instance, as depicted in Figure 10.2, a retailer will get its supply for a specific product from the city distributor of this product, who in turn will get its supply from the state distributor etc. As a result, we are assuming that the wholesalers and intermediate distributors of the company under study are not competing with each other.

Intermediate distributors and retailers incur a transportation cost and a transportation time (lead time) when they purchase products from wholesalers and intermediate distributors. We assume that the transportation costs are time-dependent, but that the transportation times are static. Nevertheless, we can relax this latter assumption by imposing additional assumptions on the functional form of the transportation time as it depends on time t although these will make the exposition more difficult to follow.

Below, we describe the inputs and the outputs of the Dynamic Pricing Model.

10.3.2 Notation

In this subsection, we provide the necessary notation. We begin with the inputs of the dynamic pricing model and then present the notation for its outputs.

Inputs of the Dynamic Pricing Model

Arc variables:

$CFR(t)$:   Shared production capacity rate, at the wholesaler level, of the company under study at time t;

$p_{(i,r)}(\cdot)$:   vector of price functions of retailers;

$D_{(i,r)}(I_{(i,r)})$ $=$ $f_{(i,r)}(I_{(i,r)}, p_{(i,r)})$, arc sojourn time function product-retailer pair, that is, the total time a newly purchased unit of product i spends in the inventory system of retailer r, given an inventory $I_{(i,r)}$ and a unit price $p_{(i,r)}(I_{(i,r)})$;

$D_a(I_a)$ $=$ $f_a(I_a, p_a)$, arc sojourn time function of a wholesaler or an intermediate distributor, that is, the total time a newly purchased unit of product spends in the inventory system of a wholesaler or an intermediate distributor a, given an inventory I_a and a unit price $p_a(I_a)$;

$c_w(t)$:   purchase cost incurred by wholesaler w at time t;

$tc_a(t)$:   transportation cost incurred by an intermediate distributor, or a product-retailer pair a at time t;

T_a :   transportation time to intermediate distributor, or product-retailer pair a;

$h_a(t)$:   inventory holding cost incurred by a wholesaler, an intermediate distributor, or a product-retailer pair a at time t.

Time variables:

t :   index for continuous time;

$[0, T]$:   wholesalers purchase period. After time T, the wholesalers cease purchasing products.

Note that the arc sojourn time functions resemble the time to traverse an arc in a transportation network.

Moreover, note that while the wholesalers' purchase cost functions $c_w(.)$ are an input of the model, the purchase cost functions $c_d(.)$ and $c_{(i,r)}(.)$ of intermediate distributors and retailers respectively are outputs of the model. This is due to the fact that the unit price functions of wholesalers and intermediate distributors, which are output of the model, are also the purchase cost functions of intermediate distributors and retailers.

Outputs of the Dynamic Pricing Model

Arc variables:

$U_w(t)$	:	cumulative production flow of wholesaler w during interval $[0, t]$;
$u_w(t)$	:	production flow rate of wholesaler w at time t;
$U_a(t)$	:	cumulative purchase flow of an intermediate distributor or a product-retailer pair a during interval $[0, t]$;
$u_a(t)$	:	purchase flow rate of an intermediate distributor or a product-retailer pair a at time t;
$V_a(t)$	:	cumulative sales flow of a wholesaler or an intermediate distributor or a product-retailer pair a during interval $[0, t]$;
$v_a(t)$	:	sales flow rate of a wholesaler or an intermediate distributor or a product-retailer pair a at time t;
$I_a(t)$	:	inventory (number of units) of a wholesaler or an intermediate distributor or a product-retailer pair a at time t;
$p_a(I_a(t))$	:	sales price of a unit of product of intermediate distributor or product-retailer pair a given an inventory $I_a(t)$;
$c_a(t)$	:	purchase cost incurred by an intermediate distributor or a product-retailer pair a at time t
	$=$	$p_{a'}(I_{a'}(t))$, where a' is the arc preceding arc a;
$s_a(t)$	:	exit time of a purchase flow of product of arc a entering at time t $(s_a(t) = t + D_a(I_a(t)))$.

Time variables:

$[0, T_\infty]$	:	analysis period. It is the interval of time from when the first unit of product is purchased by a wholesaler to the first instant all products have been sold by retailers.

Notice that the control variables are the purchase flow rates $u_a(.)$ and the unit price functions $p_a(I_a)$. The study of the general pricing model does not require any assumption on the functional form of the unit price function $p_a(I_a)$. Instead, the unit price function is an output of the model. We can consider a variety of models for the unit price functions. Examples of such models include linear functions of the type $p_a(I_a) = p_a^{max} - \frac{p_a^{max} - p_a^{min}}{C_a} I_a$ as well as nonlinear functions of the type $p_a(I_a) = \frac{p_a^{max}}{(\frac{p_a^{max}}{p_a^{min}} - 1)\frac{I_a}{C_a} + 1}$, where C_a denotes the storage capacity, p_a^{max} the maximum allowable price, and p_a^{min} the minimum allowable price. Also, notice that the unit price function $p_a(I_a(t))$ depends on time only through the time-dependence of the inventory $I_a(t)$.

10.3.3 Estimation of Sojourn Times in Practice

A few companies such as Amazon.com utilize the sojourn time information
to control their inventory levels and adjust their pricing policies. A key
motivation for introducing sojourn times in the model of this chapter is the
availability of sojourn time information in almost every company's data warehouse. Indeed, as a unit of good enters the inventory system, a barcode reader
records its entrance time. When this unit is sold, a barcode reader records
its exit time. The lag between the entrance time and the exit time is the
sojourn time.

Below, we describe how to estimate the sojourn time $D_a(I_a)$ of a wholesaler, an intermediate distributor, or a product-retailer pair a in practice.

- Extract entrance times t_a and exit times $s_a(t_a)$ of units of products
  of arc a from the data warehouse and record sojourn times $\widehat{D}_a(t_a) =$
  $s_a(t_a) - t_a$.

- Record the inventory levels $I_a(t_a)$ and the unit prices $p_a(t_a)$ at entrance
  times t_a.

- Fit the triplets $(I_a(t_a)$, $p_a(t_a)$, $\widehat{D}_a(t_a)$) into a parametric function
  $\overline{D}_a(I_a(t_a), p_a(t_a))$.

- Assume a parametric shape for the unit price function $p_a(I_a)$ and plug
  it in $\overline{D}_a(I_a(t_a), p_a(t_a))$ to derive the sojourn time function $D_a(I_a)$.

Finally, notice that the estimation procedure outlined above is easy to
implement. The parameters of the sojourn time functions $D_a(I_a)$ can be
recalibrated regularly to account for changes in customer behavior.

10.4 Formulation of the Dynamic Pricing Model

We are now ready to propose a continuous-time analytical model for the
dynamic pricing problem. We take a fluid dynamics approach by expressing
arc dynamics, flow conservation, flow propagation and boundary constraints
of wholesalers, intermediate distributors and product-retailer pairs $a \in W \cup$
$D \cup (\{1, ..., n\} \times R)$.

Arc Dynamics Equations

The arc dynamics equations express the relationship between the flow variables of an arc. That is, the change in inventory at time t is the difference
between the purchase and the sales flow rates:

$$\frac{dI_a(t)}{dt} = u_a(t) - v_a(t). \tag{10.4}$$

Flow Propagation Equations

The flow propagation equations below describe the flow progression over time. Note that a purchase flow entering arc a at time t will be sold at time $s_a(t) = t + D_a(I_a(t))$. Therefore, by time t, the cumulative sales flow on arc a should be equal to the integral of all purchase inflow rates which would have entered arc a at some earlier time z and would have been sold by time t. This relationship is expressed through the following equation:

$$V_a(t) = \int_{z \in Z} u_a(z)dz, \quad \text{where } Z = \{z : s_a(z) \leq t\}. \tag{10.5}$$

If the product exit time functions $s_a(.)$ are continuous and satisfy the strict FIFO property, then the flow propagation equations (10.5) can be equivalently rewritten as

$$V_a(t) = \int_0^{s_a^{-1}(t)} u_a(z)dz. \tag{10.6}$$

Notice that $s_a^{-1}(t)$ is the time at which a unit of flow on arc a needs to be produced so that it is sold at time t. Furthermore, under the strict FIFO condition, a unit of flow on arc a, entering the queue at time t, will be sold only after the units of flow on arc a, that entered the queue before it, are all sold. In mathematical terms, this is equivalent to the arc exit time functions $s_a(.)$ being strictly increasing. As a result, defining the purchase time $s_a^{-1}(t)$ makes sense.

Furthermore, notice $V_a(t)$ represents the cumulative demand. Equation (10.5) determines the demand from the sojourn time. It replaces the demand-price relationship used in traditional models in the literature.

Boundary Equations

Since we assume that the network is empty at time $t = 0$, we impose the following boundary conditions

$$U_a(0) = 0, \quad V_a(0) = 0, \quad I_a(0) = 0. \tag{10.7}$$

Note that it is not necessary to assume that $I_a(0) = 0$. Instead, we could assume that $I_a(0) = I_{a0} > 0$. However, we consider zero-level inventories at $t = 0$ for simplicity of notation. Hence, in the beginning, we start producing before the demand arrives. As a result, we build inventory, which is characteristic of make-to-stock systems.

Non-Negativity Conditions

We further assume that the purchase flow rate functions $u_a(.)$ are non-negative:

$$u_a(.) \geq 0. \tag{10.8}$$

Flow Conservation

For every wholesaler or intermediate distributor a, let $S(a)$ denote the set of intermediate distributors or product-retailer pairs that are immediate successors of a. From the assumptions of Subsection 10.3.1, a is the unique supplier of all the elements of set $S(a)$. The following equation expresses the conservation of flow between wholesaler or intermediate distributor a and intermediate distributors or product-retailer pairs a' of set $S(a)$ delayed by the transportation time $T_{a'}$:

$$v_a(t) = \sum_{a' \in S(a)} u_{a'}(t + T_{a'}), \quad \forall a \in W \cup D. \tag{10.9}$$

Production Capacity Constraint

We assume that at each time t, the total production flow rate of the company under study is no more than the total capacity flow rate $CFR(t)$. This can be expressed as:

$$\sum_{w \in W} u_w(t) \leq CFR(t). \tag{10.10}$$

Objective Function

The objective of the company is to maximize its profits. Profits are obtained by subtracting purchase costs, transportation costs and inventory costs from sales. As a result, the objective function can be expressed as the sum, over all arcs, of the difference between the revenue of sales and the cost of both purchase and inventory:

$$\sum_{a \in W \cup D \cup (\{1,\ldots,n\} \times R)} \int_0^{T_\infty} [p_a(I_a(t))v_a(t) - (c_a(t) + tc_a(t))u_a(t + T_a)$$

$$-h_a(t)I_a(t)]dt.$$

Note that the transportation costs and transportation times of wholesalers are assumed to be zero. Furthermore, since the unit price functions of wholesalers and intermediate distributors are also the purchase cost functions of intermediate distributors and retailers, using conservation equation (10.9) gives rise to

$$\sum_{a \in W \cup D} p_a(I_a(t))v_a(t) = \sum_{a' \in D \cup (\{1,\ldots,n\} \times R)} c_{a'}(t)u_{a'}(t + T_{a'}).$$

Therefore, the objective function simplifies to

$$\int_0^{T_\infty} \sum_{a \in (\{1,\ldots,n\} \times R)} [p_a(I_a(t))v_a(t) - tc_a(t)u_a(t + T_a) - h_a(t)I_a(t)]$$

$$-\sum_{a\in D}[tc_a(t)u_a(t+T_a)+h_a(t)I_a(t)]-\sum_{a\in W}[c_a(t)u_a(t)+h_a(t)I_a(t)]dt.$$

In summary, the continuous-time Dynamic Pricing Model (DPM) is formulated as maximizing the previous objective function subject to constraints (10.4)–(10.10). In general, the DPM is a continuous-time nonlinear optimization problem. The nonlinearity of the model comes from the unit price as a function of the inventory, as well as the integral equation (10.5). In this formulation, the known variables are the arc sojourn time functions $D_a(.)$, the wholesaler purchase costs $c_w(.)$, the transportation and inventory costs $tc_a(.)$ and $h_a(.)$, and the retailers' total capacity flow rate function $CFR_r(.)$. The unknown variables we wish to determine are $u_a(t)$, $v_a(t)$, $U_a(t)$, $V_a(t)$, $I_a(t)$, and $p_a(I_a(t))$. Notice that integral equation (10.5), which connects the purchase to the sales schedules through the delays incurred in the system due to price and inventory, makes this problem hard to solve.

The Dynamic Pricing Model:

$$\text{Maximize}\ \int_0^{T_\infty}\sum_{a\in(\{1,...,n\}\times R)}[p_a(I_a(t))v_a(t)-tc_a(t)u_a(t+T_a)-h_a(t)I_a(t)]$$

$$-\sum_{a\in D}[tc_a(t)u_a(t+T_a)+h_a(t)I_a(t)]-\sum_{a\in W}[c_a(t)u_a(t)+h_a(t)I_a(t)]dt$$

subject to:

$$\frac{dI_a(t)}{dt}=u_a(t)-v_a(t),\quad\forall a$$

$$V_a(t)=\int_{\omega\in Z}u_a(z)dz,\quad\forall a,\quad\text{where } Z=\{z:s_a(z)\le t\}$$

$$v_a(t)=\sum_{a'\in S(a)}u_{a'}(t+T_{a'}),\quad\forall a\in W\cup D$$

$$U_a(0)=0,\quad V_a(0)=0,\quad I_a(0)=0,\quad\forall a$$

$$\sum_{w\in W}u_w(t)\le CFR(t)$$

$$u_a(\cdot)\ge 0,\quad\forall a.$$

Notice that the model is general enough to account for the case where the FIFO property, defined above, is not necessarily verified (notice that equation (10.5) does not assume that the FIFO property holds). In what follows, we establish an existence result. This result illustrates that under general assumptions, the DPM possesses an optimal solution. First though, in what follows, we provide a better understanding of how the sojourn time approach connects with the more traditional demand approach.

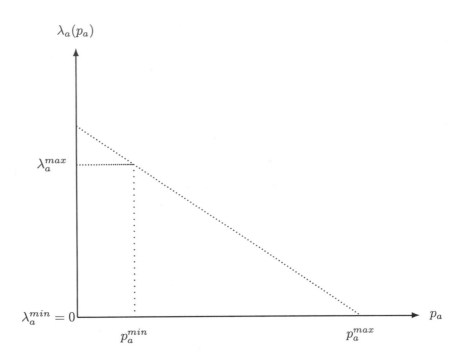

Fig. 10.3. A linear demand price relationship

10.5   Connecting Delay to Demand Models

In this section, we provide a connection between a model utilizing sojourn time as a function of inventory and price and a more traditional model where demand is a function of price.

Let us consider a linear demand price relationship (as is traditionally done in the literature); that is, consider a non-homogeneous renewal demand arrival process, with mean rate $\lambda_a(p_a)$ that is linear as a function of the price p_a. Similarly to Wold and Jureen (1953), Allen (1967), Dorfman (1978), and Tirole (1988), we assume that

$$\lambda_a(p_a) = \lambda_a^{max} \cdot \frac{p_a^{max} - p_a}{p_a^{max} - p_a^{min}}, \tag{10.11}$$

where for arc a, λ_a^{max} denotes the maximum arrival rate of demand, p_a^{max} the maximum allowable price and finally, p_a^{min} the minimum allowable price (see Figure 10.3).

Notice that when we set the minimum allowable price p_a^{min}, then it gives rise to the maximum demand rate. When we set the maximum allowable price p_a^{max}, the demand rate becomes zero.

In order to provide a connection between demand and delay models, we consider the approximation that Little's Law (cf. Little (1961)) holds for every time t, that is, $I_a(t) = \lambda_a(p_a(I_a(t))).D_a(I_a(t))$. We view $I_a(.)$ as the average length of the queue, $\lambda_a(.)$ as the arrival demand rate, and $D_a(.)$ as the average waiting time in the queue. As a result, this approximation views the sojourn time $D_a(I_a(t))$ as the expected value of $I_a(t)$ interarrivals of the renewal process, that is, $\frac{I_a(t)}{\lambda_a(p_a(I_a(t)))}$.

Notice that this approximation looks at the average state of the system. Indeed, the expression $\lambda_a(p_a(I_a(t))) = \frac{I_a(t)}{D_a(I_a(t))}$ describes the average arrival rate for product a. As a result, it is indifferent about how far or close some of the $I_a(t)$ units of product a in the inventory system are from being sold at time t. However, by looking at the system from the perspective of the sojourn time, that is the waiting in the system, the Dynamic Pricing Model formulated captures the dynamics of the $I_a(t)$ units of product a in better detail. Furthermore, quantity $v_a(t)$ describes the selling rate of product a exactly and not on average and replaces the demand rate quantity. In what follows, we consider some specific functions describing the price inventory relationship and discuss how a model with a linear demand price function gives rise to a variety of sojourn time functions.

1. Let us consider the case where the unit price function $p_a(I_a)$ is linear in terms of the inventory level I_a (see Figure 10.4 below). That is, we assume that

$$p_a(I_a) = p_a^{max} - \frac{p_a^{max} - p_a^{min}}{C_a} I_a, \qquad (10.12)$$

where C_a denotes the storage capacity. Notice that as we would expect, this function is decreasing in terms of inventory. As a result, when the inventory of product a reaches storage capacity C_a, then the price becomes the minimum price p_a^{min}. On the other hand, when the inventory of product a is zero, then the price becomes p_a^{max}.

Combining this relationship with Little's Law, gives rise to the following sojourn time function,

$$D_a(I_a) = \frac{C_a}{\lambda_a^{max}}. \qquad (10.13)$$

This result implies that under a linear price inventory relationship, a linear demand price model gives rise to a constant sojourn time function for product a. This depends on the total storage capacity as well as the maximum demand arrival rate. As a result, the higher the storage capacity the higher the sojourn time in the system. On the other hand, the higher the maximum demand arrival rate, the lower the sojourn time in the system.

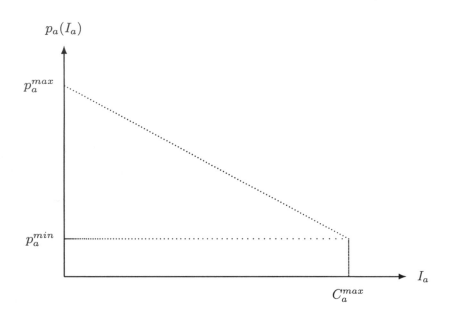

Fig. 10.4. A linear price inventory relationship

2. Let us now consider the following nonlinear price inventory relationship,

$$p_a(I_a) = \frac{p_a^{max}}{(\frac{p_a^{max}}{p_a^{min}} - 1)\frac{I_a}{C_a} + 1},$$

where C_a is the storage capacity, p_a^{max} the maximum allowable price, and p_a^{min} the minimum allowable price.

Combining this relationship with Little's Law, a linear demand price relationship gives rise to the following sojourn time function,

$$D_a(I_a) = \frac{(p_a^{max} - p_a^{min})I_a + p_a^{min}C_a}{\lambda_a^{max} p_a^{max}}. \tag{10.14}$$

Notice that in this case the sojourn time increases linearly with the inventory. Furthermore, when inventory reaches storage capacity then the sojourn time coincides with (10.13).

10.6   An Existence Result

In this section, we discuss when the dynamic pricing model we introduced in Section 10.4 is indeed reasonable by discussing conditions that guarantee existence of solution. Theorem 10.1 below summarizes our results.

Theorem 10.1: Existence
Assume that the following conditions hold:
(1) The price inventory functions $p_a(I_a)$ are continuously differentiable and bounded from above by scalars p_a^{max}.
(2) The sojourn time functions $D_a(.)$ are continuously differentiable, and there exist two non-negative constants B_{1a} and B_{2a} such that for every inventory level I_a, $0 \le B_{1a} \le D_a'(I_a) < B_{2a}$.
(3) The shared capacity flow rate function $CFR(.)$ is Lebesgue integrable, non-negative and does not exceed $\min_{1,...,n} \frac{1}{B_{2a} - B_{1a}}$.
Then, the Dynamic Pricing Model has an optimal solution.

Remarks:

- This theorem suggests that the maximum variation of the sojourn time in terms of the inventory connects with the total production capacity for all products. As a result, when the maximum variation of the delay in terms of the inventory is large (or small) then the Dynamic Pricing Model has a solution when the shared capacity (and as a result the production rate) is small (or large).

- Intuitively, properties (1) − (3) imply that the FIFO property holds which as a result implies that an optimal policy exists. Indeed, $B_{2a} - B_{1a}$ represents the maximum variation of sojourn time in terms of I_a (that is, the total number of units of product in the arc). During a time interval Δt of decrease in the number of products in the arc, the variation in the number of products $I_a(t) - I_a(t + \Delta t)$ is bounded by the quantity $CFR(t).\Delta t$. Therefore, the variation of sojourn time $D_a(I_a(t)) - D_a(I_a(t + \Delta t))$ is bounded by $(B_{2a} - B_{1a}).CFR(t).\Delta t$. Using Condition (3), it is also bounded by Δt. Hence, $s_a(t) = t + D_a(I_a(t)) \le t + \Delta t + D_a(I_a(t + \Delta t)) = s_a(t + \Delta t)$. Therefore, the FIFO property is verified in this case. On the other hand, during a time interval Δt of increase in the number of products, since the sojourn time functions are non-decreasing, $D_a(I_a(t)) \le D_a(I_a(t + \Delta t))$. Therefore, $s_a(t) \le s_a(t + \Delta t)$, and the FIFO property is also verified in this case. Conditions (1)-(3) are the minimal conditions to ensure that the FIFO property is verified (see Kachani and Perakis (2002a) for the formal proof of this statement in the single retailer case). This analysis is not formal but rather attempts to provide some intuition.

- As a special case, let us consider the case where the arc sojourn time function $D_a(.)$ is linear. Then conditions (1)-(3) of Theorem 10.1 follow. Indeed, in this case, $D_a'(.) = cst = B_{1a}$. Moreover, for any arbitrarily small positive scalar ϵ, by introducing $B_{2a} = B_{1a} + \epsilon$, Condition (2) of Theorem 10.1 is verified. Furthermore, since Condition (3) can be rewritten as $CFR(t) \le \frac{1}{\epsilon}$, $CFR(t)$ can be arbitrarily large. As a result, when the sojourn time function is a linear function of inventory, the existence of solution follows with no additional assumptions. Intuitively, when the sojourn time is linear in terms of inventory, its rate of change is constant. As a result, there is no need to look into whether the production rate is low or high.

The previous remarks provide an intuitive explanation as to why Theorem 10.1 holds. The formal proof of Theorem 10.1 follows by extending the proof of the existence of a solution in Kachani and Perakis (2002a) from the single retailer case to the distribution system case. The proof is omitted for the sake of brevity.

Notice that we can use an analysis similar to that in Kachani and Perakis (2001) in order to derive the delay functions that we use in this model (see Kachani and Perakis (2002b)). Furthermore, in the case of a single retailer, Kachani and Perakis (2002a) have introduced an algorithm for solving efficiently a discretized version of this model.

An Extension

The results in this chapter generalize to incorporate some element of competition for the company. We assume that each retailer has a number of outside competitors. In particular, we assume that the company under study is a Stackelberg leader (i.e., is a price leader) at the retail level. This means that the prices of the competitors for each retailer are also affecting the sojourn time for each product retailer pair (and as a result, the corresponding demand). Furthermore, assuming that each retailer is a Stackelberg leader implies that the prices of his/her outside competitors are functions of the prices of this retailer. This aspect is incorporated in the model through the arc sojourn time functions of product-retailer pairs. In this case the arc sojourn time functions of product-retailer pairs differ from the ones of wholesalers and intermediate distributors in that they account for the outside competitors of the retailers. As a result, if we also incorporate the vector of competitors' price functions $p_{(i,r)}^c(p_{(i,r)}(.))$ of a product-retailer pair (i,r) (which is assumed to be a function of the unit price function $p_{(i,r)}(.)$), we take into account the effect of competition in the case of product-retailer pairs. The arc sojourn time functions of product-retailer pairs can be estimated in practice using regression on the competitors' prices and the prices of the company's retailers, as illustrated in Subsection 10.3.3.

10.7   Conclusions

In this chapter, we discussed a dynamic pricing and inventory control model for distribution systems. We introduced a fluid model inspired by the Dynamic Network Loading Model. The key feature in this model is that it incorporates the delay of price and level of inventory in affecting demand, rather than a price demand relationship.

In particular, we proposed a nonlinear, continuous-time fluid dynamics model for dynamic pricing and inventory control in a distribution system with several wholesalers, intermediate distributors, and retailers, by extending the work of Kachani and Perakis (2002a) to a network environment. The model did not require the estimation of a price-demand relationship for each entity in the system. Rather, it incorporated the delay a product incurs before being sold by an entity (while kept in inventory). This delay is affected by the price and the level of inventory of the entity. The model performed joint pricing and inventory control, without considering specific price-inventory relationships for the entities in the system. We identified reasonable conditions under which determining optimal policies is possible. These policies assist the central decision-maker as well as the entities in the distribution system in coordinating their sales and production. Furthermore, we discussed how delay functions connect with demand functions; thereby providing a connection between the model in this chapter and the more traditional models in the literature.

There are several open questions that we need to explore further. Examples include: (i) studying the efficient operation of a distribution system by investigating solution approaches to the DPM that we proposed, (ii) considering the competitive aspect in fluid modeling as it connects to distribution systems, (iii) treating more general supply chain systems, and (iv) addressing distribution and supply chain problems where demand is stochastic.

Acknowledgments

We would like to thank the editor, Anna Nagurney, and the anonymous referees for their suggestions which helped us to considerably improve the exposition of this chapter. Preparation of this chapter was supported, in part, by the MIT-Singapore Alliance and the PECASE Award DMI-9984339 from the National Science Foundation.

References

Allen, C. E. (1967), *The Framework of Price Theory*, Wadsworth Publishing, Belmont, California.

Avram, F., Bertsimas, D., and Ricard, M. (1995), "Optimization of Multiclass Fluid Queueing Networks: A Linear Control Approach," in *Proceedings of the IMA*, pp. 199-234, F. P. Kelly and R. Williams, editors, Springer-Verlag, New York.

Axsater, S. (1993), "Continuous Review Policies for Multi-Level Inventory Systems with Stochastic Demand," in *Handbooks in Operations Research and Management Science*, pp. 175-197, S. C. Graves, A. H. G. Rinooy Kan, and P. H. Zipkin, editors, Elsevier, Amsterdam, The Netherlands.

Baker, W. L., Lin, E., Marn, M. V., and Zawada, C. C. (2001), "Getting Prices Right on the Web," *The McKinsey Quarterly* **2**.

Bernstein, D., and Friesz, T. (1997), "Infinite Dimensional Formulations of Some Dynamic Traffic Assignment Models," in *Network Infrastructure and the Urban Environment*, pp. 112-124, L. Lundqvist, L.-G. Mattsson, and T. J. Kim, editors, Springer-Verlag, Berlin, Germany.

Bernstein, D., and Friesz, T. (2001), "Analytical Dynamic Traffic Assignment Models," in *Handbook of Transport Modelling*, pp. 181-195, D. Hensher and K. Button, editors, Pergamon, Oxford, England.

Bernstein, F., and Federgruen, A. (1999), "Pricing and Replenishment Strategies in a Distribution System with Competing Retailers," Working Paper, Columbia University, New York.

Bertsimas, D., and Paschalidis, I. (2001), "Probabilistic Service Level Guarantees in Make-to-Stock Manufacturing Systems," *Operations Research* **49**, 119-133.

Bitran, G., and Mondschein, S. (1997), "Periodic Pricing of Seasonal Products in Retailing," *Management Science* **43**, 64-79.

Dorfman, R. (1978), *Prices and Markets*, Third Edition, Upper Saddle River, Prentice Hall, Englewood Cliffs, New Jersey.

Elmaghraby, W., and Keskinocak, P. (1997), "Dynamic Pricing: Research Overview, Current Practices and Future Directions," Working Paper, Georgia Institute of Technology, Atlanta, Georgia.

Federgruen, A., and Heching, A. (1999), "Combined Pricing and Inventory Control under Uncertainty," *Operations Research* **47**, 454-475.

Friesz, T. L., Bernstein, D., Smith, T. E., Tobin, R. L., and Wie, B. W. (1993), "A Variational Inequality Formulation of the Dynamic Network User Equilibrium Problem," *Operations Research* **41**, 179-191.

Gallego, G., and van Ryzin, G. J. (1993), "Optimal Dynamic Pricing of Inventories with Stochastic Demand over Finite Horizons," *Management Science* **40**, 990-1020.

Graves, S. (1985), "A Multi-Echelon Inventory Model for a Repairable Item with One-for One Replenishment," *Management Science* **31**, 1247-1256.

Graves, S. (1996), "A Multi-Echelon Inventory Model with Exact Replenishment Intervals," *Management Science* **42**, 1-17.

Ha, A. Y. (1997), "Optimal Dynamic Scheduling Policy for a Make-to-Stock Production System," *Operations Research* **45**, 42-53.

Kachani, S. (2000), "Analytical Dynamic Traffic Flow Models: Formulation, Analysis and Solution Algorithms," Master's Thesis, Operations Research Center, MIT, Cambridge, Massachusetts.

Kachani, S., and Perakis, G. (2001), "Modeling Travel Times in Dynamic Transportation Networks; A Fluid Dynamics Approach," Sloan School of Management, MIT, Cambridge, Massachusetts.

Kachani, S., and Perakis, G. (2002a), "A Fluid Model of Pricing and Inventory Management for Make-to-Stock Manufacturing Systems," Sloan School of Management, MIT, Cambridge, Massachusetts.

Kachani, S., and Perakis, G. (2002b), "Fluid Dynamics Models and Their Applications in Transportation and Pricing," Sloan School of Management, MIT, Cambridge, Massachusetts.

Kelly, F. P. (1994), "On Tariffs, Policing and Admission Control for Multi-service Networks," *Operations Research Letters* **15**, 1-9.

Kelly, F. P., Maulloo, A. K., and Tan, D. K. H. (1998), "Rate Control for Communication Networks: Shadow Prices, Proportional Fairness and Stability," *Journal of the Operational Research Society* **49**, 237-252.

Lilien, G., Kotler, P., and Moorthy, K. (1992), *Marketing Models*, Prentice Hall, New Jersey.

Little, J. (1961), "A Proof of the Queueing Formula $\lambda = L_W$," *Operations Research* **9**, 383-387.

Maxwell, W., and Muckstadt, J. (1985), "Establishing Consistent and Realistic Reorder Intervals in Production-Distribution Systems," *Operations Research* **33**, 1316-1341.

Meyn, S. P. (1996), "Stability and Optimization of Queueing Networks and their Fluid Models," in *Proceedings of the Summer Seminar on the Mathematics of Stochastic Manufacturing Systems*, Virginia, 17–21.

Muckstadt, J., and Roundy, R. (1993), "Analysis of Multistage Production Systems," in *Handbooks in Operations Research and Management Science* **4**, pp. 81-131, S. C. Graves, A. H. G. Rinooy Kan, and P. H. Zipkin, editors, Elsevier, Amsterdam, The Netherlands.

Nagurney, A. (1999), *Network Economics: A Variational Inequality Approach*, Second and Revised Edition, Kluwer Academic Publishers, Dordrecht, The Netherlands.

Nagurney, A., Dong, J., and Zhang, D. (2002), "A Supply Chain Network Equilibrium Model," *Transportation Research E* **38**, 281-303.

Rosling, K. A. (1989), "Optimal Inventory Policies for Assembly Systems under Random Demands," *Operations Research* **37**, 565-579.

Roundy, R. (1985), "98%-Effective Integer-Ratio Lot-Sizing for One-Warehouse Multi-Retailer Systems," *Management Science*, 1416-1430.

Sherbrooke, S. (1986), "Vari-Metric: Improved Approximations for Multi-Indenture, Multi-Echelon Availability Models," *Operations Research* **34**, 311-319.

Stadtler, H., and Kigler, C. (2000), editors, *Supply Chain Management and Advanced Planning*, Springer, Berlin, Germany.

Tayur, S., Ganeshan, R., and Magazine, M. (1998), *Quantitative Models for Supply Chain Management*, Kluwer Academic Publishers, Boston, Massachusetts.

Tirole, J. (1988), *The Theory of Industrial Organization*, The MIT Press, Cambridge, Massachusetts.

Tomlin, B. (2002), "Supply Chain Design: Capacity, Flexibility and Wholesale Price Strategies," PhD Thesis, MIT, Cambridge, Massachusetts.

Wein, L. (1992), "Dynamic Scheduling of a Multiclass Make-to-Stock Queue," *Operations Research* **40**, 724-735.

Wilson, R. (1993), *Nonlinear Pricing*, Oxford University Press, Oxford, England.

Wold, H., and Jureen, L. (1953), *Demand Analysis, A Study in Econometrics*, Wiley Publications in Statistics, John Wiley & Sons, New York.

Wu, J. H., Chen, Y., and Florian, M. (1995), "The Continuous Dynamic Network Loading Problem: A Mathematical Formulation and Solution Method," *Transportation Research B*, **32**, 173-187.

Xu, Y. W., Wu, J. H., Florian, M., Marcotte, P., and Zhu, D. L. (1999), "Advances in the Continuous Dynamic Network Loading Problem," *Transportation Science* **33**, 341-353.

Zipkin, P. H. (1999), *Foundations of Inventory Management*, Irwin McGraw-Hill, Boston, Massachusetts.

11 An Agent-Based Evolutionary Trade Network Simulation

Floortje Alkemade, J. (Han) A. La Poutré, and Hans M. Amman

11.1 Introduction

Electronic commerce and the trading of information goods significantly impact the role of intermediaries. Because the services of intermediaries are costly to consumers, the question arises as to why intermediaries are necessary. This question is particularly relevant in electronic commerce where consumers can decide to buy directly from the producer. Electronic markets facilitate direct contact between consumers and producers, thereby reducing the influence of intermediaries. On the other hand, intermediaries may be able to reduce the information overload that consumers face.

The central question of this chapter is whether intermediaries can make a profit in an information economy. Traditional intermediaries can make a profit because they trade a larger volume of goods than the average consumer, can buy at lower prices, and have better information or search capabilities. When information goods are traded over the Internet, however, this advantage disappears. Information goods differ from traditional goods because they are costly to produce but cheap to reproduce and there are no natural capacity limits for additional copies. Therefore, pricing structures for information goods are different than for traditional goods.

One possible role for the intermediary in an electronic market is the role of search expert – intermediaries are in the market for more periods of time and make more transactions than individual buyers and sellers. Such an intermediary thus gains expertise as to where the best deals are to be found. In the age of information overload, intermediaries that reduce consumer search costs may be able to make a profit in electronic markets. We investigate the conditions under which such intermediaries can attract a customer base. We use evolutionary computer simulations, a methodology from the field of agent-based computational economics (ACE) as in Tesfatsion (2001) and

Alkemade and La Poutré (2002), to study an electronic trade network where consumers, producers and intermediaries trade an information good. Agent-based computational economics studies economic phenomena as they emerge from interactions between individual, boundedly rational agents. In our case, we initialize a trade network with a fixed, user-specified number of consumers, producers, and intermediaries. Over time, the agents in the networks learn which links to form and we study the trade network that arises from those repeated local decisions.

We use a network economics approach (Shapiro and Varian (1999)) to study electronic trade networks. Network economics holds the view that individual actions, and, in turn, aggregate outcomes, are in a large part determined by the interaction structure (as in ACE). This is in contrast to the market view of the economy where buyers and sellers are anonymous and the structure of the interaction is typically considered less important. The network economics view of the economy states that there must be a connection (an information link) between buyers and sellers in order for any trade to occur. A connection between two agents means that there is a flow of relevant information between the two agents (that is, a buyer that requests price quotes from a seller or subscribes to a mailing list). If a buyer does not know about a certain seller that offers the best price, this price will not influence his purchase decision. Agents trade over the network and buyers have to decide which connections to form to the sellers. Over time, some connections may yield a higher utility than others and consumers can decide to update their link pattern. Links are a model for consumer search behavior and are costly, i.e., the buyer has to invest some resources (time, money) to find and maintain contact with potential sellers. Buyers make these strategic linking decisions based on the information that they have available. To model this boundedly rational search and learning behavior of the consumers we use an evolutionary algorithm, a learning technique inspired by the biological idea of 'survival of the fittest,' as is common in the field of ACE.

Section 11.2 describes the trading agents and the economic model. In Section 11.3 the use of an evolutionary algorithm (EA) as a model for agent learning behavior is explained. A layout of the experimental design is given in Section 11.4. Section 11.5 provides results for the agent-based simulations that we have performed. Conclusions are given in Section 11.6.

11.2   The Economic Trade Network Model

We consider a trade network game of cost-minimizing boundedly rational consumers, and profit-maximizing producers and intermediaries. The goal of this research is to investigate the influence of the network structure and information level of the agents on the level of intermediated trade in the model. In each period of the game, consumers buy a single unit of an information good, which they can buy directly from the producers or through an intermediary. Production of information goods involves high fixed but low marginal costs. In this chapter, we assume that initial production costs are sunk and that reproduction is very cheap and easy; therefore, we impose no capacity constraints on the number of goods an individual producer can supply. Trade can only occur if there is a connection, a link, between a consumer and a seller (producer or intermediary). Buyers (that is, consumers and intermediaries) strategically decide which links to form by choosing a linking strategy from their associated strategy base. This strategy base is periodically updated by an evolutionary algorithm. Producers, in turn, strategically decide what prices to charge during a trade period. The trade network thus consists of consumers, producers, intermediaries, and the links connecting them. The model is initialized with a fixed, user-specified number of consumers, producers, and intermediaries. Figure 11.1 depicts the economic model and a possible trade network.

We investigate the influence of the initial expertise level of the intermediary, that is, the influence of the number of links the intermediary initially sustains with producers, on the resulting trade network. Well-connected intermediaries have a better chance of finding a better price than intermediaries without links. We study the level of intermediation for different producer price schedules that lead to different market dynamics. Below, a more detailed description of the different types of economic agents present in the model will be given. An overview of the evolutionary algorithm that is used to learn better linking strategies is described in Section 11.3. In each trade period, the flow of goods and information follows the steps depicted in Figure 11.2. More detail is provided below.

11.2.1   Heterogeneous, Boundedly Rational Consumers

Consumers in the trade network are assumed to be cost-minimizing consumers. In each trade period, a consumer buys a single unit of a homogeneous information good. Consumers can only buy from a seller to which they have formed a link and these links are costly. Each link has a per unit cost associated with it (in the current setup these costs are taken constant for all links). The total search cost (C_s) that a consumer incurs during a single trade period is the number of links (l) he maintains times the search cost per link (c_l) (for parameter values see Table 11.1). The utility of a consumer (U_c) is then defined as the negative of this total search cost plus the purchase price (P):

$$U_c = -(l \cdot c_l + P).$$

Consumers in our model are boundedly rational (cf. Simon (1984), Newell and Simon (1972)), that is, the consumers do not have the information and the computational capabilities needed to make an optimal decision. To make a perfectly rational decision, an agent needs to know the exact price each producer will charge and then form only one link to the producer offering the

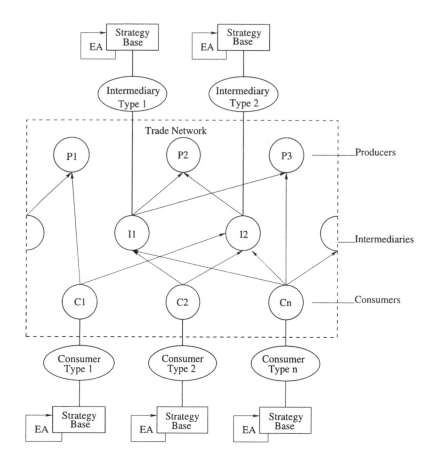

Fig. 11.1. The model and example of a possible trade network between consumers, producers, and intermediaries. The trade network is depicted within the dashed square

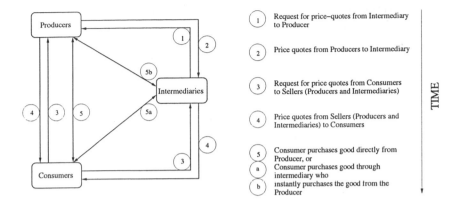

Fig. 11.2. Flow of information between consumers, producers, and intermediaries in the trade network model

lowest price. This is not a realistic scenario since the price depends on the decisions of other consumers as well. Individual consumers have no direct information about the behavior of other consumers. This is particularly true in electronic commerce where shops have no physical location and consumers do not have access to knowledge about other consumers. The consumer thus faces a trade-off between the number of costly links he forms and utility. More links mean a higher chance of finding the best price while fewer links mean lower search cost. Furthermore, since we study a model where producers change their prices over time, the optimal linking strategy for the consumer can change as well. Therefore, the consumer has to learn by trial and error (experience) which link patterns yield higher utility. A consumer's strategy determines his search behavior (which links he forms and maintains). This strategy is learned and adapted by an evolutionary algorithm. The fitness of a search strategy is equal to the utility that particular strategy yielded for the consumer.

The search strategy, hence, determines *how many* and *which* links a consumer forms to producers and intermediaries. The boundedly rational consumer then buys the product from his cheapest linked seller. However, with a small error probability ϵ the consumer purchases the information good from a randomly chosen seller. This reflects the fact that the consumer may make a mistake in selecting the cheapest seller or that the physical (Internet) connection with his preferred seller may fail. Search thus occurs at two levels; search over a link to find the best price quote and search at a more abstract level to find the best search strategy (the EA). The algorithm for the consumers is as follows:

Each trade period consumers take the following steps:

Step 1. Decide which links to form to sellers

Step 2. Choose preferred seller:

      With probability $1 - \epsilon$ (where ϵ is small)

           Preferred seller is the seller offering the lowest price

      Or, with probability ϵ

           Preferred seller is a randomly selected seller

Step 3. Buy the good from the preferred seller

Step 4. Calculate utility. Utility equals (price + total search cost)

Step 5. Update link strategy

11.2.2   Heterogeneous Adaptive Producers

At the beginning of each trade period, a producer has to decide which price to charge during that period. The prices set by the producers are the driving force behind the dynamics of the trade network. There are no capacity constraints for the producers since we are dealing with an information good. We investigate two basic adaptive price schedules, where producers adjust their prices on the basis of economic results from the previous period.

First, we consider the case where producers use a **downward sloping price demand curve** (Mas-Colell, Whinston, and Green (1995)) where price decreases as demand increases. Naive expectations are used to update beliefs about the expected demand: $Demand^{exp}(t) = Demand(t - 1)$. Expected demand for the first trade period is chosen randomly from a uniform distribution $[0, \dots, number\ of\ consumers]$. Hence, producers have heterogeneous expectations about demand. In this scenario the sellers use a basic price setting mechanism and do not recognize any market power that they may have. Since producers charge the lowest price when demand is high, this price schedule presents a coordination problem to the buyers. Buyers are best off if they all form one and only one link to the same producer. For example, a good that exhibits network effects is software.

Production of information goods involves high fixed, but low marginal costs. Some economists (see Choi, Stahl, and Whinston (1997)) argue that such a cost structure requires a pricing schedule where information goods are priced according to consumer value. We, therefore, investigate a second pricing scenario in which producers continually try to increase their profits. Producers use a so-called **derivative follower** (DF) algorithm – see Greenwald and Kephart (1999), DiMicco, Greenwald, and Maes (2001) – to determine their prices. The DF algorithm is a (local) search algorithm that dynamically adjusts the price for the offered good based on observed profits. This algorithm starts at some user-specified price level (in our case, randomly drawn) and then, step-by-step, changes the price in the same direction until the current profit drops below the profit obtained in the previous trading

Table 11.1. Parameter values used in the simulations

Economic model parameters	Value
Number of Producers	10
Number of Consumers	40
Number of Intermediaries	1
Initial network density intermediaries	$0.2, \ldots, 1.0$

period. In that case, the search direction is reversed and steps in the other direction are made. Every time the profit decreases the search direction is reversed again. The direction of change is randomly set to -1 or 1 at the beginning of the simulation. Similarly, the initial price is randomly chosen from a uniform distribution [*minimum price*, ..., *maximum price*] (heterogeneous producers). This algorithm is able to react very quickly to changes in the profit landscape. Two additional advantages of the DF algorithm are that the underlying idea of the DF is very intuitive and the DF requires very little problem-specific knowledge. The derivative follower algorithm leads to more complex price dynamics than the downward sloping price demand curve described above, so the search problem for consumers is more complex. The algorithm for the producers is as follows (for an overview of parameter values used in the experiments see Table 11.1):

Each trade period producers take the following steps:
Scenario 1: Producers using a downward sloping demand curve
      Step 1. Calculate *expected demand*,
           using: $Demand^{exp}(t) = Demand(t-1)$
      Step 2. Determine *Price*,
           using $P = a - (b * Demand^{exp}(t))$
      Step 3. Sell the good to buyers
      Step 4. Calculate actual demand $(Demand(t))$
Scenario 2: Producers using the derivative follower algorithm
      Step 1. If current profi is smaller
           than in the previous period
           Then reverse direction of price adjustment (dpa)
      Step 2. Determine *Price*,
           using: $P = P_{old} * (1 + (dpa * stepsize))$
      Step 3. Sell the good to buyers
      Step 4. Calculate actual profit

11.2.3 Profit-Maximizing Intermediaries

We investigate whether intermediaries that are experts at searching can exist and make a profit in an electronic trade network when consumers can also buy directly from the producers. To gain more insight into the role of such intermediaries we vary the level of knowledge or expertise that intermediaries have about the trade network and test whether they are able to attract customers. Intermediaries buy goods from producers and sell them to consumers. Intermediaries charge consumers a percentage (markup) of the acquisition price, so they can make a profit. Profit equals the total number of goods sold to consumers times the markup percentage minus the total link cost of the intermediary. Intermediaries can buy and sell more than one unit of the homogeneous product during a single trade period. On the consumer-side intermediaries function as the consumers described above; that is, they have a search strategy that is periodically updated by an evolutionary algorithm. The fitness of a search strategy is equal to the profit the intermediary obtained using that strategy. We assume that the intermediary only buys a product if there is a consumer he will sell it to (no stocks). The intermediary thus acts as a broker. Price quotes remain valid for the entire trade period. If an intermediary receives an attractive price quote from a producer he can purchase the information good instantly when a consumer arrives who is willing to buy the product at the price quoted by the intermediary. The algorithm for the intermediaries is as follows:

Each trade period intermediaries take the following steps:
Step 1. Decide which links to form to sellers
Step 2. Determine *Price*,
        using: $P = Acquisition\ Price * (1 + markup)$,
        Acquisition Price is the price from the
        linked seller offering the lowest price
Step 3. Calculate profit (number of units sold * markup)
Step 4. Update link strategy

In order to model the fact that the intermediary may (initially) have expert knowledge about the trade network and can use this knowledge to make a profit, we vary the initial network density of the intermediary (the number of links to producers that the intermediary sustains initially). When the intermediary has complete knowledge about the trade network, he maintains links to all producers. An initial network density of 0.6 means that at the beginning of the simulation the intermediary maintains links to (and can obtain price quotes from) 60 percent of the producers.

11.2.4 Market Dynamics

The market dynamics are driven by the prices set by producers. At each timestep of the model, the agent actions described above are executed, resulting in the model sequence described below. Initially, the numbers of producers, consumers, and intermediaries are chosen, as well as the initial network density (expertise levels) of the intermediaries. The outcome of the evolutionary agent-based simulation depends on the initial conditions and on the agent interactions.

Each trade period the economic agents take the following steps:
1. Producers choose their prices
2. Int ermediaries form links to producers (based on their search strategy)
3. Intermediaries choose their prices
4. Consumers form links to sellers (based on their search strategy)
5. Consumers buy one unit of the good from their preferred linked seller
6. Consumers calculate their utility
7. Consumer search strategies are updated by the evolutionary algorithm
8. Intermediaries calculate their profits
9. Intermediary search strategies are updated by the evolutionary algorithm
10. Producers calculate their profits
11. Producers update their prices for the next period

11.3 Agent Learning

To model the learning and search behavior of the evolutionary agents we use an evolutionary algorithm (EA), as in agent-based computational economics (McFadzean and Tesfatsion (1999), Weitzel, Wendt, and Westarp (2002), and Pingle (2000)). An evolutionary algorithm is a biologically inspired technique that uses the concept of survival of the fittest to evolve solutions for a particular problem. For an overview of EAs see Holland (1975) and Mitchell (1996). A typical EA can be described as follows (cf. Mitchell (1996)). First, a population of randomly initialized strategies is generated. The population is subsequently changed and improved upon in a number of generations by means of selection, recombination ("crossover"), and mutation. Selection chooses the better strategies (with higher accumulated payoff) that will serve as parents for the next generation of strategies. This corresponds to the concept of 'survival of the fittest' mentioned earlier and arising in nature. Offspring are then formed by pairwise recombinations of the parents. Finally, the offspring strategies are slightly changed, with a small probability (mutation), and the new population replaces the old one. Recombination is usually regarded as information exchange between strategies, while mutation can be seen as error or noise.

A schematic overview of the model is given in Figure 11.1. There are three groups of economic agents present in the model: consumers, producers, and intermediaries. There are different types of consumer agents. In the current setup agent types are heterogeneous with respect to the strategies they use. Different agent types select their strategies from a different strategy base. When a consumer of a certain type chooses a strategy, he picks a strategy out of the associated strategy base. The strategy base of a particular consumer type is periodically updated by an evolutionary algorithm. It can, therefore, happen that agents of a certain type prefer direct trade while other agent types trade through the intermediary. Similarly, each intermediary type draws strategies from a different strategy base.

11.4   Experimental Design

The goal of the experiments is to investigate how the initial expertise level of the intermediary influences the level of intermediation. We vary the initial level of expertise of the intermediary – the number of links the intermediary initially maintains to producers – and study the evolution of the trade network over several trade periods. We thus perform an agent-based computational study of an electronic trade network modeled as an evolving system of autonomous interacting agents. The resulting trade network and network dynamics are a result of the local interactions of the autonomous agents over time.

The model described above allows us to investigate the role of the intermediary in electronic trade networks where consumers can choose to buy directly from the producer or through the intermediary. The experiments are conducted under different conditions concerning the pricing mechanism for the information good and the level of expertise of the intermediary. The services of the intermediary are costly and a rational consumer with perfect information would, therefore, prefer to buy directly from the producer. However, in our model it is costly to find the cheapest producer, that is, the consumer has to invest some resources (time or money) to find a good deal. An intermediary with a good network may be able to take over the search function from the consumer and make a profit. For a consumer there is no visible difference between buying from the intermediary or buying directly from the producer. [1] To model the fact that the intermediary may have expert knowledge about the trade network and can use this knowledge to make a profit, we vary the initial network of the intermediary. In all simulations,

---

[1] In this chapter, we do not assume that intermediaries are more trustworthy than producers: the only way intermediaries can make a profit is if they are better at finding the cheapest producer than the consumers.

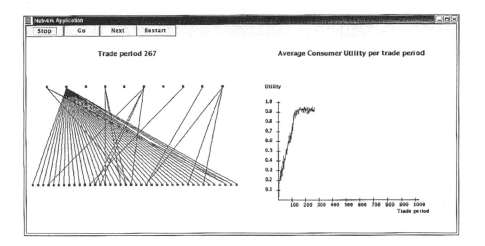

Fig. 11.3. Screenshot of the simulation environment

the consumer network is initialized with a density of 0.2. This means that the average consumer initially has links to 20 percent of the sellers (producers and intermediaries). We then introduce intermediaries in the market and the initial network density of the intermediary varies from 0.2 (no difference in knowledge between intermediaries and consumers) to 1.0 (complete knowledge about the market for the intermediary). Table 11.1 gives an overview of the parameter settings used in the experiments. We have performed a sensitivity analysis on the parameter values and found that results are robust for different parameter settings. Furthermore, we have performed 25 runs of each parameter configuration used. The results that are shown in the next section are averages over 25 runs. All experiments were initialized with 10 producers, 40 consumers, and 1 intermediary. As described above, the expertise level of the intermediary and the pricing mechanism of the producers were varied during the experiments. Additional parameter settings can be found in the Appendix.

We have also developed an agent-based simulation environment for testing and visualization of electronic trade networks. A screenshot of one of the output windows of the system is given in Figure 11.3. The system displays the architecture of the trade network at a certain point in time as well as the links that were used to purchase the good (darker links). On the right, a graph monitoring average consumer utility is shown. All economic and EA parameters can be adjusted by the user. The system can also run in batch mode allowing for more extensive simulations and statistical analysis of the results. Agent-based simulation makes it possible to investigate many new scenarios that may arise as electronic commerce increases. Agent-based computational economics studies economic phenomena as they emerge from

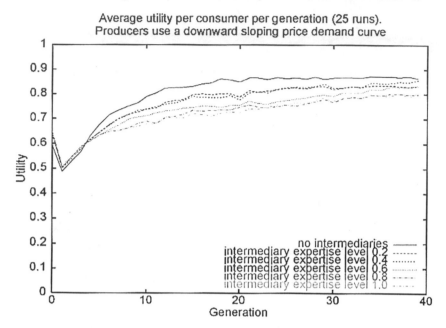

Fig. 11.4. Average consumer utilities over 25 runs for 40 update cycles of the evolutionary algorithm. Results are given for different initial expertise levels of the intermediary

interactions between individual, boundedly rational agents. Simulations can give us valuable insights in the market structures that will arise.

11.5 Results and Discussion

11.5.1 Producers Using a Downward Sloping Price Demand Curve

The price structure used by the producers in this scenario presents a coordination problem to the consumers. Consumers get the lowest price if they all purchase the information good from the same producer. The efficient[2] outcome occurs when all consumers maintain one and only one link to the cheapest producer. When a producer has succeeded in attracting a customer base of a certain threshold size, he keeps attracting new customers because he offers the lowest price. Furthermore, when the consumers have solved the coordination problem there is no incentive to change their strategy, or even to maintain outside options, so the structure of the trade network as well as the price dynamics stabilize. Figures 11.4 and 11.5 illustrate these effects.

Figure 11.4 shows the average consumer utility for different levels of the initial expertise level of the intermediary. The figure shows that consumer

---

[2]Efficiency here refers to minimum cost or maximum profit

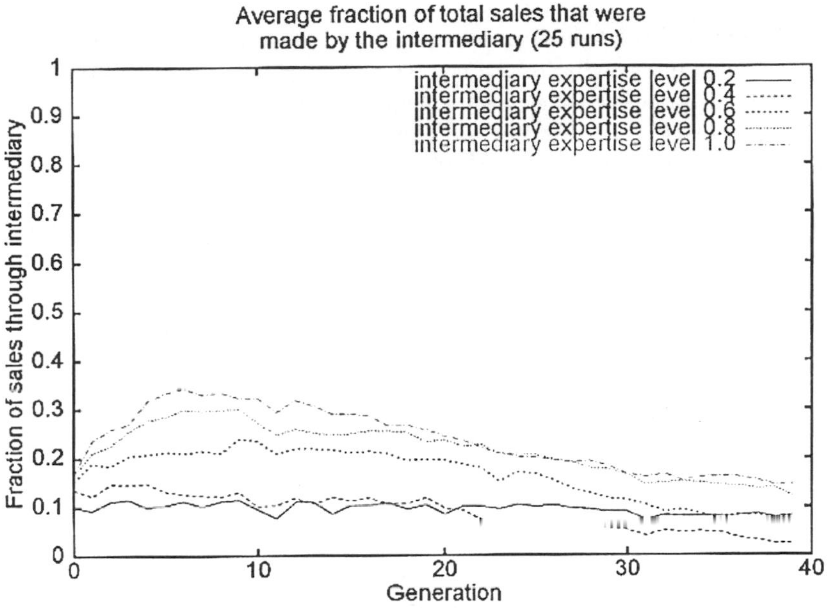

Average fraction of total sales that were
made by the intermediary (25 runs)

Fig. 11.5. Average fraction of sales by the intermediary over 25 runs. Results are given for different initial expertise levels of the intermediary

utilities are highest when no intermediaries are present in the market. The fraction of sales that occur through the intermediary is plotted in Figure 11.5. Since the intermediary starts off with a better network he attracts more consumers. However, the intermediary is not able to maintain this competitive advantage. This is caused by the fact that at the beginning of the simulation there is a lot of variance and uncertainty – prices vary, search strategies are not yet learned, and demand is greatly dispersed. It is not yet obvious which producer will 'win' (path-dependent). Under these circumstances, the intermediary presents an attractive alternative. When price dynamics stabilize, it becomes easier for the consumers to find a good strategy and most consumers learn that they can obtain higher utility by direct trade instead of intermediated trade. A comparison of Figure 11.4 and Figure 11.5 reveals that the increase in average consumer utility coincides with a decrease in intermediary activity. This is an indicator that the intermediary increases market inefficiency. Average consumer utility increases over time, which demonstrates that the evolutionary algorithm generates strategies that solve the consumer coordination problem and learn to bypass the intermediary. Note that even when the quality of the initial network of the intermediary is equal to the quality of the consumer network, the intermediary still has some market share. This is caused by the randomness in the system; consumers make mistakes, and not all newly generated search strategies are an improvement. The experiments using these price structures show that consumers are able to find the optimal solution when dynamics are simple. Furthermore, under these conditions intermediaries are not part of an efficient market structure. However, when prices fluctuate, intermediaries are a stabilizing factor and are able to attract some customers. The experiments conducted using the derivative follower algorithm are described below.

11.5.2   Producers Using the Derivative Follower Pricing Algorithm

Price dynamics caused by the derivative follower (DF) algorithm are more complex than the price dynamics discussed above. Producers continually seek to increase their profits by adjusting prices. Since the consumers now face a different problem, a trade-off between the number of links that they maintain and the total utility, it is no longer optimal in the long run to maintain just one link. In this scenario, a buyer may want to have several trade possibilities, so that he can switch when his current supplier raises his price. The results of the experiments are given below. Figure 11.6 shows the average consumer utility when producers use a DF pricing strategy, while Figure 11.7 plots the fraction of sales that occur through the intermediary. As in the experiments described above, we see that the fraction of intermediated sales increases when the quality of the initial network of the intermediary increases. However, this does not coincide with lower average consumer utility (see Table 11.2). In fact, the consumer utility remains fairly constant after an initial training period. This indicates that there is a profitable niche for the intermediary and that intermediaries can play a role in an efficient market structure. If we take a closer look at the trade patterns that arise, we see that the intermediary takes over the search function from the consumers (during the turbulent initial part of the simulation) at the cost of a slightly higher price. Initially, consumers try to form and maintain many links to different producers (network density increases from 0.2 to 0.5) but, after 10 generations, many consumers maintain only a link to the intermediary. After 20 generations, the fraction of intermediated sales decreases again and consumers learn high utility strategies for direct trade.

These experiments show that expert intermediaries can provide a valuable service to consumers when search costs are high. Furthermore, their activities have a stabilizing effect on price dynamics and the structure of the resulting trade network. However, the intermediary has to invest in a high quality network in order to attract customers. As market dynamics stabilize it becomes easier for consumers to find a good search strategy and bypass the intermediary. Electronic markets for information goods are characterized by frequent price changes; hence, we expect that specialized search intermediaries will play a role in electronic trade networks.

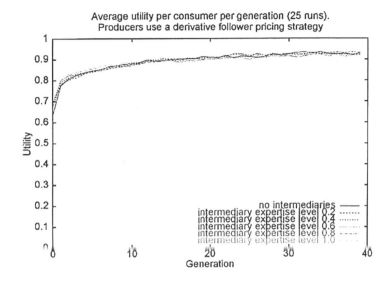

Fig. 11.6. Averages of consumer utility over 25 runs when producers use a derivative follower pricing strategy. Results are given for different initial expertise levels of the intermediary

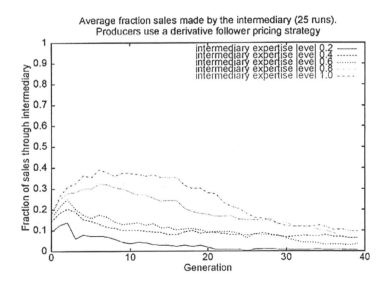

Fig. 11.7. Average fraction of sales by the intermediary over 25 runs when producers use a derivative follower pricing strategy. Results are given for different initial expertise levels of the intermediary

Table 11.2. Averages over 40 generations of 25 runs when producers use a derivative follower pricing strategy

Expert level intermediary	Fraction of intermediated sales	Average consumer utility
no intermediary	0	0.89 (0.05)
0.2	0.03 (0.04)	0.89 (0.05)
0.4	0.09 (0.03)	0.89 (0.05)
0.6	0.10 (0.06)	0.89 (0.04)
0.8	0.19 (0.08)	0.89 (0.05)
1.0	0.25 (0.10)	0.89 (0.04)

11.6 Conclusions

In this chapter, we have addressed the question of whether intermediaries will still exist and be able to make a profit if consumers can make direct connections with producers, as is often the case in electronic commerce. We have performed agent-based simulations to study the performance of intermediaries under different market conditions. We modeled an electronic trade network where an information good is traded over the network. In each trade period, cost-minimizing consumers have to decide which links to form to sellers (i.e., producers and intermediaries), and the good can only be purchased if a link between the buyer and the seller exists. Links, thus, represent trading possibilities, with the flow on them consisting of relevant information (i.e., price quotes in our case between potential buyers and sellers). The consumers, in turn, have to make a strategic decision about which (costly) links to form. We have used an evolutionary algorithm to model the search and learning behavior of the buyers. Our main finding is that if market dynamics are sufficiently complex, intermediaries that have better knowledge about the market than the average consumer are initially able to increase their market share and make a profit. Our conclusions are summarized below:

- Intermediaries that are experts at finding the best price quotes can initially survive (and even increase their market share) in an electronic trade network in which consumers can also form direct links to producers.

- Ultimately, most consumers bypass the intermediary if direct trade is more profitable.

- However, when producers change their prices in an adaptive way to increase their profits (derivative follower) consumers face a trade-off between maintaining many costly links and getting the best price.

- In such types of markets, there is a profitable niche for the intermediary and we find that many consumers choose to trade through the intermediary.

- Consumers compensate for the higher purchase price by maintaining fewer links – this has a stabilizing effect on the architecture of the electronic trade network.

These findings suggest that intermediaries will still be needed when consumers trade on complex dynamic electronic trade networks. To test this hypothesis, we are currently conducting experiments with more realistic trade networks, where new producers can enter the market and producers that fail to make a profit will leave the market. Agent-based simulation makes it possible to investigate many new scenarios that may arise as electronic commerce increases. Simulations can give us valuable insights into the market structures that will arise. The simulations discussed in this chapter are a first step in that direction. However, there are many interesting and open problems in the future of electronic trade networks and we intend to extend our models to incorporate more complex dynamics and agents. In particular, we are investigating intermediaries that use more sophisticated acquisition strategies, such as spreading the demand to influence market dynamics.

Acknowledgments

The authors would like to thank two anonymous referees for their helpful comments. This research is part of the project, "Evolutionary Exploration Systems for Electronic Markets," funded by the Netherlands Organization for Scientific Research (NWO), Project 612-60-008.

References

Alkemade, F., Amman, H. M., and La Poutré, J. A. (2002), "The Separation of Economic versus EA Parameters in EA-Learning," CWI Technical Report, Amsterdam, The Netherlands.

Alkemade, F., and La Poutré, J. A. (2002), "Heterogeneous, Boundedly Rational Agents in the Cournot Duopoly," in *Heterogeneous Agents, Interactions and Economic Performance*, pp. 3-17, R. Cowan and N. Jonard, editors, *Lecture Notes in Economics and Mathematical Systems* **521**.

Choi, S. Y., Stahl, D. O., and Whinston, A. B. (1997), *The Economics of Electronic Commerce*, Macmillan Technical Publishing, Indianapolis, Indiana.

DiMicco, J. M., Greenwald, A., and Maes, P. (2001), "Dynamic Pricing Strategies Under a Finite Time Horizon," in *Proceedings of the 3rd ACM Conference on Electronic Commerce*, pp. 95-104, ACM Press, New York.

Greenwald, A. M., and Kephart, J. O. (1999), "Shopbots and Pricebots," in *Proceedings of the 16th Joint Conference on Artificial Intelligence (IJCAI-99)*, Tockholm, Sweden, pp. 506-511.

Holland, J. H. (1975), *Adaptation in Natural and Artificial Systems*, University of Michigan Press, Ann Arbor, Michigan.

McFadzean, D., and Tesfatsion, L. (1999), "A C++ Platform for the Evolution of Trade Networks," *Computational Economics* **14**, 109-134.

Mas-Colell, A., and Whinston, M. D., and Green, J. R. (1995), *Microeconomic Theory*, Oxford University Press, Oxford, England.

Mitchell, M. (1996), *An Introduction to Genetic Algorithms*, MIT Press, Cambridge, Massachusetts.

Newell, A., and Simon, H. A. (1972), *Human Problem Solving*, Prentice-Hall, Englewood Cliffs, New Jersey.

Pingle, M. (2000), "The Effect of Decision Costs on the Formation of Market-Making Intermediaries: A Pilot Experiment," *Journal of Economic Behavior and Organization*, **41**, 1-24.

Simon, H. A. (1984), *Models of Bounded Rationality*, MIT Press, Cambridge, Massachusetts.

Spulber, D. F. (1999), *Market Microstructure: Intermediaries and the Theory of the Firm*, Cambridge University Press, Cambridge, England.

Shapiro, C., and Varian, H. R. (1999), *Information Rules: A Strategic Guide to the Network Economy*, Harvard Business School Press, Boston, Massachusetts.

Tesfatsion, L. (2001), "Introduction to the Special Issue on Agent-Based Computational Economics," *Journal of Economic Dynamics and Control* **25**, 281-293.

Weitzel, T., Wendt, O., and Westarp, F. V. (2002), "Reconsidering Network Effect Theory," in *Proceedings of the 8th European Conference on Information Systems (ECIS 2002)*, Vienna, Austria, pp. 484-491.

Appendix: Parameter Values

A sensitivity analysis was performed and we found that results were robust to changes in the EA parameters (within the range of generally suggested values). The parameter values are given in Table 11.3.

Table 11.3. Economic parameter values for consumers, producers, and intermediaries and the evolutionary algorithm parameter values

Parameter	Value
Economic model parameters	
Producers	
Number of producers	10
Maximum price	12.0
Minimum price	0.0
Producer price setting mechanism	
Downward sloping demand curve	$P = a - b * Demand^{exp}$
a	12
b	0.3
Derivative follower	$P = P * (1 + (dir * step\ size))$
Direction	$\{-1, 1\}$
Step size	0.1
Consumers	
Number of consumers	40
Number of consumer types	10
Link costs	1
Error constant ϵ	0.05
Initial network density consumers	0.2
Intermediaries	
Number of intermediaries	1
Link costs	1
Initial network density intermediaries	$0.2, \ldots, 1.0$
Intermediary markup	5%
EA parameters	
EA	Simple GA
Mutation rate	0.02 per bit
Crossover rate	1.0
Size of strategy base/population size	20

12 Evolution of Worker-Employer Networks and Behaviors under Alternative Non-Employment Benefits: An Agent-Based Computational Study

Mark Pingle and Leigh Tesfatsion

12.1 Introduction

Determining the effects of labor institutions on macroeconomic performance is a central concern of economic policymakers. Differences in labor institutions have been conjectured to be a key explanation for observed cross-country differences in the level and persistence of unemployment, in the distribution of income and wealth, and in growth rates for labor productivity and GDP.

For example, as discussed by Blau and Kahn (1999), Ljungqvist and Sargent (1998), and Nickell and Layard (1999), European OECD countries over the past twenty years have tended to rely on administered wages and legislated job protection and have experienced sluggish job growth and persistently high unemployment. In contrast, the United States has had a relatively more flexible, less regulated labor market and has achieved much greater job growth and relatively lower unemployment rates. This has led many European policymakers to argue the need for reforms in their labor institutions.

Unfortunately, as discussed by Acemoglu and Shimer (2000), Blau and Kahn (1999), and Freeman (1998), it is difficult to obtain conclusive empirical results regarding how labor institutions affect economic performance.

Regression methods relating changes in labor institutions to economic outcomes quickly tax degrees of freedom. This problem is compounded if one
institution's impact depends on the presence or absence of other institutions.
Also, labor institutions are inherently endogenous. For example, governments continually revise labor institutions in response to economic and political pressures. This endogeneity makes it difficult to interpret the validity
of empirical investigations.

In recognition of these difficulties, Freeman (1998, pp. 19-20) suggests that
agent-based computational modeling might offer a promising additional way
to study the impact of labor institutions, particularly from a market design
perspective. Tesfatsion (1998, 2001, 2002a) reports some preliminary work
along these lines. An *agent-based computational economics (ACE)* framework is used to study path dependence, market power, and market efficiency
outcomes for a labor market under systematically varied concentration and
capacity conditions. ACE is the computational study of economies modeled
as evolving systems of autonomous interacting agents (Tesfatsion (2002b,
2003)).[1]

In this study we conduct an ACE labor market experiment to test the sensitivity of labor market outcomes to changes in the level of a non-employment
payment. Our ultimate objective is to understand how the basic features of
real-world unemployment benefit programs affect labor market performance.[2]
However, as will be clarified below, a human subject experiment was run in
parallel to this computational experiment as a check on the reliability of our
findings and the adequacy of the learning representations for our computational workers and employers. To facilitate this initial benchmark check, a
deliberately simplified experimental design is used.

Specifically, we consider a balanced labor market with equal numbers
of workers and employers. In each trade cycle (work period), every worker
has one work offer to make and every employer has one job opening to fill.
An employer can reject a work offer received from a worker on two possible
grounds: unacceptable past work history; or capacity limitations.

The workers repeatedly submit their work offers to preferred employers
until either they succeed in being hired or they become discouraged by re-
jections and exit the job market. A worker must pay a small transaction
cost each time he submits a work offer to an employer. As in MacLeod and
Malcomson (1998), each matched worker and employer individually chooses

---

[1] See http://www.econ.iastate.edu/tesfatsi/ace.htm for extensive resources related
to ACE, including surveys, an annotated syllabus of readings, research area sites, software,
teaching materials, and pointers to individual researchers and research groups.

[2] For example, in the US, unemployment benefits are *financed by taxes on employers* and
are intended to provide *temporary* financial assistance to workers who become unemployed
through no fault of their own and who *continue to seek work.* Understanding the separate
and combined impacts of these and other unemployment benefit program features on labor
market performance over time is an extremely challenging problem. A detailed discussion
of theoretical and empirical labor market studies focusing on unemployment benefits and
related issues can be found in Pingle and Tesfatsion (2001).

to shirk or cooperate on the work-site, and these choices are made simultaneously so that neither has a strategic informational advantage. Any worker or employer who does not enter an employment relationship during the trade cycle in question receives an exogenously specified non-employment payment. Workers and employers evolve their work-site behaviors over time on the basis of past experiences in an attempt to increase their earnings.

In this labor market, then, full employment with no job vacancies is possible. Nevertheless, the unemployment rate and the particular set of workers and employers in employment relationships endogenously evolve over the course of successive trade cycles. Two interdependent choices made repeatedly by the workers and the employers shape this evolutionary process: namely, their choices of work-site partners; and their behavioral choices in interactions with these partners.

Three non-employment payment (NEP) treatments are experimentally studied: a zero NEP; a low NEP; and a high NEP. As reported in Table 12.1, one main finding is that the average utility levels attained by workers and employers do not substantially change as the NEP is increased from zero to high. As will be clarified in Section 12.4, although the increase in the NEP increases the worker unemployment rate and the employer vacancy rate, this greater loss of productive activity is offset in part by the higher NEP and in part by the increased levels of mutual cooperation exhibited by the workers and employers who manage to match.

Another main finding reported in Table 12.1 is that a somewhat higher average utility level for workers and employers is attained with a low NEP than with either a zero or a high NEP in the short and intermediate runs (generations 1 through 50). As will be explained more carefully in Section 12.4, a zero NEP encourages shirking on the work-site (low risk of quits or firings in reponse to defections) while a high NEP results in a high risk of lost earnings due to coordination failure (high risk of quits or firings in response to defections). Interestingly, however, average utility tends to increase over time under each NEP treatment as the workers and employers become better at sustaining mutual cooperation on the work-site. Moreover, this movement towards higher average utility is strongest under the high NEP treatment. Thus, in the long run (generation 1000), the average utility level attained by workers and employers with a high NEP exceeds the average utility levels attained with a zero or low NEP.

On the other hand, program costs should be taken into account as well as utility benefits in order to obtain a more accurate measure of economic efficiency. Let net earnings be measured by the average (per agent) utility level attained by workers and employers minus the average NEP paid to these workers and employers. Define efficiency to be the ratio of actual net earnings to maximum possible net earnings. As indicated in Table 12.1, although a high NEP results in a high average utility level, it also results in a significantly lower efficiency level than either the zero or low NEP due to high program

Table 12.1. Summary of aggregate outcomes: average agent utility level (with standard deviation), worker unemployment rate, employer vacancy rate, and efficiency level for each non-employment payment (NEP) treatment

	Generation 12	**Generation** 50	**Generation** 1000
ZeroT **NEP=0**	Utility 33.8 (5.9) Unemp 0% Vacancy 0% Efficiency 85%	Utility 35.2 (2.8) UnEmp 0% Vacancy 0% Efficiency 88%	Utility 35.8 (3.6) UnEmp 0% Vacancy 0% Efficiency 90%
LowT **NEP=15**	Utility 35.4 (3.6) UnEmp 1% Vacancy 2% Efficiency 88%	Utility 37.2 (2.0) UnEmp 0% Vacancy 1% Efficiency 93%	Utility 35.7 (1.8) UnEmp 2% Vacancy 3% Efficiency 88%
HighT **NEP=30**	Utility 34.6 (1.0) Unemp 48% Vacancy 50% Efficiency 50%	Utility 35.7 (0.5) Unemp 36% Vacancy 36% Efficiency 62%	Utility 36.4 (0.6) UnEmp 32% Vacancy 33% Efficiency 67%

costs. Overall, considering the short, intermediate, and long run, the low NEP delivers the highest overall efficiency level. Consequently, evaluated in terms of efficiency, our findings indicate that a low NEP is preferable to either a zero or a high NEP.

The aggregate outcomes reported in Table 12.1, while interesting, are only the tip of the iceberg. A careful study of individual experimental runs indicates that the response of the ACE labor market to changes in the NEP is much more intricately structured than this table suggests. As reported in Figure 12.1, the 20 runs generated for each NEP treatment tend to gravitate towards one of two "attractor states." The configuration of these two attractor states is similar under the zero and low NEP treatments: the first attractor state is characterized by latched pairs of mutually cooperative workers and employers, while the second attractor state is characterized by latched pairs of workers and employers who intermittently defect and cooperate. In contrast, under the high NEP treatment, one attractor state is characterized by latched pairs of mutually cooperative workers and employers while the other attractor state is a state of economic collapse in which each worker and employer ultimately becomes inactive. This apparent existence of multiple attractor states suggests caution in interpreting the aggregate outcomes reported in Table 12.1, since these outcomes could be based on inappropriately pooled data.

The existence of multiple attractor states for each NEP treatment is due to strong network and learning effects. Starting from the same initial structural conditions, chance differences in the initial interaction patterns among the workers and employers can cause the labor market to evolve towards persistent interaction networks supporting sharply distinct types of expressed behaviors. For example, with a high NEP, the labor market evolves either towards a highly efficient economy in which all workers and employers are in long-run mutually cooperative relationships or towards economic collapse with 100% unemployment. Thus, while a change in the level of the NEP can be expected to have substantial systematic effects on key labor market outcomes such as efficiency and unemployment, our findings suggest that these effects will be in the form of spectral (multiple peaked) distributions with large standard deviations.

These computational experiment findings can be compared to findings reported in Pingle and Tesfatsion (2002) for a human-subject experiment using a similarly structured labor market but with a smaller number of workers and employers participating in a much smaller number of trade cycles per experimental session. In the human-subject experiment, as in the computational experiment, a higher NEP resulted in higher average unemployment and vacancy rates as well as higher average utility levels among those who successfully matched. In the human-subject experiment, however, most relationships that formed between workers and employers were either short-lived or intermittent, with only modest amounts of behavioral coordination in evidence. In contrast, in the computational experiment almost all workers and employers who succeeded in matching ended up in long-run relationships with one partner in which the behaviors of the partners were highly coordinated.

As detailed more carefully in Pingle and Tesfatsion (2002), this difference in findings raises interesting questions. To what extent are the human-subject and computational experiments capturing the same economic structure but reporting over different time scales, short run versus long run? In particular, could it be that the "shadow of the past" weighs heavily on human subjects over the necessarily shorter human-subject trials, biasing behaviors towards unknown past points of reference? If so, the computational experiment might be providing the more accurate prediction of what would happen in actual labor markets over a longer span of time. Alternatively, the two experiments might differ structurally in some fundamental way so that differences in outcomes would be observed regardless of time scale. In particular, is the representation of agent learning in the computational experiment too inaccurate to permit valid comparisons with human-subject labor market experiments? Are the observed differences in types of network formations due to the different frequencies with which transaction costs are incurred due to scale effects?

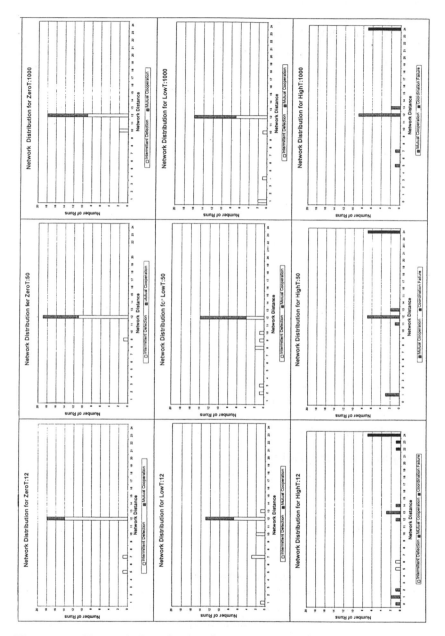

Fig. 12.1. Network distribution by treatment and generation

Careful additional studies, both empirical and experimental, will be needed to resolve these questions.

The ACE labor market model is presented in Section 12.2. Section 12.3 outlines the experimental design of our study, and Section 12.4 provides a detailed report of our experimental findings. Concluding remarks are presented in Section 12.5.

12.2   The ACE Labor Market Model

Overview

The ACE labor market comprises 12 workers and 12 employers. Each worker can work for at most one employer at any given time, and each employer can employ at most one worker at any given time. The workers and employers repeatedly seek preferred work-site partners using a modified form of a matching mechanism (Gale and Shapley (1962)) that has been observed to evolve in various real-world labor market settings (Roth and Sotomayor (1992)). The workers and employers who successfully match then engage in risky work-site interactions modeled as prisoner's dilemma games. At regular intervals the workers and employers separately update their work-site rules of behavior on the basis of the past earnings obtained with these rules.

The computational experiment is implemented by means of the *Trade Network Game Laboratory (TNG Lab)*, an agent-based computational laboratory developed by McFadzean, Stewart, and Tesfatsion (2001) for studying the evolution of trade networks via real-time animations, tables, and graphical displays.[3] The specific TNG parameter settings used for the experiment at hand are described below. All other TNG parameter settings are the same as in Tesfatsion (2001).

Implementation Details

As depicted in Table 12.2, ACE labor market activities are divided into a sequence of 1000 generations. Each generation in turn is divided into three parts: (a) a trade cycle loop consisting of successive trade cycles during which work-site interactions take place; (b) an environment step in which each worker and employer assesses their current utility (fitness) level as a function of their accumulated earnings to date; and (c) an evolution step in which the workers and employers separately evolve their work-site rules of behavior on the basis of the past earnings attained with these rules.

Each worker and employer in the initial generation is assigned a work-site rule in the form of a randomly specified pure strategy for playing an iterated prisoner's dilemma game with an arbitrary partner an indefinite number of times. This work-site rule governs the behavior of the agent in his work-site interactions throughout the entire trade cycle loop for the initial

---

[3]See http://www.econ.iastate.edu/tesfatsi/tnghome.htm for source code, executables, user instructions, tutorials, and research related to the TNG Lab.

Table 12.2. Flow of activities in the ACE labor market

```
int main () {
    InitiateEconomy();        // CONSTRUCT initial subpopulations of
                              //    workers and employers with random
                              //    work-site rules of behavior.
    For (G = 1,...,1000) {    // ENTER THE GENERATION CYCLE LOOP
                              // GENERATION CYCLE:
        InitiateGen();        //    Configure workers and employers
                              //       with user-supplied parameter values
                              //       (initial expected utility assessments,
                              //       minimum tolerance levels, )
        For (TC = 1,...,150) { //   ENTER THE TRADE CYCLE LOOP
                              //    TRADE CYCLE:
            MatchTraders();   //       Workers and employers determine
                              //          their work-site partners, given
                              //          their expected utility assessments,
                              //          and record job search and
                              //          inactivity costs.
            Trade();          //       Workers and employers engage
                              //          in work-site interactions and
                              //          record their work-site payoffs.
            UpdateExp();      //       Workers and employers update their
                              //          expected utility assessments, using
                              //          newly recorded costs and work-site
                              //          payoffs, and begin a new trade cycle.
        }
                              // ENVIRONMENT STEP:
        AssessFitness();      //    Each worker and employer assesses
                              //    his utility (fitness) level.
                              // EVOLUTION STEP:
        EvolveGen();          //    Workers and employers separately
                              //       evolve their work-site rules,
                              //       and a new generation cycle begins.
    }
    Return 0;
}
```

generation. Each work-site rule is represented by means of a "finite state automaton"[4] with 16 internal states. Thus, the set of feasible work-site rules for each worker and employer, while extremely large, is nevertheless finite. Each worker and employer in the initial generation also assigns an initial expected utility assessment U^o to each of his possible work-site partners, where U^o is equal to the mutual cooperation payoff.[5]

The workers and employers in the initial generation then participate in a trade cycle loop consisting of 150 successive trade cycles. In each trade cycle they engage in two main activities: (1) a matching process during which they search for preferred work-site partners on the basis of their current expected utility assessments for these partners; and (2) an employment process during which each matched worker-employer pair engages in one work-site interaction. Throughout these processes the workers and employers update their current expected utility assessments for each other every time they obtain a payoff from an interaction with each other.

Each worker and employer also has an exogenously specified minimum tolerance level, assigned as part of the initial generation configuration process. In the current experiment, these minimum tolerance levels are set equal to the non-employment payment. Thus, entering into a risky work-site interaction is viewed as a tolerable gamble if and only if it is expected to yield at least as high a payoff as would be earned through inactivity. If the expected utility assessment assigned to an employer by a worker ever falls below the minimum tolerance level, the worker will stop directing work offers to this employer. Similarly, if the expected utility assessment assigned to a worker by an employer ever drops below the minimum tolerance level, the employer will stop accepting work offers from this worker.

The manner in which workers direct work offers to employers during the matching process for each trade cycle proceeds as follows. Each worker and employer has a preference ranking over possible partners, determined by his current expected utility assessments. Each worker starts by directing a work offer to a most preferred tolerable employer. Each employer receiving at least one tolerable work offer places his most preferred tolerable work offer on his work offer list and refuses all the rest. Each worker having a work offer refused then redirects this work offer to a next most preferred tolerable employer who has not yet refused him in the current matching process, if any such employer exists. Once employers stop receiving new work offers, they accept the work offers currently on their work offer lists and the matching process comes to a close. Throughout this process, ties are broken by random

---

[4] A *finite state automaton* is a system comprising a finite collection of internal states together with a state transition function that gives the next state of the system as a function of the current state and other current system inputs. For the application at hand, the latter inputs are the actions selected by a worker and employer engaged in a work-site interaction.

[5] This is not an innocuous specification, since it strongly affects the extent to which the workers and employers engage in experimentation with new partners. This issue is further considered in Section 12.3.

selection.

Once a worker and employer are matched, they enter into a work-site interaction. This interaction is modeled as a prisoner's dilemma game with cooperation interpreted as meeting all work-site obligations and defection interpreted as shirking with regard to these obligations. As depicted in Table 12.3 below, one of four possible payoffs can be earned in each work-site interaction: a low payoff L=10, earned by an agent who cooperates against a defecting partner; a mutual defection payoff D=20; a mutual cooperation payoff C=40; or a high payoff H=60 earned by an agent who defects against a cooperating partner. Also, a worker incurs an offer cost OC=1.0 each time he directs a work offer to an employer, whether or not the work offer is accepted. A worker or employer who is not matched earns a non-employment payment (NEP) for the trade cycle. Each worker and employer records all payoffs he receives during the course of each trade cycle, including work-site payoffs, negative payoffs due to offer costs, and non-employment payments.

Each worker and employer uses a simple reinforcement learning algorithm to update his expected utility assessments for possible partners in response to new payoffs. Recall that each agent (worker or employer) initially assigns an initial expected utility assessment $U^o=C$ to each possible work-site partner. Subsequently, each time an agent v interacts with an agent z, agent v forms an updated expected utility assessment for z by summing U^o together with all payoffs received to date from interactions with z and dividing this sum by one plus the total number of these interactions. The payoffs included in this summation include work-site payoffs and negative payoffs due to offer costs. Consequently, an updated expected utility assessment for any agent z is the average of all payments received to date in interactions with z, augmented to include U^o as a virtual additional payoff. Under this method, if an agent interacts repeatedly with another agent for a sufficient length of time, his expected utility assessment for z will eventually approach his true average payoff level from interactions with z.[6]

At the end of the initial generation, the workers and employers enter into an environment step in which each agent calculates his utility (fitness) level. This utility level is taken to be the average total net payoffs per trade cycle that the agent earned during the course of the preceding trade cycle loop, i.e., the agent's total net payoffs divided by 150 (the number of trade cycles per loop). The workers and employers then enter into an evolution step in which they use their attained utility levels to evolve (structurally update) their work-site rules via both inductive and social learning. Inductive learning takes the form of experimentation; agents perturb their work-site rules by introducing random modifications. Social learning takes the form of mimicry;

---

[6]See McFadzean and Tesfatsion (1999) for more details. Briefly, this long-run consistency property follows from the finite state automaton representation for work-site rules which ensures that the action pattern between any two agents who repeatedly interact must eventually enter into a cycle as the number of their interactions becomes sufficiently large.

agents deliberately modify their work-site rules to more closely resemble the work-site rules used by more successful (higher utility) agents of their own type. Thus, workers imitate other more successful workers, and employers imitate other more successful employers.

Experimentation and mimicry are separately implemented for workers and for employers by means of genetic algorithms involving commonly used elitism, mutation, and recombination operations. Elitism ensures that the most successful work-site rules are retained unchanged from one generation to the next. Mutation ensures that workers and employers continually experiment with new work-site rules (inductive learning). Recombination ensures that workers and employers continually engage in mimicry (social learning).[7]

At the end of the evolution step, each worker and employer has a potentially new work-site rule. The memory of each worker and employer is then wiped clean of all past work-site experiences. In particular, initial expected utility assessments for possible partners are re-set to the mutual cooperation payoff level without regard for past work-site experiences. The workers and employers then enter into a new generation and the whole process repeats, for a total of 1000 generations in all.[8]

12.3   The Computational Experiment

The computational experiment focuses on only one treatment variable, the non-employment payment (NEP). The three tested treatments for NEP are NEP=0, NEP=15, and NEP=30. These three treatments are referred to as ZeroT, LowT, and HighT, respectively.

The interest in these three alternative treatments is seen by comparing them with the work-site payoffs depicted in Table 12.3. In treatment ZeroT, non-employment during a trade cycle results in the payment NEP=0. This is

---

[7] See McFadzean and Tesfatsion (1999) and Tesfatsion (2001) for detailed discussions of this use of genetic algorithms to implement the evolution of work-site rules.

[8] A final technical remark about implementation should also be noted, in case others wish to replicate or extend this experiment. The minimum tolerance level is hardwired to zero in the TNG Lab, the software used to implement the computational experiment. Thus, to retain the non-employment payment NEP equal to the minimum tolerance level, experiments were actually run with each work-site payoff normalized by subtraction of NEP. In addition, for better TNG Lab visualization, the work-site payoffs were further normalized by multiplication by 0.10. For example, $C* = 0.10[C-NEP]$ was used in place of the mutual cooperation payoff C, and similarly for the other work-site payoffs. The corresponding normalized non-employment payment then equaled $NEP* = 0.10[NEP-NEP] = 0$. Finally, to maintain consistency with this normalization, the offer cost OC was normalized to $OC*=0.10$. Note that it would *not* be consistent to subtract NEP from OC, since OC is a cost per work offer. For example, a worker who is refused k times and never hired during a trade cycle receives a total payoff NEP-kOC at the end of the trade cycle, and this is the payoff from which NEP must then be subtracted to implement the payoff normalization. This subtraction occurs automatically when $NE*=0$ is used in place of NEP. In all data tables presented below, utility levels and market power levels are translated back into non-normalized form prior to reporting, for easier comparison with the human-subject experimental findings reported in Pingle and Tesfatsion (2002).

Table 12.3. Payoff matrix for the work-site prisoner's dilemma game

Employer

		c	d
	c	(40,40)	(10,60)
Worker			
	d	(60,10)	(20,20)

the worst possible trade cycle payoff, worse even than the sucker payoff L=10 that results from cooperating with a defecting work site partner. In treatment ZeroT, then, unemployment or vacancy is never an attractive alternative to employment or hiring, and the workers and employers will be willing to put up with defections to avoid unemployment or vacancy.

In contrast, in treatment LowT non-employment during a trade cycle results in the payment NEP=15. This payment is strictly higher than the sucker payoff L=10, meaning agents will prefer non-employment to being suckered. Thus, each agent who defects against a cooperative partner to attain a high payoff now faces a risk of future non-employment if this current partner chooses not to interact with him in the future. Finally, in treatment HighT non-employment results in the payment NEP=30. This payment dominates both the sucker payoff L=10 and the mutual defection payoff D=20. Consequently, agents will tend to be much more sensitive to defections, preferring unemployment or vacancy in preference to defecting back against a defecting partner.

For each NEP treatment, 20 runs were generated using 20 different seeds for the TNG Lab pseudo-random number generator: namely, {0, 5, 10, ..., 95}. In the data tables reported in Section 12.4, each run is identified by its corresponding seed value. Each run consists of 1000 generations in total. To investigate evolutionary change, the twenty runs for each treatment are sampled at three different points in time: generation 12, generation 50, and generation 1000. For each sampled generation, data is collected regarding network formation, market non-participation rates, work-site behaviors, welfare (utility and market power) outcomes, and persistent relationship type counts.

Before reporting our experimental findings in detail, it is important to explain carefully the descriptive statistics that have been constructed to help characterize the one-to-many mapping between treatment and outcomes.

Measurement of Persistent Relationships

As previously noted (see footnote 4), work-site rules are represented as finite state automata, implying that the actions undertaken by any one agent in repeated work-site interactions with another agent must eventually cycle. Consequently, the actions of any one agent in interactions with another agent during a trade cycle loop can be summarized in the form of a work-site history H:P. The "handshake" H is a (possibly null) string of work-site actions that form a non-repeated pattern, while the "persistent portion" P is a (possibly null) string of work-site actions that are cyclically repeated. For example, letting c denote cooperation and d denote defection, the work-site history ddd:dc for an agent v in interactions with another agent z indicates that v defected against z in his first three work-site interactions with z and thereafter alternated between defection and cooperation.

A worker and employer are said to exhibit a *persistent relationship* during a given trade cycle loop if two conditions hold. First, their work-site histories with each other during the course of this loop each have non-null persistent portions. Second, accepted work offers between the worker and employer do not permanently cease during this loop either by choice (a permanent switch away to a strictly preferred partner) or by refusal (one agent becomes intolerable to the other because of too many defections).

A persistent relationship between a worker and employer in a given trade cycle loop is said to be *latched* if the worker works continually for the employer (i.e., in every successive trade cycle) during the persistent portions of their work-site histories. Otherwise, the persistent relationship is said to be *recurrent*.

Measurement of Market Non-Participation Rates

A worker or employer who fails to form any persistent relationship during a given trade cycle loop is classified as *persistently non-employed* for that trade cycle loop. The percentage of workers who are persistently non-employed constitutes the *persistent unemployment rate* for that trade cycle loop. Similarly, the percentage of employers who are persistently non-employed constitutes the *persistent vacancy rate* for that trade cycle loop.

Classification of Networks by Competitive Distance

We will next construct a distance measure that permits the classification of experimentally observed "interaction networks" into alternative types. This distance measure will calculate the distance between an experimentally observed interaction network and an idealized interaction network capable of supporting a competitive (full employment) market outcome.

Recall from Table 12.2 that each generation G of the ACE labor market model consists of a single trade cycle loop plus an environment step and an evolution step. The *interaction network* N(G,R) for a particular generation G in a particular experimental run R refers to the observed pattern of interactions occurring among workers and employers in the trade cycle loop for that generation and run.

Each interaction network N(G,R) is represented in the form of a directed graph. The vertices V of the graph represent the workers and employers. The edges of the graph (directed arrows) represent work offers directed from workers to employers. Finally, the edge weight on any edge denotes the number of accepted work offers between the worker and employer connected by the edge. The reduced-form network PN(G,R) derived from N(G,R) by eliminating all edges of N(G,R) that correspond to non-persistent relationships is referred to as the *persistent network* corresponding to N(G,R).

In a standard competitive equilibrium situation, workers are indifferent among employers offering the same working conditions and employers are indifferent among workers offering identical labor services. Moreover, workers offering the same labor services have the same ex ante expected employment rate and employers offering the same working conditions have the same ex ante expected vacancy rate.

In the current labor market model, these same market characteristics would tend to prevail if all workers and employers always cooperated. In the latter case, due to indifference, workers would randomly distribute their work offers across all employers and employers would randomly select work offers from among all work offers received. The resulting interaction pattern would therefore tend to be fully recurrent (no latching and no persistent non-employment) with equal ex ante expected employment rates and vacancy rates for workers and employers, respectively. For these reasons, the following interaction pattern among workers and employers is referred to below as a *competitive interaction pattern*: each worker is recurrently directing work offers to employers, and every worker and employer has at least one persistent relationship.

The *network distance* for any persistent network PN(G,R) is then defined to be the number of vertices (agents) in PN(G,R) whose edges (persistent relationships) fail to conform to the competitive interaction pattern. By construction, then, a distance measure of 0 indicates zero deviation and a distance measure of 24 (the total number of workers and employers) indicates maximum deviation. In particular, a perfectly recurrent persistent network has a network distance of 0, a perfectly latched persistent network has a network distance of 12, and a perfectly disconnected persistent network (no persistent relationships) has a network distance of 24.

Classification of Work-Site Behaviors

A worker or employer in generation G of a run R is called a *never-provoked defector (NPD)* if he ever defects against another agent that has not previously defected against him. The percentages of workers and employers who are NPDs measure the extent to which these agents behave opportunistically in work-site interactions with partners who are strangers or who so far have been consistently cooperative.

A worker or employer in generation G of a run R is referred to as a *per-*

sistent intermittent defector (IntD) if he establishes at least one persistent relationship for which his persistent portion consists of a non-trivial mix of defections and cooperations. The agent is referred to as a *persistent defector (AllD)* if he establishes at least one persistent relationship and if the persistent portion of each of his persistent relationships consists entirely of defections. Finally, the agent is referred to as a *persistent cooperator (AllC)* if he establishes at least one persistent relationship and if the persistent portion of each of his persistent relationships consists entirely of cooperations. By construction, an agent in generation G of a run R satisfies one and only one of the following four agent-type classifications: persistently non-employed; a persistent intermittent defector; a persistent defector; or a persistent cooperator.

Two important points can be made about this classification of agent types. First, in contrast to standard game theory, the agents coevolve their types over time. This coevolution is in response to past experiences, starting from initially random behavioral specifications. Thus, agent typing is endogenous. Second, agent typing is measured in terms of persistently expressed behaviors, not in terms of work-site rules. An agent may have coevolved into an AllC in terms of expressed behaviors with current work-site partners, based on past work-site experiences with these partners, while still retaining the capability of defecting against a new untried partner. Indeed, work-site rules continually coevolve in the evolution step through mutation and recombination operations even if expressed behaviors appear to have largely stabilized. This ceaseless change in work-site rules makes any apparent stabilization in the distribution of agent types all the more surprising and interesting.

Measurement of Utility and Market Power Outcomes

The utility level of a worker or employer at the end of generation G in a run R is measured by the average total net payoffs per trade cycle that the agent earns during the course of the trade cycle loop for generation G.

With regard to market power, we adopt the standard industrial organization approach: namely, market power is measured by the degree to which the actual utility levels attained by workers and employers compare against an idealized competitive yardstick. We take as this yardstick a situation in which there is absence of strategic behavior, symmetric treatment of equals, and full employment. Specifically, we define *competitive market conditions* for the ACE labor market to be a situation in which each worker is recurrently directing work offers to employers, and each worker and employer is a persistent cooperator (AllC).

Ignoring offer costs, the utility level that each worker and employer would attain under these competitive market conditions is simply the mutual cooperation payoff level, C. Therefore, as in Pingle and Tesfatsion (2001, 2002), we define the *market power (MPow)* of each worker or employer in generation G of a run R to be the extent to which their attained utility level, U, differs from C: that is, $MPow = (U-C)/C$.

Classification of Persistent Relationship Types

A persistent relationship between a worker and employer in generation G of a run R is classified in accordance with the persistent behaviors expressed by the two participants in this particular relationship.

If both participants are persistent intermittent defectors (IntDs), the relationship is classified as *mutual intermittent defection (M-IntD)*. If both participants are persistent defectors (AllDs), the relationship is classified as *mutual defection (M-AllD)*. If both participants are persistent cooperators (AllCs), the relationship is classified as *mutual cooperation (M-AllC)*. Note that the relative shirking rates for an M-IntD relationship can be deduced for the participant worker and employer by examining their relative market power levels.

A persistent relationship in which the worker and employer express distinct types of behaviors is indicated in hyphenated form, with the worker's behavior indicated first. For example, a persistent relationship involving a worker who is an IntD and an employer who is an AllC is indicated by the expression IntD-AllC.

12.4   Experimental Findings

Overview

The results for the computational experiment display a startling degree of regularity. This regularity is visible as early as the twelfth generation and persists through generation 1000.

For each of the three NEP treatments ZeroT, LowT, and HighT, the twenty trial runs tend to cluster into two distinct attractor states. Each attractor state supports a distinct configuration of market non-participation rates, work-site behaviors, utility levels, market power outcomes, and persistent relationship types. These attractor states can be Pareto-ranked, in the sense that the average utility levels attained by workers and by employers are both markedly higher in one of the two attractor states. The exact form of the attractor states varies systematically across the three NEP treatments.

Network Formation

For each of the twenty runs corresponding to each treatment ZeroT, LowT, and HighT, the form of the persistent network was determined at three sampling points: generation 12; generation 50; and generation 1000. Using the network distance measure defined in Section 12.3, the distribution of these persistent networks across runs was then plotted, conditional on treatment and sampled generation. Thus, a total of nine network distributions were plotted, three for each of the three treatments.

These nine network distributions are depicted in Figure 12.1. Network distance is measured along the horizontal axes and the number of runs clustered at this network distance is indicated on the vertical axes. Recall that a network distance of 0 corresponds to a perfectly recurrent ("competitive") persistent network, a network distance of 12 corresponds to a perfectly latched persistent network, and a network distance of 24 corresponds to a perfectly disconnected persistent network (no persistent relationships).

In treatment ZeroT, perfectly latched networks are strongly dominant even by generation 12. For each sampled generation, all but one or two of the twenty runs exhibit persistent networks consisting of perfectly latched worker-employer pairs. This is indicated by the sharp peak in the network distribution at network distance 12.

In treatment LowT, perfectly latched networks are again dominant. Nevertheless, at each sampled generation, the network distribution is less sharply peaked at network distance 12 than it was for treatment ZeroT.

In treatment HighT, a new phenomenon arises. For each sampled generation, seven runs out of twenty lie at network distance 24, indicating that the workers and employers in these runs have failed to form any persistent relationships. At generation 12, the remaining 13 runs are scattered over network distances from 0 to 23. By generation 1000, however, the network distribution displays two sharp peaks, one at network distance 12 (latching) and one at network distance 24 (complete coordination failure).

Figure 12.1 also indicates the behavioral modes supported by each network distribution. For example, consider the 19 runs clustered at network distance 12 for the ZeroT treatment sampled at generation 50. Figure 12.1 indicates that workers and employers generally attained M-IntD (mutual intermittent defection) relationships in 11 of the runs and M-AllC (mutual cooperation) relationships in the remaining 8 runs.

Overall Utility and Efficiency Levels

As indicated in Table 12.1 above, the following results are obtained for the average (per agent) utility achieved by workers and employers across treatments. For generations 12 and 50, average utility is highest in treatment LowT. By generation 1000, however, average utility is actually highest in treatment HighT. The latter finding results from the high NEP for inactive agents as well as the previously noted observation that workers and employers who do manage to match under treatment HighT become increasingly more successful over time at coordinating on persistent mutual cooperation (the first attractor state) rather than persistent non-employment (the second attractor state). Although this evolution over time of increased cooperative behavior between matched workers and employers is observed under all three NEP treatments, it is observed most strongly for treatment HighT.

On the other hand, consider the overall level of economic efficiency attained under each NEP treatment, where efficiency takes into account both utility benefits and program costs. Specifically, for each NEP treatment, let net earnings be measured as the average utility level attained by workers and employers minus the average NEP paid to workers and employers. Ignoring offer costs, the maximum possible net earnings under each NEP treatment is

Table 12.4. Utility and efficiency outcomes: average utility levels (with standard deviations) attained by workers and by employers in the two attractors and overall, together with the general efficiency level, for each nonemployment payment (NEP) treatment

	Generation 12		Generation 50		Generation 1000	
	w	e	w	e	w	e
ZeroT **NEP=0**	CoopAtt. 35.4	40.1	CoopAtt. 39.1	40.7	CoopAtt. 36.4	39.9
	(6.6)	(5.5)	(1.5)	(1.4)	(2.7)	(3.6)
	IntDAtt. 32.2	33.1	IntDAtt. 31.8	32.8	IntDAtt. 33.2	34.2
	(5.9)	(6.0)	(2.7)	(2.8)	(4.1)	(3.2)
	Overall 32.5	35.1	Overall 34.0	36.3	Overall 34.7	36.8
	(5.9)	(5.8)	(2.3)	(2.5)	(3.6)	(3.6)
	Efficiency=85%		Efficiency=88%		Efficiency=90%	
	w	e	w	e	w	e
LowT **NEP=15**	CoopAtt. 38.3	40.1	CoopAtt. 38.9	40.8	CoopAtt. 38.5	38.8
	(2.3)	(2.3)	(1.4)	(1.4)	(0.8)	(1.5)
	IntDAtt. 33.6	36.7	IntDAtt. 28.0	40.5	IntDAtt. 34.2	33.9
	(4.3)	(4.4)	(2.3)	(3.1)	(2.1)	(2.2)
	Overall 34.0	36.8	Overall 35.7	38.6	Overall 36.0	35.3
	(3.6)	(3.6)	(2.0)	(2.0)	(1.5)	(2.0)
	Efficiency=88%		Efficiency=93%		Efficiency=88%	
	w	e	w	e	w	e
HighT **NEP=30**	CoopAtt. 38.1	40.2	CoopAtt. 38.9	40.2	CoopAtt. 38.9	41.3
	(2.0)	(1.6)	(0.7)	(0.5)	(0.5)	(0.5)
	CFailAtt. 30.2	30.3	CFailAtt. 30.0	30.1	CFailAtt. 30.0	30.1
	(0.4)	(0.3)	(0.0)	(0.0)	(0.0)	(0.0)
	Overall 33.5	35.7	Overall 35.5	35.9	Overall 35.5	37.2
	(0.9)	(1.1)	(0.5)	(0.4)	(0.6)	(0.5)
	Efficiency=50%		Efficiency=62%		Efficiency=67%	

the mutual cooperation payoff 40, attained by mutually cooperative workers and employers in latched pairings. For each NEP treatment, let *efficiency* be measured by actual net earnings as a percentage of 40. As indicated in Table 12.1, efficiency is substantially lower under treatment HighT than under treatments ZeroT or LowT. In particular, the relatively higher average utility level attained under treatment HighT at generation 1000 is more than offset by the higher average NEP to unemployed workers and vacant employers. In contrast, program costs are miniminal at all sampled generations under treatments ZeroT and LowT since unemployment and vacancy rates remain close to zero. As Table 12.1 indicates, evaluated in terms of efficiency, the best program option overall turns out to be the low NEP.

Table 12.4 provides a breakdown of the average utility levels reported in Table 12.1 by agent type (workers and employers) and by attractor state for each of the three NEP treatments. The generally higher average utility levels attained by employers reflects in part the structural asymmetry that workers shoulder all of the offer (transaction) costs associated with network formation and maintenance. As detailed below, in some cases this structural asymmetry also appears to provide employers a strategic advantage in their work-site interactions.

Market Non-Participation Rates, Work-Site Behaviors, Utility Levels, and Market Power Levels

Table 12.5 reports market non-participation rates, work-site behaviors, utility levels, and market power outcomes for the twenty runs constituting treatment ZeroT, each sampled at generation 12. These descriptive statistics are reported separately for each of the twenty individual runs comprising this treatment. More precisely, for each run, the following descriptive statistics are given: Persistent unemployment rate for workers (UnE-w); Persistent vacancy rate for employers (Vac-e); A count of never-provoked defectors for workers (NPD-w) and employers (NPD-e); A count of intermittent defectors for workers (IntD-w) and employers (IntD-e); A count of always-defectors for workers (AllD-w) and employers (AllD-e); A count of always-cooperators for workers (AllC-w) and employers (AllC-e); Mean utility level for workers (Util-w) with standard deviation (Util-w SD); Mean utility level for employers (Util-e) with standard deviation (Util-e SD); Mean market power level attained by workers (MPow-w); Mean market power level attained by employers (MPow-e).

The twenty runs in Table 12.5 are grouped together, first in accordance with their network distance (NetD), and second in accordance with the type of work-site behaviors expressed by the workers and employers. This grouping reveals that the runs are essentially clustered into two distinct *attractor states* comprising 18 runs in total, each run exhibiting a perfectly latched persistent network pattern (NetD=12). The remaining two runs $\{5, 7\}$ comprise a mix of recurrent and latched relationships and appear to be transition states between the two attractor states. The workers attain very low mean market power levels in the transition-state runs. This is due to the substantial offer costs they accumulate from refused work offers in the course of maintaining their recurrent relationships.

In the first attractor state comprising four runs $\{30, 50, 90, 65\}$, 77% of the workers and 71% of the employers are AllCs (persistent cooperators). Despite the prevalence of AllC agent types, the employers attain an average mean market power level (MPow-e = -0.00) that is markedly higher than the corresponding level obtained by the workers (Mpow-w = -0.12). This is due to the offer costs incurred by workers in the process of forming and sustaining the persistent latched networks and to the modestly higher percentages of NPD (non-provoked defection), IntD (persistent intermittent defection), and AllD (persistent defection) exhibited by employers.

Table 12.5. Non-participation rates, work-site behaviors, and welfare outcomes – ZeroT treatment, generation 12

NetD	Run	UnE-w	Vac-e	NPD-w	NPD-e	IntD-w	IntD-e	AllD-w	AllD-e	AllC-w	AllC-e	Util-w	Util-w SD	Util-e	Util-e SD	MPow-w	MPow-e	NETWORK PATTERNS
5	40	0	0	0	8	9	7	0	2	3	3	32.5	3.7	37.6	4.1	-0.19	-0.06	Mix of latched pairs and recurrent relations
7	45	0	0	0	12	10	6	0	2	3	4	25.6	6.5	40.9	6.2	-0.36	0.02	
	Average	0.00	0.00	0.00	10.00	9.50	6.50	0.00	2.00	2.50	3.50	29.1	5.0	39.3	5.2	-0.27	-0.02	
	%	0%	0%	0%	83%	79%	54%	0%	17%	21%	29%							
12	30	0	0	0	11	2	1	0	4	10	7	28.2	9.4	45.1	6.1	-0.29	0.13	Perfect latched pairs with high percentage of AllC Cooperators.
12	50	0	0	2	3	5	6	0	0	7	6	34.2	5.9	42.0	2.3	-0.15	0.05	
12	90	0	0	12	4	2	3	0	0	10	9	36.2	4.5	37.2	3.7	-0.10	-0.07	
12	65	0	0	2	0	0	0	2	0	10	12	42.8	6.6	36.2	9.9	0.07	-0.10	
	Average	0.00	0.00	4.00	4.50	2.25	2.50	0.50	1.00	9.25	8.50	35.4	6.6	40.1	5.5	-0.12	-0.00	
	%	0%	0%	33%	38%	19%	21%	4%	8%	77%	71%							
12	60	0	0	7	12	11	11	0	1	1	0	28.1	5.7	39.6	5.3	-0.28	-0.01	Perfect latched pairs with high percentage of Int-Defectors
12	35	0	0	1	12	9	9	1	1	2	2	30.9	5.6	36.3	4.7	-0.25	-0.09	
12	95	0	0	5	12	10	9	0	1	2	2	30.4	5.3	35.6	2.8	-0.24	-0.11	
12	75	0	0	12	12	11	9	0	2	1	1	28.0	7.5	35.1	8.3	-0.30	-0.12	
12	15	0	0	6	11	10	9	1	2	1	0	30.9	6.6	35.5	6.5	-0.23	-0.12	
12	55	0	0	7	6	12	12	0	0	1	0	31.6	3.3	34.4	3.7	-0.21	-0.13	
12	85	0	0	6	8	11	12	0	0	1	0	31.5	3.6	34.1	4.6	-0.21	-0.13	
12	5	0	0	5	12	11	11	1	0	0	0	29.7	5.2	33.2	5.1	-0.26	-0.15	
12	10	0	0	1	10	7	8	2	0	3	4	36.6	7.0	33.2	8.2	-0.09	-0.18	
12	20	0	0	11	8	9	10	2	0	1	2	35.9	5.4	30.7	6.4	-0.10	-0.23	
12	80	0	0	5	8	10	10	1	0	1	1	37.4	7.2	30.5	6.5	-0.07	-0.24	
12	25	0	0	8	5	9	11	2	0	0	1	36.0	6.1	29.3	8.6	-0.10	-0.27	
12	0	0	0	2	11	8	8	4	3	0	0	31.5	8.2	29.0	6.4	-0.21	-0.28	
12	70	0	0	11	12	9	10	3	2	0	0	32.2	5.7	28.1	6.3	-0.20	-0.37	
	Average	0.00	0.00	6.21	9.93	9.79	9.93	1.21	0.93	1.00	1.14	32.2	5.9	33.1	6.0	-0.20	-0.17	
	%	0%	0%	52%	83%	82%	83%	10%	8%	8%	10%							
	Total Average	0.00	0.00	5.15	8.85	8.25	8.10	0.95	1.05	2.80	2.85	32.5	5.9	36.1	5.8	-0.19	-0.12	
	Total %	0%	0%	43%	74%	69%	68%	8%	9%	23%	24%							

In the second attractor state comprising fourteen runs $\{60, 35, ..., 70\}$, very high percentages of the workers and the employers are NPDs and IntDs. Interestingly, the workers and employers obtain similar average mean market power levels in this second attractor state (-0.20 for workers and -0.17 for employers). However, these levels are substantially lower than the average mean market power levels they attain in the first attractor state. Thus, in terms of this market power measure, the first attractor state Pareto-dominates the second attractor state.

In parallel to Table 12.5, Table 12.6 reports persistent relationship type counts for treatment ZeroT sampled at generation 12. As in Table 12.5, data are reported for the two transient-state runs $\{5, 7\}$ plus the eighteen remaining runs grouped into the two attractor states.

The most striking aspect of Table 12.6 is the almost complete lack of mixed persistent relationships, i.e., relationships in which the participant worker and employer are expressing distinct types of behaviors. In particular, Table 12.6 reveals that the first attractor state comprising four runs $\{30, 50, 90, 65\}$ is dominated by mutual cooperation (M-AllC) whereas the second attractor state comprising 14 runs $\{60, 35, ..., 70\}$ is dominated by mutual intermittent defection (M-IntD). Mutual defection (M-AllD) is almost entirely absent.

The mean market power levels reported in Table 12.6 reveal, however, that the shirking rates expressed by the workers and employers in their M-IntD relationships in the second attractor state are not generally balanced in any given run. Rather, in about half the runs the workers shirk more than the employers, and in the remaining half the employers shirk more than the workers. Thus, although the average mean market power levels attained by workers and employers in this second attractor state are very close, this hides an underlying volatility in relative shirking rates across runs.

The characteristics reported in Table 12.5 and Table 12.6 for treatment ZeroT sampled at generation 12 are largely maintained in generation 50 and in generation 1000. One interesting observation, however, is that individual runs can traverse from one attractor state to another as time proceeds. For example, run 30 is in the first attractor state in generation 12, appears as a transition state in generation 50, and ends up in the second attractor state by generation 1000. Conversely, run 60 is in the second attractor state in generation 12 but ends up in the first attractor state by generation 1000.

A second interesting observation is that the number of runs lying in each attractor state evens out over time. In generation 12, the cooperative first attractor state comprises only four runs while the second attractor state dominated by intermittent defection comprises fourteen runs. By generation 50, the first attractor state comprises eight runs while the second attractor state comprises 11 runs. By generation 1000, each attractor state comprises exactly nine runs. Thus, on average, agents over time are improving their ability to coordinate on mutual cooperation.

Table 12.6. Persistent relationship type counts – ZeroT treatment, generation 12

NetD	Run	MUTUALITY			MIXED CASES (w - e)						MARKET POWER		NETWORK PATTERNS
		M-IntD	M-AllD	M-AllC	IntD-AllD	IntD-AllC	AllD-IntD	AllD-AllC	AllC-IntD	AllC-_IID	MPow-w	MPow-e	
5	40	10	1	6	0	0	0	0	–	–	-0.19	-0.06	Mix of latched pairs and recurrent relations
7	45	7	1	3	2	2	0	2	–	–	-0.36	0.02	
	Average	**8.50**	**1.00**	**4.50**	**1.00**	**1.00**	**0.00**	**1.00**	**1.00**	**0.50**	**-0.27**	**-0.02**	
12	30	0	0	7	2	0	0	0	–	–	-0.29	0.13	Perfect latched pairs with high percentage of AllC Cooperators
12	50	5	0	6	0	0	0	0	–	–	-0.15	0.05	
12	90	2	0	9	0	0	0	0	–	–	-0.10	-0.07	
12	65	0	0	10	0	0	0	2	0	–	0.07	-0.10	
	Average	**1.75**	**0.00**	**8.00**	**0.50**	**0.00**	**0.00**	**0.50**	**0.75**	**0.50**	**-0.12**	**-0.00**	
12	60	10	0	0	1	0	0	0	–	–	-0.28	-0.01	Perfect latched pairs with high percentage of Int-Defectors
12	35	9	1	2	0	0	0	0	0	–	-0.23	-0.09	
12	95	9	2	0	1	0	0	0	0	–	-0.24	-0.11	
12	75	9	0	0	1	1	0	0	0	–	-0.30	-0.12	
12	15	9	1	0	0	1	0	0	0	–	-0.23	-0.12	
12	55	12	0	0	0	0	0	0	0	0	-0.21	-0.13	
12	85	11	0	0	0	0	0	0	1	0	-0.21	-0.13	
12	5	11	1	0	0	0	0	0	0	0	-0.26	-0.15	
12	10	7	0	3	0	0	1	1	0	0	-0.09	-0.18	
12	20	8	0	1	0	1	2	0	0	0	-0.10	-0.23	
12	80	10	0	1	0	0	0	1	0	0	-0.07	-0.24	
12	25	9	0	0	0	0	2	0	0	0	-0.10	-0.27	
12	0	8	3	0	0	0	0	1	0	0	-0.21	-0.28	
12	70	9	2	0	0	0	1	0	0	0	-0.20	-0.37	
	Average	**9.36**	**0.71**	**0.57**	**0.21**	**0.21**	**0.43**	**0.21**	**0.14**	**0.14**	**-0.20**	**-0.17**	
	Total Average	**7.75**	**0.60**	**2.45**	**0.35**	**0.25**	**0.30**	**0.35**	**0.35**	**0.25**	**-0.19**	**-0.12**	

As in treatment ZeroT, the twenty runs comprising treatment LowT, sampled at generation 12, can be clustered into two attractor states together with a collection of transition states. The first attractor state comprises six runs characterized by perfect latching and a high percentage of AllC agent types in M-AllC relationships. The second attractor state comprises eight runs characterized by almost perfect latching and a high percentage of IntD agent types in M-IntD relationships. The six transition-state runs each comprise a mix of latched and recurrent relationships and have a high percentage of IntD agent types in M-IntD relationships.

In contrast to treatment ZeroT, however, the number of transition-state runs is larger (six runs instead of two) for treatment LowT sampled at generation 12. This is consistent with the network distribution data reported in Figure 12.1. The latter data reveal that, for each sampled generation, the peak at network distance 12 (latching) for treatment LowT is less pronounced than the peak at distance 12 for treatment zeroT. This indicates that the workers and employers in treatment LowT take longer on average to coordinate into perfect latched networks than the workers and employers in treatment ZeroT.

Also in contrast to treatment ZeroT, the average mean market power levels attained by workers and employers in treatment LowT, sampled at generation 12, are not balanced in the second attractor. The employers attain a level of -0.08, whereas the workers attain a markedly lower level of -0.16. The second attractor is dominated by latched relationships, indicating that each worker is persistently incurring only one offer cost per trade cycle. Since each offer cost is small relative to trade payoffs, only 1.0, it follows that accumulation of offer costs does not explain this large discrepancy in market power. Rather, since the second attractor state is dominated by M-IntD relationships, this discrepancy indicates that the employers are managing to shirk at a substantially higher rate than the workers in these M-IntD relationships.

The outcomes for treatment LowT sampled at generation 1000 closely resemble the outcomes reported in Table 12.5 and Table 12.6 for treatment ZeroT sampled at generation 12. The first attractor state comprises nine runs strongly dominated by M-AllC relationships, and the second attractor state comprises seven runs strongly dominated by M-IntD relationships. (Hence, an increase in the size of the first attractor state is observed for treatment LowT in moving from generation 12 to generation 1000.) Mixed types of relationships are almost entirely absent in the two attractor states. In the first attractor state the workers and employers attain average mean market power levels of -0.04 and -0.03, respectively. In the second attractor state the workers and employers attain uniformly lower but balanced average mean market power levels of -0.15. As for treatment ZeroT, this balance hides an underlying volatility in shirking rates across runs.

Table 12.7 reports market non-participation rates, work-site behaviors, utility levels, and market power outcomes for the twenty runs constituting treatment HighT, sampled at generation 12. Table 12.8 reports persistent relationship type counts for these same runs, again sampled at generation 12. As for the previous two treatments, the twenty runs can be clustered into two attractor states together with a scattering of transition states. Moreover, once again the runs in the first attractor state exhibit perfectly (or almost perfectly) latched persistent networks with a high percentage of AllC agent types. Nevertheless, the nature of the second attractor state is dramatically different. Whereas in the previous two treatments the second attractor state was dominated by M-IntD relationships, now the second attractor state corresponds to complete or almost complete coordination failure. More precisely, the network distance for the runs in the second attractor state varies from 22 (only two persistent relationships) to 24 (no persistent relationships). With a high non-employment payment, agents are opting for non-employment rather than choosing to remain in M-IntD relationships.

As also seen for treatments ZeroT and LowT, increased coordination on the first attractor state occurs over time for treatment HighT. In generation 12, the first attractor state comprises five runs, the second attractor state comprises 9 runs, and the six remaining runs are scattered across transition states. Also, in the first attractor state, an average of 9.8 out of the 12 persistent relationships in each run are M-AllC. By generation 1000, however, the first attractor state comprises 11 runs, the second attractor state comprises seven runs, and only two runs are in a transition state. Moreover, in the first attractor state, an average of 10.73 out of the 12 persistent relationships in each run are M-AllC.

Summarizing the relative market power outcomes of workers and employers in each treatment, the following regularities are observed. For every treatment, in each sampled generation, the employers consistently attain a higher average market power level than workers in the cooperative first attractor state. This difference is attributable to the relatively higher (although small) incidence of NPD, IntD, and AllD behaviors among employers and to the fact that offer costs are borne solely by the worker. Also, for treatments ZeroT and HighT, the workers and employers attain essentially the same average market power levels in the second attractor state in each sampled generation; and the same is true for treatment LowT when sampled in generation 1000. A balanced market power level in the second attractor state indicates either that workers and employers have essentially the same shirking rates on average (treatments ZeroT and LowT) or that all agents are persistently non-employed (treatment HighT).

With regard to market power in the cooperative first attractor state compared across treatments, the workers attain a modestly negative average market power level in each treatment in each sampled generation; the levels range from -0.12 to -0.02. Interestingly, treatments LowT and HighT have a lower average incidence of NPD behavior and a higher average percentage of M-

Table 12.7. Non-participation rates, work-site behaviors, and welfare outcomes – HighT treatment, generation 12

NetD	Run	UnE-w	Vac-e	NPD-w	NPD-e	IntD-w	IntD-e	AllD-w	AllD-e	AllC-w	AllC-e	Util-w	Util-w SD	Util-e	Util-e SD	MPow-w	MPow-e	NETWORK PATTERNS
0	45	0	0	0	1	1	1	0	0	11	11	38.6	0.6	40.7	1.0	-0.04	0.02	Mostly recurrent relations. High percentage of AllC Cooperators.
1	0	0	1	0	1	0	0	0	0	12	11	35.4	0.4	40.5	1.7	-0.12	0.01	
1	65	0	0	1	1	0	0	0	0	12	11	35.4	0.4	40.5	1.5	-0.12	0.01	
2	35	0	2	0	2	0	0	0	0	12	10	33.2	0.7	39.9	2.5	-0.17	-0.00	
5	75	0	3	0	5	1	2	0	0	11	7	32.6	0.7	40.5	1.7	-0.19	0.01	
6	40	4	2	2	12	8	10	0	0	0	0	34.0	1.8	37.2	1.9	-0.15	-0.07	
Average		0.67	1.50	0.33	3.67	1.67	2.17	0.00	0.00	9.67	8.33	34.9	0.8	39.9	1.7	-0.13	-0.00	
%		6%	13%	3%	31%	14%	18%	0%	0%	81%	69%							
12	5	0	0	0	0	0	0	0	0	12	12	39.8	0.0	41.0	0.0	-0.01	0.03	Mostly latched relations. High percentage of AllC Cooperators.
13	10	1	1	1	0	0	0	0	0	11	11	39.1	2.3	40.2	1.6	-0.02	0.01	
13	50	1	1	1	0	0	0	0	0	11	11	39.0	2.7	40.2	1.6	-0.03	0.01	
13	80	1	1	1	0	0	0	0	0	11	11	39.0	2.7	40.2	2.1	-0.03	0.01	
14	85	3	4	5	4	3	5	0	0	6	3	33.3	2.5	39.6	2.7	-0.17	-0.01	
Average		1.20	1.40	1.60	0.80	0.60	1.00	0.00	0.00	10.20	9.60	38.1	2.0	40.2	1.6	-0.04	0.01	
%		10%	12%	13%	7%	5%	8%	0%	0%	85%	80%							
22	20	10	10	12	10	2	2	0	0	0	0	30.9	1.9	31.3	0.2	-0.23	-0.22	Almost complete coordination failure.
23	15	11	11	12	11	1	1	0	0	0	0	30.5	1.6	30.8	0.1	-0.24	-0.23	
24	25	12	12	12	12	0	0	0	0	0	0	30.0	0.0	30.1	0.0	-0.25	-0.25	
24	30	12	12	12	12	0	0	0	0	0	0	30.0	0.0	30.1	0.0	-0.25	-0.25	
24	55	12	12	12	12	0	0	0	0	0	0	30.0	0.0	30.1	0.0	-0.25	-0.25	
24	60	12	12	12	12	0	0	0	0	0	0	30.0	0.0	30.1	0.0	-0.25	-0.25	
24	70	12	12	12	12	0	0	0	0	0	0	30.0	0.0	30.1	0.0	-0.25	-0.25	
24	90	12	12	12	12	0	0	0	0	0	0	30.0	0.0	30.1	0.0	-0.25	-0.25	
24	95	12	12	12	12	0	0	0	0	0	0	30.0	0.0	30.1	0.0	-0.25	-0.25	
Average		11.67	11.67	12.00	11.67	0.33	0.33	0.00	0.00	0.00	0.00	30.2	0.4	30.3	0.0	-0.25	-0.24	
%		97%	97%	100%	97%	3%	3%	0%	0%	0%	0%							
Total Average		5.75	6.05	5.90	6.55	0.80	1.05	0.00	0.00	5.45	4.90	33.5	0.9	35.7	0.9	-0.16	-0.11	
Total %		48%	50%	49%	55%	7%	9%	0%	0%	45%	41%							

AllC relationships per run than treatment ZeroT in this first attractor state. Nevertheless, these advantages are offset (in market power terms) by the higher average offer costs incurred by workers due to the longer time taken within each generation to establish a persistent network. (For example, as seen in Table 12.7 for treatment HighT sampled at generation 12, only one run in the first attractor state attains a network distance of 12, i.e., a perfectly latched persistent network.) In contrast to the workers, employers do not incur offer costs, hence they attain close to a zero average market power level in each treatment at each sampled generation in the cooperative first attractor state; the levels range from -0.02 to +0.03.

With regard to market power in the second attractor state compared across treatments, in each sampled generation both the workers and the employers attain their lowest average levels in treatment HighT. The second attractor state in treatment HighT is characterized by complete or nearly complete coordination failure.

Never-Provoked Defection

The importance of stance toward strangers and first impressions for determining subsequent outcomes in sequential interactions has been stressed by Orbell and Dawes (1993) and by Rabin and Schrag (1999). In the present computational experiment, two sharply differentiated attractor states exist for each treatment, the first dominated by persistent mutual cooperation and the second dominated either by persistent intermittent defection or by persistent non-employment. Thus, outcomes are strongly path dependent, and stance towards strangers and first impressions could play a critical role in determining these outcomes. These aspects of agent behavior are captured by counts of never-provoked defection (NPD).

In treatments ZeroT and LowT, NPD is commonly observed in all sampled generations, particularly in the second attractor state dominated by persistent intermittent defection (IntD). For example, as seen in Table 12.5, for treatment ZeroT sampled at generation 12, 33% of workers and 38% of employers engage in NPD in the first attractor state, and these percentages rise to 52% and 83%, respectively, for the second attractor state. It would appear that these high percentages for NPD in the second attractor state might actually be inducing the resulting predominance of IntD as agents engage in retaliatory defections. Because the non-employment payment is lower than the mutual defection payoff in these two treatments, agents tend to defect back against defecting partners rather than simply refusing to interact with them.

Another interesting observation regarding treatments ZeroT and LowT is that the incidence of NPD for each agent type in each attractor state tends to be higher in treatment ZeroT than in treatment LowT. In treatment ZeroT, the non-employment payment 0 lies below all work-site payoffs, including the sucker payoff L=10 earned by an agent who cooperates against a defecting partner. Consequently, there is no risk of refusal on the basis of bad behavior

Table 12.8. Persistent relationship type counts – HighT treatment, generation 12

NetD	Run	MUTUALITY			MIXED CASES (w-e)						MARKET POWER		PATTERNS
		M-IntD	M-AllD	M-AllC	IntD-AllD	IntD-AllC	AllD-IntD	AllD-AllC	AllC-IntD	AllC-AllD	MPow-w	MPow-e	
0	45	1	0	37	0	0	0	0	0	0	-0.04	-0.02	Mostly recurrent Relations. High percentage of AllC Cooperators.
1	0	0	0	79	0	0	0	0	0	0	-0.12	0.01	
1	65	0	0	80	0	0	0	0	0	0	-0.12	0.01	
2	35	0	0	99	0	0	0	0	0	0	-0.17	-0.00	
5	75	1	0	60	0	0	0	0	1	0	-0.19	0.01	
6	40	21	0	0	0	0	0	0	0	0	-0.15	-0.07	
Average		3.83	0.00	59.17	0.00	0.00	0.00	0.00	0.17	0.00	-0.13	-0.00	
12	5	0	0	12	0	0	0	0	0	0	-0.01	0.03	Mostly latched relations. High percentage of AllC Cooperators.
13	10	0	0	11	0	0	0	0	0	0	-0.02	-0.01	
13	50	0	0	11	0	0	0	0	0	0	-0.03	-0.01	
13	80	0	0	11	0	0	0	0	0	0	-0.03	-0.01	
14	85	3	0	4	0	0	0	0	2	0	-0.17	-0.01	
Average		0.60	0.00	9.80	0.00	0.00	0.00	0.00	0.40	0.00	-0.04	0.01	
22	20	2	0	0	0	0	0	0	0	0	-0.23	-0.22	Almost complete coordination failure.
23	15	1	0	0	0	0	0	0	0	0	-0.24	-0.23	
24	25	0	0	0	0	0	0	0	0	0	-0.25	-0.25	
24	30	0	0	0	0	0	0	0	0	0	-0.25	-0.25	
24	55	0	0	0	0	0	0	0	0	0	-0.25	-0.25	
24	60	0	0	0	0	0	0	0	0	0	-0.25	-0.25	
24	70	0	0	0	0	0	0	0	0	0	-0.25	-0.25	
24	90	0	0	0	0	0	0	0	0	0	-0.25	-0.25	
24	95	0	0	0	0	0	0	0	0	0	-0.25	-0.25	
Average		0.33	0.00	0.00	0.00	0.00	0.00	0.00	0.00	0.00	-0.25	-0.24	
Total Average		1.45	0.00	20.20	0.00	0.00	0.00	0.00	0.15	0.00	-0.16	-0.11	

alone, but only from unfavorable comparisons with other agents. In contrast, in treatment LowT the non-employment payment 15 lies between the sucker payoff and the mutual defection payoff D=20. In this case, then, an opportunistic agent faces a higher risk of refusal since non-employment is preferred to a sucker payoff.

In treatment HighT the non-employment payment 30 lies above the mutual defection payoff for the first time, and the impact of this change in payoff configuration is substantial. For example, as reported in Table 12.5, only 13% of workers and 7% of employers in generation 12 engage in NPD in the first attractor state characterized by mutual cooperation. In contrast, 100% of workers and 97% of employers engage in NPD in the second attractor state characterized by complete or almost complete coordination failure. The same pattern holds at generation 50 and generation 1000. Agents are now much pickier with regard to their partners; an early defection from a partner drops that partner's expected utility assessment below the non-employment payoff and hence below minimum tolerability.

12.5   Concluding Remarks

As detailed by Roth (2002), recent advances in experimental methods and game theory using both human subjects and computational agents are now permitting economists to study a wide variety of complex phenomena associated with decentralized market economies. Examples include inductive price discovery, imperfect competition, buyer-seller matching, and the open-ended co-evolution of individual behaviors and economic institutions.

One interesting branch of this literature is the attempt to exploit synergies between experiments with human subjects and experiments with computational agents by means of parallel experimental designs. The few parallel experimental studies to date have largely focused on financial market issues.[9] However, we conjecture that parallel experiments will ultimately prove to be even more valuable when applied to economic processes such as labor markets in which face-to-face personal relationships play a potentially strong role in determining market outcomes.

The preliminary ACE labor market study at hand highlights the need to carefully align parallel experimental designs to ensure valid comparability. For example, transaction costs must be properly scaled across experiments to ensure comparable agent incentives, and horizons need to be aligned to ensure that short-run and long-run effects are properly distinguished.

In future ACE labor market studies, we intend to calibrate our parallel experimental designs to empirical data. Salient aspects of actual unemployment benefit programs will be incorporated, and findings from previous empirical studies of unemployment benefit programs will be used wherever possible.

---

[9]See http://www.econ.iastate.edu/tesfatsi/aexper.htm for pointers to research using parallel experiments.

In addition, the recent construction of linked employer-employee (LEE) data sets is an exciting development facilitating the empirical study of outcomes generated by worker-employer interactions; see Hammermesh (1999). LEE data sets complement beautifully the focus of ACE labor market studies on worker-employer interaction patterns. Consequently, LEE data should permit careful empirical testing of computational findings related specifically to interaction effects, such as strong path dependence and the existence of multiple attractors.

Acknowledgments

The authors are grateful for helpful comments received from an anonymous referee, from Peter Orazem, from Marshall Van Alstyne and other participants in the UCLA Computational Social Sciences Conference held in May 2002 at Lake Arrowhead, California, and from Richard Freeman and other participants in the Harvard University Colloquium on Complexity and Social Networks held on April 7, 2003.

References

Acemoglu, D., and Shimer, R. (2000), "Productivity Gains from Unemployment Insurance," *European Economic Review* **44**, 1195-1223.

Blau, F. D., and Kahn, L. M. (1999), "Institutional Differences in Male Wage Inequality: Institutions versus Market Forces," in *Handbook of Labor Economics* Volume 3A, pp. 1399-1461, O. Ashenfelter and D. Card, editors, Elsevier Science B.V., Amsterdam, The Netherlands

Freeman, R. (1998), "War of the Models: Which Labour Market Institutions for the 21st Century?" *Labour Economics* **5**, 1-24.

Gale, D., and Shapley, L. L. (1962), "College Admissions and the Stability of Marriage," *American Mathematical Monthly* **69**, 9-15.

Hammermesh, D. (1999), "LEEping into the Future of Labor Economics: The Research Potential of Linking Employer and Employee Data," *Labour Economics* **6**, 25-41.

Ljungqvist, L., and Sargent, T. J. (1998), "The Unemployment Dilemma," *Journal of Political Economy* **106**, 514-550.

MacLeod, W. B., and Malcomson, J. (1998), "Motivation and Markets," *American Economic Review* **88**, 388-411.

McFadzean, D., Stewart, D., and Tesfatsion, L. (2001), "A Computational Laboratory for Evolutionary Trade Networks," *IEEE Transactions on Evolutionary Computation* **5**, 546-560.

McFadzean, D., and Tesfatsion, L. (1999), "A C++ Platform for Evolutionary Trade Networks," *Computational Economics* **14**, 108-134.

Nickell, S., and Layard, R. (1999), "Labor Market Institutions and Economic Performance," in *Handbook of Labor Economics*, pp. 3029-3084, O. C. Ashenfelter and D. Card, editors, Volume 3C, Elsevier Science B.V., Amsterdam, The Netherlands.

Orbell, J., and Dawes, R. M. (1993), "Social Welfare, Cooperator's Advantage, and the Option of Not Playing the Game," *American Sociological Review* **58**, 787-800.

Pingle, M., and Tesfatsion, L. (2001), "Non-Employment Benefits and the Evolution of Worker-Employer Cooperation: Experiments with Real and Computational Agents," Iowa State University Economic Report No. 55, Ames, Iowa, June.

Pingle, M., and Tesfatsion, L. (2002), "Non-Employment Benefits and the Evolution of Worker-Employer Cooperation: A Human-Subject Experiment," Working Paper, Iowa State University, Ames, Iowa, October.

Rabin, M., and Shrag, J. (1999), "First Impressions Matter: A Model of Confirmatory Bias," *Quarterly Journal of Economics* **114**, 37-82.

Roth, A., and Sotomayor, M. A. (1992), *Two-Sided Matching: A Study in Game-Theoretic Modeling and Analysis*, Cambridge University Press, Cambridge, United Kingdom.

Roth, A. (2002), "The Economist as Engineer: Game Theory, Experimentation, and Computation as Tools for Design Economics," *Econometrica* **70**, 1341-1378.

Tesfatsion, L. (1998), "Preferential Partner Selection in Evolutionary Labor Markets: A Study in Agent-Based Computational Economics," in *Evolutionary Programming VII*, pp. 15-24, V. Porto, N. Saravanan, D. Waagan, and A. E. Eiben, editors, Springer-Verlag, Berlin, Germany.

Tesfatsion, L. (2001), "Structure, Behavior and Market Power in an Evolutionary Labor Market with Adaptive Search," *Journal of Economic Dynamics and Control* **25**, 419-457.

Tesfatsion, L. (2002a), "Hysteresis in an Evolutionary Labor Market with Adaptive Search," in *Evolutionary Computation in Economics and Finance*, pp. 189-210, S.-H Chen, editor, Physica-Verlag, Heidelberg, Germany.

Tesfatsion, L. (2002b), "Economic Agents and Markets as Emergent Phenomena," *Proceedings of the National Academy of Sciences U.S.A.*, Volume 99, Supplement 3, 7191-7192.

Tesfatsion, L. (2003), "Agent-Based Computational Economics," in *Agent-Based Theories, Languages, and Practices*, F. Luna, A. Perrone, and P. Terna, editors, Routledge Publishers, to appear.

13 Capacity Provision Networks: A Technology Framework and Economic Analysis of Web Cache Trading Hubs

Xianjun Geng, Ram Gopal, R. Ramesh, and Andrew B. Whinston

13.1 Introduction

The world of the Web consists of numerous players. Broadly, they can be classified into content providers, content consumers and an array of service providers. The rapid advances in the technologies for digital content distribution have impacted all these players in a most fundamental way: *increasing opportunities for content creation, distribution and consumption have led to strong externalities in each of these constituencies.* While this is a desirable effect from the points of view of both digital business and the consumers' need for digital information, it is also deeply straining the fundamental infrastructure of the Internet in adequately supporting digital content delivery. Quality of Service (QoS) at the customers' end is of paramount importance to both content and other service providers, and the network externality effect is not helping them in this dimension. If network bandwidths and server capacities were infinite, then this would not be a problem; however, unfortunately, this is not the case in reality. Given the externality effect in all the categories of players in the Web, ensuring acceptable performance and reliability is referred to as the *Web Scalability Problem* (Rabinovich and Spatscheck (2002)). Several approaches to the web scalability problem have been proposed and some have even been implemented. For instance, the Internet Protocol; IP version 6; is intended to incorporate QoS features in packet routing; Internet Service Providers (ISPs) and other Network Service Providers (NSPs) attempt to increase their bandwidths and server capacities; several content providers employ replicated servers with proxies; many unique service providers such as Akamai (cf. Akamai Technologies Inc.(2000a)), for example, enable content providers to distribute and bring their content closer to the end users through Content Delivery Networks (CDN), and many such innovative solutions to the web scalability problem are constantly evolving. Principal among these solutions is the idea of *Web caching*, where content from origin servers is strategically and partially replicated at numerous other servers with a view to reducing traffic in the Internet core and maximizing web accesses at the edge of the network.

The idea of caching content itself is not new. In fact, caching is a central component of most operating systems that attempt to minimize disk input/outputs (I/O). Caching is also used quite effectively in the Internet context. For instance, a web browser usually caches websites visited by a user in the local computer, and when the user visits a previously visited site, it is accessed from the local cache. Although this minimizes Internet traffic, this also leads to the problems of *Cache Consistency* and *Cache Capacity*. The consistency problem arises when the contents at the origin servers change over time and the cache may become obsolete as a result, and the capacity problem arises due to the storage limitations in a computer, and the consequent restrictions on the extent of content caching. However, these problems also point to several innovative caching strategies. We outline some of these opportunities as follows.

First, when multiple users access the same web objects either concurrently or within a short time interval, caching these objects at a common server and feeding the users from this proxy would (i) reduce the bandwidth required to serve these users, (ii) reduce the latencies in accessing the required information, (iii) reduce the overhead in maintaining several TCP connections by the origin server (Barish and Obraczka (2000)). Second, when proxies are used as *interceptors* of a single stream from an origin server and *broadcasters* to several concurrent users could yield significant bandwidth savings and latency reduction in multimedia streaming presentations. This suggests a unique opportunity for ISPs and NSPs operating at the edge of the Internet: *local caching at the user's computer level will not yield such savings; some kind of a centralized cache that serves multiple users is needed.* This however, does not solve the consistency and capacity problems associated with caching. While several solutions have been proposed for the consistency problem (Dilley (1999), Dilley et al. (1999), Nottingham (1999), and Yin et al. (1999)), the capacity problem still remains. Some of the popular solutions to the consistency problem include *time to live* (TTL) modeling, asynchronous and piggyback cache validations, tradeoffs in delayed versus immediate updates and cooperative cache consistency mechanisms, to name a few. As of now, the only solution to the capacity problem seems to be to increase the bandwidth and storage capacities as required when customer demands increase over time. This however, is a difficult if not an unacceptable decision for many service providers for the following reasons.

The network externality of the customer base is mostly a gradual effect; the base does not expand overnight. As a result, an ISP should look into the future as much as possible in determining a scalable server configuration, and this is extremely difficult. Note that when a distributed system of caches cooperate to maintain a set of web objects (which include those pre-fetched as well as usage-driven), it is important to maintain some supporting services for object location, maintaining consistency among copies of objects held and coordinating policies of replacement among the caches. Even if a scalable configuration is determined, there will be a significant period of under-utilization of the capacity resources as it takes time for the demand to build up to the planned capacity levels. Next, the users' web access behavior is very uneven. Spikes and troughs in volume access occur frequently, and combined with the variety in web objects accessed, pose serious challenges in coordinating cache consistency maintenance policies and the supporting services within an available capacity space. The tradeoff in this regard is clear: *increasing capacity would yield greater flexibility in consistency maintenance, but at a significant cost* since buying capacity is more costly than renting capacity only when necessary, as we will shortly discuss. Finally, customer churn rates are closely linked to performance, especially in the ISP market (Akamai Technologies Inc. (2000b)). This follows from the widely held eight-second rule that after eight seconds of waiting for a web page to be downloaded, a customer becomes impatient and will likely abandon the site (Gutzman (2000)). An increasing frequency of such abandonment leads to poor evaluations of an ISP's performance by a customer who may ultimately decide to seek another service. As a result, churn rates put a premium on performance, especially in uncertain ISP markets.

Putting it all together, the above analysis adds up to the following conclusions. An ISP should (a) carefully determine a scalable capacity solution, (b) coordinate caching strategies to maintain as much consistency as possible within the capacity constraints most of the time, and (c) ensure capacity utilization levels yielding adequate returns on investments, all with a view to providing an acceptable level of service to the customers. These strategic decisions are quite challenging from the point of view of a single ISP, especially when the ISP is a small to medium enterprise with little hold on its market share in a competitive environment. Errors in these decisions, both predictable and unpredictable, could cost the ISP significantly. As a result, it is only logical to expect cooperative agreements even among locally competing ISPs to share their caching resources in order to achieve these objectives in a collective sense. With the increasing demands for publishing and receiving digital content over the Internet, we envision the emergence of networks of service providers who share cache capacities through bilateral and other forms of trade agreements with a view to maximizing service performance to the customers and cache capacity utilizations[1] at the same time. We term a network of cache servers[2] owned, operated and coordinated through capacity trading by different ISPs as a *Capacity Provision Network* (CPN). At the outset, we differentiate a CPN from a CDN: while the focus of a CDN is *replication* of content from specifically contracted content providers, the focus of a CPN is *caching* of content as accessed by users in any random fashion from the world of content servers; while a CDN could be wholly owned and operated by a single company, a CPN is based on capacity sharing arrangements among several service providers, and consequently, operates via a trading hub; finally, a CDN services the *supply-side* of content distribution, whereas a CPN services the *demand-side*.

We develop a technology framework for a CPN and present an economic analysis in this chapter. A CPN hub consists of a set of participating ISPs, where each ISP serves a local customer base. The demand for cache capacity at each ISP usually varies over time depending on the access behavior of the customers. The performance of a cache is basically determined by two factors: *object replacement policies of the ISP* and the *object access behavior of the users*. While the former factor is controllable, the latter is not. As a result, significant fluctuations in the effective internal utilization of a cache could result. Therefore, in order to provide a manageable level of service, an ISP could resort to establishing a *capacity contract* with some of its customers as follows: for a certain fee, a customer could reserve a certain block of cache space at the ISP's cache server for his own caching needs. This can be implemented by caching the web objects accessed by the customer in his reserved space, while managing their currency by appropriate replacement policies.[3] Another form of contracting is the *performance contract*. This is based on the service level approach, where a customer is guaranteed an appropriate level of service. This implies that for a given fee, an ISP commits to satisfy a buyer's caching demand no matter what the realized demand is; if the ISP fails to satisfy the demand then he is penalized appropriate to the unsatisfied demand. Such contracts can be more common, since an estimation of the cache capacity needed is usually difficult, especially for customers whose access behaviors are quite random. Therefore, an ISP faced with a shortfall situation could either decide to pay the penalty or secure the needed additional capacity from elsewhere. This leads to the notion of *capacity trading*, which is central to a CPN. In a CPN, a participating ISP

---

[1] We employ two notions of capacity utilization in this chapter, termed *internal* and *external*. Internal utilization refers to the consistency of a cache; that is, how useful are the cached web objects to a real-time user. External utilization refers to the usefulness of any unused capacity to an ISP by generating revenues from trading it with other ISPs. In the rest of the chapter, we refer only to external utilization as our main focus is on capacity trading. For internal utilization, refer to Rabinovich and Spatschek (2002).

[2] We use the term *cache servers* and *proxy servers* interchangeably throughout the chapter

[3] The replacement policies can be determined either by the ISP or the customer or jointly.

could either buy additional capacity from other participants or sell any excess capacity to them as and when needed in real-time.

Using the service level performance contracts results in the problem of optimal capacity planning by an ISP when faced with stochastic demands. However, the opportunities to buy and sell cache capacity through a CPN trading hub tend to alleviate the costs associated with errors in capacity planning to some extent. Alternatively, in the absence of such trading hubs, an ISP operating in isolation is faced with the full burden of these costs. Thus the concept of a CPN is both intuitively appealing and makes sound business sense to its participants. We demonstrate this through an economic modeling and analysis of bilateral and multilateral trading behavior among CPN participants. While capacity planning is a strategic decision for ISPs where scalable server configurations and cache tradability among the CPN participants are predominant considerations, customer contracting, capacity trading and capacity pricing are tactical/operational decisions where costs and levels of customer service are the principal concerns. In this chapter, we develop an implementation framework for a CPN trading hub that operationalizes the CPN trading activities, addresses some of the strategic/tactical/operational decisions of the CPN participants, and provides a business and technical architecture for realizing a CPN hub.

Besides cooperative caching, another important cooperative mechanism for effective content delivery is cooperative Internet peering. The proposed CPN model has a close relationship with the peering model and also significantly enhances its viability. One of the main challenges in realizing a peering relationship is in establishing *mutual acceptance* of the relationship by the ISPs (Norton (2001, 2002)). A common question asked in the numerous discussions on ISP-peering is: what incentives do ISPs have to enter into such a relationship? For a peering relationship to succeed, it is important that each party in the relationship should be able to offer some unique or cost-effective service to the other. In this regard, it is important to note that piggybacking or free-riding would be counter-productive to a peering relationship. A phrase often heard in this context is "Why should I haul your traffic around the globe for free?"

The CPN model provides a unique mechanism for peering ISPs to be of significant service to each other. By enabling trades of cache services, the CPN model provides sound incentives for ISPs to agree to peer with each other. Faced with limited cache capacities, changing customer demand patterns and network externality factors, the ISPs face major challenges in the dynamic management of web objects to yield desirable QoS and cache management efficiencies. As a result, the option of cache procurement at short notice without incurring any fixed costs to sustain an acceptable QoS will be quite attractive to many ISPs. This option would also strongly incentivize ISPs to peer, which could yield other benefits as well. It is also important to note that peering is not necessary for a CPN to operate; a CPN could work equally well with transit arrangements. However, CPN by itself would provide good motivation for peering relationships to materialize and sustain. In this regard, we also note that CPN is somewhat a *futuristic* concept. We feel that ISPs considering peering and other options to collaborate in resource sharing will employ the notion of sharable and tradable cache services contained in the CPN model as a viable reason for innovative new business relationships in the future. Finally, given an existing peering arrangement among ISPs, the implementation of sharable and tradable cache services on top of the peering networks is relatively easy. If ISPs enter into cache trading and cooperative cache management over peering networks, then clearly the volume of traffic using transit lines would decrease. A quantification of the benefits to the QoS as a result of this depends on the cache architectures used, the cooperative cache management policies used and the access behaviors of customers for static as well as dynamic web content. A study of these factors is beyond the scope of this chapter and is a potential and important area for future research.

The organization of this chapter is as follows. Section 13.2 develops the proposed CPN model. Section 13.3 presents the economic foundations of a CPN. Section 13.4 develops two tactical trading models in CPN operation. The conclusions and directions for future research are presented in Section 13.5.

13.2 The CPN Model

An excellent literature resource on web caching is Rabinovich and Spatscheck (2002). Web caching primarily involves replicating digital content at some intermediary proxy servers between the users and content/service providers. Caching on the supply-side employs a set of *reverse proxy servers*, and on the demand side uses a set of *forward proxies* (cf. Barish and Obraczka (2000)). Accordingly, a CPN can be viewed as a collection of interconnected forward proxies, whereas a CDN is a network of reverse proxies. Supply-side caching is more predictable than demand-side caching since it is initiated and controlled by content providers, while the demand-side is subject to the random access behavior of the users.

Figure 13.1 illustrates a CPN with three ISPs with cache trading agreements. In this figure, first each ISP sets aside a certain portion of the available cache for local use. Next, the remaining capacity is traded. In this instance, ISP 1 sells excess capacity to ISPs 2 and 3, and ISP 2 sells some of its capacity to ISP 3, and in some respects acts like an intermediary in a trilateral capacity trade. When traded, each ISP maintains a control link with the capacity it sells, while allowing the buyers' proxies to access their allocated spaces for their respective use. When a certain cache capacity is traded to an ISP, the management of the contents of this cache is entirely relegated to the buying ISP. As a result, the buyer determines what objects are to be

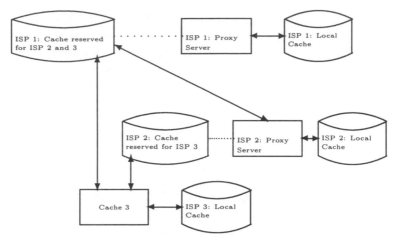

Fig. 13.1. An example of a CPN operation

cached and for how long, except that the seller's proxy maintains a link to the traded capacity resources and the buyer's proxy is enabled access to the cache via the seller's proxy. In some sense, the capacity bought from another ISP can be regarded as an extension of the local cache at the buyer's proxy, however located at a remote location. The trades are bound in time, and we could also expect each trade to occur in different time windows.

The objective of CPN caching is to reduce network latency, improve server load balancing, realize bandwidth savings, and most importantly, improve the performance of content delivery to the customers through content distribution. Network latency can be classified into two types: *internal* and *external*. Internal latency is experienced in transferring objects from a cache server to a client, and the external latency occurs between the cache and origin servers. External latency is by and large predominant as a bulk of this data transmission could occur through the core of the Internet. Strategies for proxy deployment, cache consistency maintenance and optimization of internal/external cache utilization essentially attempt to minimize these latencies (Tewari et al. (1999), Gautam (2002)). Proxy deployment can be broadly classified into two types: *transparent* and *nontransparent*. In transparent deployment, the client software is unaware of the existence of the proxy intermediaries, whereas it is aware in nontransparent deployment. Transparent proxies are also known as *interceptors*, which receive client requests directed at a unique URL and redirect them to other content servers. Several interception mechanisms at various layers of the OSI model have been proposed, implemented and evaluated in practice with different degrees of performance (Barish and Obraczka (2000), and Rabinovich and Spatscheck (2002)). In the nontransparent arena, the suggested mechanisms include explicit client configuration, auto-configuration and auto-discovery of proxies by clients (Rabinovich and Spatscheck (2002)). In all these mechanisms, a network of intermediary cache proxies are used, all collaborating to minimize network latencies especially in the Internet core.

A classical tradeoff in the design of proxy networks is between the internal and external latencies, since latency is proportional to geographical distances. Therefore, the central issues in cooperative proxy network design are *location management, proxy pruning* and *global cache replacement policies*. Location management refers to updating each proxy on the content available at other proxies at any given time. This is an important issue, since the proxies must know in real-time whom to approach for a requested content if it is not locally available. Therefore, inter-proxy protocols for updating proxies about their current content are needed for location management. Such updates can be periodic or instantaneous. Proxy pruning refers to the selection of a server from an available set that can potentially serve the required content. Algorithms for network traffic and server load assessments are needed for pruning. The rules governing what is to be cached, where it should be cached and how long the contents should be maintained collectively by a set of cooperating proxies constitute the global replacement policies. These rules are central to optimal internal/external cache utilizations among the set of proxies, and have a direct impact on their service performance.

Several cooperative caching schemes have been developed in the literature and some of them have been implemented and tested (such as Harvest and Squid, for example). Of particular interest in this area are the hierarchical, distributed, geographical and hybrid architectural schemes. We agree that it is debatable which caching architecture can achieve the optimal performance in minimizing the expected latency in retrieving web documents. For example, hierarchical caching has been shown to require shorter connection times than distributed caching, whereas distributed caching has shorter transmission times and higher bandwidth usage (Wang (1999)). Accordingly, the ultimate goal of user level latency minimization (a major QoS criterion) has been addressed in the literature specifically in terms of various surrogate measures (such as TCP connection latencies, bandwidth latencies, object currency levels, etc.) and other systemic measures (such as system availability, secure transactions, dynamic content delivery capabilities etc.). Consequently, the literature abounds in various techniques to address the different facets of this criteria space, including strategies such as cache server configurations, cache network configurations, web object management (including pre-fetching, leases, invalidation techniques etc), access protocols and cache object location algorithms etc. Therefore, in a CPN context, since we deal with a network of cache servers cooperating to perform tasks such that the desired objectives of the ISPs are met, we should take a broader view of the design problem that includes these solution strategies, their associated design parameters and expected performances. While cooperative caching is a major component of this architecture, we need to consider these various other important parameters as well, since they affect the final QoS measures significantly. In this respect, some of the key design parameters include: cache network topology, cache management protocols and policies, coordination strategies for distributed web object replacement, service protocols and other control functions. We can envision a multitude of design strategies for cache system architectures with various performance tradeoffs. This in fact is the primary reason for the sustained thrust in research and development of cache networks in both academia and industry. The architecture of a caching system should be carefully configured to achieve the desired objectives in a given deployment environment, taking into account the characteristics of the caching strategies used and the performance tradeoffs among the various design options. In this chapter, we do not advocate any single architecture, but instead focus on the coordination among a network of caches.

Cooperative proxy caching is appropriate in a tightly coupled proxy network. In such networks, the options for location management include broadcast protocols, hierarchical caching, URL hashing and directory-based cooperation (see Chankhunthod et al. (1996), Wessels and Claffy (1997), Krishnan and Sugla (1998), and Gadde, Chase, and Rabinovich (1999)). In the pruning area, techniques such as cache routing with routing tables, vicinity caching and integrated cache hierarchies are commonly employed (Grimm et al. (1998), Michel et al. (1998), Rabinovich, Chase, and Gadde (1998)). Several consistency maintenance algorithms and replacement policies have been proposed for cooperative proxies. These include cache validation/invalidation techniques, skulking versus immediate update procedures, volume maintenance of web objects and several other replacement policies including prefetching web contents (Venkataramani et al. (2001)). A comprehensive survey of current web caching technologies is given in Barish and Obraczka (2000).

Both CDN and CPN employ cooperative proxy caching; however, with a difference. Due to the uniqueness of ownership, fairly centralized management and contractual agreements with content providers, CDN proxies tend to be somewhat tightly coupled. The distributed nature of ownership, and consequently the decentralized management of the proxy network and customer-driven contractual agreements, mean that CPN proxies tend to be rather loosely coupled. As a result, CDN involves fairly structured proxy deployments and usage, and CPN is mostly operated through different forms of cache trading contracts among the owners of the proxies. However, the loose coupling and distributed ownership lead to several innovative ways to manage a CPN effectively. We outline a broad strategy for this as follows.

13.2.1   Location Management

Location management in CPN is based on the cache trading arrangements among the participating ISPs. For example, consider a trade agreement between ISPs 1 and 2 where ISP 1 sells C units of cache capacity to ISP 2 for a period of time T. During this period, ISP 1 would set aside this capacity for

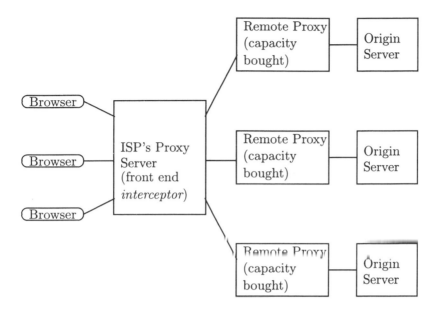

Fig. 13.2. Transparent proxy deployment in CPN

the exclusive use of ISP 2. As a result, the management of the traded capacity comes under the purview of ISP 2 during this period. In essence, this implies that ISP 2 controls what is stored in the cache bought and its replacement policies. In a CPN with several participants, we can envision an ISP buying capacity from several others for a given period of time. Clearly, the storage of web objects at multiple remote caches all intended for the service of the customers of a single ISP requires substantial coordination from the ISP's proxy servers. This implies that a certain level of central management of the ISP's distributed cache resources is needed. Given several such ISPs operating simultaneously and together by exercising their respective central management of various cache resources under their control at any given time, a loosely coupled system of location management comprised of different areas of autonomous cache control is required for a CPN. This can be implemented using either the transparent or nontransparent deployment strategies. In a transparent deployment, all client requests can be handled by a front end proxy server that will either direct the requests to a remote server holding the required web objects or obtain them first from the remote proxies and then serve them to the clients. This model is illustrated in Figure 13.2. In the nontransparent mode, the client can be either explicitly configured to access specific remote proxies or the users can be given a choice of the nearest server for replicated content or the browsers can be auto-configured to select a proxy at run-time. Implicit in this model is that the front end knows exactly what is stored in the other proxies throughout the period T. This model is shown in Figure 13.3. In either model, the entire CPN operates

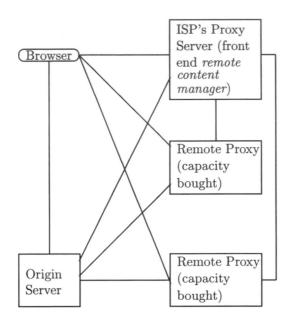

Fig. 13.3. Nontransparent proxy deployment in CPN

as a set of disjoint and autonomously managed collections of remote caches where each collection serves the customers of an ISP.

13.2.2   Proxy Pruning

Proxy pruning can be implemented in different ways, depending on whether the deployment is transparent or otherwise. We first consider the transparent case as follows. Note that every web object cached has an identifier. The identifier is a composite of source server URL, cache server URL and the IP address of the site originating the request. An ISP could decide to organize the set of remote caches under its management either hierarchically or otherwise. In *hierarchical structuring*, each cache represents a node of the hierarchy and could have parent-child as well as peer-to-peer relationships with others. Accordingly, directories of web object identifiers can be maintained at different levels of granularity. For instance, a dense entry would represent a high level aggregation of the entries. The granularity can be progressively decreased from the root of the hierarchy in a top-down manner, ending at the leaves. Accordingly, when a user requests an object, the request is first processed at the front-end proxy interceptor, and then assigned to the hierarchy for determining where the object could be found if it exists in the cache. Several coordinated search mechanisms are possible in this process. For instance, the interceptor could serve as the root of the hierarchy, and proceed with the search in a top-down manner. On the other hand, the interceptor could start from a leaf node and progress the search bottom-up followed by a top-down process, until the required cache holding the web object can be found. In this case, each user could be assigned to a *home base* cache server at the leaf level and all requests from a user would be directed to his home base. Starting at the home base, search could percolate upwards in the hierarchy and then downwards until either the required object is found or is determined to be not available in the cache system. In some respects, this model is similar to operations of PSTN and cellular telephone networks. The top-down and bottom-up pruning models are illustrated in Figure 13.4. The access paths in given instances are illustrated using bold lines in this figure. Directory structures at the cache nodes whose granularity is based on the hierarchy and with partitioning/replication capabilities and potential hash-based search opportunities would enhance the performance of this search.

Several alternatives to the hierarchical structuring of remote caches are possible. These include *network structures*, *hub and spoke structures* and *real-time client assignments*. A network structure is a peer-to-peer generalization of the hierarchy. This is a flat organization of the caches, and pruning takes the form of broadcast requests of required web objects, URL hashing and directory mechanisms. A hub and spoke model is essentially a flat hierarchy with two levels, where the interceptor could serve as the hub and caches as the spoke terminals. Pruning in hub and spoke architectures could also follow the same mechanisms in addition to round robin and other possible protocols that a circular set of caches would allow. In real-time client assignments, each client could be assigned a specific cache or a set of caches – either local or remote – and all caching needs for a particular session of the client could be provided from the chosen caches. The advantage with this approach is that no pruning is necessary. A requested object is either found in the assigned cache or not. If it is not found, then the query can be transmitted to the origin server. These structures are illustrated in Figure 13.5.

13.2.3   Cooperative Replacement

Several metrics have been used in formulating policies for replacement of web objects in the cache systems. Some of the important metrics include hit rate, byte hit rate, bandwidth savings, latency reduction, disk performance and CPU performance (Aggarwal, Wolf, and Yu (1999)). Since the need for web objects exists in the customer base, these performance metrics could become highly indeterminate. Additional options for caching such as pre-fetching in anticipation of customer needs would only increase this indeterminacy. At the outset, we consider caching and replacement along two dimensions: user level and session level. In the user level, we basically differentiate between the caching required to satisfy a single user versus multiple users. In the session level, we distinguish between the caching required for a single user's specific session versus multiple sessions for either a single user or multiple users.

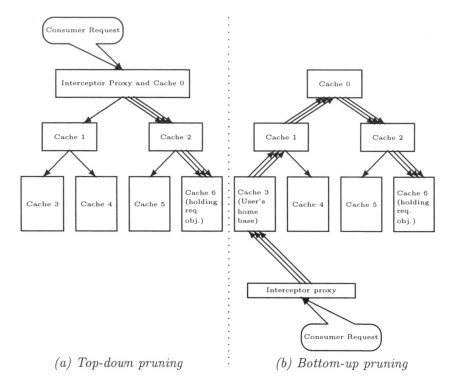

(a) Top-down pruning   (b) Bottom-up pruning

Fig. 13.4. CPN pruning strategies with hierarchical caches and transparent proxy deployment

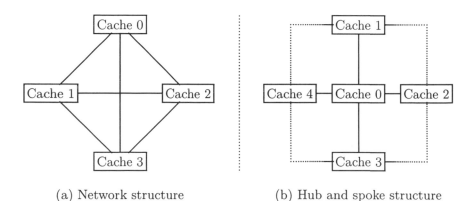

(a) Network structure   (b) Hub and spoke structure

Fig. 13.5. Alternative pruning and proxy deployment strategies

The essential characteristics of the cache replacement strategies in each of these cases are developed in Geng et al. (2002a). The replacement policies should be closely tied to user distribution, URL distribution of web objects assessed, lifetimes of web objects as determined by the content providers (which eventually affects the consistency of a cached object with the original) and location management and pruning models employed.

13.2.4 CPN Trading Hub Model

A CPN, because of its decentralized nature of network components ownership and management, is centered on a trading hub where all capacity trades are carried out prior to putting into effect the capacities bought and sold for real-time customer service operations. The trading hub can be conceptualized as a marketplace for cache trading where ISPs and other cache capacity owners participate as registered members. The cache market is a virtual organization consisting of numerous participants who have an interest in buying or selling cache capacity or serving as an intermediary in a cache trade. An intermediary could be an ISP who sells some of his own capacity to others while also buying capacity from some others to meet his own requirements. In general, three necessary requirements for participation are: (a) registered membership in the hub, (b) possession of web cache capacity, and (c) availability of a proxy server that can either host software for directing and redirecting traffic to specific destinations or reconfigurable according to cache sharing needs. Membership could entail either a subscription or commissions per trade facilitated by the hub according to their nature. The value proposition of the hub is essentially twofold: a matchmaker for cache trading opportunities and provider of appropriate software services for trade management as well as implementation of run-time distributed cache operations. We outline the structure of the hub and present a model of its scope and operations together with a framework of its technical architecture below.

The trading hub is centrally managed and it coordinates a variety of trades among sellers and buyers of cache capacity both in real-time and batch modes with a range of buyer-seller contract types, economic exchange mechanisms and other trade practices. Since most of these tasks can be standardized, we envision the hub to be almost entirely managed and operated by a set of intelligent agents. However, several types of agents will be necessary to implement a CPN fully. At the outset, we organize them into two broad categories: *trade level agents* and *operational agents*. The set of trade level agents are essentially responsible for managing the hub and conducting the trading activities. The operational agents are implementation agents that take over from the trade level agents once a contract between a buyer and a seller is finalized. We outline the broad functional details of these agents in the following discussion. The more specific technical details are provided in Geng et al. (2002b).

A CPN hub is maintained by a hierarchy of agents to facilitate trades, and for simplicity, we denote the top agent as the *Hub Manager*. The trades in a CPN can be characterized along two dimensions: *temporal modes* and *trade mechanisms*. The temporal mode defines the time dimension of trades – whether they are completed in real-time or batch mode. The trade mechanisms define how the trades are accomplished – through bargaining or auctions or any type of matchmaking between buyers and sellers. In the real-time temporal mode, potential buyers and sellers enter the hub in real-time and post their needs and availabilities. The hub manager could then instantly match potential buyers with sellers and facilitate immediate trades. The hub manager could also skulk these requests in short time intervals so that a set of trades can be collectively arranged for optimal service levels. In general, participants entering the real-time trade mode would either want to sell their excess capacity or buy some capacity immediately. In the batch mode, the participants could be posting their requirements for some future trade. In this case, the hub manager could collect these requests and periodically arrange trades with a view to optimize costs and revenues in the future. In the operations of a CPN hub, each participant would be represented by a secure, authorized agent who is provided with the necessary information such as capacity available/needed, reservation prices, time windows for availability/requirement, choice of trade mechanism and other details. On the hub side, different sets of agents would manage the different temporal modes and exchange mechanisms. The agents managing different exchange mechanisms would employ appropriate underlying trade models; these are described in Geng et al. (2002b) and summarized in the next section. Furthermore, capacity providers and buyers can be clustered and segregated geographically, and a complete set of agents for each segregated cluster could be employed. In this case, we envision simultaneous but independent sets of trades segregated by geographical domains to occur within the trading hub.

The operational agents implement the contracts established by the trade level agents in conjunction with the participating ISPs. For example, consider ISP 3 who buys capacity from ISPs 1 and 2 in Figure 13.1. The CPN hub would provide agent software to the three ISPs that would be installed and run on their respective proxies. The agent at ISP 3 would coordinate with the other two agents for location management, pruning and content replacement operations. The agents could be developed in shell mode, and could be implemented with the parametric choices of the participating ISPs at runtime. This is a workable agent configuration for transparent deployment of the proxies, and in the case of nontransparent deployment, either additional agents for the client platforms can be used or their browsers be appropriately reconfigured. The agents provided by the hub to the participants could also entail an appropriate fee structure. Accordingly, the revenue model of the trading hub is derived from the fixed fee structures associated with membership, charges for trade facilitation and operationalization through the software agents provided and possibly, royalty payments from members based on each successfully completed trade to sustain the hub as a viable business entity in the long run.

13.3   Economic Foundations of CPN

We summarize the key results from our study on the economic foundations of CPN markets in this section. The details of these analyses can be found in Geng et al. (2002a, b). Each ISP serves a local customer base, and the demand for capacity is assumed to be random. Hence, each ISP is first faced with the problem of how much cache capacity should be planned for, in order to satisfy the contracted service. Next, once the demand is realized, the ISP should decide on how the demand is to be met, either wholly from the available capacity or by buying additional capacity from other service providers if necessary. In planning for the capacity to build, an ISP should consider the option of trading. Sometimes an ISP could plan to build less with a view to buy additional capacity if necessary; sometimes an ISP could plan for more with a view to sell the excess capacity if any. Similarly, when the demand is realized, an ISP should decide whether to buy or sell, and from or to whom and at what price. Capacity planning is a strategic decision, while allocation and trading decisions pertain to continuous tactical process management. Subsequently, the implementation of the capacity allocations and customer service provisioning deal with the operational management level. The three stages of management and decision-making from an ISP's point of view are summarized in Figure 13.6.

13.3.1   Modeling Cache Trading Efficiencies

We characterize efficiencies in web capacity trading among remote servers and develop the intuitions and convexity properties of web capacity trading efficiencies. In particular, we model the *reduced performance problem*: given a choice between a certain amount of local caching capacity and the same level of capacity available at a remote location, an ISP would always prefer the local caching capacity since the performance of any remote capacity can be negatively affected by the delay between the two ISPs. The farther the remote cache, the more likely are delays in retrieving the data. The reduced performance can be captured by using the concept of a *discount factor*. We define the discount factor between any pair of ISPs as follows. In general, let N denote the set of ISPs in a CPN. Given $n, m \in N$, we define a discount factor $\delta_{n,m}$ between ISPs n and m if, from ISP n's perspective, one unit of capacity from ISP m is equivalent to $\delta_{n,m}$ units of ISP n's local capacity. Let the average delay for accessing content directly from the origin server be t_0. Let the average delay be t_c if the content is fetched from an ISP's local cache.

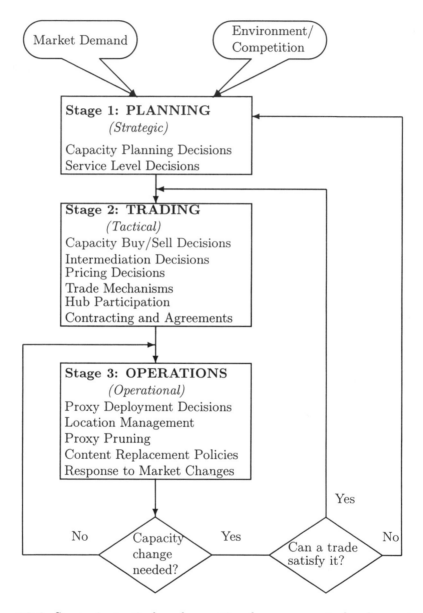

Fig. 13.6. Strategic, tactical, and operational management of cache services

If the average delay between these two ISPs is $t_{n,m}$, then, immediately we have

$$\delta_{n,m} = \frac{t_0 - t_{n,m}}{t_0 - t_c}. \tag{13.1}$$

The discount factors satisfy the following properties: (i) $\delta_{n,m} \in (0,1]$, $\delta_{n,m} = 1$, and $\delta_{n,m} = \delta_{m,n}$, (ii) given any three different ISPs n, m, and l, suppose that the least delay path between n and l contains m, i.e. $t_{n,l} = t_{n,m} + t_{m,l}$, then $\delta_{n,l} < \delta_{n,m}\delta_{m,l}$, and (iii) $\delta(t)$ is monotonically decreasing and concave. The discount factors provide a basis for evaluating the efficiencies of remote caches while trading under both non-competitive and competitive situations.

13.3.2   A Bilateral Cache Trading Model

Using the concept of discounting, we outline a stochastic two ISP-CPN model for capacity planning with a bilateral cache trading option. For simplicity, we model the total demand for capacity by consolidating all individual demands into a single *aggregate buyer's demand*, x. Assume that the ISP establishes a *performance contract* with his customers. This implies that for a given price, p, the ISP commits to satisfy the aggregate buyer's caching demand no matter what the realization of the demand is; if the ISP fails to satisfy the demand, he is penalized by the buyer based on the amount of unsatisfied demand. Let $F(x)$ and $f(x)$ on $[0, \infty)$ denote the distribution and density functions of x.

Users' access behaviors can be random in several instances and are subject to spikes and troughs in access patterns over time. We can generally characterize user behavior as either "surfing" where many different URLs are referenced or "conservative" where frequent re-references to the same URLs are used. Note that this is a general simplified characterization of user behavior and the behavior could assume more complex forms in practice. Moreover, unpredictable environmental factors (e.g. congestion) can also cause spikes and troughs. Further, externality factors which suggest that both the Internet traffic and web content grow exponentially over time would only compound this effect (Rabinovich and Spatscheck (2002)). All of these contribute to certain uneven access patterns that underly our modeling of user demand as a random variable.

Given the performance contract, the ISP selects his caching capacity, s. Since it takes time to construct the capacity, the ISP should decide on and build the capacity s in the planning stage. Let the unit cost of building the capacity be a positive constant c. The performance contract also includes penalties if the ISP fails to provide the promised service as follows. Let the penalty for each unsatisfied unit of demand be b. If the ISP is unable to provide enough capacity when the demand is realized, then a total penalty r is paid to the buyer, and is determined as follows. Let $x^+ = \max(x, 0)$. Then, $r = b(x - s)^+$.

Now, in an isolated market where no trading is involved, an ISP's profit function in the service period is: $\pi = p - cs - b(x - s)^+$. In the contracting period, the ISP will choose the capacity to maximize his expected profit as follows:

$$\max_s E(\pi) = p - cs - bE(x - s)^+ = p - cs - b\int_0^\infty (x - s)f(x)ds. \quad (13.2)$$

The first order condition is $\frac{\partial E(\pi)}{\partial s} = -c + b(1 - F(s)) = 0$, and, therefore, the optimal capacity choice $\hat{s}$, satisfies $F(\hat{s}) = 1 - c/b$, if $c < b$, or $\hat{s} = 0$, if $c \geq b$. In particular, if x is uniformly distributed, then, $\hat{s} = 1 - c/b$, if $c < b$, or $\hat{s} = 0$ if $c \geq b$. If the penalty is too small, i.e. $c \geq b$, it is optimal for the ISP not to build any cache capacity at all. Consequently, it does not make sense to provide any caching service at all to the consumers, which is not the case in reality. Therefore, hereafter we assume $c/b < 1$.

Next, we develop a bilateral trading model outlined as follows. Without loss of generality, consider ISPs 1 and 2 with discount factor δ. Let s_1 and s_2 denote the cache capacities at the two ISPs. Let x_1 and x_2 be the random variables denoting the demands at the two ISPs. Capacity trading is done in the service period after x_1 and x_2 have been observed. To begin with, it is straightforward to see that each ISP would first try to satisfy all the local demand with the locally available capacity, given the discount factor. If local demand is satisfied and if any extra capacity is available, then an ISP would sell as much as possible. So in the service period, the trading scenarios and the amounts of capacity traded between the ISPs are as shown in Figure 13.7. Once the demands are realized, the trades are based on the capacities available at the two ISPs. The six regions shown in the figure represent the combinations of x_1 and x_2 values in relation to the two capacities s_1 and s_2. In regions 1 and 6, clearly no trade is possible. In regions 2 and 3, ISP 1 would sell excess capacity to ISP 2, and vice versa in regions 4 and 5.

Assume a social optimization scenario with the two ISPs *integrated* with a central planner. The central planner coordinates both ISPs to maximize their total expected profit. Let π^t denote the total profit. Then:

$$E(\pi^t) = E(\pi_1) + E(\pi_2) = p_1 + p_2 - c(s_1 + s_2)$$

$$-b\left[\int_{s_1}^\infty \int_{s_2}^\infty (x_1 - s_1) + (x_2 - s_2)f_1(x_1)f_2(x_2)dx_2dx_1\right.$$

$$+ \int_0^{s_1} \int_{s_2+\delta s_1-\delta x_1}^\infty (x_2 - s_2 - \delta(s_1 - x_1))f_1(x_1)f_2(x_2)dx_2dx_1$$

$$\left.+ \int_0^{s_2} \int_{s_1+\delta s_2-\delta x_2}^\infty (x_1 - s_1 - \delta(s_2 - x_2))f_1(x_1)f_2(x_2)dx_1dx_2\right]. \quad (13.3)$$

After some tedious algebra and calculus, the first-order conditions yield:

$$\int_0^{s_1} (1 - F_2(s_2 + \delta s_1 - \delta x_1))f_1(x_1)dx_1 = \int_0^{s_2} (1 - F_1(s_1 + \delta s_2 - \delta x_2))f_2(x_2)dx_2$$

$$(13.4)$$

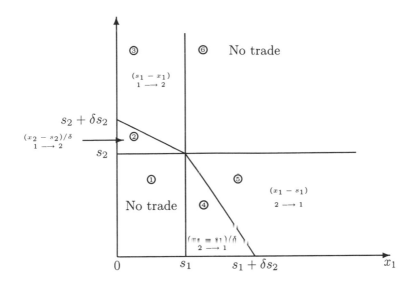

Fig. 13.7. Bilateral cache trading space

The above equation is concise and symmetric on both ends. In fact, if $f_1 \equiv f_2$, then only symmetric solutions exist. This is shown in the following lemma.

Lemma 13.1:
Let $f_1 = f_2 = f$. Let s_1^* and s_2^* denote the optimal cache capacity allocation to the two ISPs by the central planner. Then, $s_1^* = s_2^*$.

Proof: Let F denote the distribution function corresponding to f. Assume that in the optimal solution $s_1^* > s_2^*$. Rewrite (13.4) as

$$\int_{s_2^*}^{s_1^*} (1 - F(s_2^* + \delta s_1^* - \delta x)) f(x) dx$$

$$+ \int_0^{s_2^*} (F(s_1^* + \delta s_2^* - \delta x) - F(s_2^* + \delta s_1^* - \delta x)) f(x) dx = 0.$$

However, both terms on the left side are positive, which leads to contradiction. A similar result can be obtained if we assume $s_1^* < s_2^*$. Therefore, we must have $s_1^* = s_2^* = s^*$. $\square$

The solution to the above symmetric problem is given by $s_1^* = s_2^* = s^*$, where s^* satisfies

$$-c + b(1 + F^2(s^*)) - (1 - \delta)F(s^*) - (1 + \delta)\int_0^{s^*} F((1 + \delta)s^* - \delta x)f(x)dx) = 0.$$
$$(13.5)$$

The following lemma establishes that the profit for each ISP is higher when the social trading option is exercised than otherwise.

Lemma 13.2:
If $s_1^* \neq \hat{s}_1$ or $s_2^* \neq \hat{s}_2$, then the expected total profit of the two ISPs under an integrated trading option with a central planner is greater than the expected total profit when they operate in isolation.

Proof: Let $v(s_1, s_2)$ and $w(s_1, s_2)$ denote the expected total profit of the two ISPs with capacities s_1 and s_2, under an integrated trading option with a central planner and under isolated operation, respectively. Since $s_1^* \neq \hat{s}_1$ or $s_2^* \neq \hat{s}_2$, we only need to show that $v(s_1^*, s_2^*) \geq w(\hat{s}_1, \hat{s}_2)$. Since (s_1^*, s_2^*) are the optimal capacities with a central planner, we have $v(s_1^*, s_2^*) \geq v(\hat{s}_1, \hat{s}_2)$. Furthermore, given $(\hat{s}_1, \hat{s}_2)$, by having the trading option the two ISPs can do at least as well as the case where they are isolated, i. e., $v(\hat{s}_1, \hat{s}_2) \geq w(\hat{s}_1, \hat{s}_2)$. So we have $v(s_1^*, s_2^*) \geq w(\hat{s}_1, \hat{s}_2)$. $\square$

Using the above characterization of the trading scenarios, Geng et al. (2002a) model the expected profit profiles under *social optimization with a central planner* and *independent optimizations through bargaining*, respectively. The expected profitability with the trading option under each of these scenarios is evaluated in comparison with the case when the ISPs operate in isolation. The key results of this analysis are as follows: (i) When the demands are iid random variables, a central planner would allocate equal capacity to the ISPs under optimality, (ii) the expected total profit of the two ISPs under an integrated trading option with a central planner is greater than that when they operate in isolation, (iii) if the demands are iid random variables and capacity is procured using an exogenously determined market price, then the two ISPs would make identical capacity decisions at optimality, (iv) if the ISPs can negotiate the capacity trading price, they will agree on the price that a central planner would have chosen, thus maximizing their joint profit.

13.3.3   Multilateral Cache Trading

In the multilateral trading scenario, we investigate the capacity planning problem when more than two ISPs participate in trading. We first extend the model to a 3-ISP case to study the impact of intermediation on trading decisions and outcomes. Next, we study the general case of a *network* of ISPs mutually trading capacity. Successive trading through intermediaries has strong implications for capacity trading between ISPs who are geographically far removed from each other. Typically, a consortium of intermediaries could generate such markets that are otherwise either too expensive to operate or even impossible. The behavior of the discount factors determines the intermediary options. Successive trading also gives rise to arbitrage opportunities for the intermediaries when the transfer prices are negotiated. The arbitrage arises due to the geographic advantages of the intermediaries, and this has been observed in the related area of bandwidth trading in the telecom industry. A study of the market equilibrium under arbitrage in web caching is suggested for future research. We have also carried out extensive computational investigations on the bilateral and multilateral trading models using computer simulations of trading behavior among three or more ISPs.

13.3.4   Major Conclusions from the Analysis

The major conclusions of the study in Geng et al. (2002a) can be summarized as follows. (a) total cost under social optimization decreases with improvement in the efficiency of cache sharing among ISPs, (b) the velocity of trading increases with the sharing efficiency, (c) in a cooperative setting, cache sharing occurs not only between capacity suppliers and buyers, but could also involve third-party intermediaries who could be exploited for sharing advantages due to geographic proximity and capacity availability, and finally, (d) the lower bounds on expected costs per ISP progressively decrease as additional ISPs join the trading network. The last result especially suggests a positive network externality effect on web cache trading groups, and signals the arrival of web exchanges and other mechanisms for large-scale capacity trading. Unlike classical mechanism design issues in economics where a proposed mechanism is not industry specific, the proposed design of the CPN market is closely tied to the characteristics of Internet caching technology, namely, the positive network externality and the convexity property of capacity sharing with geographically separated cache sites. In this market, trading is not limited to a capacity provider and a capacity buyer, but other related ISPs can provide significant value-added via intermediary services. At the center of mechanism design are the incentive questions: what are the participation incentives for the involved parties and what is the optimal incentive structure that leads to the maximum aggregated profit? Compared to a CDN solution that is usually operated by a global company that has little knowledge of local markets, a CPN solution incorporates local ISPs' knowledge about their local markets into the trading process. This leads to better resource allocation decisions and can result in rational expectation equilibria in the trading markets.

The research in Geng et al. (2002a) has developed the foundations of the market mechanisms that would enable ISPs to plan their capacity investments ahead and meet stochastic demands for their services through bilateral and multilateral capacity trading among them. We show; using a CPN trading model; that: (a) each ISP would gain by agreeing to buy/sell the additionally needed/excess capacities rather than by going alone in meeting the market demands, and consequently, (b) it is profitable to take into account the trading option while planning for cache capacities. These observations hold under both social optimization and bargaining scenarios. As a result, when the CPN market develops, we can see a great deal of cooperation among ISPs in cache resource sharing. Furthermore, these results hold under non-competitive as well as competitive situations. In a non-competitive situation, each ISP has a captive market and neither competes in the other's market; in the competitive case, both ISPs could target the same market. An interesting conclusion from this analysis is that regardless of competition the ISPs would cooperate, which is analogous to business practices in bandwidth trading and service level provisioning among telecom service providers. A key insight derived from the caching situation is that cooperation and coordination are advantageous even to competitors when faced with a sharable resource that could be relatively expensive to build and whose non-availability could lead to higher customer churn rates. The higher returns on social welfare among the ISPs and the existence of bargaining equilibria demonstrate these effects. In conclusion, this study demonstrates the practical business viability of a cooperative CPN market. The technological viability of CPN has already been shown in the industry through CDN. Consequently, we can see a rapid emergence of the CPN market with several innovative business models.

13.4   Tactical Trading Models of CPN

The fundamental objective of the CPN trading hub is to facilitate cache capacity trading which is economically beneficial to the participating ISPs. While a plethora of trade mechanisms can be implemented, the unique characteristics of cache trading, namely the presence of network externalities and capacity arbitrage, need to be incorporated in order to design an effective and efficient trading platform.

Consider a scenario where the CPN hub is implemented, as a simple 'bulletin board' comprised of a compilation of participating ISPs. In this case, an ISP can initiate negotiations with another participating ISP, and settle a mutually beneficial trade agreement via a bilateral negotiation. In a CPN hub of more than two ISPs this mechanism yields sub-optimal outcomes as effective trading patterns could be much more complex than a set of simple bilateral trades. These patterns could potentially result in more efficient capacity allocation since each ISP can trade with two or more other ISPs; they also open up significant opportunities for arbitrage. An intermediary could serve as a bridge for capacity trading among other ISPs, which could be beneficial to the ISPs when the discount factor is a decreasing and concave function of distance.

Consider a trade between ISP 1 and ISP 2. In the absence of an intermediary, the two ISPs would engage in a bilateral trade. Now, assume that a third ISP is strategically positioned in the Internet segment connecting the two ISPs. This implies that the capacity trades between ISPs 1 and 2 occur through this intermediary. The third ISP could be the owner of a backbone and routers that link the other two. Call the intermediary ISP 3. By virtue of its strategic location, ISP 3 could facilitate the capacity transfer without actually participating in the trade. Consider a situation where ISP 1 sells a capacity t^* to ISP 2. While this can be accomplished without involving ISP 3 directly in the trade, the following transfer strategy is also possible: ISP 1 sells capacity t^* to ISP 3, and then ISP 3 sells capacity $\delta_{1,3}t^*$ to ISP 2. Note that the capacity t^* originating from ISP 1 first depreciates to $\delta_{1,3}t^*$ when it is realized at ISP 3. Since ISP 3 does not participate in the trade, he simply transfers the incoming capacity $\delta_{1,3}t^*$ to ISP 2. As a result, when the capacity is made available at ISP 2, its total depreciated value is $\delta_{1,3}\delta_{3,2}t^*$. Without the use of the intermediary, ISP 2 would have realized a capacity of $\delta_{1,2}t^*$. When $\delta_{1,3}\delta_{3,2} > \delta_{1,2}$, it is beneficial for ISPs 1 and 2 to engage the transfer services of ISP 3 in realizing the trade between them.

Geng et al. (2002b) have developed two trade mechanisms termed the *Market Maker (MM) Model* and the *Double Auction (DA) Model* to facilitate effective cache trading via the CPN hub. These models can be implemented individually; or can also be implemented in a symbiotic fashion that provides greater flexibility to the participants. We have further developed a suite of risk-management tools that include futures contracts and options. We outline the two mechanisms in the following discussion.

In the MM model, the CPN hub acts as a trusted third party market maker. The participating ISPs provide full information to the hub; the information includes the available capacity, realized demand and the penalty costs. The market maker computes socially optimal trade routes and suggests prices to the participants. These prices are termed MSRP (Market-maker Suggested Rational Price). The prices are developed in a fashion that provides economic incentives for all the participants and are *coalition-proof*. Coalition-proof prices ensure that no subset of the ISPs has an incentive to forego the CPN hub and form private deals amongst themselves. Such prices validate the role of a CPN hub as a robust and viable market mechanism.

The DA model environment is designed for participants who do not want to provide full information for competitive reasons. The DA model employs a double-auction methodology. The participants provide buy and sell prices they desire and the amount of capacity they wish to trade with. Based on the supply and demand conditions, the DA model can be implemented in a near-continuous time. Table 13.1 provides highlights of the two trade methodologies.

Table 13.1. Characteristics of the two tactical trading models

	MM Model	DA Model
Mode	Trusted Third Party	Auction House
Time	Periodic	Near Continuous
Prices	Model-Generated MSRP	Dictated by the ISPs
Trade Capacities	Model-Generated Cache Trades	Model-Generated Cache Trades

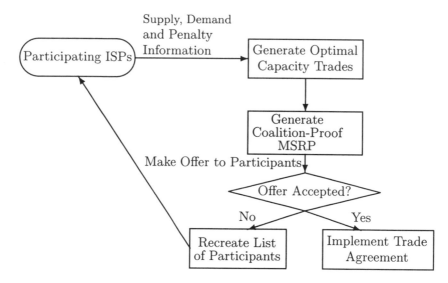

Fig. 13.8. The Market Maker (MM) Process Model

13.4.1   MM Model

Figure 13.8 provides the MM process model. Given the membership of participating ISPs the MM model operates in two critical steps. The first step involves the creation of socially optimal capacity trades so that the total surplus of the membership is maximized. The second step involves the production of MSRPs that are coalition-proof. We present the model underlying the first step in the following discussion and refer the reader to Geng et al. (2002b) for coalition-proof pricing strategies.

Consider a set of N ISPs. Let C_i be the capacity available at node i (ISP i), and D_i be the realized demand. In terms of making its own capacity available for others, an ISP would simply identify a portion of its own capacity for use by other ISPs. Let C_{ij} denote the capacity made available by ISP i

for use by ISP j. To simplify notation, let C_{ii} denote the capacity allocated by ISP i for its own use. Therefore, it follows that:

$$\sum_{j=1}^{N} C_{ij} + C_i, \quad \forall i. \tag{13.6}$$

Now, let δ_{ij} denote the *direct* discount factor (i.e. the discount factor without the use of any other intermediate ISP's caching systems). The amount of capacity for ISP i for its own use comes from (a) C_{ii} (own space allocated for its own use) and (b) space allocated by other ISPs for ISP i to use. If we let $\delta_{ii} = 1$, we have that the

$$\text{amount of capacity for ISP } i = \sum_{j=1}^{N} \delta_{ji} C_{ji}. \tag{13.7}$$

Let E denote the set of nodes with excess capacity (all i, where $C_i = D_i$) and F denote the set of nodes with excess demand (all i where $C_i < D_i$).

Note that ISPs that belong to E should never face a shortfall. This follows from the fact that capacity that is shipped out is always discounted. Therefore, in making the capacity trading decisions we have the constraint

$$\sum_{j=1}^{N} \delta_{ji} C_{ji} \geq D_i, \quad \forall i \in E. \tag{13.8}$$

Similarly, for each node that belongs to F, the effective capacity that is provided should not exceed what is required. Otherwise, it results in unnecessary transport. This results in the constraint

$$\sum_{j=1}^{N} \delta_{ji} C_{ji} \leq D_i, \quad \forall i \in F. \tag{13.9}$$

Hence, the problem faced by the CPN hub in making the capacity decisions is to choose the C_{ij} values to minimize the total penalty paid, subject to constraints (13.6), (13.8), and (13.9). The total penalty paid is given by

$$\sum_{i \in F} b(D_i - \sum_{j=1}^{N} \delta_{ji} C_{ji}).$$

Hence, the MM Model Trade Capacity formulation is:

$$\text{Minimize} \quad \sum_{i \in F} b(D_i - \sum_{j=1}^{N} \delta_{ji} C_{ji})$$

subject to:

$$\sum_{j=1}^{N} C_{ij} = C_i, \quad \forall i,$$

$$\sum_{j=1}^{N} \delta_{ji} C_{ji} \geq D_i, \quad \forall i \in E,$$

$$\sum_{j=1}^{N} \delta_{ji} C_{ji} \leq D_i, \quad \forall i \in F,$$

$$C_{ij} \geq 0, \quad \forall i.$$

The above trade capacity formulation can be solved as a linear programming problem and, hence, is computationally efficient. Let C_{ij}^* denote the optimal results from solving the above. Then we have:

(i) A node i is a *pure supply* node if:

$$\sum_{j, j \neq i}^{N} C_{ji}^* = 0 \quad \text{and} \quad \sum_{j, j \neq i}^{N} C_{ij}^* > 0,$$

(ii) A node i is a *pure demand* node if:

$$\sum_{j, j \neq i}^{N} C_{ji}^* > 0 \quad \text{and} \quad \sum_{j, j \neq i}^{N} C_{ij}^* = 0,$$

(iii) A node i is an *intermediary* node if:

$$\sum_{j, j \neq i}^{N} C_{ji}^* > 0 \quad \text{and} \quad \sum_{j, j \neq i}^{N} C_{ij}^* > 0.$$

13.4.2   The Double Auction Model

In the MM model the market maker plays an active role in analyzing demand-supply information and suggesting prices. In cases where ISPs are reluctant to reveal their demand information to the market maker or other ISPs, or in cases where the CPN market is heavily decentralized and no such active market maker exists, the Double Auction (DA) Model is an appropriate candidate for solving the trading problem. The DA model is illustrated in Figure 13.9.

Unlike the MM model, in the DA model the market maker does not directly suggest prices to the ISPs. Instead, each ISP is able to submit a limit order into the DA market. Suppose the CPN contains N ISPs. A limit order from ISP i takes the form (z_i, η_i) , where z_i is a bundle presented in a column

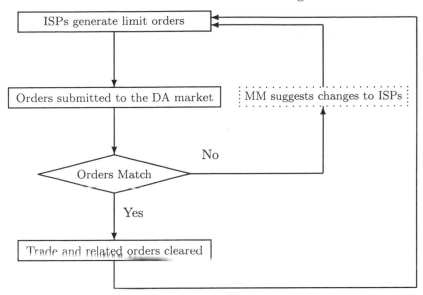

Fig. 13.9. The Double Auction (DA) Process Model

vector of size $N+1$ and $\eta_i > 0$ is a limit quantity. $z_i = (z_{1i}, z_{2i}, \ldots, z_{Ni}, p_i)^T$, where z_{ji} is the amount of capacity ISP i wants from ISP j in each unit of the bundle (a negative z_{ji} means ISP i wants to send capacity to ISP j), and p_i is the minimum price ISP i charges for this unit bundle (for a negative p_i, the absolute value of p_i is the maximum price ISP i would pay for this unit bundle).

Once all ISPs submit their limit orders into the market, the market maker will try to find a solution $y = (y_1, y_2, \ldots, y_N)^T$, where y_i is the amount of unit bundles for ISP i, and $0 \le y_i \le \eta_i$, such that $(z_1, z_2, \ldots, z_N)y \le 0$.

Once a feasible solution y is found, the market maker finishes the according trades. The limit order constraint reflects that each ISP only has limited local cache for trading. ISPs who are involved in the trades accordingly reduce their remaining local cache volume. If a feasible solution cannot be found, or if a feasible solution is found and the according trades are finished, ISPs generate the next round of limit orders. Intuitively, in the first round an ISP would like to submit a limit order that addresses the path that has the largest arbitrage opportunity, and explore the second largest arbitrage opportunity in the second round, and so on.[4] If the market maker fails to find a solution y, there could be two kinds of reasons. The first possibility is that the limit order submitted mismatches the current supply-demand situa-

---

[4]Alternatively, we can also consider the scenario where each ISP is able to submit multiple limit orders. Nevertheless, its local capacity constraint makes the market clearing process somewhat complicated as there could be cases where the limit orders submitted by a certain ISP become mutually exclusive to each other.

tion. Consider a three-ISP case where ISP 1 has extra capacity, ISP 2 needs capacity, and ISP 3 intermediates between ISP 1 and 2. If ISP 3 submits a limit order which requires capacity from ISP 2 and sends to ISP 1, the trade will never happen as this limit order contradicts the actual direction of trading demands. The second possibility is that some ISPs ask for high shares of the benefit from trading, and the market maker cannot simply satisfy all of them.

One solution to the above market failure problem is to let the market maker suggest changes to the ISPs. Whenever an ISP submits a limit order that only demands (supplies) capacity, the market maker will know that this ISP is a pure demand (supply) node. Therefore the market maker can learn about directions for trading flows. He can then suggest appropriate forms of limit orders to relevant ISPs to guide their submissions. Moreover, the market maker can also suggest reduction on p_i to any ISP i.

13.5   Conclusion

In this chapter, we introduce Capacity Provision Networks as a market mechanism for demand-side Web cache trading. The need for demand-side cache trading is supported by the fact that there exist positive network externalities across individual ISPs who provide caching services to their respective local users. The need for a CPN market is further supported by the existence of convexity in capacity discounting and the consequential potential for intermediation in cache trading.

We introduce three critical components in an implementation of a CPN: the technical framework for CPN operation, the economic foundations of a CPN, and tactical models of real-time trading. The economic foundations justify why a decentralized market mechanism could potentially achieve joint optimality for all participating ISPs. In the tactical trading area, we introduce two potential market mechanisms, the Market Maker Model and the Double Auction Model. The former requires an active market maker who provides MSRPs to ISPs to enable trading, and the latter enables ISPs to propose prices and the market maker plays a more passive role in matching orders and providing suggestions. The MM model fits well in cases where ISPs agrees to reveal their demand information a priori to the market maker. The DA model fits when ISPs prefer to keep their demand information private. Some of the major extensions of this work for future research include futures contracts, options, and development of indices as instruments for ISPs to coordinate capacity decisions in the planning stage when distribution of demand is private information.

Acknowledgments

We thank the anonymous reviewers for their comments on an earlier version of this paper.

References

Akamai Technologies, Inc. (2000a), "Delivering the Profits," White Paper, http://www.akamai.com/en/html/services/register_to_view.cfm.

Akamai Technologies, Inc. (2000b), "Internet Bottlenecks," White Paper, http://www.akamai.com/en/html/services/register_to_view.cfm.

Aggarwal, C., Wolf, J. L., and Yu, P. S. (1999), "Caching on the World Wide Web," IEEE Transactions on Knowledge and Data Engineering 11, 94-107.

Barish, G., and Obraczka, K. (2000), "World Wide Web Caching: Trends and Techniques," IEEE Communications 38, 178-184.

Chankhunthod, A., Danzig, P. B., Neerdaels, C., Schwartz, M. F., and Worrell, K. J. (1996), "A Hierarchical Internet Object Cache," in Proceedings of the USENIX Technology Conference, San Diego, California, January.

Dilley, J. (1999), "The Effect of Consistency on Cache Response Time," Technical Report HPL-1999-107, Hewlett-Packard Labs, http://www.hpl.hp.com/techreports/1999/HPL-1999-107.html.

Dilley, J., Arlitt, M., Perret, S., and Jin, T. (1999), "The Distributed Object Consistency Protocol," Technical Report HPL-1999-109, Hewlett-Packard Labs, http://www.hpl.hp.com/techreports/1999/HPL-1999-109.html.

Gadde, S., Chase, J., and Rabinovich, M. (1999), "CRISP Distributed Web Proxy," http://www.cs.duke.edu/ari/cisi/crisp/.

Gautam, N. (2002), "Performance Analysis and Optimization of Web Proxy Servers and Mirror Sites," European Journal of Operational Research 142, 396-418.

Geng, X., Gopal, R., Ramesh, R., and Whinston, A. B. (2002a), "Capacity Provision Networks: Foundations of Markets for Internet Caching," Working Paper, Center for Research in Electronic Commerce, University of Texas at Austin, Austin, Texas.

Geng, X., Gopal, R., Ramesh, R., and Whinston. A. B. (2002b), "Capacity Provision Networks: An Implementation Framework for Web Cache Trading Hubs," Working Paper, Center for Research in Electronic Commerce, University of Texas at Austin, Austin, Texas.

Grimm, C., Neitzner, M., Pralle, H., and Vockler, J. S. (1998), "Request Routing in Cache Meshes," Computer Networks and ISDN Systems 30, 2269-2278.

Gutzman, A. (2000), "Living with the Eight Seconds Rule," Internet.com, November 22, http://ecommerce.internet.com/news/insights/ectech/article/0,,9561_518111,00.html.

Krishnan, P., and Sugla, B. (1998), "Utility of Co-operating Web Proxy Caches," *Computer Networks and ISDN Systems* **30**, 195-203.

Michel, S., Nguyen, K., Rosenstein, A., Zhang, L., Floyd, S., and Jacobson, V. (1998), "Adaptive Web Caching: Towards a New Global Caching Architecture," *Computer Networks and ISDN Systems* **30**, 2169-2177.

Norton, W. B. (2001), "A Business Case for ISP Peering," White Paper, Equinix, Inc., http://arneill-py.sacramento.ca.us/ipv6mh/ABusinessCaseforISPPeering1.2.pdf.

Norton, W. B. (2002), "Internet Service Providers and ISP Peering," White Paper, Equinix Inc., available via email from author at wbn@euinix.com.

Nottingham, M. (1999), "Optimizing Object Freshness Controls in Web Caches," in *Proceedings of the 4th Web Caching and Content Delivery Workshop*, San Diego, California.

Rabinovich, M., Chase, J., and Gadde, S. (1998), "Not All Hits Are Created Equal: Cooperative Proxy Caching over a Wide-Area Network," *Computer Networks and ISDN Systems* **30**, 2253-2259.

Rabinovich, M., and Spatscheck, O. (2002), *Web Caching and Replication*, Addison-Wesley, Boston, Massachusetts.

Tewari, R., Dahlin, M., Vin, H., and Kay, J. (1999), "Design Considerations for Distributed Caching on the Internet," in *The 19th IEEE International Conference on Distributed Computing Systems (ICDCS)*, May, Austin, Texas.

Venkataramani A., Yalagandula, P., Kokku, R., Sharif, S., and Dahlin, M. (2001), "Potential Costs and Benefits of Long-Term Prefetching for Content-Distribution," 2001 Web Cache Workshop, June, Boston, Massachusetts.

Wang, J. (1999), "A Survey of Web Caching Schemes for the Internet," *ACM SIGCOMM Computer Communication Review* **29**, 36-46.

Wessels, D., and Claffy, K. (1997), "RFC 2186: Internet Cache Protocol (ICP), Version 2," http://www.ieft.org/rfc/rfc2186.txt.

Yin, J., Alvisi, L., Dahlin, M., and Lin, C. (1999), "Volume Leases for Consistency in Large-Scale Systems," *IEEE Transactions on Knowledge and Data Engineering* **11**, 563-576.

Index